# RECORD OF COMMISSIONS OF OFFICERS IN THE TENNESSEE MILITIA, 1796-1815

*Compiled by*
MRS. JOHN TROTWOOD MOORE

With a New Introduction
By Robert M. McBride
Editor, Tennessee Historical Quarterly

*And an Index for the Years 1812-1815
By Anita Comtois*

GENEALOGICAL PUBLISHING CO., INC.
BALTIMORE

The first section of this work, covering the years 1796 to 1811, was originally published in the *Tennessee Historical Quarterly*, Volumes I-VI (1942-1947), and then consolidated and reprinted in a single volume by the Tennessee Historical Commission in 1947 as a sesquicentennial publication. Mrs. Moore continued her contributions to the *Quarterly*, however, and in Volumes VII-IX and XV (1948-1950, 1956), she extended the period of coverage from 1812 to 1815.

With the permission of the Tennessee Historical Commission and the Tennessee Historical Society, and the cooperation of Robert M. McBride, editor of the *Quarterly*, the Genealogical Publishing Co., Inc. has consolidated this final group of articles and combined them with the book-length publication of 1947 to make this comprehensive reprint edition.

Reprinted with an Added Index
Genealogical Publishing Co., Inc.
Baltimore, 1977

Library of Congress Catalogue Card Number 76-53147
International Standard Book Number 8063-0756-0

Copyright © 1977
Tennessee Historical Commission
and Tennessee Historical Society,
Nashville, Tennessee
and
Genealogical Publishing Co., Inc.
Baltimore, Maryland
All Rights Reserved

*Made in the United States of America*

# Record of Commissions of Officers in the Tennessee Militia, 1796-1811

Compiled By
MRS. JOHN TROTWOOD MOORE
*Librarian and Archivist*
*State of Tennessee*

*Reprinted from Tennessee Historical Quarterly*
*By*
*The Adjutant General of the State of Tennessee*

Issued by the Tennessee Historical Commission
as a Sesquicentennial Publication
**1947**

# CONTENTS

INTRODUCTION TO THE ENLARGED EDITION — vii

PART I — 3
    1796-1801 — 4
    1807-1811 — 37
    INDEX — 133

PART II — 169
    1812 — 169
    1813 — 196
    1814 — 219
    1815 — 244
    INDEX — 261

# INTRODUCTION

The early Tennessee militia organizations, as well as those of the Southwest Territory, were based on the militia laws of the State of North Carolina. Under these laws each county had a separate regiment of militia, divided into Captain's Companies, each regiment being designated by the name of its county—"The Washington County Regiment of Militia of this State," for example. From the time of the earliest regiment until 1811, with a single exception, there was only one regiment in each county in the State. In 1797 the General Assembly ordered that there be a regiment of militia on the south side of the Cumberland River to be designated as the First Regiment of Davidson County, and one on the north side of the Cumberland River to be designated as the Second Regiment of Davidson County. In each of the other counties their regiment was designated as the "First Regiment of the County."

Under the Militia Law of 1803, the General Assembly adopted a numerical system of identification, assigning a number to each regiment in each county; again, however, these regiments were known locally as the First Regiment of the County. The two regiments in Davidson County, for example, were officially designated as the 19th and 20th regiments.

It was not until the latter part of 1810 that the increase in population made it necessary, under the law, to organize an additional regiment in some of the counties. These were known as the "Second Regiment" of the county and were assigned a regimental number in the order in which they were organized by the General Assembly in 1811.

Commissions of officers in the Tennessee Militia were listed in a series of manuscript books, beginning with the creation of the State in 1796 and extending for many years thereafter. The earliest of these are:

> 1796-1801: The original is in the Tennessee State Archives. It was printed serially in the *Tennessee Historical Quarterly*, Volume I and II (1942-43)

1801-1806: The original has never been located and presumably is lost. No known copy of it exists.

1807-1815: The original was printed in Volume II-IX, and XV (1943-1949, 1956) of the *Tennessee Historical Quarterly*.

1815-1827: The original is in the Tennessee State Archives. It has not been printed.

The militia commissions in these manuscripts are listed in chronological order, with a name index.

In 1942 Mrs. John Trotwood Moore, then Tennessee State Librarian and Archivist, began a project of serial publication of the militia commissions. Mrs. Moore's methodology was to abstract all names, with rank and date of commission, and to arrange them alphabetically by county for selected time periods, and to publish them as described above.

After the Records of Commissions had been so published through the year 1811, it was decided, in 1946, as a feature of Tennessee's Sesquicentennial Celebration to publish the compiled list in hard cover. The result was *Record of Commissions of Officers in the Tennessee Militia, 1796-1811*, compiled by Mrs. John Trotwood Moore (Nashville, Tennessee Historical Commission, 1947). The commission records for 1812-1815 were not printed.

The volume for 1796-1811 has long been out-of-print, and it seems desirable to reissue it, with the addition of commissions for the years 1812-1815, which were also compiled by Mrs. Moore. There follows herewith a facsimile reproduction of Mrs. Moore's remarks and the 1947 listing of commissions, plus the listings for 1812-1815, with an index for those years.


Robert M. McBride
Editor, *Tennessee Historical Quarterly*
November 1, 1976

# PART I

## RECORD OF COMMISSIONS OF OFFICERS IN THE TENNESSEE MILITIA, 1796-1811

# RECORD OF COMMISSIONS OF OFFICERS IN THE TENNESSEE MILITIA, 1796-1801

COMPILED BY MRS. JOHN TROTWOOD MOORE

At the suggestion of the Chairman of the Tennessee Historical Commission, this record of the names of the men commissioned as officers in the Tennessee Militia after the admission of the state to the Union in 1796 has been compiled for serial publication. The information on which the present list is based is to be found in a manuscript volume entitled, Commission Book, 1796-1800, which is now in the Tennessee State Archives. Despite the terminal date of 1800 in the title, the volume contains a record of a few commissions issued in 1801.

This volume is the first of a series into which has been copied a complete record, arranged in chronological order, of all military appointments to office for which the governors issued commissions. A second volume, which apparently covered the years 1801 through 1806, has not been found. Two other volumes, covering the periods from 1807 to May, 1815, and from 1815 to 1827, respectively, are in the State Archives, and will be used for the compilation of similar lists for those periods.

The present list undertakes to include only the commissions issued to militia officers during the first three terms of Governor John Sevier. The names are arranged in alphabetical, rather than chronological, order and are grouped by counties. The counties, in turn, are arranged in alphabetical order, and the publication will present the officers of each county as a unit. It should be kept in mind that the counties in existence at the beginning of statehood were later divided in the establishing of new counties; therefore, the name of the same officer will sometimes be found in his original county and later in the new county where he resided.

It is hoped that the compilation of such a list will facilitate the preparation and publication of county histories, an object which the Historical Commission has set itself to encourage and promote. The roster should also aid in tracing the men from Tennessee who served in campaigns outside of the state, such as: Doherty's march toward New Orleans in 1803; Jackson's campaign to Natchez in 1812-1813; the Creek Wars; the battles against Great Britain on the Gulf Coast under Jackson in 1814-1815; and the war against the Seminole Indians in Florida. It is a tradition in Tennessee that no other state has equalled it in the proportion of its manpower sent to fight wars beyond the state boundary, and the names of the officers who led these men are worthy of being recorded. It is believed, also, that the publication of these rosters may prove to be of interest and assistance to genealogists and biographers.

The spelling as it appears in the original record has been followed throughout, although in many cases it is obviously erroneous.

### Blount County Regiments
### Commissioned

| | | |
|---|---|---|
| Adams, Thomas | Lieutenant | March 29, 1799 |
| Alexander, John | Lieutenant in cavalry regiment, Hamilton District | October 4, 1796 |
| Alexander, John | Captain | October 10, 1796 |
| Alexander, Joseph | Lieutenant | September 17, 1800 |
| Allison, John | Captain | September 17, 1800 |
| Bice, Jonathan | Ensign | March 29, 1799 |
| Bigham, Nathaniel | Ensign | September 17, 1800 |
| Black, Given | Lieutenant | October 10, 1796 |
| Bogle, Hugh | Ensign | January 6, 1801 |
| Bogle, Samuel | Captain | October 10, 1796 |
| Boyd, Robert | Captain in cavalry volunteers | November 8, 1796 |
| Bradley, John | 2nd Major | October 4, 1796 |
| Broyls, George | Ensign | May 25, 1799 |
| Casteele, Edmond | Ensign | March 29, 1799 |
| Cochran, James | Lieutenant | October 10, 1796 |
| Coldwell, David | Captain | March 29, 1799 |
| Colvill, Joseph | Captain | October 10, 1796 |
| Cowan, John | Captain | September 26, 1799 |
| Craig, David | Lieutenant-Colonel Commandant | October 4, 1796 |
| Cunningham, James | Captain in cavalry regiment, Hamilton District | October 4, 1796 |
| Dearmond, Richard | Ensign in Captain Rhea's company, vice John Kelly | June 8, 1797 |
| Dearmond, Richard | Lieutenant | May 25, 1799 |
| Dearmond, Richard | Captain | October 23, 1799 |
| Donaldson, Robert | Ensign | September 17, 1800 |
| Durham, William | Ensign | March 29, 1799 |
| Durham, William | Lieutenant | January 6, 1801 |
| Gailey, James | Ensign | September 17, 1800 |
| Gallaher, James | Lieutenant | October 10, 1796 |
| Gamble, Andrew | Ensign | October 10, 1796 |
| Gillespie, James | Captain | June 8, 1797 |
| Gillespie, James | Captain | September 17, 1800 |

IN THE TENNESSEE MILITIA, 1796-1811    5

| | | |
|---|---|---|
| Griffiths, Eli | Ensign | April 8, 1800 |
| Guin (?), Norton | Lieutenant | June 8, 1797 |
| Hall, Luke | Ensign | June 8, 1797 |
| Hannah, Andrew | Ensign | June 16, 1801 |
| Hess, John | Lieutenant | October 10, 1796 |
| Hoge, Samuel | Ensign | September 17, 1800 |
| Holloday, William | Ensign | October 10, 1796 |
| Hues, Moses | Lieutenant | September 17, 1800 |
| Jones, Prettyman | Ensign | September 26, 1799 |
| Kelley, John | Captain | September 17, 1800 |
| Kelly, John | Ensign | October 10, 1796 |
| Lacky, Archibald | Captain | October 10, 1796 |
| Lovelice, David | Lieutenant | June 16, 1801 |
| McCampbell, Solomon | Ensign | October 10, 1796 |
| McCampbell, Solomon | Lieutenant | September 17, 1800 |
| McClanahan, Matthew | Lieutenant | June 16, 1801 |
| McClenahan, Matthew | Ensign | May 25, 1799 |
| McGinley, James | Captain | September 17, 1800 |
| McRandels, John | Ensign | September 17, 1800 |
| Montgomery, Alexander | Captain | September 26, 1799 |
| Montgomery, Murphrey | Lieutenant | March 29, 1799 |
| Moore, James | Captain | October 10, 1796 |
| Morrisson, Thomas | Lieutenant | May 25, 1799 |
| Nelson, Lewis | Captain | March 29, 1799 |
| Norwood, Samuel | Lieutenant | September 26, 1799 |
| Parsons, Robert | Ensign | September 17, 1800 |
| Reagan, Ahimaaz | Ensign | June 16, 1801 |
| Reves, Moses | Ensign | September 17, 1800 |
| Rhea, Robert | Captain | October 10, 1796 |
| Rogers, Reuben | Ensign | May 25, 1799 |
| Rogers, Reuben | Lieutenant | June 8, 1800 |
| Scott, James | Captain | October 10, 1796 |
| Sherrell, John | Lieutenant | May 25, 1799 |
| Sherrill, John | Lieutenant in cavalry regiment | November 8, 1796 |
| Singleton, John | 1st Major | October 4, 1796 |
| Sloan, William | Cornet in cavalry regiment, Hamilton District | October 4, 1796 |
| Smith, John | Ensign | October 10, 1796 |
| Snider, George | Cornet in cavalry volunteers | November 8, 1796 |
| Snider, Peter | Ensign | June 16, 1801 |
| Taylor, James | Ensign | January 6, 1801 |
| Tedford, George | Lieutenant | October 10, 1796 |
| Walker, John | Lieutenant | October 10, 1796 |
| Walker, William | Lieutenant | September 17, 1800 |
| Wallace, Joel | Lieutenant | October 10, 1796 |
| Wattson, James | Lieutenant | September 17, 1800 |

Wear, James ..............Ensign ................October 10, 1796
Weir, James ..............Lieutenant ..........September 17, 1800
Williams, John ...........Ensign ................October 10, 1796
Woods, John ..............Ensign ................October 23, 1799

*Carter County Regiments*
*Commissioned*

Anderson, Thomas .........Captain .............December 17, 1798
Borough, Valentine .......Ensign ..................June 16, 1801
Brantstter(?), Peter .......Captain ..............October 10, 1796
Buck, Abraham ............Lieutenant ..........September 26, 1800
Campbell, Isaac ..........Lieutenant ............October 10, 1796
Campbell, William ........Ensign ...............January 22, 1799
Campbell, William ........Lieutenant ...............June 16, 1801
Carriger, Godfrey .........Lieutenant ............October 10, 1796
Carter, John ..............Brigade Major of
                          Washington District .February 5, 1797
Carter, Landon ............Brigadier-General of Wash-
                          ington District .....November 9, 1796
Crossen, Asa(?) ..........Lieutenant .....,......October 10, 1796
Crossen, Samuel ..........Lieutenant ............October 10, 1796
Cunningham, Aaron ........Ensign ................October 10, 1796
Cunningham, John .........Captain .............December 17, 1798
Dugger, Julius ............Captain ..............October 10, 1796
Ford, Jacob ...............Ensign ................October 10, 1796
Ford, Joseph ..............Captain ..............October 10, 1796
Ford, Joseph ..............Captain ...............August 2, 1798
Greer, Alexander ..........Lieutenant-Colonel
                          Commandant ........October 4, 1796
Griffin, Solomon ...........Ensign .............December 17, 1798
Hawn, Abraham ..........Ensign .............September 26, 1800
Heaton, John ..............Captain .............September 28, 1799
Hinson, John .............Lieutenant ..............August 2, 1798
Howerd, John ............Ensign ................October 10, 1796
Jinkins. William ..........Ensign .............September 28, 1799
Lacy, James ..............Ensign .............December 17, 1798
Lewis, Thomas ............Lieutenant ............October 10, 1796
Love, John ...............Captain .................June 16, 1801
McNabb, Absolom ........Lieutenant ..........September 26, 1800
McNabb, Baptiste .........Ensign ................October 10, 1796
McNabb, Baptiste .........Lieutenant ..........December 17, 1798
Mason, Joseph ............Ensign .............December 17, 1798
Maxwell, Thomas ..........2nd Major ...........October 4, 1796
Pearson, Abel .............Ensign ..................June 16, 1801
Reynolds, Moses ..........Lieutenant ............October 10, 1796
Shelly, John ..............Lieutenant ...............June 16, 1801
Skippeth, Needham .......Ensign ................October 10, 1796

Smith, Daniel .............Ensign ................October 10, 1796
Storm, John ...............Lieutenant ..........September 28, 1799
Taylor, Nathaniel ..........1st Major .............October  4, 1796
Tipton, Jonathan ..........Captain ..............October 10, 1796
Tipton, Thomas ...........Captain .............December 17, 1798
Tompkins, James ..........Lieutenant ..........September 28, 1799
Vannoy, William ..........Lieutenant ............October 10, 1796
Western, William ..........Captain ..............October 10, 1796
Whitson, Isaac ............Ensign .............September 26, 1800
Williams, Archibald ........Captain ..............October 10, 1796
Wills, Peter ...............Lieutenant ..........September 28, 1799

*Cocke County Regiments*
*Commissioned*

Adams, William ...........Captain ................April 12, 1798
Allen, Isaac ...............Captain .................June 16, 1800
Allen, Reuben .............Lieutenant ..............April  5, 1798
Bragg, William ............Ensign .............December 11, 1798
Campbell, William ........Captain .............December 11, 1798
Clark, Thomas ............Lieutenant ..............April  5, 1798
Clevengher, Richard ......Ensign ................April 12, 1798
Cooper, Joel ..............Lieutenant ..............April  5, 1798
Croslin, Samuel ...........Ensign .............December 11, 1798
Denton, John .............Captain .............December 11, 1798
Fine, Ledgerd ............Lieutenant in cavalry regiment,
                          Hamilton District ..December 22, 1798
Fine, Peter ...............1st Major .............January 11, 1798
Harle, Baldwin ............1st Major in cavalry regiment,
                          Hamilton District, vice Charles
                          McClung, resigned ....October 10, 1800
Henry, George ............Ensign ..................April  5, 1798
Holland, Thomas ..........Captain .................April  3, 1800
Hutchans, Smith ..........Captain .................April  5, 1798
Inman, Daniel ............Lieutenant ...........December  3, 1798
Inman, John ..............Captain .............December 11, 1798
Jack, William .............Captain ..................July  8, 1800
Jones, Thomas ............Captain in cavalry regiment,
                          Hamilton District ..December 22, 1798
Lammons, Samuel .........Captain .................April  3, 1800
Lewis, John ...............Ensign ..................April  5, 1798
Lillard, James .............2nd Major ............January 18, 1798
Lillard, John ..............Captain .................April  5, 1798
Lillard, William ...........Lieutenant-Colonel
                          Commandant ........January 18, 1798
McGlolen, John ...........Captain .................April  5, 1798
McMullin, Samuel .........Captain .................April  5, 1798
McPherson, Henry .........Ensign ..................April  5, 1798
McPherson, Joseph ........Ensign ..................April  3, 1800

Matthews, Obadiah .......Lieutenant ...........December 11, 1798
Maybary, Frederick .......Lieutenant ...............April  5, 1798
Mitchell, Nathaniel .......Lieutenant ...............April  3, 1800
Neely, William Washington .Lieutenant ...............June 16, 1800
Ogdon, John .............Lieutenant ...............April  5, 1798
Rector, John ............Captain .................April  5, 1798
Scott, William ............Ensign ..................April  5, 1798
Seduskes, James ..........Cornet in cavalry regiment,
                          Hamilton District ..December 22, 1798
Snelson, James ...........Lieutenant ................July  8, 1800
Snodgrass, James .........Ensign ...................July  8, 1800
Stinnet, William ..........Ensign ..................June 16, 1800
Styers, Henry ............Ensign ..................April  5, 1798
Williams, Thomas ........Lieutenant ...............June 16, 1800
Yoacham, Solomon ........Lieutenant ...............April 12, 1798

*Davidson County Regiments*
*Commissioned*

Able, Ezekiel .............Captain ...............October 10, 1796
Baker, Nathaniel M. .......Ensign,
                           Second Regiment ...December 22, 1800
Baker, Zacheus ...........Captain,
                           Second Regiment .....October 20, 1800
Beevers, James ...........Ensign, First Regiment ....May 14, 1800
Bell, John ................Lieutenant,
                           First Regiment .....December 10, 1800
Benge, Obediah M. ........Captain,
                           First Regiment .....November  7, 1799
Blackmore, William ........2nd Major,
                           Second Regiment ........May  5, 1798
Blair, Samuel .............Captain ...............August 15, 1797
Brown, Joseph ............Lieutenant .............October 10, 1796
Brown, Joseph ............Captain,
                           Second Regiment ...December 17, 1798
Boyd, Harrison ...........Ensign ................October 10, 1796
Boyd, John ...............Lieutenant .............October 10, 1796
Boyd, John, Junior ........Captain,
                           vice John Parks ....September 25, 1797
Campbell, David ..........Ensign,
                           First Regiment ........August 16, 1798
Cartwright, Thomas .......Ensign,
                           Second Regiment .....October 20, 1800
Castleman, John ..........Lieutenant ...............May 10, 1797
Chambers, Alexander .......Ensign,
                           Second Regiment .....October  1, 1798
Childress, Stephen .........Captain,
                           First Regiment ........May 14, 1800

Collinsworth, James ........Lieutenant,
　　　　　　　　　　　　　　First Regiment ..........July 25, 1798
Connoly, Andrew ..........Ensign, First Regiment ....April  2, 1798
Cotton, James .............Ensign ................October 10, 1796
Cox, Thomas ..............Lieutenant,
　　　　　　　　　　　　　　First Regiment .........April  2, 1798
Cross, John ...............Ensign ................October 10, 1796
Cross, John B. .............Captain,
　　　　　　　　　　　　　　First Regiment ..........June 14, 1799
Cross, Maclin .............Lieutenant, vice John Boyd,
　　　　　　　　　　　　　　promoted ..........September 25, 1797
Curry, Samuel .............Ensign, First Regiment ...April 15, 1800
Demose, James ............Captain ..............October 12, 1797
Dillehunty, William .......Lieutenant,
　　　　　　　　　　　　　　First Regiment .........April  2, 1798
Earheart, David ..........Captain,
　　　　　　　　　　　　　　Second Regiment ...December 22, 1800
Edwards, Owen ............Captain,
　　　　　　　　　　　　　　First Regiment ....November 12, 1800
Enochs, Isaac .............Ensign,
　　　　　　　　　　　　　　Second Regiment .....October  1, 1798
Enochs, Isaac .............Lieutenant,
　　　　　　　　　　　　　　Second Regiment .....October  9, 1799
Evans, Robert .............Lieutenant ............October 10, 1796
Ewing, William ............Captain ...............October 10, 1796
Fambrow, Stewart .........Ensign,
　　　　　　　　　　　　　　Second Regiment ...December 17, 1798
Frazer, Daniel .............1st Major of
　　　　　　　　　　　　　　Mero District ........October  8, 1799
Frazor, Daniel .............Captain in Cavalry Regiment,
　　　　　　　　　　　　　　Mero District ........October  4, 1796
Going, William ............Lieutenant .........September  1, 1797
Harney, Thomas ...........Captain ..............October 10, 1796
Harney, Thomas ...........1st Major,
　　　　　　　　　　　　　　Second Regiment ........May  5, 1798
Hay, David ................1st Major ............October  4, 1796
Hay, Joseph ...............Lieutenant,
　　　　　　　　　　　　　　First Regiment ......January 27, 1801
Hays, Robert ..............Lieutenant-Colonel commanding
　　　　　　　　　　　　　　cavalry, Mero District.January 13, 1797
Heaton, Enoch ............Lieutenant,
　　　　　　　　　　　　　　Second Regiment ...December 17, 1798
Hewit, Robert .............Ensign, First Regiment .....July 25, 1798
Hill, James ................Ensign,
　　　　　　　　　　　　　　First Regiment .....November  7, 1799
Hinton, Jeremiah .........Lieutenant,
　　　　　　　　　　　　　　Second Regiment .....October  9, 1799

| | | |
|---|---|---|
| Hooper, Ennis | Captain, Second Regiment | October 1, 1798 |
| Johnson, Peter | Ensign, Second Regiment | October 1, 1798 |
| Johnston, John | Lieutenant | October 10, 1796 |
| Josseling, Benjamin | Captain | October 10, 1796 |
| Kerr, Samuel | Ensign, Second Regiment | October 9, 1799 |
| London, William | Lieutenant, First Regiment | June 14, 1799 |
| McCrory, Thomas | Captain, First Regiment | April 2, 1798 |
| McEwing, David | Captain, First Regiment | August 16, 1798 |
| McGaugh, John | Ensign | October 10, 1796 |
| McKnight, John | Captain, Second Regiment | October 1, 1798 |
| Mackey, William | Lieutenant, First Regiment | August 16, 1798 |
| Maclin, James C. | Adjutant General | May 10, 1797 |
| Manifee, Nimrod | Ensign | September 1, 1799 |
| Manifee, Nimrod | Lieutenant, First Regiment | November 7, 1799 |
| Miller, John | Captain, Second Regiment | October 1, 1798 |
| Moore, Alexander | Captain | October 10, 1796 |
| Motherall, John | Captain, Second Regiment | May 10, 1799 |
| Motherel, John | Lieutenant | October 10, 1796 |
| Nance, Bird | Ensign | August 15, 1797 |
| Neeley, William | Captain in Cavalry Regiment, Mero District | May 30, 1800 |
| Neely, George | Ensign | October 10, 1796 |
| Neely, William | Lieutenant-Colonel, Cavalry Regiment, Mero District | October 4, 1796 |
| Nolen, Robert | Ensign | October 12, 1797 |
| Orsbon, Icabud | Ensign | October 10, 1796 |
| Orton, William | Ensign, First Regiment | April 2, 1798 |
| Parker, David | Lieutenant, Second Regiment | December 22, 1800 |
| Parks, John | Captain | October 10, 1796 |
| Patton, Alexander | Lieutenant | October 12, 1797 |
| Payne, George | Lieutenant, Second Regiment | October 1, 1798 |
| Payne, Matthew | Ensign, First Regiment | January 9, 1800 |
| Phenix, Henry | Captain, First Regiment | February 24, 1801 |
| Phillips, Jonathan | Cornet in Cavalry Regiment, Mero District | October 4, 1796 |
| Phillips, Samuel | Ensign, First Regiment | January 9, 1800 |

In the Tennessee Militia, 1796-1811    11

Pillow, Gideon ............Ensign,
                          First Regiment .....December 17, 1798
Pillow, William ...........Lieutenant ............October 10, 1796
Pillow, William ...........Captain,
                          vice William Ewing .....May 17, 1797
Pipkin, Phillip ............Lieutenant,
                          First Regiment .....December 17, 1798
Pipkin, Philip ...........Captain,
                          First Regiment .....November 12, 1800
Pursley, David ...........Ensign ..................May 10, 1797
Radford, Edward .........Ensign, First Regiment ....July 25, 1798
Rains, John ..............Captain .............,.....October 10, 1796
Rains, William ...........Captain, First Regiment ...April 15, 1800
Ray, William .............Lieutenant ...........October 10, 1796
Reader, Jacob ............Lieutenant, First Regiment.April 15, 1800
Reeder, Jacob ............Ensign ................August 16, 1798
Roberts, Isaac ............Lieutenant-Colonel
                          Commandant ........October 4, 1796
Robertson, Jonathan F. .....2nd Major,
                          First Regiment .....December 17, 1798
Scott, William ............Captain,
                          Second Regiment .....October 9, 1799
Shannon, David ..........Captain ..............October 10, 1796
Shannon, Thomas .........Captain, First Regiment ...April 2, 1798
Shaw, Hugh ..............Lieutenant in Cavalry Regiment,
                          Mero District ..........May 30, 1800
Shous, John ..............Captain,
                          First Regiment ......January 27, 1801
Smith, William ...........Captain ..............October 10, 1796
Stramler, George ..........Ensign,
                          First Regiment ....September 25, 1799
Stump, John ..............Ensign ................October 10, 1796
Stump, John ..............Lieutenant,
                          Second Regiment ...December 17, 1798
Stump, Jonathan ..........Ensign,
                          Second Regiment ...December 17, 1798
Tarkinton, Jesse ..........Lieutenant,
                          First Regiment .........May 14, 1800
Taylor, John .............Ensign ................August 15, 1797
Thompson, James .........Lieutenant,
                          First Regiment .......August 16, 1798
Thompson, Samuel ........Cornet in Cavalry Regiment,
                          Mero District ..........May 30, 1800
Thompson, Thomas .......Lieutenant ............October 10, 1796
Thompson, Thomas .......Captain, First Regiment, vice
                          John Rains, resigned .....July 25, 1798
Thompson, William .......Captain .............September 1, 1797
Tilley, John ..............Ensign ................October 10, 1796

Tracy, Evan ..............Lieutenant ..............October 10, 1796
Walker, Abraham ..........Captain,
                          Second Regiment .....October 1, 1798
Ward, John ..............Lieutenant,
                          Second Regiment .....October 1, 1798
Weakley, Robert ..........Lieutenant-Colonel commanding
                          Second Regiment ......March 18, 1798
White, Jacob .............Ensign,
                          Second Regiment .....October 9, 1799
Williams, Rite ............Ensign ................October 10, 1796
Williamson, John ..........Captain ..................May 10, 1797
Williamson, Thomas .......Lieutenant,
                          First Regiment ......January 9, 1800
Williamson, Thomas .......Captain,
                          First Regiment .....September 29, 1800
Wills, James .............Lieutenant ..............August 15, 1797

*Grainger County Regiments*
*Commissioned*

Adkins, James ............Ensign ...................April 12, 1797
August, John .............Ensign ...................June 20, 1797
Baker, Samuel ............Ensign ...................June 26, 1800
Bean, Ellis ...............Lieutenant ...............May 31, 1798
Bean, George .............Captain ...............October 10, 1796
Berton, John .............Cornet in cavalry
                          volunteers ........September 29, 1800
Bird, John ...............Lieutenant ............October 10, 1796
Blair, James .............Cornet in cavalry regiment,
                          Hamilton District, vice
                          Thomas Davis .......August 16, 1797
Blair, James, Jr. ..........Lieutenant in cavalry regiment,
                          Hamilton District ......April 1, 1800
Boman, William ..........Captain .................April 12, 1797
Bowen, James ............Cornet in cavalry regiment,
                          Hamilton District ......April 1, 1800
Bowen, John .............Lieutenant ............October 10, 1796
Boyd, Robert ............Lieutenant in cavalry regiment,
                          Hamilton District ....October 4, 1796
Brown, John .............Lieutenant, vice, Cutburd
                          Shelton, resigned ........April 5, 1798
Bruten, Samuel ..........Lieutenant ...............April 12, 1797
Camron, Ezra ............Ensign ...................June 16, 1800
Cantabury, John ..........Lieutenant ...............June 16, 1800
Chilton, William ..........Ensign ................October 1, 1800
Chisum, James ...........Captain ..................June 16, 1800
Churchman, Edward ......Ensign ................October 10, 1796
Cocke, John .............Brigade Major of Hamilton
                          District ..............April 26, 1797

| | | |
|---|---|---|
| Combs, George | Captain in cavalry volunteers | September 29, 1800 |
| Cooke, Markes | Ensign | August 2, 1798 |
| Cox, Thomas | Captain | June 20, 1797 |
| Davis, Thomas | Cornet in cavalry regiment, Hamilton District | October 4, 1796 |
| Duke, John | Lieutenant in cavalry volunteers | September 29, 1800 |
| English, James | Ensign | June 16, 1800 |
| Ginens, Ryal | Captain | May 31, 1798 |
| Graham, Spencer | Captain | June 16, 1800 |
| Grimes, George | Lieutenant | June 16, 1800 |
| Haffaker, Peter | Captain | April 12, 1797 |
| Halffaker, Peter | Lieutenant | October 10, 1796 |
| Hamilton, William | Captain | November 13, 1799 |
| Harrelson, John | Ensign | June 20, 1797 |
| Harrison, Solomon | Captain | October 10, 1796 |
| Hayley, David | First Major | October 4, 1796 |
| Henderson, William | Captain in cavalry regiment, Hamilton District, vice Thomas Mitchell | August 16, 1797 |
| Hill, Joab | Lieutenant, vice Matthew McKee, resigned | August 2, 1798 |
| Hoddge, John | Lieutenant | June 20, 1797 |
| Hodge, Moses | Lieutenant | June 16, 1801 |
| Horner, John | Captain, vice Isaac Stroud, removed out of the county | April 5, 1798 |
| Howard, William | Lieutenant | September 24, 1800 |
| Howell, Caleb | Ensign | June 16, 1801 |
| Howell, Henry | Second Major | October 4, 1796 |
| Howell, Malachia | Ensign | October 10, 1796 |
| Inglish, James | Captain | April 12, 1797 |
| Ivey, Henry | Captain | June 16, 1801 |
| Keef, John | Ensign | June 20, 1797 |
| Kettwell, John | Captain | October 10, 1796 |
| Kitchen, Jesse | Ensign | September 24, 1800 |
| Kitchen, John | Lieutenant | June 20, 1797 |
| Lain, Isaac | Captain | October 10, 1796 |
| Langham, Abel | Lieutenant | June 20, 1797 |
| Lea, John | Captain | September 23, 1800 |
| McKee, Matheia | Captain, vice John Kidwell, | |
| McKee, Mathew | Lieutenant October 10, 1796 removed | August 2, 1798 |
| Mitchell, Thomas | Captain in cavalry regiment, Hamilton District | October 4, 1796 |
| Morriss, Shadrach | Captain | June 26, 1800 |
| Ore, James | Lieutenant-Colonel Commandant | October 4, 1796 |

Perrin, Joel .................Lieutenant ............October 10, 1796
Perry, Samuel ..............Captain .............September 24, 1800
Poils, Conrath .............Ensign, vice Richard Terry,
                                removed ..............April  5, 1798
Ricks, Sandrus ............Lieutenant ..............April 12, 1797
Robertson, Hughes ........Ensign ................October 10, 1796
Shelton, Cutburd .........Lieutenant ............October 10, 1796
Shelton, David ............Captain ..............October 10, 1796
Sims, Mathew .............Ensign ................October 10, 1796
Skidmore, Henry .........Captain ..............October  9, 1799
Smith, Ezekiel .............Lieutenant ...............June 16, 1800
Stroud, Isaac ..............Captain ..............October 10, 1796
Talbert, Frederick ........Lieutenant ...............June 26, 1800
Taylor, Daniel ............Captain ................June 20, 1797
Terry, Richard ............Ensign ................October 10, 1796
Vanbibber, John ..........Captain .................June 16, 1800
Venbeber, Peter ..........Lieutenant ..............April 12, 1797
Wever, Benjamn ..........Ensign .................April 12, 1797
Whittle, Robert ...........Ensign ..................May 31, 1798
Williams, Silas ............Captain .................June 16, 1800
Williams, William ........Ensign ................October 10, 1796
York, William ............Ensign ..................June 16, 1800

*Greene County Regiments*
*Commissioned*

Allison, Ewen .............Second Major ..........October  4, 1796
Bigham, Andrew .........Ensign ................October 10, 1796
Bigham, Andrew .........Lieutenant ...............May 10, 1798
Breatherton, William .....Lieutenant ............October 10, 1796
Brewer, Samuel ..........Cornet in cavalry regiment,
                                Washington District ..January 27, 1801
Brown, Hugh .............Ensign ................October 10, 1796
Brown, Thomas ..........Ensign ................October 10, 1796
Bryant, Andrew ..........Ensign ................October 16, 1799
Buland, John .............Ensign .............December  5, 1800
Bullard, Christopher ......Captain ..............October 10, 1796
Carr, James ...............Lieutenant ............October 10, 1796
Carter, Ezekiel ............Lieutenant ...............June 16, 1800
Carter, Jesse ..............Ensign ................October 16, 1799
Condray, James ..........Lieutenant ............October 16, 1799
Conway, Christopher .....Captain in cavalry
                                volunteers ..........January 13, 1798
Conway, George ..........Major-General of the
                                State ............November  4, 1797
Conway, William .........Second Major, cavalry regiment,
                                Washington District ..October 13, 1796
Couch, George ............Lieutenant ............October 16, 1799

Crawford, William ......... Lieutenant ............ October 10, 1796
Crow, Benjamin ........... Lieutenant-Colonel Commandant ............ October 4, 1796
Davis, William ............ Lieutenant ............ October 10, 1796
Dill, Leonard ............. Ensign .................. May 10, 1798
Dill, Leonard ............. Lieutenant ............ October 16, 1799
Dodd, John ............... Captain ............... November 7, 1799
Easterly, Cunrod .......... Ensign .................. May 1, 1799
Edmondson, Samuel ....... Ensign .................. June 16, 1800
Fearnsworth, George ...... Captain ............... February 2, 1801
Frenary, Richard .......... Ensign ................ October 16, 1799
Gibson, John .............. Captain ............... October 10, 1796
Gibson, John .............. Captain ............... January 15, 1801
Goldman, John ............ Ensign ............... November 7, 1799
Gragg, John .............. Captain ............... October 10, 1796
Gregg, Samuel ............ First Major ........... October 4, 1796
Gullick, Reese ............ Captain ............... October 10, 1796
Guttary, James ........... Captain ............... May 10, 1798
Hair, Jacob ............... Lieutenant ............. May 1, 1799
Harman, George ........... Lieutenant ............ October 16, 1799
Harmon, John ............. Captain ............... October 10, 1796
Harrison, Edmund ......... Adjutant ............... June 16, 1801
Harrison, Isaiah .......... Lieutenant ............ October 10, 1796
Henderson, Daniel ......... Ensign ............... October 16, 1799
Henninger, Jacob .......... Captain ............... October 10, 1796
Hickson, Andrew .......... Ensign ............... October 10, 1796
Hickson, Ephraim ......... Ensign .................. June 16, 1800
Howard, William .......... Ensign ................... May 1, 1799
Johnson, Zaphre .......... Ensign .............. December 5, 1800
Jones, John .............. Captain .................. July 3, 1799
Kasterson, John ........... Captain .................. July 3, 1799
Kelley, William ........... Ensign ................... May 1, 1799
Kelley, William ........... Lieutenant .............. June 16, 1800
King, John ............... Lieutenant ............ November 7, 1799
King, William ............ Lieutenant ............ October 10, 1796
King, William ............ Adjutant ............... April 20, 1797
Laderdale, James .......... Captain ............... October 10, 1796
Landrum, Younger ....... Lieutenant ............... July 3, 1799
Lettrell, John ............ Lieutenant ............ October 10, 1796
Lowry, Alexander ......... Lieutenant ............ October 10, 1796
McCopen, Alexander ...... Lieutenant, cavalry regiment, Washington District .. October 4, 1796
McGill, Hugh ............. Lieutenant ............ October 10, 1796
McMurtry, Joseph ......... Ensign .................. May 10, 1798
McMurtry, Joseph ......... Lieutenant .............. June 16, 1800
Mahan, James ............ Captain ............... October 10, 1796
Milburn, Jonathan ........ Lieutenant ............ October 16, 1799
Morris, Shadrach ......... Captain ............... October 10, 1796

| | | |
|---|---|---|
| Newman, John | Ensign | May 10, 1798 |
| Nicholson, Richard | Lieutenant | October 10, 1796 |
| Parson, George | Adjutant, vice William King | May 10, 1798 |
| Patterson, William | Ensign | December 5, 1800 |
| Penney, James | Captain | October 10, 1796 |
| Pettet, Nehemiah | Lieutenant | May 1, 1799 |
| Reed, James | Ensign | June 16, 1800 |
| Reed, Robert | Ensign | June 16, 1800 |
| Reeves, James | Ensign | October 10, 1796 |
| Resterson, John | Lieutenant | May 1, 1799 |
| Rice, David | Lieutenant in cavalry regiment | January 13, 1798 |
| Roberts, John | Ensign | October 10, 1796 |
| Robertson, John | Cornet in cavalry regiment, Washington District | October 4, 1796 |
| Robertson, John | Ensign | October 10, 1796 |
| Russell, John | Cornet in cavalry regiment | January 13, 1798 |
| Self, Thomas | Ensign | May 10, 1798 |
| Shoemaker, Leonard Clabourne | Lieutenant | October 10, 1796 |
| Smith, Cornelious | Ensign | October 10, 1796 |
| Smith, Cornelius | Lieutenant | November 7, 1799 |
| Stanburg, William | Ensign | October 10, 1796 |
| Stanfield, John | Captain | June 16, 1800 |
| Steal, Andrew | Captain | May 1, 1799 |
| Stephenson, James | Captain in cavalry regiment, Washington District | October 4, 1796 |
| Sterns, John | Lieutenant | October 10, 1796 |
| Tate, David | Lieutenant | May 10, 1798 |
| Tate, David | Captain | October 16, 1799 |
| Tate, Edward | Captain | October 10, 1796 |
| Temple, James | Cornet in cavalry regiment, Washington District | June 24, 1799 |
| Temple, James | Captain in cavalry regiment, Washington District | January 27, 1801 |
| Temple, Thomas | Lieutenant in cavalry regiment, Washington District | January 27, 1801 |
| Thorlaton, Robert | Ensign | October 10, 1796 |
| Thorlaton, Robert | Quartermaster | May 10, 1798 |
| White, William | Captain | October 10, 1796 |
| Whithead, John | Captain | May 1, 1799 |
| Willoughby, Elijah | Ensign | October 10, 1796 |
| Woolse, Stephen | Ensign | October 10, 1796 |

## In the Tennessee Militia, 1796-1811

### Hawkins County Regiments
#### Commissioned

| | | |
|---|---|---|
| Bailey, Britan | Ensign | October 10, 1800 |
| Bailey, Britton | Lieutenant | June 16, 1801 |
| Bailey, Thomas | Captain | October 10, 1800 |
| Bailey, William | Captain | October 10, 1796 |
| Barnet, Gilbert | Ensign | August 15, 1797 |
| Bartlett, Joseph | Captain | April 1, 1800 |
| Berry, James | Second Major, vice Joel Dyer, resigned | November 30, 1798 |
| Berry, Thomas | Lieutenant-Colonel Commandant | October 4, 1796 |
| Brown, William | Ensign | October 10, 1796 |
| Bryan, Joseph | Lieutenant | August 15, 1797 |
| Burras, John | Ensign | August 15, 1797 |
| Byrd, John | Ensign | April 5, 1798 |
| Carmack, John | Ensign | September 16, 1798 |
| Center, Willes Stephen | Lieutenant | October 10, 1796 |
| Chestnut, Henry | Lieutenant | April 1, 1800 |
| Cloud, Benjamin | Captain | June 16, 1801 |
| Coke, Richard | Ensign | October 10, 1796 |
| Cooper, John | Captain | October 10, 1796 |
| Cox, Daniel | Lieutenant | October 10, 1796 |
| Craft, Jacob | Ensign | October 10, 1796 |
| Cross, Joseph | Ensign | February 18, 1800 |
| Dardis, James | Lieutenant in cavalry volunteers | March 29, 1797 |
| Dardis, James | Lieutenant in cavalry volunteers | September 16, 1798 |
| Davies, John | Lieutenant | October 10, 1796 |
| Dodson, Olliver | Lieutenant | October 10, 1796 |
| Dodson, Olliver | Captain | August 15, 1797 |
| Dodson, Rolley | Ensign | August 15, 1797 |
| Dyer, Henry | Captain | July 8, 1800 |
| Dyer, Joel | Second Major | October 4, 1796 |
| Etter, George H. | Cornet in cavalry volunteers | July 30, 1800 |
| Fowler, Jacob | Lieutenant | August 15, 1797 |
| Gast, Moses | Lieutenant | September 25, 1799 |
| Gillingwaters, Thomas | Lieutenant | April 1, 1800 |
| Golden, William | Ensign | May 9, 1798 |
| Goodrey, George | Ensign | October 10, 1796 |
| Guthrey, Francis | Lieutenant in cavalry regiment, Washington District | October 4, 1796 |
| Haines, John | Ensign | October 10, 1796 |
| Hall, John | Cornet in cavalry volunteers | March 29, 1797 |

Hamilton, James .......... Cornet in cavalry regiment,
  Captain .................. June 16, 1801
Hamilton, John ........... Ensign ................... June 16, 1801
Hamilton, Johnston ....... Lieutenant ............... July  9, 1800
Hammons, Thomas ........ Captain ................ April  5, 1798
Haney, Spencer .......... Captain ............... August 15, 1797
Harrison, John ............  Washington District .. October  4, 1796
Haynes, Christopher ....... Ensign ................... June 12, 1800
Henderson, William ....... Captain ........... September 26, 1800
Hickey, John .............. Lieutenant ........... October 10, 1800
Hogan, James ............. Captain ............... October 10, 1796
Hord, William ........... First Major, vice Joseph
  McMinn, resigned .. November 30, 1798
Hurcherson, William ...... Captain .................. July  9, 1800
Ice, Frederick ............ Ensign ................... July  9, 1800
Johnson, William ......... Ensign .................. April  1, 1800
Kellensworth, John ....... Ensign ............... August 15, 1797
Koyle, William ........... Lieutenant ............ August 15, 1797
Lane, William ............ Lieutenant ............... May  9, 1798
Lawson, Isham ........... Ensign .................. April  1, 1800
Lawson, Jacob ............ Lieutenant ............ August 15, 1797
Lawson, Jacob ............ Captain ................. April  1, 1800
Lebow, John .............. Ensign ............... August 15, 1797
Lee, Cader ................ Lieutenant ............. March 29, 1799
Lee, Needam .............. Lieutenant ........... October 10, 1800
Lee, Needham ............ Lieutenant ........... October 10, 1796
Lines, Jacob .............. Ensign ............... August 15, 1797
Looney, Robert ........... Lieutenant in cavalry regiment,
  Washington District ..... July 30, 1800
McCollough, William ...... Lieutenant .......... February 18, 1800
McCraw, Dancey ......... Lieutenant ............... July  8, 1800
McDonald, Randolph ..... Captain ............. September 25, 1799
McGeehee, William ....... Lieutenant ........... October 10, 1796
McKain, Robert .......... Ensign ............... October 10, 1796
McKain, Robert .......... Lieutenant ............ August 15, 1797
McKain, Robert .......... Captain ............... March 29, 1799
McMinn, Joseph ......... First Major .......... October  4, 1796
Markham, Josiah ......... Captain ............. November 30, 1798
Miller, Jacob ............. Ensign .................. April  1, 1800
Mitchell, Edward ......... Captain ............... October 10, 1796
Mitchell, William ......... Lieutenant in
  cavalry volunteers ....... July 30, 1800
Morgan, James ........... Lieutenant ............... June 16, 1801
Nelson, Alexander ........ Captain in
  cavalry volunteers ..... March 29, 1797
Nelson, Alexander ........ Captain in
  cavalry volunteers . September 16, 1798

IN THE TENNESSEE MILITIA, 1796-1811 19

Nelson, Alexander .........Captain in
 cavalry volunteers .......July 30, 1800
Patterson, Robert ..........Lieutenant .............August 15, 1797
Perriman, James ..........Ensign ..................June 16, 1801
Riddle, John .............Lieutenant ..............April 1, 1800
Roberts, George ..........Lieutenant ...........January 8, 1798
Saunders John ............Captain ..............October 10, 1796
Senter, Talbert ............Ensign ..................July 8, 1800
Sicks, John ...............Ensign .............September 25, 1799
Smith, Alexander .........Ensign ...............October 10, 1796
Smith, Allan .............Ensign .................June 16, 1801
Smith, John ..............Lieutenant ...........October 10, 1796
Smith, Joseph ............Captain ..............October 10, 1796
Smith, Samuel ............Captain .............August 15, 1797
Stacy, Mashak ............Ensign ...................July 9, 1800
Stubblefield, William .......Captain in cavalry regiment,
 Washington District ..October 4, 1796
Sumpter, John ............Captain ................June 16, 1801
Surguine, James ..........Captain .............August 15, 1797
Taylor, John .............Lieutenant ...............July 9, 1800
Thompson, John ..........Lieutenant ...........October 10, 1796
Thompson, John ..........Captain ............September 16, 1798
Walling, James ............Captain ..............October 10, 1796
Webster, John ............Captain ............August 15, 1797
Williams, James ..........Captain ............October 10, 1796
Williams, Joseph .........Lieutenant ...............June 16, 1801
Willson, Michael ..........Ensign ...............October 10, 1796
Wilson, Michael ..........Lieutenant .........September 16, 1798
Young, William ..........Captain in cavalry regiment,
 Washington District .....July 30, 1800

*Jefferson County Regiments*
*Commissioned*

Allan, Reuben .............Ensign .................March 17, 1797
Arnold, William ..........Ensign ...............October 10, 1796
Bates, Matthew ..........Ensign ..................April 4, 1799
Bird, Abraham ...........Captain in cavalry regiment,
 Hamilton District ....October 4, 1796
Braselton, William ........Captain .................April 5, 1799
Brendley, Frazer ..........Lieutenant ...........October 10, 1796
Carlock, Abraham .........Cornet in cavalry regiment,
 Hamilton District ....October 4, 1796
Carr, Andrew .............Ensign ...............October 10, 1796
Carson, Adam ............Ensign ...............October 10, 1796
Carson, Robert ...........Captain ..............October 10, 1796
Carthey, George ..........Lieutenant ...........October 10, 1796
Cooper, Joel .............Ensign ............February 23, 1797

Copland, Zachariah ........Captain ...............October 10, 1796
Cowan, James .............Lieutenant ..........September 25, 1799
Cunningham, James ........Lieutenant in cavalry regiment,
 Hamilton District ....October 4, 1796
Damran, Joseph ...........Captain ...............October 10, 1796
Deroset, Samuel ...........Captain ...............October 10, 1796
Doherty, George ...........Lieutenant-Colonel
 Commandmant ......October 22, 1799
Doherty, James ............Second Major, vice Hugh Kelso,
 resigned ...........December 10, 1800
Eldridge, Simion ...........Ensign ................October 10, 1796
Fansher, James ............Captain ............September 25, 1799
George, Edward ...........Lieutenant ................April 1, 1800
Hanes, John ..............Captain ...............October 10, 1796
Harman, Jacob ............Captain .................April 5, 1799
Hill, John ................Captain in cavalry regiment,
 Hamilton District .....August 6, 1798
Hill, Samuel ..............Cornet in cavalry regiment,
 Hamilton District .....August 6, 1798
Hodges, Charles ...........Captain ...............October 12, 1797
Inman, Daniel .............Ensign ................October 10, 1796
Inman, David .............Ensign ................October 10, 1796
Inman, James .............Captain ...............October 10, 1796
Jentry, Martin ...........Lieutenant in cavalry regiment,
 Hamilton District .....August 6, 1798
Kelso, Alexander ..........Lieutenant ............October 10, 1796
Kelso, Alexander ..........Captain ..................April 1, 1800
Kelso, Hugh ..............Second Major ..........October 22, 1799
Kirkpatrick, Hugh .........Lieutenant ............October 10, 1796
Lane, Tidence ............Captain ...............October 10, 1796
Leeth, George ............Ensign ................October 10, 1796
Lillard, James ............Captain ............February 23, 1797
Longacre, Benjamin .......Lieutenant ............October 10, 1796
Lowry, James ............Ensign ................October 10, 1796
Luburn, John .............Lieutenant .................April 4, 1799
McCoy, Moses ............Lieutenant .............March 17, 1797
McCuistion, James ........Lieutenant ................April 1, 1800
McDannell, John ..........Ensign .............September 25, 1799
McDonald, James .........Lieutenant ............October 10, 1796
McDonel, James ..........Captain .................April 4, 1799
McDonel, John ...........Lieutenant ................April 4, 1799
McFarland, Robert ........First Major ...........October 22, 1799
McSpaden, Samuel ........Captain ...............October 10, 1796
Mendinhall, Martin ........Ensign ................October 12, 1797
Murphey, David ..........Lieutenant ............October 10, 1796
Myers, James ............Lieutenant ..........September 25, 1799
Myres, David ............Ensign .............September 25, 1799
Nicholson, Jeremiah .......Ensign .................Aprill 1, 1800

IN THE TENNESSEE MILITIA, 1796-1811  21

Nicholson, Joseph ......... Ensign ................. April 1, 1800
Pangle, Frederick .......... Ensign ................ October 10, 1796
Peck, Jacob ............... Lieutenant .............. April 5, 1799
Pryer, William ............ Lieutenant ........... February 23, 1797
Rankin, James ............ Ensign ................. April 5, 1799
Ratherford, Thomas ....... Captain ............... March 17, 1797
Reno, Thomas ............ Captain ............... October 10, 1796
Sellards, Samuel .......... Ensign ................. April 5, 1799
Shield, William ........... Captain ............... October 10, 1796
Sively, Jacob ............. Ensign ................. April 4, 1799
Trotter, John ............. Lieutenant ............. October 10, 1796
Turner, James ........... Captain ................ April 4, 1799
Vance, John .............. Lieutenant ............ October 10, 1796
Veech, Elijah ............. Ensign ................ October 10, 1796
Walters, John ............ Lieutenant ............. April 4, 1799
Winton, William .......... Lieutenant ............ October 10, 1796

*Knox County Regiments*
*Commissioned*

Aike, Joseph ............. Captain ............... October 10, 1796
Aldridg, William ......... Lieutenant .............. April 26, 1797
Anderson, Thomas ........ Lieutenant ........... October 10, 1796
Armstrong, John .......... Ensign ................ October 10, 1796
Armstrong, John .......... Ensign .............. November 1, 1797
Armstrong, John .......... Lieutenant ............. June 16, 1801
Armstrong, Robert ........ Lieutenant ........... October 10, 1796
Atkinson, William ........ Ensign ................. May 30, 1799
Bailey, David ............ Lieutenant ............. June 16, 1801
Bartlet, Joseph ........... Ensign ............... October 10, 1796
Bayless, Hezekiah ........ Captain .............. October 10, 1796
Bird, Stephen ............ Captain ............... October 10, 1796
Birden, William .......... Ensign ............... October 10, 1796
Bishop, David ............ Ensign ............ September 29, 1800
Blackely, Alexander ....... Captain ............... January 28, 1801
Blackley, Alexander ....... Ensign ................. April 8, 1800
Bowen, John ............. Lieutenant ............. March 13, 1797
Bowen, John ............. Captain ................ May 31, 1798
Brazeal, Valentine ........ Ensign ............ September 29, 1800
Brown, Thomas ........... Lieutenant ............. June 16, 1801
Burdon, William .......... Ensign ............... October 10, 1796
Butler, James ............ Captain .............. August 10, 1799
Campbell, Alexander ...... Captain .............. October 10, 1796
Campbell, David ......... Second Major ......... October 4, 1796
Campbell, David ......... Lieutenant-Colonel Commandant,
                          vice, John Sawyers.. December 20, 1800
Campbell, John ........... Lieutenant ........... October 10, 1796
Campbell, Richard ........ Adjutant ............... June 16, 1801

Carmicle, Alexander ........ Lieutenant ............. October 10, 1796
Cavett, Richard ........... Ensign .............. September 29, 1800
Chapman, Asahel .......... Lieutenant .............. May 31, 1798
Chisolm, James ........... Lieutenant ........... January 28, 1801
Cobb, Asa ............... Ensign ................. June 16, 1801
Colker, William .......... Ensign ............. September 29, 1800
Conway, Charles .......... Ensign ............... August 15, 1797
Cowan, Wallace .......... Cornet in cavalry regiment,
                              Hamilton District ..... August 22, 1800
Cox, Samuel .............. Lieutenant ........... October 10, 1796
Crain, Benjamin ........... Ensign ............. September 29, 1800
Crawford, John ........... First Major ........... October 4, 1796
Crelly, William ............ Lieutenant ............ August 10, 1799
Crowford, English ........ Lieutenant .......... September 25, 1799
Crozier, Arthur ........... Captain ................. May 30, 1799
Crozier, Arthur ........... First Major, vice John Crawford,
                              resigned ................ May 11, 1801
Crozier, John ............. Captain in cavalry
                              volunteers ........ November 8, 1796
Crozier, John ............. Captain in cavalry
                              volunteers ........... January 12, 1798
Crozier, John ............. Captain in cavalry
                              volunteers ........... January 18, 1800
Davis, Nathaniel .......... Captain ............. September 29, 1800
Davis, Thomas ............ Lieutenant ............ January 28, 1801
Davis, Wilson ............. Ensign ................ October 10, 1796
Dillingham, Absalom ...... Lieutenant ........... August 10, 1799
Douglass, James .......... Ensign ............. September 29, 1800
Duncan, Joseph ........... Ensign ............... October 10, 1796
Eldridge, Nathan .......... Ensign ............... October 10, 1796
England, John ............. Captain .............. October 16, 1799
Ferrel, Charles ............ Ensign ............. September 25, 1799
Flenniken, James Wallace .. Captain ............. September 29, 1800
Ford, Zachary ............. Captain ............. November 7, 1799
Frazor, Julian ............. Lieutenant .............. June 16, 1801
Friley, Martin ............. Cornet in Cavalry regiment,
                              Hamilton District .... October 4, 1796
Fristoe, William .......... Captain ............. September 29, 1800
Fronier, N. H. S. .......... Surgeon in cavalry regiment,
                              Hamilton District... February 7, 1797
Frost, Edward ............ Ensign ................. April 26, 1797
Frost, Samuel ............. Lieutenant ........... October 10, 1796
Fulton, Thomas ........... Ensign ................. June 16, 1801
Gamble, John ............. Lieutenant ........... October 10, 1796
Gamble, John ............. Captain .............. October 12, 1798
Gardinhire, William ....... Lieutenant ........... October 14, 1797
Geerin, John .............. Ensign ................ June 16, 1801
Gentry, Jesse ............. Captain .............. October 16, 1799

In the Tennessee Militia, 1796-1811    23

Gerin, Solomon ............Lieutenant ...........October 10, 1796
Gibbs, John ...............Lieutenant ...........October 10, 1796
Green, Jesse ..............Captain ...............October 10, 1796
Green, Joseph .............Captain ...............October 10, 1796
Grills, Elliott .............Captain ...............August 10, 1799
Hail, Nathan ..............Captain ...............January 28, 1801
Hale, Nathan ..............Ensign ................August 10, 1799
Hall, Samuel ..............Ensign ................October 10, 1796
Hambright, John .........Lieutenant ..........September 29, 1800
Hankins, John .............Ensign .............September 29, 1800
Hardin, James ............Captain ...............October 16, 1799
Harlson, John .............Ensign ................October 10, 1796
Harlson, Paul .............Captain ...............October 10, 1796
Havens, William ..........Captain ..................June 16, 1801
Hays, Nathaniel ..........Adjutant ..............October 10, 1796
Hendrex, Luke ............Captain ...............October 10, 1796
Hines, Levi ...............Captain ...............January 28, 1801
Hobbs, James .............Ensign ................October 16, 1799
Hobbs, Joel ...............Captain .................April 26, 1797
Hurd, James ..............Lieutenant ..........September 29, 1800
Hutchens, Smith ..........Captain .............September 29, 1800
Irwin, Francis ............Lieutenant ..........November 7, 1799
Jefferey, Jeremiah ........Captain ...............August 10, 1799
Johnson, William .........Ensign ................August 10, 1799
Lavender, John ...........Lieutenant in cavalry
                          volunteers ........November 8, 1796
Lavender, John ...........Lieutenant in cavalry
                          volunteers ..........January 12, 1798
Lea, Joseph ...............Lieutenant ............August 10, 1799
Lea, Zachariah ............Lieutenant ............October 16, 1799
Lonas, Jacob ..............Ensign ..................June 16, 1801
Long, William .............Ensign ..................June 16, 1801
Looney, Peter .............Lieutenant ............October 16, 1799
Love, John ................Lieutenant ............October 12, 1798
Low, Aquala ...............Lieutenant ..........September 25, 1799
Low, Aquila ...............Captain .................June 16, 1801
Low, John .................Lieutenant ............August 15, 1797
Low, John .................Captain ...............August 10, 1799
Low, John .................Lieutenant ..........September 29, 1800
McAffry, Terence ..........Lieutenant ..............June 16, 1801
McAnier, David ...........Lieutenant ............August 15, 1797
McBeth, Robert ...........Ensign .............September 29, 1800
McCampbell, William ......Captain .............September 29, 1800
McCamy, John .............Ensign .................March 13, 1797
McCamy, John .............Lieutenant ...........January 28, 1801
McClellan, Abraham .......Lieutenant in cavalry regiment,
                          Hamilton District ....October 4, 1796

| | | |
|---|---|---|
| McClellan, John | Lieutenant-Colonel Commandant in cavalry regiment, Hamilton District | October 13, 1796 |
| McClellan, Samuel | Captain in cavalry regiment, Hamilton District | October 4, 1796 |
| McClellan, Samuel | Second Major in cavalry regiment, Hamilton District, vice Joseph Evans, removed | August 3, 1799 |
| McClung, Charles | First Major in cavalry regiment, Hamilton District | October 13, 1796 |
| McCorry, Thomas | Cornet in cavalry volunteers | November 8, 1796 |
| McDonald, Daniel | Captain | September 25, 1799 |
| McKamy, William | Ensign | September 29, 1800 |
| McKorkle, Robert | Ensign | October 16, 1799 |
| McNutt, William | Lieutenant | September 29, 1800 |
| McRee, William | Lieutenant | June 1, 1799 |
| Martin, James | Lieutenant in cavalry regiment, Hamilton District | August 22, 1800 |
| Masterson, Aaron | Ensign | September 29, 1800 |
| Merrow, Richard | Ensign | August 15, 1797 |
| Miller, John | Captain | October 10, 1796 |
| Miller, Robert | Lieutenant | September 29, 1800 |
| Nelson, David | Ensign | January 28, 1801 |
| Oliver, Richard | Lieutenant | September 29, 1800 |
| Oliver, Richard | Captain | June 16, 1801 |
| Owens, Edward | Ensign | May 30, 1799 |
| Parker, Benjamin C. | Cornet in cavalry volunteers | January 18, 1800 |
| Preston, George | Captain | September 29, 1800 |
| Preston, George | Second Major, vice David Campbell, resigned | December 20, 1800 |
| Preston, James | Lieutenant | May 31, 1799 |
| Preston, James | Captain | June 16, 1801 |
| Prewett, Jacob | Captain | September 29, 1800 |
| Price, Reuben | Ensign | October 10, 1796 |
| Pride, Benjamin | Ensign | October 10, 1796 |
| Pruet, Jacob | Captain | March 13, 1797 |
| Reynolds, Robert | Ensign | October 10, 1796 |
| Reynolds, Robert | Lieutenant | May 30, 1799 |
| Reynolds, Robert | Captain | September 25, 1799 |
| Roberts, Nathan | Ensign | June 16, 1801 |
| Rogers, Jeremiah | Captain | October 10, 1796 |
| Sample, Samuel | Captain | October 10, 1796 |
| Sawyers, John | Lieutenant-Colonel Commandant | October 4, 1796 |
| Scaggs, Elie | Ensign | October 10, 1796 |

IN THE TENNESSEE MILITIA, 1796-1811    25

Scott, Laurence ............Ensign ...............February 23, 1801
Shote, John ...............Lieutenant ............October 16, 1799
Smith, Joseph .............Ensign ..................June 16, 1801
Smith, Reuben ............Captain ..............January 28, 1801
Standefer, Samuel ........Lieutenant ...........February 23, 1801
Standefor, Samuel ........Ensign ..............September 25, 1799
Stanley, Rodes ............Ensign ................August 10, 1799
Stone, John ...............Captain ..............October 10, 1796
Taylor, Joseph ............Captain ..............October 10, 1796
Tempel, William ..........Captain in cavalry regiment, Hamilton
                           District, vice Samuel McClellan,
                           promoted .............August 22, 1800
Terry, Jesse ..............Lieutenant ............October 10, 1796
Terry, Samuel .............Ensign ...............October 16, 1799
Thompson, Robert .........Ensign ................August 10, 1799
Ussery, William ...........Lieutenant ..........September 29, 1800
Warnar, Stephen ..........Ensign ...............October 16, 1799
Watson, John ..............Lieutenant ...............April 8, 1800
Wetzel, John H. ...........Lieutenant ...............May 30, 1799
Wetzell, John H. ..........Captain ..................June 16, 1801
Wheeler, John .............Lieutenant ...........October 10, 1796
White, Andrew ............Lieutenant in cavalry
                           volunteers ...........January 18, 1800
White, James ..............Brigadier-General, Hamilton
                           District ............November 9, 1796
White, Moses ..............Cornet in cavalry
                           volunteers ...........January 12, 1798
Whiteside, Abraham ........Surgeon in cavalry
                           volunteers ...........January 18, 1800
Wilson, Benjamin ..........Lieutenant ...............June 16, 1801
Woodward, Thomas .......Lieutenant ............October 10, 1796

*Montgomery County Regiments*
*Commissioned*

Beaty, John ...............Ensign ..............September 29, 1797
Beaty, John ...............Lieutenant ..........December 22, 1798
Beaty, Samuel .............Ensign ..................June 16, 1801
Beeasun, William ..........Lieutenant in cavalry regiment,
                           Mero District .........June 6, 1799
Bell, William .............First Major ..............May 14, 1800
Brantley, Charles .........Lieutenant ..........September 29, 1797
Brown, Darden .............Ensign ..............September 29, 1797
Campbell, James ...........Captain .............September 29, 1797
Carns, Alexander ..........Captain ..................June 16, 1801
Choat, Aaron ..............Lieutenant ..........September 29, 1797
Choat, Joseph .............Ensign ..............September 29, 1797
Cocke, John ...............Ensign ..............December 22, 1798

Cocke, Richard ...........Lieutenant ..........December 22, 1798
Edmonston, John ..........Captain in cavalry regiment,
                          Mero District ........October  4, 1796
Elliott, John ..............Lieutenant ..........November 18, 1800
Ford, James ...............Lieutenant-Colonel
                          Commandant ........October  4, 1796
Gibson, Witson ............Captain .............September 29, 1797
Greson, William ...........Ensign ..............September 29, 1797
Hambleton, Alexander ......Cornet in cavalry regiment,
                          Mero District ........October  4, 1796
Harris, John ..............Lieutenant ..........September 29, 1797
Harriss, Thompson .........Captain .............December 22, 1798
Hollis, James .............Captain .............September 29, 1797
Hutcheson, Thomas .......Lieutenant ................June 16, 1801
McCollum, Hugh ..........Second Major in cavalry regiment,
                          Mero District ........October 28, 1797
Miles, Richard ............First Major ............October  4, 1796
Mitcheson, William .......Second Major ..........October  4, 1796
Peterson, Isaac ............Captain .............September 29, 1797
Rogers, Larkin ............Lieutenant ..........September 29, 1797
Teas, William .............Cornet in cavalry regiment,
                          Mero District ...........June  6, 1799
Tenen, Thomas .............Captain .............November 18, 1800
Thomas, Benjamin .......Captain .............September 29, 1797
Trousdale, Alexander ......Lieutenant ..........September 29, 1797
Wells, Archelas ...........Lieutenant in cavalry regiment,
                          Mero District ........October  4, 1796
Wells, Archelus ............Second Major .........October 20, 1800
Wells, Archibald ...........Captain .............December 22, 1798
Williams, Henry ...........Ensign ..............September 29, 1797

*Robertson County Regiments*
*Commissioned*

Blackwell, James ..........Captain ...............October 18, 1800
Bounds, Thomas ...........Captain ...............January 9, 1800
Briscoe, John ..............Ensign ................August 15, 1797
Bryant, John ..............Captain ..............February 23, 1801
Carr, Lawrence ............Lieutenant .............August 10, 1799
Caughran, John ...........Captain ...............October 10, 1796
Cheathem, Edward .........Captain .............December 17, 1798
Clap, Adam ................Ensign ................October 10, 1796
Colgan, Charles ............Lieutenant ............August 15, 1797
Crombwell, Dawsey .......Lieutenant .............October 1, 1798
Curry, Robert B. ...........Lieutenant in cavalry regiment,
                          Mero District .........October 1, 1800
Dakerson, Nathaniel .......Ensign ................October 10, 1796

IN THE TENNESSEE MILITIA, 1796-1811 27

Dardin, Jonathan .......... Captain .............. November 12, 1800
Dorris, John ............... Ensign ................ October 10, 1796
Dortch, Isaac .............. Captain ............... August 10, 1799
Duncan, Martin ........... Captain ............... October 10, 1796
Fort, Josiah ............... Lieutenant ............ August 10, 1799
Grimes, William ........... Ensign ................ August 10, 1799
Groom, Valentine ......... Ensign ................... May 21, 1800
Haggard, William .......... Captain in cavalry regiment,
             Mero District ........ October 4, 1796
Hamilton, Isaiah ........... Captain ................. May 21, 1800
Hampelton, David ........ Lieutenant .......... September 22, 1797
Haynes, James ............ Lieutenant ............ October 10, 1796
Henry, Hugh .............. Second Major, vice James Norfleet
             resigned ................. July 30, 1800
Henry, Thomas ............ Lieutenant in cavalry regiment,
             Mero District ........ October 4, 1796
Hutchison, Thomas ....... Captain ............... August 15, 1797
James, John ............... Lieutenant, vice Charles
             Colgan ................. July 23, 1798
Johnson, John ............. Ensign ............. September 22, 1797
Johnson, Thomas ......... Lieutenant-Colonel
             Commandant ........ October 4, 1796
Johnson, William ......... Ensign ................ October 10, 1796
Johnson, William ......... Captain .............. February 14, 1798
Jones, Eli ................. Ensign ............... February 14, 1798
Jones, Jesse .............. Captain .................. June 16, 1801
Killgore, Charles .......... Ensign ................ August 22, 1800
Killgore, Thomas ......... Lieutenant ............ August 22, 1800
Krisel, John ............... Ensign ............... February 18, 1800
Krisel, John ............... Lieutenant .......... February 23, 1801
Lancaster, Robert ......... Lieutenant ............ October 10, 1796
Lawson, Epephoditus ..... Lieutenant .......... November 12, 1800
Lockhart, James .......... Captain ............... October 10, 1796
Mathews, Sampson ........ Captain in cavalry regiment,
             Mero District ........ October 1, 1800
Matthews, Sampson ....... Cornet in cavalry regiment,
             Mero District ........ October 4, 1796
Menees, Benjamin, Jr. ..... Ensign .................. May 31, 1798
Menees, Isaac ............. Lieutenant ............ October 10, 1796
Messer, John ............. Captain ............. September 22, 1797
Miles, William ............ First Major in cavalry regiment,
             Mero District ........ October 28, 1797
Norfleet, James ........... Second Major .......... October 4, 1796
Osborn, Icabud ........... Lieutenant ............... May 31, 1798
Owens, Benjamin .......... Ensign .................. May 21, 1800
Oyler, Jonathan ........... Cornet in cavalry regiment,
             Mero District ........ October 1, 1800
Patterson, David .......... Lieutenant ............ October 10, 1796

Perry, Robert ..............Ensign ...............February 23, 1801
Phillips, Isaac .............Captain ..............October  1, 1798
Rawls, Shadrach ...........Lieutenant ..........December 17, 1798
Simmons, Charles ..........Ensign ...............January  9, 1800
Walton, Meredith ..........Lieutenant ...........February 14, 1798
Weakley, Benjamin ........Captain .................May 21, 1800
Weakley, David ...........Lieutenant ..............May 21, 1800
Williams, Pierce ..........Lieutenant ..............May 21, 1800
Young, Abraham ...........Captain ..............October 10, 1796
Young, John ...............First Major ...........October  4, 1796

*Sevier County Regiments*
*Commissioned*

Alexander, Archibald .......Ensign ................October 10, 1796
Barns, Jeremiah ...........Captain ..................June 16, 1801
Blair, Samuel ..............Lieutenant ............October 10, 1796
Bryan, Peter ..............First Major ............October  4, 1796
Campbell, John ............Lieutenant .............October 10, 1796
Campbell, Ralph ...........Ensign ................October 10, 1796
Clarke, Isaac, Jr. ...........Cornet in cavalry regiment,
                            Hamilton District .......April 20, 1801
Cowan, Andrew ............Captain ...............October 10, 1796
Creaton, James ............Ensign ................October 10, 1796
Crowson, Richard ..........Lieutenant .............October 10, 1796
Dickson, Joseph ...........Lieutenant .............October 10, 1796
Duggan, Daniel ............Ensign ...................May  1, 1799
Evans, Joseph .............Captain in cavalry regiment,
                            Hamilton District ....October  4, 1796
Evans, Joseph .............Second Major in cavalry regiment,
                            Hamilton District ....October 13, 1796
Fost, Adam ................Captain ...............October 10, 1796
Handy, James .............Lieutenant .............October 10, 1796
Henderson, Robert .........Cornet in cavalry regiment,
                            Hamilton District ....October  4, 1796
Henderson, Robert .........Captain in cavalry regiment,
                            Hamilton District, vice William
                            Henderson, resigned....August 22, 1800
Henderson, William ........Lieutenant in cavalry regiment,
                            Hamilton District ....October  4, 1796
Henderson, William, Jr. .....Captain in cavalry regiment,
                            Hamilton District, vice Joseph
                            Evans, promoted ......August 16, 1797
Higens, Philemon ..........Ensign ................October 10, 1796
Layman, Jacob ............Captain .................July 30, 1800
Lemon, Daniel .............Ensign ................October 10, 1796
Lovelady, Jesse ............Ensign ..................June 16, 1801
Lovelady, Stephen .........Lieutenant ..............June 16, 1801

IN THE TENNESSEE MILITIA, 1796-1811 29

McClung, John ............Captain ..............October 10, 1796
McDaniel, David .........Ensign ..................May  1, 1799
McGauhy, James .........Ensign ..................April  4, 1799
McGill, Robert ...........Captain ..............October 10, 1796
McLaughlin, Alexander .....Captain ..............October 10, 1796
Mahan, John .............Captain .................April  4, 1799
Mahon, John .............Second Major ............May  3, 1800
Mathews, Obediah ........Lieutenant ..............July 30, 1800
Miller, William, Jr. .........Lieutenant in cavalry regiment,
                        Hamilton District .......April 20, 1801
Mulendore, Abraham .......Ensign ..................April  4, 1799
Nicholas, Flail ............Captain .................June 16, 1801
Pate, Thomas ............Ensign ..................July 30, 1800
Prentice, Robert ..........Ensign ...............October 10, 1796
Richardson, William .......Captain ..............October 10, 1796
Rodgers, Josiah ...........Captain ..............October 10, 1796
Rogers, George ...........Lieutenant ............October 10, 1796
Shields, James ............Captain .................May  1, 1799
Simmons, Henry ..........Lieutenant ...............May  1, 1799
Thomas, Grieph ..........Lieutenant ............October 10, 1796
Walroud, William .........Ensign ...............October 10, 1796
Wear, Samuel ............Lieutenant-Colonel
                        Commandant ........October  4, 1796
Williams, John ............Lieutenant ..............April  4, 1799
Woldridge, Edmond ........Ensign ..................July 30, 1800

*Smith County Regiments*
*Commissioned*

Ballow, James ............Captain ..................May 11, 1801
Black, Josiah .............Lieutenant ..............June 16, 1801
Casey, Levi ..............Captain ..................June 16, 1801
Coapland, Joseph .........Lieutenant ..............June 16, 1801
Cotton, Allen .............Ensign ..................May 11, 1801
Donoho, Patrick ..........Lieutenant ..............May 11, 1801
Draper, Thomas ..........First Major ............August  6, 1800
Gifford, Jabues ...........Captain .................May 11, 1801
Greer, Andrew ............Second Major .........August  6, 1800
Hargiss, William ..........Ensign ..................May 11, 1801
Hart, Moris ..............Lieutenant ..............June 16, 1801
Lilly, Noah ...............Lieutenant ..............May 11, 1801
Lowrey, Alexander ........Captain .................June 16, 1801
McMurry, Charles ........Ensign ..................May 11, 1801
Ozburn, Michael ..........Ensign ..................May 11, 1801
Pate, Stephen ............Lieutenant ..............May 11, 1801
Pate, Willecoy ............Captain .................May 11, 1801
Patterson, John ..........Captain .................May 11, 1801

| | | |
|---|---|---|
| Piper, John | Ensign | May 11, 1801 |
| Prewet, William | Ensign | June 16, 1801 |
| Russell, William | Captain | June 16, 1801 |
| Sanders, William | Lieutenant Colonel Commandant | August 6, 1800 |
| Seehorn, John | Ensign | June 16, 1801 |
| Settle, Edward | Captain | May 11, 1801 |
| Turner, Jirasha | Lieutenant | May 11, 1801 |
| White, Samuel | Ensign | June 16, 1801 |
| Young, Samuel | Lieutenant | May 11, 1801 |

### Sullivan County Regiments
### Commissioned

| | | |
|---|---|---|
| Allen, Daniel | Captain | October 10, 1796 |
| Allison, John | Captain | October 12, 1797 |
| Barton, Hugh | Captain in cavalry regiment Washington District vice David Brigham | May 10, 1798 |
| Berry, Francis | First Major | October 4, 1796 |
| Birdwell, William | Lieutenant | October 10, 1796 |
| Bockman, Nathaniel | Ensign | October 10, 1796 |
| Booher, John | Lieutenant | October 10, 1796 |
| Bowman, John | Ensign | October 10, 1796 |
| Bresheers, Samuel | Captain | October 10, 1796 |
| Brigham, David | Captain | October 4, 1796 |
| Brittain, Abraham | Cornet in cavalry regiment Washington District vice Benjamin Downs elected by error | October 12, 1797 |
| Carithers, Samuel | Lieutenant in cavalry regiment Washington District | October 4, 1796 |
| Carithers, Samuel | Lieutenant | October 10, 1796 |
| Christian, William | Lieutenant | October 10, 1796 |
| Cloud, Jeremiah | Captain | October 10, 1796 |
| Craft, Thomas | Captain | October 10, 1796 |
| Cross, Elijah | Captain | October 10, 1796 |
| Downs, Benjamin | Cornet in cavalry regiment Washington District | October 4, 1796 |
| Dredin, David | Captain | October 10, 1796 |
| Dullany, Elkanah | Second Major vice Robert Rutledge, resigned | June 16, 1801 |
| Dunsmore, Samuel | Ensign | October 10, 1796 |
| Gains, Ambrose | Captain | January 11, 1799 |
| Gains, Edmond | Ensign | October 10, 1796 |
| Gallian, George | Ensign | January 11, 1799 |
| Gifford, Jabus | Ensign | October 10, 1796 |
| Goodson, John | Captain | October 10, 1796 |

| | | |
|---|---|---|
| Hale, Alexander | Ensign | October 10, 1796 |
| Hannah, Andrew | Captain | October 10, 1796 |
| Housley, Robert | Ensign | October 10, 1796 |
| Housley, Robert | Lieutenant | January 11, 1799 |
| James, Walten | Ensign | October 10, 1796 |
| King, Isaac | Ensign | October 10, 1796 |
| King, John | Captain | October 10, 1796 |
| King, Phillip | Lieutenant | October 23, 1799 |
| Knidever, Jacob | Captain | October 10, 1796 |
| Lewis, William | Lieutenant | October 10, 1796 |
| Lewis, William | Captain | October 12, 1797 |
| McCrabb, Alexander | Cornet, vice Abraham Brittain | May 10, 1798 |
| McMahan, Michael | Lieutenant | October 23, 1799 |
| Magert, Henry | Ensign | January 11, 1799 |
| Margin, Solomon | Ensign | January 11, 1799 |
| Miller, John | Ensign | January 11, 1799 |
| Moore, Samuel | Lieutenant | January 11, 1799 |
| Morrel, Thomas | Lieutenant | October 10, 1796 |
| Morrel, Thomas | Captain | January 11, 1799 |
| Prothro, David | Lieutenant | October 10, 1796 |
| Punch, John | Lieutenant | October 10, 1796 |
| Rhea, Joseph | Lieutenant | October 10, 1796 |
| Rutledg, Robert | Second Major | October 4, 1796 |
| Rutledge, George | Brigadier General Washington District "in the room of Landon Carter, deceased" | December 20, 1800 |
| Scott, John | Lieutenant Colonel Commandant | October 4, 1796 |
| Shell, Frederick | Lieutenant | October 10, 1796 |
| Snodgrass, William | Captain | October 10, 1796 |
| Snodgrass, William | First Major vice Francis Berry, resigned | June 16, 1801 |
| Taylor, John | Lieutenant | October 10, 1796 |
| Tipton, John | Lieutenant Colonel Commandant vice John Scott, resigned | June 16, 1801 |
| Tyner, Lewis | Ensign | October 10, 1796 |
| Walker, James | Captain | January 11, 1799 |
| Wallen, Stephen | Captain | October 10, 1796 |
| Ware, James | Lieutenant | January 11, 1799 |
| Webb, Aaron | Ensign | October 10, 1796 |
| Webb, Abel | Ensign | October 12, 1797 |
| Webb, Benjamin | Ensign | October 10, 1796 |
| Webb, Benjamin | Lieutenant | October 12, 1797 |
| Whitnell, Josiah | Lieutenant | October 10, 1796 |
| Work, Jacob | Captain in cavalry regiment Washington District | June 19, 1800 |

## RECORD OF COMMISSIONS OF OFFICERS

### Sumner County Regiments
### Commissioned

| | | |
|---|---|---|
| Alexander, Silas | Ensign | December 10, 1798 |
| Badget, Jonathan | Ensign | July 5, 1800 |
| Bailey, Samuel | Ensign | December 8, 1798 |
| Ballow, James | Captain | December 15, 1798 |
| Barns, Solomon | Ensign | July 5, 1800 |
| Bishop, Jones | Ensign | December 4, 1798 |
| Bishop, Joseph | Lieutenant | December 4, 1798 |
| Black, Gabriel | Captain | July 5, 1800 |
| Bradly, Isua | Ensign | November 4, 1800 |
| Bradly, Thomas | Captain | December 4, 1798 |
| Briggance, George S. | Cornet in cavalry regiment Mero District | October 4, 1796 |
| Briggance, William | Ensign | October 10, 1796 |
| Britten, Richard | Lieutenant | December 5, 1798 |
| Browner, Thomas | Ensign | July 5, 1800 |
| Cage, Wilson | Lieutenant in cavalry regiment Mero District | October 4, 1796 |
| Cantrell, Stephen | Captain | October 10, 1796 |
| Carr, John | Captain | December 5, 1798 |
| Cavett, Joseph | Lieutenant | December 7, 1798 |
| Douglass, Edward | Lieutenant Colonel Commandant | October 4, 1796 |
| Douglass, Reuben | Captain in cavalry regiment Mero District | October 4, 1796 |
| Franklin, John | Ensign | October 10, 1796 |
| Frazor, James | First Major | October 4, 1796 |
| Garret, George | Lieutenant | July 5, 1800 |
| Gibson, John | Lieutenant | July 5, 1800 |
| Gibson, Joseph | Ensign | July 5, 1800 |
| Gifford, Jabes | Ensign | December 5, 1798 |
| Ginkins, William | Ensign | July 5, 1800 |
| Green, Zachariah | Lieutenant | October 10, 1796 |
| Guin, John | Ensign | November 4, 1800 |
| Guin, William | Captain | November 4, 1800 |
| Guinn, Alexander | Lieutenant | July 5, 1800 |
| Hall, William | Second Major | October 4, 1796 |
| Hamlinton, Robert | Captain | October 10, 1796 |
| Haney, Jesse | Captain | July 5, 1800 |
| Hankins, William | Lieutenant | October 10, 1796 |
| Hankins, William | Captain | December 9, 1798 |
| Hansborough, Smith | Captain | October 10, 1796 |
| Harpole, Solomon | Captain | December 4, 1798 |
| Harrison, Nathaniel | Ensign | October 10, 1796 |
| Kirkpatrick, David | Ensign | December 6, 1798 |

| | | | |
|---|---|---|---|
| Kirkpatrick, James | Lieutenant | December | 6, 1798 |
| Kirkpatrick, James | Captain | July | 5, 1800 |
| Lacy, Amos | Ensign | December | 15, 1798 |
| Latimer, Griswold | Captain | July | 5, 1800 |
| Latimore, Griswold | Lieutenant | October | 10, 1796 |
| Lattimer, Joseph | Ensign | October | 10, 1796 |
| Lieuney, Peter | Captain | October | 10, 1796 |
| Lilly, Noah | Lieutenant | December | 15, 1798 |
| Love, David | Captain | December | 8, 1798 |
| Lyon, John | Lieutenant | December | 8, 1798 |
| McConnell, Montgomery | Ensign | May | 10, 1797 |
| McDowell, James | Lieutenant | November | 4, 1800 |
| McKee, John | Ensign | December | 7, 1798 |
| McKinney, Henry | Lieutenant | May | 10, 1797 |
| McKorkle, William | Lieutenant | October | 10, 1796 |
| McMurrey, David | Lieutenant | July | 5, 1800 |
| McNight, Alexander | Lieutenant | July | 5, 1800 |
| Madden, Champ | Lieutenant | December | 4, 1798 |
| Murray, William | Captain | August | 15, 1797 |
| Neeley, Joseph | Captain | December | 10, 1798 |
| Parker, Isaac | Lieutenant | December | 10, 1798 |
| Pearce, Isaac | Ensign | October | 10, 1796 |
| Reed, William | Captain | October | 10, 1796 |
| Scoby, Matthew | Lieutenant | November | 4, 1800 |
| Shaw, Robert | Captain | July | 5, 1800 |
| Smith, John | Lieutenant | July | 5, 1800 |
| Snoddy, William | Captain | October | 10, 1796 |
| Steel, Joseph | Lieutenant | October | 10, 1796 |
| Stephenson, Moore | Captain | October | 10, 1796 |
| Sterns, John | Ensign | October | 10, 1796 |
| Stewart, John | Lieutenant | July | 5, 1800 |
| Stone, Eusebius | Lieutenant | July | 5, 1800 |
| Stubbelfield, George | Ensign | December | 4, 1798 |
| Vinson, James | Captain | December | 6, 1798 |
| Walton, Isaac | Lieutenant | October | 10, 1796 |
| White, David | Lieutenant | October | 10, 1796 |
| White, David | Lieutenant | August | 15, 1797 |
| White, Robert | Ensign | August | 15, 1797 |
| Whitsett, James | Ensign | October | 10, 1796 |
| Whittsets, Lawrence | Captain | July | 5, 1800 |
| Williams, Sampson | Captain | May | 10, 1797 |
| Willis, Richard | Ensign | July | 5, 1800 |
| Wilson, James | Captain | October | 10, 1796 |
| Wilson, William | Ensign | October | 10, 1796 |
| Winchester, James | Brigadier General Mero District | November | 9, 1796 |

## Washington County Regiments
## Commissioned

| | | |
|---|---|---|
| Adams, John | Captain in cavalry regiment Washington District | October 4, 1796 |
| Aiken, Matthew | Lieutenant | July 16, 1800 |
| Aiken, Matthew | Captain | February 11, 1801 |
| Allison, Robert | Captain | October 10, 1796 |
| Ball, Amous | Lieutenant | October 10, 1796 |
| Bayles, William | Ensign | January 9, 1800 |
| Bean, Edmund | Second Major | October 4, 1796 |
| Biddle, Thomas | Captain | October 10, 1796 |
| Blair, Brice | Captain in cavalry regiment Washington District | April 1, 1800 |
| Boring, Absolom | Lieutenant | October 10, 1796 |
| Brown, Benjamin | Lieutenant | October 10, 1796 |
| Brown, Benjamin | Captain | June 16, 1801 |
| Brown, Jacob | First Major | October 4, 1796 |
| Brown, John | Ensign | October 10, 1796 |
| Calvert, William | Captain | October 10, 1796 |
| Campbell, Richard | Adjutant | October 10, 1796 |
| Carithers, Jonathan | Ensign | September 26, 1799 |
| Clark, John | Lieutenant | October 10, 1796 |
| Collum, Jonathan | Ensign | October 10, 1796 |
| Collums, George | Ensign | September 26, 1799 |
| Conly, David | Lieutenant in cavalry regiment Washington District | October 4, 1796 |
| Crabtree, Barnet | Ensign | April 5, 1798 |
| Davis, George | Lieutenant | October 10, 1796 |
| Davis, Nathaniel, Jr. | Lieutenant | October 10, 1796 |
| Deakins, John | Lieutenant | October 10, 1796 |
| Duncan, Joseph | Captain | October 10, 1796 |
| Edwards, John | Lieutenant | September 26, 1799 |
| Edwards, Jonathan | Ensign | October 10, 1796 |
| Fain, John | Ensign | December 6, 1800 |
| Fuston, John | Lieutenant | September 26, 1799 |
| Gallahor, William | Cornet in cavalry regiment | February 8, 1797 |
| Gann, Nathan | Captain vice Robert Allison resigned | June 5, 1797 |
| Gann, Nathan | Captain | September 26, 1799 |
| Gates, Jacob | Lieutenant vice Lieutenant Davis resigned | April 5, 1798 |
| Gillespie, Allen | Captain in volunteer cavalry regiment | February 8, 1797 |
| Gillespie, Allen | Captain in volunteer cavalry regiment | January 13, 1798 |

| | | |
|---|---|---|
| Gillespie, George | Lieutenant Colonel Commandant | October 4, 1796 |
| Gillespie, James | Cornet in volunteer cavalry | January 13, 1798 |
| Glascock, Archibald | Captain | September 26, 1799 |
| Glasscock, Archibald | Lieutenant | October 10, 1796 |
| Gott, Lott | Lieutenant | September 26, 1799 |
| Gray, James | Lieutenant in cavalry regiment Washington District | December 6, 1800 |
| Gristham, John | Ensign | October 10, 1796 |
| Haile, Thomas | Ensign | September 26, 1799 |
| Hale, Shadrack | Ensign | June 23, 1800 |
| Handly, John | Lieutenant | June 23, 1800 |
| Hannah, Andrew | Captain | October 10, 1796 |
| Harle, Baldwin | First Major in cavalry regiment Washington District | October 13, 1796 |
| Harrison, Michael | Lieutenant Colonel Commandant in cavalry regiment Washington District | October 13, 1796 |
| Harrold, John | Ensign | October 10, 1796 |
| Hunt, Uriah | Lieutenant | October 10, 1796 |
| Jobe, Abraham | Cornet in cavalry regiment Washington District | December 6, 1800 |
| Johnston, John, Jr. | Cornet in cavalry regiment Washington District | October 4, 1796 |
| Jones, Nathaniel | Ensign | October 10, 1796 |
| Kelson, John | Cornet in cavalry regiment Washington District vice John Johnston | May 10, 1798 |
| Kincheloe, Elijah | Lieutenant | September 26, 1799 |
| Lane, Tidance | Captain | February 11, 1801 |
| Longmires, John | Captain | October 10, 1796 |
| Lowry, Adam | Lieutenant | October 10, 1796 |
| Lowry, Adam | Adjutant | June 23, 1800 |
| McAdams, Hugh | Ensign | September 26, 1799 |
| McAllister, John | Captain | July 16, 1800 |
| McCollister, John, Jr. | Ensign | October 10, 1796 |
| McGee, George | Ensign | October 1, 1798 |
| Maines, Thomas | Ensign | October 10, 1796 |
| Marks, David | Ensign | October 10, 1796 |
| Melven, Thomas | Ensign | June 16, 1801 |
| Mercer, Jones | Ensign | September 26, 1799 |
| Mitchell, William | Captain in cavalry regiment Washington District | December 6, 1800 |
| Moore, Alexander | Captain | October 1, 1798 |
| Morrouson, Joseph | Captain | October 10, 1796 |
| Neal, William | Ensign | June 23, 1800 |

Norward, John ............ Captain vice William York
  resigned .............. April 5, 1798
Parker, Josiah ............. Ensign ................ October 1, 1798
Rallings, Moses ........... Lieutenant .......... February 11, 1801
Robertson, Charles ......... Captain ............... October 10, 1796
Sevier, Valentine .......... Ensign .................. July 16, 1800
Shields, Henry ............ Ensign ............... October 10, 1796
Shields, Joseph ............ Lieutenant in cavalry regiment
  Washington District .... April 1, 1800
Shipley, Nathan ........... Captain ............... October 10, 1796
Sidner, Martin ............ Lieutenant .......... September 26, 1799
Sidnor, Martin ........... Ensign ................ October 10, 1796
Squibb, John .............. Captain ............. September 26, 1799
Stepherson, Matthew ....... Ensign ................. October 1, 1798
Taylor, Henry ............ Captain ............... October 1, 1798
Taylor, William ........... Captain .................. July 4, 1799
Waddill, Charles .......... Lieutenant in volunteer
  cavalry ............ February 8, 1797
Waddill, Charles .......... Lieutenant in volunteer
  cavalry ............. January 13, 1798
Wallice, Thomas ......... Lieutenant .......... September 26, 1799
Wear, George ............. Cornet in cavalry regiment
  Washington District .... April 1, 1800
Wood, James .............. Lieutenant ............ October 1, 1798
Wood, William .......... .. Lieutenant ........... October 10, 1796
Wright, Isaac ............. Ensign ............. September 26, 1799
York, William ....... ..... Captain ............... October 10, 1796
Young, Joseph ............ Captain ............... October 10, 1796

### *Williamson County Regiments*
### *Commissioned*

Campbell, Patrick ........ Lieutenant .......... November 12, 1800
Chambers, John .......... Ensign .............. November 12, 1800
Crocket, Samuel .......... Captain ............. November 12, 1800
Dooley, William .......... Captain ............. November 12, 1800
Gentry, George .......... Ensign .............. November 12, 1800
Hill, John ............... Captain ............. November 12, 1800
Jones, Azor .............. Ensign .............. November 12, 1800
McCrory, Thomas ........ Lieutenant Colonel
  Commandant .......... June 23, 1800
McKinney, John .......... First Major .......... June 23, 1800
McMillen, William ....... Lieutenant .......... November 12, 1800
Nelson, Samuel .......... Captain ............. November 12, 1800
Nolen, Berry ............ Captain ............. November 12, 1800
Porter, Joseph ........... Second Major .......... June 23, 1800
Reid, William ........... Ensign .............. November 12, 1800

IN THE TENNESSEE MILITIA, 1796-1811    37

Rutledge, William ........Lieutenant ..........November 12, 1800
Sommers, Abraham .......Lieutenant ..........November 12, 1800
Webb, Able ..............Ensign ..............November 12, 1800
Wombill, Readin .........Lieutenant ..........November 12, 1800

*Wilson County Regiments*
*Commissioned*

Allen, Theophilus .........Lieutenant ...............May 30, 1800
Anderson, James ..........Captain ..................May 30, 1800
Bishop, Jones ............Ensign ...................May 30, 1800
Bishop, Joseph ...........Lieutenant ...............May 30, 1800
Cavanaugh, Charles .......Lieutenant ...............May 30, 1800
Dillard, Elisha ...........Captain ..................May 30, 1800
Eikols, John .............Lieutenant ...............May 30, 1800
Eikols, Kanah ............Captain ..................May 30, 1800
Harpole, Martin ..........Ensign ...................May 30, 1800
Harpole, Solomon .........Captain ..................May 30, 1800
Lancaster, William .......Captain ..................May 30, 1800
Mitchell, Edward .........First Major ..............April 1, 1800
Smith, Robert ............Ensign ...................May 30, 1800
Spickant, Jacob ..........Lieutenant ...............May 30, 1800
Steele, Samuel ...........Ensign ...................May 30, 1800
Steele, William ...........Second Major ............April 1, 1800
Tedford, Hugh ............Ensign ...................May 30, 1800
Wynne, John .... ........Lieutenant Colonel
                         Commandant ..........April 1, 1800

The military commissions published in the previous pages of this volume date from 1796 through June 16, 1801. There is a gap in the file of Commission books from June 1801 to May 1807. These books were not among the original files placed in the state archives in 1903, nor have they been located since.

A number of original military returns are on file in the archives and from these manuscript returns an effort is being made to compile a list covering the gap for future publication.

*Anderson County Regiments*
*Commissioned*

Gray, Joseph .............Lieutenant 13th regiment...June 23, 1807
Kirkpatrick, James ........Lieutenant
                         Light Infantry ...August 22, 1807
Kirkpatrick, John .........Ensign Light Infantry....August 22, 1807
McGee, James ............Captain 13th regiment......June 23, 1807
Macey, Charles ...........Ensign 13th regiment.......June 23, 1807
Quin, Morton .............Captain Light Infantry...August 22, 1807
Tunnell, James ...........Ensign 13th regiment.......June 23, 1807
Underwood, John .........Captain regiment of
                         cavalry 3d brigade....October 1, 1807

## Blount County Regiments
### Commissioned

Beaty, Aaron .............. Ensign 12th regiment .. September 12, 1807
Forrester, William ......... Captain 12th regiment. September 25, 1807
Franks, Samuel ............ Ensign 12th regiment .. September 25, 1807
Green, William ............ Lieutenant
    12th regiment ...... September 25, 1807
Ish, John ................. Lieutenant
    12th regiment ...... September 25, 1807
McCoy, William (McCag) ... Lieutenant
    12th regiment ...... September 25, 1807
Reed, John ................ Ensign 12th regiment .. September 12, 1807
Right, William ............ Ensign 12th regiment .. September 25, 1807
Robertson, Michael ........ Lieutenant
    12th regiment ...... September 25, 1807

## Campbell County Regiments
### Commissioned

Brock, Joshua ............. Ensign ............... October 24, 1807
Canterberry, Zachariah ..... Captain .............. October 24, 1807
Clap, Ludwick ............. Lieutenant regiment .... October 24, 1807
Cunningham, James ........ Lieutenant ............ October 24, 1807
Dougherty, Andrew ........ Captain .............. October 7, 1807
Huffacre, Michael .......... Captain .............. October 24, 1807
Martin, Nathaniel .......... Captain .............. October 24, 1807
Murrey, Jacob ............. Lieutenant ............ October 24, 1807
Sharp, Joseph ............. Ensign ............... October 24, 1807
Smith, James .............. Ensign ............... October 24, 1807
Smith, Patrick ............. Ensign ............... October 24, 1807
Yandell, **Henry** ........... Lieutenant ............ October 24, 1807

## Carter County Regiments
### Commissioned

Arrendell, James .......... Ensign 5th regiment .. November 10, 1807
Brown, Jesse .............. Lieutenant 5th regiment .... May 30, 1807
Cole, Jesse ................ Captain 5th regiment ...... May 30, 1807
Keys, James ............... Second Major
    5th regiment ....... November 5, 1807
McIntirff, David ........... Ensign 5th regiment ... September 23, 1807
Profitt, Pleasent ........... Ensign 5th regiment ........ May 30, 1807
Stoydell, John ............. Lieutenant
    5th regiment ....... September 23, 1807
Wilson, Tapley ............ Lieutenant
    5th regiment ....... November 10, 1807

IN THE TENNESSEE MILITIA, 1796-1811

*Cocke County Regiments
Commissioned*

Allen, Isaac ...............Second Major 8th regiment...July 13, 1807
Blackston, Youngue ........Ensign 8th regiment .......July 13, 1807
Caffee, William ...........Lieutenant regiment of
　　　　　　　　　　　　　　cavalry 2d brigade.......July 13, 1807
Dreneron, Robert ..........Ensign 8th regiment........July 13, 1807
Fine, David ...............Lieutenant 8th regiment....July 13, 1807
Fowler, Thomas ...........Captain 8th regiment....October 9, 1807
Gregg, Samuel .............Lieutenant 8th regiment..October 9, 1807
Large, Samuel .............Captain 8th regiment ......July 13, 1807
Lax, Solomon ..............Ensign 8th regiment........July 13, 1807
Moon, William ............Lieutenant Light Infantry
　　　　　　　　　　　　　　8th regiment .........October 9, 1807
Newland, Thomas ..........Captain regiment of cavalry
　　　　　　　　　　　　　　2d brigade...............July 13, 1807
Rice, John ...............Captain 8th regiment ......July 13, 1807
Sandusky, Emanually ......Cornet regiment of cavalry
　　　　　　　　　　　　　　2d brigade .............July 13, 1807
Sutton, Joseph ............Lieutenant 8th regiment ....July 13, 1807
West, William ............Lieutenant 8th regiment ....July 13, 1807
Witson, Stephen ...........Captain Light Infantry
　　　　　　　　　　　　　　8th regiment .........October 9, 1807

*Davidson County Regiments
Commissioned*

Boyles, James .............Lieutenant 20th regiment...July 24, 1807
Bradshaw, John C. .........Captain 19th regiment .....July     1807
Burnham, John ............Lieutenant
　　　　　　　　　　　　　　19th regiment ......November 7, 1807
Campbell, Philip ..........Lieutenant
　　　　　　　　　　　　　　19th regiment ......November 7, 1807
Conger, John .............Captain 20th regiment......May 30, 1807
Cupper, James ............Ensign 19th regiment..November 7, 1807
Demoss, John .............Captain
　　　　　　　　　　　　　　19th regiment ......November 7, 1807
Doak, John ...............Captain 20th regiment......May 30, 1807
Evans, William ...........Ensign 19th regiment..November 7, 1807
Gord, Samuel .............Lieutenant
　　　　　　　　　　　　　　20th regiment ......November 11, 1807
Grizard, William ..........Ensign 20th regiment.......May 30, 1807
Harwell, James ...........Lieutenant 19th regiment....July     1807
Holms, Drury ............Lieutenant 20th regiment ...May 30, 1807
Hughes, Robert ...........Second Major 19th regiment.July 13, 1807
James, Joshua ............Lieutenant 19th regiment...May 30, 1807
Johnston, Robert ..........Captain 19th regiment.November 7, 1807

Jones, Daniel .............. Ensign 19th regiment.. November 7, 1807
Lee, Braxton .............. Captain 20th regiment...... July 24, 1807
Lentz, William ............. Ensign in Independent Company Infantry of the Town of Nashville .......... October 9, 1807
McConnel, Samuel ......... Ensign 19th regiment ...... July 1807
McConnell, John P.......... First Major 19th regiment.. July 13, 1807
Mitchell, John ............. Lieutenant 20th regiment ... May 30, 1807
Robertson, Christopher ..... Captain 19th regiment. November 7, 1807
Thompson, Jacob .......... Captain 19th regiment ..... May 30, 1807
Weaver, Christian .......... Captain 20th regiment. November 11, 1807
Williamson, John S. ........ Lieutenant 19th regiment... July 24, 1807
Wortham, John ............ Ensign 19th regiment .... October 2, 1807

*Dickson County Regiments*
*Commissioned*

Alston, John ............... Captain 25th regiment ..... May 30, 1807
Crawford, Sebret .......... Ensign 25th regiment ...... July 17, 1807
Dickson, Molton ........... Captain Light Infantry 25th regiment .......... June 13, 1807
Haily, Thomas ............. Captain 25th regiment ..... July 17, 1807
Irvine, David .............. Lieutenant Light Infantry 25th regiment .......... June 13, 1807
Jermin, Robert ............ Captain 25th regiment.... August 22, 1807
Jones, Thomas ............. Ensign 25th regiment.. November 7, 1807
Lewis, James .............. Lieutenant 25th regiment ... July 17, 1807
Moseley, James ............ Lieutenant 25th regiment ...... November 7, 1807
Nusbell, John .............. Ensign Light Infantry 25th regiment .......... June 13, 1807
Parker, William ............ Lieutenant 25th regiment. August 22, 1807
Pearsall, Edward ........... Ensign 25th regiment .... August 22, 1807
Tatum, James ............. Ensign 25th regiment ....... July 31, 1807
Thomas, Nathaniel ......... Captain 25th regiment. November 7, 1807

*Grainger County Regiments*
*Commissioned*

Allison, John .............. Cornet regiment of cavalry 2nd brigade ............ July 1, 1807
Counts, David ............. Captain regiment of cavalry 2nd brigade ............ July 1, 1807
Jack, John F. .............. Aide to Major General 1st Division .......... October 22, 1807
Windham, William ......... Lieutenant regiment cavalry 2nd brigade ............ July 1, 1807

## Greene County Regiments
### Commissioned

| | | |
|---|---|---|
| Bell, John | Cornet regiment of cavalry 1st brigade | October 16, 1807 |
| Guardner, Conrad | Ensign 3rd regiment | October 3, 1807 |
| Jeffers, William | Lieutenant 3rd regiment | October 3, 1807 |
| Justice, Thomas | Ensign 3rd regiment | October 3, 1807 |
| Karbough, John | Ensign 3rd regiment | October 3, 1807 |
| Kilday, Henry | Ensign 3rd regiment | October 3, 1807 |
| Logan, David | Captain 3rd regiment | October 3, 1807 |
| Morse, George | Lieutenant 3rd regiment | October 3, 1807 |
| Neel, Benjamin | Captain 3rd regiment | October 3, 1807 |
| Neil, Hamilton | Lieutenant regiment of cavalry 1st brigade | October 16, 1807 |
| Tarben, John | Ensign 3rd regiment | October 3, 1807 |
| Winters, Christopher | Captain regiment of cavalry 1st brigade | October 16, 1807 |

## Hawkins County Regiments
### Commissioned

| | | |
|---|---|---|
| Dalzall, Francis | Captain volunteer troop of Horse 1st brigade | November 9, 1807 |
| Lawrance, Randolph | Captain 4th regiment | November 18, 1807 |
| Lee, Edward | Ensign 4th regiment | October 16, 1807 |
| McWilliams, Andrew | Captain 4th regiment | October 16, 1807 |
| Myers, Jacob | Lieutenant volunteer troop of Horse 1st brigade | November 9, 1807 |
| Reynolds, George | Ensign | October 16, 1807 |

## Jackson County Regiments
### Commissioned

| | | |
|---|---|---|
| Barnett, Elijah | Ensign 18th regiment | July 17, 1807 |
| Dale, John | Captain 18th regiment | July 17, 1807 |
| East, Mathew | Ensign 18th regiment | November 11, 1807 |
| Edwards, Thomas | Captain 18th regiment | November 11, 1807 |
| Graham, William | Ensign 18th regiment | November 11, 1807 |
| Holeman, James | Captain 18th regiment | November 11, 1807 |
| James, John | Lieutenant 18th regiment | November 11, 1807 |
| Pryar, Jonathan | Lieutenant 18th regiment | July 17, 1807 |
| Rutledge, William | Lieutenant 18th regiment | November 11, 1807 |
| Scott, Andrew | Ensign 18th regiment | August 22, 1807 |
| Terrel, Laten | Lieutenant 18th regiment | November 11, 1807 |
| Woodfork, William | First Major 18th regiment | June 5, 1807 |

## Record of Commissions of Officers

### Jefferson County Regiments
### Commissioned

Baker, George .............Ensign 6th regiment .....August 22, 1807
Bradford, Hamilton ........Captain regiment of cavalry
                           2nd brigade .............June 19, 1807
Bradford, Henry ...........First Major regiment of
                           cavalry 2nd brigade....August 22, 1807
Cate, John ................Captain 6th regiment ......July 24, 1807
Denton, Joel ..............Captain 6th regiment ......May 30, 1807
Ellis, James ..............Ensign 6th regiment .....August 15, 1807
Goens, Mashack ...........Ensign 6th regiment .......June 26, 1807
Goens, Shadrick ...........Lieutenant 6th regiment....June 26, 1807
Graham, William ..........Lieutenant 6th regiment ..August 15, 1807
Hindman, John ............Lieutenant
                           6th regiment .......September 12, 1807
House, Gabrial ...........Captain 6th regiment ......June 26, 1807
Inman, Ezekiel ...........Captain 6th regiment ....August 15, 1807
Leeth, James .............Lieutenant 6th regiment....May 30, 1807
Longacre, Andrew .........Lieutenant regiment of cavalry
                           2nd brigade .............June 19, 1807
McClennehan, William .....Cornet in regiment of cavalry
                           2nd brigade .............June 19, 1807
McMeans, Thomas .........Lieutenant Light Infantry
                           6th regiment ............June 26, 1807
Malcolm, Robert ..........Ensign 6th regiment .......May 30, 1807
Pangle, Isaac .............Lieutenant
                           6th regiment .......November 11, 1807
Rankin, Samuel S. .........Ensign 6th regiment ......August 15, 1807
Reed, Robert .............Lieutenant 6th regiment ....July 31, 1807
Tate, William ............Ensign Light Infantry
                           6th regiment ............June 26, 1807
Taylor, Argyle ............Captain Light Infantry
                           6th regiment ............June 26, 1807

### Knox County Regiments
### Commissioned

Ashworth, John ...........Cornet regiment of cavalry
                           3rd brigade ........September 5, 1807
Bishop, Jacob .............Lieutenant 10th regiment ...July 31, 1807
Bond, Isaac ...............Ensign 10th regiment.......July 24, 1807
Booth, Edwin E. ..........First Major 10th regiment..May 8, 1807
Bowman, John .............Captain 10th regiment....August 15, 1807
Brown, William ...........Lieutenant 10th regiment.August 15, 1807
Campbell, Robert .........Lieutenant 10th regiment.October 15, 1807
Clift, Henry ..............Captain 10th regiment .....July 24, 1807
Davis, Clayton ...........Ensign 10th regiment.......July 22, 1807

Dowler, Francis ............Ensign 10th regiment.......May 30, 1807
Dunn, Jonathan ..........Lieutenant 10th regiment....July 31, 1807
Fryas, William ............Lieutenant 10th regiment....July 24, 1807
Gillaspie, Thomas ..........Ensign 10th regiment....October 15, 1807
Ham, Jacob ...............Lieutenant 10th regiment...June 5, 1807
Hemby, Dennis ............Ensign 10th regiment ....August 15, 1807
Hill, John ................Lieutenant 10th regiment....July 22, 1807
Hill, John ................Captain 10th regiment ...October 15, 1807
Kearns, Philip ............Ensign 10th regiment.......June 5, 1807
Long, William ............Lieutenant 10th regiment...May 30, 1807
McPherron, William .......Lieutenant 10th regiment....July 22, 1807
Miller, John ..............Captain 10th regiment......July 22, 1807
Smith, William J. ..........Captain 10th regiment......May 30, 1807
Snodgrass, William ........Ensign 10th regiment..September 18, 1807
Taylor, Henry .............Ensign 10th regiment.......July 22, 1807
Thompson, Lyle ..........Ensign 10th regiment ......July 31, 1807
William, John ............Ensign 10th regiment ......July 31, 1807

*Montgomery County Regiments*
*Commissioned*

Batie, Andrew .............Captain 24th regiment .....June 26, 1807
Baxter, James ............Captain Light Infantry
                          24th regiment ..........June 24, 1807
Black, Peter ..............Lieutenant 24th regiment...June 26, 1807
Duff, Barney .............Lieutenant 24th regiment...June 26, 1807
Ogwin, Stephen ............Ensign 24th regiment ......June 26, 1807
Pucket, Lewis ............Captain regiment of cavalry
                          6th brigade ........December 3, 1807
Thomas, Grant (?) .........Lieutenant 24th regiment ...June 26, 1807
Tinnen, Alexander ........Lieutenant regiment of cavalry
                          6th brigade ........December 3, 1807
Vance, Samuel ............Captain 24th regiment .....June 26, 1807

*Overton County Regiments*
*Commissioned*

Armstrong, John ..........Lieutenant ...............May 30, 1807
Baxter, Alexander .........Ensign .................May 30, 1807
Cannon, Benjamin ........Lieutenant .............October 13, 1807
Copeland, John ...........Captain .................May 30, 1807
Copeland, Richard, Junior...Lieutenant .............May 30, 1807
Copeland, Stephen ........Lieutenant Colonel
                          Commandant ..........May 30, 1807
Cross, John B. .............First Major ..............May 30, 1807
Derham, Josiah ...........Ensign .................May 30, 1807
Goodpasture, James .......Captain .................May 30, 1807
Groger, Spencer ..........Ensign .................May 30, 1807

Record of Commissions of Officers

Harrison, James, Junior.....Ensign ................October 13, 1807
Hickey, Michael ...........Captain ...............October 13, 1807
Hill, Thomas ..............Ensign ................October 13, 1807
Jones, John ...............Lieutenant ...............May 30, 1807
Levingston, William .......Ensign ..................May 30, 1807
Martin, Menai .............Lieutenant ............October 13, 1807
Mathews, James ...........Captain ...............October 13, 1807
Matlock, Charles ..........Captain ..................May 30, 1807
Maxwell, James M.........Lieutenant ...............May 30, 1807
Morriss, John .............Ensign ..................May 30, 1807
Norman, Joseph ..........Lieutenant ............October 13, 1807
Oneal, Robert ............Captain ..................May 30, 1807
Sevier, Charles ...........Second Major ............May 30, 1807
Swallow, Jacob ...........Ensign ................October 13, 1807
Turner, James ............Captain ..................May 30, 1807
Williams, Peter ...........Lieutenant ...............May 30, 1807
Williams, Peter ...........Captain ...............October 13, 1807
Witt, James ..............Ensign ................October 13, 1807
Young, William ...........Captain ..................May 30, 1807

*Roane County Regiments*
*Commissioned*

Howard, John ............Captain 14th regiment .....June 5, 1807
Kearns, James ...........Lieutenant 14th regiment...June 5, 1807
Stokes, Benjamin .........Ensign 14th regiment ......June 5, 1807

*Robertson County Regiments*
*Commissioned*

Atkins, James ............Ensign 23rd regiment ......July 13, 1807
Blackwell, James ..........Captain 23rd regiment......July 13, 1807
Cheatham, Peter ..........Cornet regiment cavalry
                          6th brigade ........December 3, 1807
Cheatham, Thomas ........Lieutenant regiment cavalry
                          6th brigade ........September 25, 1807
Darr, Henry ..............Ensign 23rd regiment ......July 13, 1807
Fikes, Nathan ............Ensign 23rd regiment..September 25, 1807
Gardner, Jesse ...........Lieutenant
                          23rd regiment ......September 25, 1807
Gardner, Joshua ..........Lieutenant
                          23rd regiment ........October 9, 1807
Harrington, Whitmill ......Captain 23rd regiment .....July 13, 1807
Lawson, Eppaphroditus ....Captain 23rd regiment.September 25, 1807
Rawles, Abel .............Lieutenant 23rd regiment ...July 13, 1807
Swan, Thomas ............Captain regiment cavalry
                          6th brigade ........September 25, 1807

In the Tennessee Militia, 1796-1811 45

*Rutherford County Regiments
Commissioned*

| | | |
|---|---|---|
| Armstrong, James L. | Captain 22nd regiment | October 16, 1807 |
| Blount, Benjamin | Ensign 22nd regiment | October 16, 1807 |
| Carr, Benjamin | Lieutenant 22nd regiment | October 16, 1807 |
| Carrol, Stephen | Ensign 22nd regiment | October 16, 1807 |
| Cooper, Zacheus | Lieutenant 22nd regiment | October 16, 1807 |
| Country, George | Captain 22nd regiment | October 16, 1807 |
| Country, Isaac | Lieutenant 22nd regiment | October 16, 1807 |
| Denton, Thomas | Lieutenant 22nd regiment | October 16, 1807 |
| Doake, Robert | Captain 22nd regiment | October 16, 1807 |
| Dyer, Robert Henry | Lieutenant regiment of cavalry 5th brigade | July 28, 1807 |
| Ellis, John | Ensign 22nd regiment | October 16, 1807 |
| Henderson, James | Captain regiment of cavalry 5th brigade | July 28, 1807 |
| Henderson, James | Ensign 22nd regiment | October 16, 1807 |
| Higginbotham, William | Ensign 22nd regiment | October 16, 1807 |
| Houstion, John | Lieutenant 22nd regiment | October 16, 1807 |
| Laughlin, James | Captain 22nd regiment | October 16, 1807 |
| Litton, James | Lieutenant 22nd regiment | October 16, 1807 |
| McBride, Francis | Ensign 22nd regiment | October 16, 1807 |
| McBride, Samuel | Second Major 22nd regiment | July 31, 1807 |
| McEwen, Alexander | Captain 22nd regiment | October 16, 1807 |
| Moore, Edward | Captain 22nd regiment | October 16, 1807 |
| Morrow, William | Lieutenant 22nd regiment | October 16, 1807 |
| Morton, James | Captain 22nd regiment | October 16, 1807 |
| Ramsey, Robert | Ensign 22nd regiment | October 16, 1807 |
| Ramsey, William | Lieutenant 22nd regiment | October 16, 1807 |
| Searcy, William W. | First Major 22nd regiment | June 6, 1807 |
| Sharp, James | Captain 22nd regiment | October 16, 1807 |
| Sharp, Marcus | Lieutenant 22nd regiment | October 16, 1807 |
| Smith, Nathaniel | Ensign 22nd regiment | October 16, 1807 |
| Ward, Burrel | Ensign 22nd regiment | October 16, 1807 |
| Wilbourne, James | Lieutenant 22nd regiment | October 16, 1807 |
| Wright, Richard | Captain 22nd regiment | October 16, 1807 |

### Sevier County Regiments
#### Commissioned

Baker, Abraham B. .........Ensign 11th regiment ......June 5, 1807
Jinkins, John .............Ensign 11th regiment..September 5, 1807
Montgomery, James .......Lieutenant Light Infantry
    11th regiment ........October 12, 1807
Mullindore, Abraham ......Captain 11th regiment .....June 5, 1807
Murphey, Samuel ..........Lieutenant
    11th regiment ........October 30, 1807
Preston, Alexander ........Captain Light Infantry
    11th regiment ........October 12, 1807
Ruth, John ................Lieutenant
    11th regiment ......September 5, 1807
Varnille, Joseph ............Ensign Light Infantry
    11th regiment ........October 12, 1807
Waddle, David ............Lieutenant 11th regiment...July 24, 1807
Williams, Isaac ............Captain 11th regiment.September 5, 1807

### Smith County Regiments
#### Commissioned

Blair, Solomon .............Lieutenant
    16th regiment ......November 18, 1807
Canter, Zachariah ..........Ensign 16th regiment..November 18, 1807
Cochran, James ............Captain
    16th regiment ......November 18, 1807
Corum, Robert ............Ensign 16th regiment..November 18, 1807
Davidson, John ............Lieutenant
    16th regiment ......November 18, 1807
Furlong, Martin ...........Captain
    16th regiment ......November 18, 1807
Gifford, Gibbs .............Captain
    16th regiment ......November 18, 1807
Gray, Frederick ............Lieutenant
    16th regiment ......November 18, 1807
Gregory, Laben ............Ensign 16th regiment..November 18, 1807
Harper, Mathew ...........Lieutenant
    16th regiment ......November 18, 1807
Hogun, William ............Lieutenant
    16th regiment ......November 18, 1807
Kirby, Caleb ..............Lieutenant
    16th regiment ......November 18, 1807
Lamberson, John ..........Ensign 16th regiment..November 18, 1807
Looney, John .............Captain
    16th regiment ......November 18, 1807
Mitcalf, Anthony ..........Captain
    16th regiment ......November 18, 1807

IN THE TENNESSEE MILITIA, 1796-1811      47

Owen, William ............Ensign 16th regiment..November 18, 1807
Paty, Jesse ...............Ensign 16th regiment..November 18, 1807
Piper, John ...............Captain
                          16th regiment ......November 18, 1807
Rhea, George .............Ensign 16th regiment..November 18, 1807
Robertson, Jonathan B......Second Major
                          16th regiment ........August 22, 1807
Touson, William J.........Ensign 16th regiment..November 18, 1807
Voden, William ...........Captain
                          16th regiment.......November 18, 1807
Witcher, Lay .............Ensign 16th regiment..November 18, 1807
Young, Milton ............Captain
                          16th regiment ......November 18, 1807

*Sullivan County Regiments*

Acuff, Isaac ..............Lieutenant Light Infantry
                          2nd regiment ..........June 13, 1807
Baker, Endemion .........Captain regiment of cavalry
                          1st brigade ........September 28, 1807
Brasheers, Sampson .......Lieutenant 2nd regiment.October  3, 1807
Copus, John ..............Captain 2nd regiment ......May 30, 1807
Cox, John ................Ensign 2nd regiment ....October  3, 1807
Goshue, Jacob ............Lieutenant
                          2nd regiment .......November 10, 1807
Jennings, John ............Captain 2nd regiment....August 15, 1807
Keen (Kun), Enoch ........Lieutenant
                          2nd regiment .......December 17, 1807
Keen, Harper .............Ensign 2nd regiment .......May 30, 1807
King, Harvey .............Captain 2nd regiment ......July 17, 1807
Ladey, Henry ............Lieutenant
                          2nd regiment .........August 15, 1807
Lady, John ...............Ensign Light Infantry
                          2nd regiment ..........June 13, 1807
Leture, Christopher .......Ensign 2nd regiment ....October  3, 1807
Lourey, John, Junior ......Lieutenant regiment cavalry
                          1st brigade ........September 28, 1807
McBride, John ............Ensign 2nd regiment ..December 17, 1807
McVaughan, John .........Captain 2nd regiment .November 10, 1807
Martin, Hugh ............Captain 2nd regiment..December 17, 1807
Melone, Jesse ............Lieutenant 2nd regiment.October  3, 1807
Neil, Patrick .............Cornet regiment cavalry
                          1st brigade ........September 28, 1807
Owen, John ...............Lieutenant 2nd regiment....May 30, 1807
Rogers, Joseph ...........Captain 2nd regiment....October  3, 1807
Snyder, Henry ...........Ensign 2nd regiment...November 10, 1807
Thomas, David ...........Ensign 2nd regiment .......July 17, 1807

White, Thomas ...........Lieutenant 2nd regiment....July 17, 1807
Whitten, Archibald ........Ensign 2nd regiment.....August 15, 1807

### Sumner County Regiments

Cunningham, John ........Lieutenant
    15th regiment ........August 8, 1807
Davis, John ..............Lieutenant
    15th regiment ........August 8, 1807
Montgomery, William .....Captain 15th regiment....August 8, 1807
Pirtle, Nathaniel ..........Ensign 15th regiment ....August 8, 1807
Rice, Elijah .............Ensign 15th regiment ....August 8, 1807
Walton, Josiah ............Captain 15th regiment ...August 8, 1807
Williams, Elijah ..........Lieutenant 15th regiment.August 8, 1807
Wright, John .............Ensign 15th regiment ....August 8, 1807

### Washington County Regiments

Brown, William ...........Lieutenant 1st regiment..August 8, 1807
Casady, James ............Ensign 1st regiment.....October 16, 1807
Clark, William ...........Lieutenant 1st regiment..October 16, 1807
Dillard, John .............Ensign 1st regiment .....August 8, 1807
Elliot, John ..............Cornet regiment of cavalry
    1st brigade .............June 26, 1807
Fain, William ............Captain regiment of cavalry
    1st brigade .............June 26, 1807
Myers, John ..............Ensign 1st regiment .....October 16, 1807
Robertson, Charles .. ......Lieutenant regiment of cavalry
    1st brigade ........September 28, 1807
Ruble, Jacob ..............Ensign Light Infantry
    1st regiment ..........August 8, 1807
Starns, Jesse ..............Ensign 1st regiment......August 8, 1807

### White County Regiments

Anderson, Joseph .........Lieutenant .............August 8, 1807
Anderson, Robert G. ........Captain ................August 8, 1807
Brady, Alexander .........Lieutenant .............August 1, 1807
Burlesson, Joseph .........Captain ................October 12, 1807
Cartwright, Joshua ........Ensign ................October 12, 1807
Ervin, William ............Captain ................July 31, 1807
Ferrill, Charles ...........Lieutenant .............July 31, 1807
Friley, Caleb .............Captain ................August 8, 1807
Hammons, Leroy ..........Captain ................August 1, 1807
Humphries, John ..........Captain ................July 31, 1807
Isbells, James ............Ensign ................August 1, 1807
Isbels, Zachariah .........Ensign ................August 1, 1807
Kane, James ..............Lieutenant .............October 12, 1807
Lewis, Benjamin ...........Ensign ................August 8, 1807

IN THE TENNESSEE MILITIA, 1796-1811 49

Lindville, Warley ..........Lieutenant ................July 31, 1807
McDannold, William ......Lieutenant ............August 1, 1807
Milton, Joel ...............Ensign ................August 8, 1807
Mitchell, Spencer .........Lieutenant ............August 8, 1807
Nations, Nathaniel .........Ensign ..................July 31, 1807
Seratt, John ..............Captain ...............August 1, 1807
Still, Daniel ..............Ensign ..................July 31, 1807

*Williamson County Regiments*

Allen, Charles .............Ensign 21st regiment .......July 24, 1807
Baxter, Robert .............Captain 21st regiment......July 24, 1807
Bay, John .................Lieutenant
                       21st regiment ......November 7, 1807
Benton, James .............Lieutenant 21st regiment...July 31, 1807
Brooks, Thomas, Senior.....Ensign 21st regiment ......July 31, 1807
Brunk, Solomon ...........Captain 21st regiment .....July 24, 1807
Buckly, Joab ..............Ensign 21st regiment .......July 24, 1807
Clark, John ...............Lieutenant 21st regiment....July 24, 1807
Cooper, Abraham .........Ensign 21st regiment .......July 24, 1807
Copeland, James ..........Lieutenant 21st regiment....July 24, 1807
Cowser, Freeland .........Ensign 21st regiment ..November 7, 1807
Craig, John ................Ensign 21st regiment .......July 24, 1807
Craig, William .............Captain 21st regiment ......July 24, 1807
Daniel, William ...........Captain 21st regiment ......July 24, 1807
Dennis, John ..............Captain 21st regiment ......July 31, 1807
Eames, Jonathan ..........Lieutenant 21st regiment....July 25, 1807
Gillespie, Alexander .......Ensign 21st regiment .......July 24, 1807
Goodrich, Samuel E. ......Lieutenant 21st regiment....July 24, 1807
Gunter, Francis ...........Ensign 21st regiment .......July 24, 1807
Hatgrove, James ..........Captain 21st regiment ......July 25, 1807
Helton, Abraham .........Ensign 21st regiment .......July 24, 1807
Hinch, John ...............Lieutenant 21st regiment....July 24, 1807
Holaday, Peter ............Lieutenant 21st regiment....July 24, 1807
Holloway, John ...........Ensign 21st regiment .......July 24, 1807
Jones, Lewis ..............Lieutenant 21st regiment....July 24, 1807
Love, John ................Lieutenant 21st regiment....July 24, 1807
McCrady, Alexander ......Lieutenant 21st regiment....July 31, 1807
McGee, William ..........Lieutenant 21st regiment....July 24, 1807
Mackey, William .........Captain 21st regiment.November 7, 1807
May, James ...............Captain 21st regiment ......July 24, 1807
Montgomery, Alexander ...Captain 21st regiment.November 7, 1807
Neely, John ...............Captain 21st regiment ......July 31, 1807
Philips, William ...........Ensign 21st regiment .......July 25, 1807
Reed, Joseph .............Ensign 21st regiment .......July 31, 1807
Simmons, Thomas ........Lieutenant 21st regiment....July 24, 1807
Smith, Ebenezer ..........Ensign 21st regiment .......July 24, 1807

Warner, John ..............Ensign 21st regiment .......July 31, 1807
Watkins, Daniel ...........Lieutenant 21st regiment....July 31, 1807
Whitacer, John, Junior......Lieutenant 21st regiment....July 25, 1807
Whitacer, John, Senior......Ensign 21st regiment .......July 25, 1807
White, Stephen F. ..........Ensign 21st regiment .......July 24, 1807
Williams, Joshua ...........Captain 21st regiment ......July 24, 1807
Woodrich, Josiah ...........Ensign 21st regiment .......July 24, 1807
Woods, Daniel T. ..........Captain 21st regiment ......July 25, 1807

### Wilson County Regiments

Alexander, Joshua ..........Ensign 17th regiment ......July 13, 1807
Alexander, Robert .........Captain 17th regiment .....July 13, 1807
Doak, Robert ..............Lieutenant 17th regiment ...July 13, 1807
Hunter, James A. ..........Captain 17th regiment .....July 13, 1807
Joiner, Cornelius ...........Captain 17th regiment .....July 13, 1807
Moore, William ............Ensign 17th regiment ......July 13, 1807
Pittman, William ..........Captain 17th regiment .....July 13, 1807
Rickett, Jonathan .........Lieutenant 17th regiment ...July 13, 1807
Smith, Josiah .............Lieutenant 17th regiment ...July 13, 1807
Taylor, John ..............Ensign 17th regiment ......July 13, 1807
Walker, John ..............Ensign 17th regiment ......July 13, 1807
Warnock, William ..........Ensign 17th regiment ......July 13, 1807
William, John .............Lieutenant 17th regiment ...July 13, 1807
Wilson, William ...........Captain 17th regiment .....July 13, 1807

### Anderson County Regiments

Arnold, James .............Ensign 13th regiment.......May 30, 1808
Barton, Hugh ..............Captain Volunteer Company of
                            Riflemen 13th regiment.March 30, 1808
Bowling, Larkin ............Captain 13th regiment......July 12, 1808
Branham, Ephraim .........Ensign 13th regiment.......June  8, 1808
Heard, Stephen ............Lieutenant Colonel Commandant
                            13th regiment .........March 30, 1808
Horton, John ..............Lieutenant Volunteer Company of
                            Riflemen 13th regiment.March 30, 1808
Jones, Sugar ...............Ensign 13th regiment.......July 12, 1808
Loy, John .................Captain 13th regiment .....July 12, 1808
Morton, Quin ..............First Major 13th regiment.March 30, 1808
Oliver, Lunsford ...........Captain 13th regiment......May 30, 1808
Parks, John ...............Captain 13th regiment.September 27, 1808
Scruggs, James ............Ensign 13th regiment..September 27, 1808
Taylor, Walter .............Lieutenant 13th regiment...May 30, 1808
Wall, Daniel ..............Lieutenat 13th regiment....July 12, 1808
Wyatt, John ...............Ensign 13th regiment.......May 30, 1808
Wyatt, Samuel ............Lieutenant 13th regiment...May 30, 1808

## Bedford County Regiments

| | | |
|---|---|---|
| Loy, William | Captain regiment of cavalry 5th brigade | September 28, 1808 |
| Oneal, James | Cornet regiment of cavalry 5th brigade | September 28, 1808 |
| Robertson, James | Lieutenant regiment of cavalry 5th brigade | September 28, 1808 |

## Bledsoe County Regiments

| | | |
|---|---|---|
| Anderson, John | Captain regiment of cavalry 3rd brigade | December 6, 1808 |
| Birden, Hawkins | Ensign 31st regiment | July 5, 1808 |
| Burress, William | Lieutenant 31st regiment | July 5, 1808 |
| Chilton, Thomas | Second Major 31st regiment | March 30, 1808 |
| Coulter, Thomas | Lieutenant Colonel Commandant 31st regiment | March 30, 1808 |
| Follet, David | Ensign 31st regiment | July 5, 1808 |
| Hankins, John | Lieutenant 31st regiment | July 5, 1808 |
| Hixon, Ephraim | Captain 31st regiment | July 5, 1808 |
| Johnson, William | First Major 31st regiment | March 30, 1808 |
| Lea, John | Ensign 31st regiment | July 5, 1808 |
| Looney, Peter | Captain 31st regiment | July 5, 1808 |
| Lovelady, John | Ensign 31st regiment | July 5, 1808 |
| McCoy, William | Captain 31st regiment | July 5, 1808 |
| Oliver, Durrett | Ensign Light Infantry Company 31st regiment | July 5, 1808 |
| Rogers, Elisha | Lieutenant 31st regiment | July 5, 1808 |
| Rogers, John | Lieutenant 31st regiment | July 5, 1808 |
| Rogers, Joseph | Lieutenant regiment of cavalry 3rd brigade | December 6, 1808 |
| Spring, Valentine | Cornet regiment of cavalry 3rd brigade | December 6, 1808 |
| Stephens, Isaac | Captain Light Infantry Company 31st regiment | July 5, 1808 |
| Tharp, Levi | Lieutenant Light Infantry Company 31st regiment | July 5, 1808 |
| Thurman, Eli | Captain 31st regiment | July 5, 1808 |

## Blount County Regiments

| | | |
|---|---|---|
| Allen, Edwin | Captain 12th regiment | May 28, 1808 |
| Barr, Constant O. | Ensign Light Infantry 12th regiment | December 26, 1808 |
| Buchannon, Edward | Captain 12th regiment | May 28, 1808 |
| Conner, William | Ensign 12th regiment | April 13, 1808 |
| Cook, Mathias | Ensign 12th regiment | May 28, 1808 |

Cook, William ............. Lieutenant 12th regiment...May 28, 1808
Cowan, Samuel ............ Captain regiment cavalry
                                       3rd brigade ........ September 10, 1808
Cox, George ............... Lieutenant
                                       12th regiment ...... September 13, 1808
Dickson, Eli ............... Captain 12th regiment ..... May 28, 1808
Gardner, William .......... Captain 12th regiment.December 26, 1808
Harris, Alexander .......... Lieutenant regiment cavalry
                                       3rd brigade ........ September 10, 1808
Hart, Alexander ............ Lieutenant Light Infantry Company
                                       12th regiment ...... December 26, 1808
Houston, John P. ........... Captain 12th regiment...... May 28, 1808
Houston, Robert .......... Cornet regiment of cavalry
                                       3rd brigade ........ September 10, 1808
McCamey, David .......... Lieutenant 12th regiment...May 28, 1808
McGinley, James .......... First Major 12th regiment..April 11, 1808
McMahan, John .......... Lieutenant 12th regiment...April 13, 1808
Means, William ............ Ensign 12th regiment....... May 28, 1808
Nichol, John .............. First Major regiment of cavalry
                                       3rd brigade ........ September 10, 1808
Rhea, James ............... Ensign 12th regiment..December 26, 1808
Rhea, John ................ Ensign 12th regiment....... May 28, 1808
Roddy, James .............. Ensign 12th regiment....... April 13, 1808
Taylor, John ............... Lieutenant
                                       12th regiment ...... September 13, 1808
Taylor, William S. ......... Captain Light Infantry Company
                                       12th regiment ....... December 26, 1808
Thompson, Samuel ........ Captain 12th regiment..... April 13, 1808
Tipton, James ............. Lieutenant 12th regiment...April 13, 1808
Tipton, John .............. Ensign 12th regiment....... May 28, 1808
Tipton, John .............. Lieutenant
                                       12th regiment ...... December 26, 1808
Walker, William ........... Second Major 12th regiment.April 11, 1808
Wear, Hugh ............... Lieutenant 12th regiment...May 28, 1808
Wear, Hugh ............... Ensign 12th regiment..September 13, 1808
Weldon, John .............. Lieutenant 12th regiment...May 28, 1808

## Campbell County Regiments

Bruton, John ............. Captain 33rd regiment.September 28, 1808
Dosset, Moses ............ Ensign 33rd regiment..September 28, 1808
Fenley, James ............ Lieutenant
                                       33rd regiment ...... September 28, 1808
Grant, James ............. Lieutenant Colonel Commandant
                                       33rd regiment ........ January 27, 1808
Grant, James, Jr. ........... Ensign 33rd regiment..September 28, 1808
Gray, Joseph ............. Lieutenant
                                       33rd regiment ...... September 28, 1808

Haynes, Michael ........... Ensign 33rd regiment..September 28, 1808
Howard, Johnson .......... Lieutenant
                           33rd regiment ...... September 28, 1808
Johnson, John ............. Lieutenant
                           33rd regiment ...... September 28, 1808
Keck, Philip ............... Ensign 33rd regiment..September 28, 1808
Magee, James C. .......... Second Major 33rd regiment.April 8, 1808
Polly, Elijah .............. Captain 33rd regiment.September 28, 1808
Sharp, Isaac ............... Captain 33rd regiment.September 28, 1808
Smith, Robert ............. First Major 33rd regiment..April 8, 1808

### Carter County Regiments

Carrigar, Christian ........ Lieutenant Colonel Commandant
                            5th regiment ....... December 21, 1808
Emmert, George ........... First Major
                            5th regiment ....... December 21, 1808
Emmert, John ............. Lieutenant regiment of cavalry
                            1st brigade ....... September 5, 1808
Hendrix, Nathan .......... Captain regiment cavalry
                            1st brigade ....... September 5, 1808
Howard, Stephen .......... Captain 5th regiment
                            1st brigade ............. July 19, 1808
James, Joseph ............. Ensign 5th regiment ... December 31, 1808
Profit, Pleasant ........... Lieutenant
                            5th regiment ....... December 31, 1808

### Claiborne County Regiments

Arnold, Thomas ............ Ensign 9th regiment...September 21, 1808
Brag, Hugh ................ Lieutenant 9th regiment..October 12, 1808
Davis, Moses .............. Captain 9th regiment....October 12, 1808
Devald, Henerey .......... Captain 9th regiment..September 21, 1808
Gennings, William ......... Ensign 9th regiment....... March 31, 1808
Gosuage, William .......... Lieutenant
                            9th regiment ....... September 21, 1808
Horncock, John ............ Captain 9th regiment..September 21, 1808
Kenney, James ............ Ensign 9th regiment...September 21, 1808
Lebow, Daniel ............. Lieutenant 9th regiment...March 31, 1808
Lebow, John ............... Captain 9th regiment..... March 31, 1808
McCarty, Thomas ......... Lieutenant
                            9th regiment ....... September 21, 1808
Maddy, James ............. Lieutenant 9th regiment..October 12, 1808
Murphey, William ......... Ensign 9th regiment...September 21, 1808
Neal, Peter ................ Ensign 9th regiment ...... March 31, 1808
Renney, Jesse ............. Lieutenant
                            9th regiment ....... September 21, 1808
Watson, William .......... Ensign 9th regiment...September 21, 1808

## Cocke County Regiments

Barnett, William ...........Ensign Volunteer Rifle Company
    8th regiment........September 28, 1808
Drenon, Robert ............Lieutenant
    8th regiment .......September 28, 1808
Guinn, Bartholomew ........Captain 8th regiment..September 28, 1808
Jennings, Thomas ..........Ensign 8th regiment...September 28, 1808
Jones, William D. ..........Lieutenant Volunteer Rifle Company
    8th regiment .......September 28, 1808
Lamb, John ...............Captain 8th regiment..September 28, 1808
McClennehan, Joshua .......Lieutenant 8th regiment..October 5, 1808
Mitchell, Thomas ..........Captain Volunteer Rifle Company
    8th regiment .......September 28, 1808
Neel, David ...............Ensign 8th regiment.....October 5, 1808
Odell, Nehemiah ...........Ensign 8th regiment ..September 28, 1808
Penell (Perrel), George .....Ensign 8th regiment...September 28, 1808
Sutton, Joseph ............Captain 8th regiment..September 28, 1808

## Davidson County Regiments

Allen, Carter .............Ensign 20th regiment.......July 8, 1808
Baker, William ...........Lieutenant regiment cavalry
    5th brigade ..........October 22, 1808
Ballow, William ...........Lieutenant 20th regiment...May 21, 1808
Bell, Robert ..............Captain 19th regiment......June 6, 1808
Bell, William .............Lieutenant 19th regiment...June 6, 1808
Booth, James .............Lieutenant 20th regiment....July 5, 1808
Camp, Thomas ............Ensign 20th regiment.....March 5, 1808
Camp, Thomas ............Lieutenant 20th regiment...July 8, 1808
Clemons, Isaac ............Ensign 20th regiment.......May 21, 1808
Ervin, William ............Lieutenant
    19th regiment ......September 28, 1808
Ferguson, William .........Ensign 20th regiment.......July 5, 1808
Hackney, William .........Ensign 20th regiment.......July 5, 1808
Hail, George ..............Captain 19th regiment......July 8, 1808
Hunter, Manuel ...........Ensign 20th regiment..December 26, 1808
McGlaughlin, Samuel ......Ensign 19th regiment.......June 6, 1808
Mills, David ..............Lieutenant 19th regiment...July 8, 1808
Moore, Edwin S. ..........Captain regiment of cavalry
    5th brigade ..........August 6, 1808
Morris, Demsey ...........Ensign 20th regiment.....March 5, 1808
Phelen, Richard C. ........Ensign 20th regiment ......May 21, 1808
Phillips, Merrel ...........Second Major
    20th regiment ......December 8, 1808
Reeves, James ............Lieutenant
    20th regiment ......December 26, 1808
Roulston, John ............Lieutenant 20th regiment....May 21, 1808

IN THE TENNESSEE MILITIA, 1796-1811          55

Stump, John ..............First Major
                         20th regiment ......December  8, 1808
Taylor, Samuel ...........Captain 20th regiment .....May 21, 1808
Winfrey, Valentine ........Captain 20th regiment......May 21, 1808
Woodard, Benjamin ........Lieutenant
                         19th regiment ......September 28, 1808

*Dickson County Regiments*

Gilmore, Mathew .........Captain 25th regiment.December 26, 1808
Hogan, David .............Second Major
                         25th regiment .........March  5, 1808
Irwin, David .............First Major
                         24th regiment ......September 28, 1808

*Franklin County Regiments*

Hunt, James ..............Second Major
                         32nd regiment......September 28, 1808
Metcalf, William ..........Lieutenant Colonel Commandant
                         32nd regiment......September 28, 1808
Rogers, John .............First Major
                         32nd regiment......September 28, 1808

*Grainger County Regiments*

Boman, Elisha ............Lieutenant 7th regiment..August  9, 1808
Branson, Nathaniel ........Ensign 7th regiment........June  8, 1808
Bryant, Joseph ...........Lieutenant 7th regiment..August  9, 1808
Coats, Richard ............Captain 7th regiment ......June  8, 1808
Conn, James ..............First Major regiment of
                         cavalry 2nd brigade....August  6, 1808
Fears, James .............Ensign 7th regiment.......June 20, 1808
Giffard, George ...........Captain 7th regiment....August  9, 1808
Gifford, George ...........Lieutenant 7th regiment ..March  5, 1808
Griffit, Griffe .............Ensign 7th regiment......March  5, 1808
Hodges, Moses ............Second Major
                         7th regiment .........August 27, 1808
James, Thomas ............Lieutenant 7th regiment....June  8, 1808
Jones, Aquilla .............Captain 7th regiment....August  9, 1808
Joy, John ................Ensign 7th regiment......March  5, 1808
McAnally, Jesse ...........Captain 7th regiment.....March  5, 1808
Martin, Joel ..............Ensign 7th regiment........June  8, 1808
Martin, Robert ...........Lieutenant 7th regiment....June  8, 1808
Massengale, Robert ........First Major
                         7th regiment .........August 27, 1808
Moody, Martin ...........Lieutenant Volunteer Company
                         7th regiment ...........July 13, 1808

Moore, John ..............Captain Volunteer Company
    7th regiment ............July 13, 1808
Morrow, George ............Ensign 7th regiment.......April 6, 1808
Oneal, John ..............Ensign 7th regiment.......April 6, 1808
Peters, Brewton ............Lieutenant 7th regiment...April 6, 1808
Sharp, Thomas ............Captain 7th regiment......June 20, 1808
Vineyard, John, Jr. .........Lieutenant 7th regiment....June 20, 1808
Williams, Isaac ............Ensign Volunteer Company
    7th regiment ............July 13, 1808
Wilson, Abraham ...........Captain 7th regiment......April 6, 1808
Young, Francis ............Cornet regiment of cavalry
    2nd brigade .............July 13, 1808

### Greene County Regiments

Baker, Jacob ..............Ensign 3rd regiment..September 23, 1808
Baker, William ............Lieutenant
    3rd regiment ......September 23, 1808
Bible, Adam ..............Ensign in Light Infantry
    Company 3rd regiment...June 18, 1808
Brown, Jothan .............Ensign Light Infantry
    Company 3rd regiment...June 18, 1808
Duncan, Banjamin .........Captain Light Infantry
    Company 3rd regiment...June 18, 1808
Earnest, Henry ............Lieutenant Colonel Commandant
    regiment of cavalry
    1st brigade ............July 18, 1808
Easterly, John .............Lieutenant Light Infantry
    Company 3rd regiment...June 18, 1808
Evens, Even ..............Lieutenant Volunteer Rifle Company 3rd regiment..September 23, 1808
Harman, Peter ............Lieutenant Light Infantry
    Company 3rd regiment...June 18, 1808
Jamison, Robert W. ........Captain Volunteer Rifle Company
    3rd regiment ......September 23, 1808
Loyd, John ...............Lieutenant Light Infantry
    Company 3rd regiment...June 18, 1808
Profit, Robert .............Ensign Light Infantry Company
    3rd regiment ..........June 18, 1808
Smith, Thomas ............Ensign 3rd regiment...September 23, 1808
Wilson, Thomas ...........Captain 3rd regiment..September 23, 1808
Woods, Richard M. .........Ensign Volunteer Rifle Company
    3rd regiment ......September 23, 1808

### Hawkins County Regiments

Argenbright, George ........Captain Volunteer Rifle Company
    4th regiment ......September 17, 1808
Gibbons, Epps .............Lieutenant
    4th regiment .......September 17, 1808

Gillenwaters, William ....... Captain 4th regiment..September 17, 1808
Gregory, John ............ Lieutenant
    4th regiment ....... September 17, 1808
Hale, John ............... Captain 4th regiment..September 17, 1808
Harmon, Thomas .......... Captain 4th regiment..September 17, 1808
Larkin, Henry S. .......... Ensign 4th regiment..September 17, 1808
Looney, Absalom .......... Lieutenant Colonel Commandant
    4th regiment ............ July 30, 1808
McCans, James ............ Cornet Volunteer Cavalry
    1st brigade ............. May 9, 1808
McCraw, Gabriel ......... Second Major 4th regiment.July 30, 1808
McVay, James ............ Lieutenant Volunteer Rifle Company 4th regiment..September 17, 1808
Miller, Michael ............ Ensign Volunteer Rifle Company
    4th regiment ....... September 17, 1808
Powell, Samuel ............ Captain Volunteer Cavalry
    1st brigade ............. May 9, 1808
Rock, John ............... Ensign 4th regiment...September 17, 1808
Sysemore, Edward ......... Lieutenant
    4th regiment ....... September 17, 1808

### Hickman County Regiments

Holland, John ............ Lieutenant Colonel Commandant
    36th regiment ........ October 22, 1808
Inman, Joseph ............ Second Major
    36th regiment ........ October 22, 1808
Wilson, Joseph ............ First Major
    36th regiment ........ October 22, 1808

### Jackson County Regiments

Anderson, Thomas ........ Lieutenant 18th regiment...May 7, 1808
Cook, James ............. Captain Volunteer Rifle Company
    18th regiment ..... September 28, 1808
Davis, Cadwalader ........ Lieutenant Volunteer Rifle Company 18th regiment..September 28, 1808
McDannold, William ...... Ensign 18th regiment....... May 7, 1808
Meeole, James ............ Ensign Volunteer Rifle Company
    18th regiment ..... September 28, 1808
Thomas, Ephraim .......... Lieutenant
    18th regiment ...... September 28, 1808
Young, James ............ Captain 18th regiment..... April 2, 1808

### Jefferson County Regiments

Bradford, Henry .......... Lieutenant Colonel Commandant
    regiment of cavalry
    2nd brigade .......... August 6, 1808
Butler, Colier ............. Ensign 6th regiment........ June 4, 1808
Corder, Jesse ............. Ensign 6th regiment...September 17, 1808

Denniston, John ............Captain 6th regiment.......July  5, 1808
Doss, John ...............Ensign 6th regiment........May  7, 1808
Elder, Samuel ............Ensign 6th regiment...September 17, 1808
Gregory, George ..........Lieutenant 6th regiment....May  7, 1808
McCuiston, Thomas ........Captain 6th regiment......May  7, 1808
McSpaden, John ..........Lieutenant 6th regiment....May 30, 1808
Mount, Humphrey ........Captain 6th regiment..September 17, 1808
Neely, James .............Lieutenant 6th regiment....July 18, 1808
Nelson, John .............Ensign 6th regiment.......May 30, 1808
Sewell, George ...........Ensign 6th regiment........July  2, 1808
Snoddy, James ............Ensign 6th regiment........July 18, 1808
Sterns, Jacob .............Ensign 6th regiment........July  5, 1808
Sterns, Jacob ............Lieutenant
                          6th regiment .......September 17, 1808
Vanhoozer, Valentine .......Lieutenant
                          6th regiment .......September 17, 1808

*Knox County Regiments*

Allred, Eli ................Ensign 10th regiment......April  1, 1808
Armstrong, Francis ........Captain 10th regiment.December 26, 1808
Ayers, Jonathan ...........Lieutenant 10th regiment...June  6, 1808
Bowan, Randal ............Ensign 10th regiment......June  4, 1808
Bowman, Abraham ........Captain 10th regiment.December 26, 1808
Bright, John .............Cornet Volunteer Cavalry
                          3rd brigade ........September 10, 1808
Couch, Jonathan ...........Ensign 10th regiment..September  3, 1808
Cowan, William W. .........Captain 10th regiment.....April 23, 1808
Dunlop, Samuel ...........Ensign 10th regiment.......July  2, 1808
Edmondson, Samuel .......Lieutenant 10th regiment...April  1, 1808
McClintock, Robert .......Lieutenant 10th regiment...April 23, 1808
Miller, Thomas ...........Ensign 10th regiment.......July 11, 1808
Mitchell, Hiram ..........Lieutenant 10th regiment...July  2, 1808
Pate, Stephen .............Ensign 10th regiment......April 23, 1808
Roach, Littleton ..........Ensign 10th regiment.......June  6, 1808
Robertson, Andrew ........Lieutenant 10th regiment...July  2, 1808
Thompson, David .........Lieutenant 10th regiment...June  4, 1808

*Maury County Regiments*

Bills, Isaac ................Captain 27th regiment.December 26, 1808
Booker, John .............Ensign 27th regiment..December 26, 1808
Coldwell, Amos ...........Ensign 27th regiment..December 26, 1808
Crawford, Samuel .........Lieutenant
                          27th regiment ......December 26, 1808
Daniel, William ...........Captain 27th regiment.December 26, 1808
Darnell, David ...........Ensign 27th regiment..December 26, 1808

Davidson, John E. .......... Lieutenant
 27th regiment ...... December 26, 1808
Demwood, Henry .......... Lieutenant
 27th regiment ...... December 26, 1808
Edgar, John ............... Ensign 27th regiment.. December 26, 1808
Frierson, Elias ............. Captain 27th regiment. December 26, 1808
Garagas, John ............. Ensign 27th regiment.. December 26, 1808
Gholston, John ............. Ensign 27th regiment.. December 26, 1808
Graham, Nimrod ........... Lieutenant
 27th regiment ...... December 26, 1808
Hendricks, Abner .......... Ensign 27th regiment.. December 26, 1808
Hinnegan, James .......... Lieutenant
 27th regiment ...... December 26, 1808
Job, James ............... Lieutenant
 27th regiment ...... December 26, 1808
Kirk, William .............. Ensign 27th regiment.. December 26, 1808
McGaughey, George W. ..... Captain 27th regiment. December 26, 1808
Pillow, William ............ Lieutenant Colonel Commandant
 27th regiment .......... May 7, 1808
Polk, William .............. Captain 27th regiment. December 26, 1808
Ramsey, Joshua ............ Lieutenant
 27th regiment ...... December 26, 1808
Reynolds, Benjamin ....... Lieutenant
 27th regiment ...... December 26, 1808
Riley, Andrew ............. Captain 27th regiment. December 26, 1808
Rutledge, James .......... Captain 27th regiment. December 26, 1808
Sellers, Lard ............... Captain 27th regiment. December 26, 1808
Simpson, William ......... Lieutenant
 27th regiment ...... December 26, 1808
Smith, Moses ............. Captain 27th regiment. December 26, 1808
Srigly, Samuel ............ Ensign 27th regiment.. December 26, 1808
Steele, Robert ............. First Major 27th regiment.. May 7, 1808
Welch, James ............. Second Major
 27th regiment .......... May 7, 1808

*Montgomery County Regiments*

Bryan, Henry H. ........... Captain 24th regiment..... May 21, 1808
Bryan, Henry H. ........... First Major
 24th regiment ...... December 29, 1808
Bryant, William .......... Lieutenant 24th regiment... May 21, 1808
Cocke, John ............... Lieutenant Colonel Commandant
 24th regiment ...... December 29, 1808
Cocke, William ............ Ensign Volunteer Rifle Company
 24th regiment .......... June 4, 1808
Duff, Barney ............. Ensign 24th regiment....... May 21, 1808
Duvall, Moilmore ......... Captain Volunteer Rifle
 Company ............... June 4, 1808

Frost, Ebenezer ............Captain 24th regiment.December 26, 1808
Harman, Adam, Jr. .........Captain 24th regiment..February 27, 1808
Hawkins, Samuel C. ........Lieutenant 24th regiment...June 4, 1808
Holms, Simon ..............Lieutenant
  24th regiment ......December 26, 1808
Jackson, Brice .............Ensign 24th regiment..December 26, 1808
McGowan, James ..........Ensign 24th regiment......June 18, 1808
McGowan, William .........Ensign 24th regiment......May 21, 1808
Newel, William ............Ensign 24th regiment.......June 18, 1808
Niblet, Edward ............Lieutenant Volunteer Rifle
  Company 24th regiment..June 4, 1808
Porter, William ............Captain 24th regiment.December 26, 1808
Rochel, Amos ..............Lieutenant
  24th regiment .......February 27, 1808
Rushing, John .............Ensign 24th regiment..February 27, 1808
Ryborne, Thomas ..........Ensign 24th regiment......June 4, 1808
Shelby, Isaac ..............Second Major
  24th regiment .......February 27, 1808
Smith, Robert ..............Lieutenant
  24th regiment ......December 26, 1808
Trotter, John ..............Ensign 24th regiment..December 26, 1808
Weakley, John .............Captain 24th regiment......June 4, 1808
Whitfield, Needham ........Captain 24th regiment.December 26, 1808
Whitworth, Philman ........Lieutenant 24th regiment...June 4, 1808

*Overton County Regiments*

Babb, Matthew ............Ensign 34th regiment..September 28, 1808
Brown, Daniel .............Captain 35th regiment.September 21, 1808
Brown, Daniel .............Captain 35th regiment...October 15, 1808
Callahan, William ..........Ensign .................March 22, 1808
Copeland, William ........Lieutenant 35th regiment October 15, 1808
Dale, Thomas ..............Lieutenant
  35th regiment ......September 21, 1808
Daniel, William ............Lieutenant
  34th regiment ......September 28, 1808
Early, Michael ............Lieutenant
  34th regiment ......September 28, 1808
Elsey, John ................Ensign 35th regiment....October 15, 1808
Evans, William ............Captain ................March 22, 1808
Fannon, Middleton ........Lieutenant
  35th regiment ......September 15, 1808
Gilliland, James ...........Ensign 35th regiment..September 15, 1808
Hudspeath, William ........Lieutenant
  35th regiment ......September 15, 1808
Katron, Charles ............Captain 34th regiment.September 28, 1808
McCord, William ..........Ensign 35th regiment..September 15, 1808
Mayberry, Jacob ..........Lieutenant .............March 22, 1808

IN THE TENNESSEE MILITIA, 1796-1811 61

Oaks, Isaac ................Captain ................March 22, 1808
Poteet, Squire .............Captain 35th regiment.September 15, 1808
Rawlings, John ............Lieutenant
    35th regiment ......September 15, 1808
Smith, Iri ................Ensign ................March 22, 1808
Walker, William ...........Ensign 35th regiment....October 15, 1808
Weaver, Elijah ............Captain 34th regiment.September 28, 1808
Williams, David ..........Captain 35th regiment.September 15, 1808
Williams, John .............Lieutenant .............March 22, 1808
Willis, Abel ...............Captain 35th regiment.September 15, 1808
Willis, Henry ..............Ensign 34th regiment..September 28, 1808
Windell, Joseph Hawkins ....Adjutant ..............March 26, 1808

### Rhea County Regiments

Barr, Daniel ...............Lieutenant
    30th regiment ......December 26, 1808
Campbell, James ...........Lieutenant
    30th regiment ......December 26, 1808
Gamble, Charles ...........Second Major
    30th regiment ...........May 21, 1808
Johnson, William ...........Lieutenant Colonel Commandant
    30th regiment ...........May 21, 1808
Ladderdale, John ...........Lieutenant
    30th regiment ......December 26, 1808
Leich, George ..............Captain 30th regiment.December 26, 1808
Leister, William ............Ensign 30th regiment..December 26, 1808
Lewis, John ...............Lieutenant
    30th regiment ......December 26, 1808
Mitchell, James ............Captain 30th regiment.December 26, 1808
Parker, John ...............Ensign 30th regiment..December 26, 1808
Reigle, George ............Captain 30th regiment.December 26, 1808
Smith, John A. .............Captain 30th regiment.December 26, 1808
Spurgin, John .............Ensign 30th regiment..December 26, 1808
Walker, John ..............Ensign 30th regiment..December 26, 1808
Worley, George ...........First Major 30th regiment..May 21, 1808

### Roane County Regiments

Avery, John ................Ensign 14th regiment.......July 5, 1808
Bevely, John .............Lieutenant 14th regiment...May 7, 1808
Blanton, Thomas ..........Ensign 14th regiment.......July 5, 1808
Brown, John ...............Lieutenant Colonel Commandant
    14th regiment ......February 26, 1808
Coleman, John .............Captain 14th regiment......May 7, 1808
Cook, George ..............Ensign 14th regiment.......July 5, 1808
Cox, Nathaniel ............First Major
    14th regiment .......January 14, 1808
Eddington, Luke ..........Captain 14th regiment......July 5, 1808

England, John .............Lieutenant
            14th regiment ........October 15, 1808
Hall, Samuel .............Captain 14th regiment...October 15, 1808
Holly, William Tyrrell ......Ensign 14th regiment.......July  5, 1808
Huett, Robert .............Lieutenant 14th regiment...July  5, 1808
Jones, John ...............Lieutenant
            14th regiment ......November 14, 1808
King, Robert .............Ensign 14th regiment....October 15, 1808
Lane, Jorden .............Lieutenant 14th regiment...July  5, 1808
Lavender, Daniel ..........Captain 14th regiment......July  5, 1808
McClellan, David .........Second Major
            14th regiment .......February 26, 1808
McMullen, James .........Captain 14th regiment......July  5, 1808
Sargant, John H. ...........Ensign 14th regiment.......July  5, 1808
Tippet, James .............Captain 14th regiment......July  5, 1808
Wallace, Oliver ...........Lieutenant 14th regiment...July  5, 1808
White, William ...........Captain 14th regiment...October 15, 1808
Wilson, Stephen ...........Lieutenant 14th regiment...July  5, 1808

*Rutherford County Regiments*

Abbot, David .............Captain 22nd regiment.....April  2, 1808
Barefield, James ..........Ensign 22nd regiment...October 21, 1808
Barr, Silas ...............Captain 22nd regiment..October 21, 1808
Blount, Benjamin .........Lieutenant
            22nd regiment ........October 21, 1808
Brown, Joshua ............Ensign 22nd regiment...October 21, 1808
Carty, John ..............Ensign 22nd regiment...October 21, 1808
Freeman, James ...........Ensign 22nd regiment...October 21, 1808
Gitton, John ..............Lieutenant
            22nd regiment ........October 21, 1808
Humphreys, William .......Ensign 22nd regiment......April  2, 1808
Kerr, Benjamin ...........Captain 22nd regiment..October 21, 1808
McBride, Francis ..........Lieutenant
            22nd regiment ........October 21, 1808
McMicken, Andrew ........Captain 22nd regiment.....May  7, 1808
Peake, John M. ...........Lieutenant 22nd regiment...May  7, 1808
Rucker, James ............Lieutenant 22nd regiment..April  2, 1808

*Sevier County Regiments*

Benton, Samuel ...........Ensign 11th regiment .......July 8 1808
Bryan, Thomas ...........Lieutenant Volunteer Rifle Company
            11th regiment ......December  9 1808
Clabough, William ........Ensign Light Infantry Company
            11th regiment ...........July  8 1808
Countz, Michael ..........Ensign 11th regiment ......May  7 1808
Denton, George ...........Lieutenant 11th regiment ..April  2 1808
Elder, John ..............Lieutenant 11th regiment ...May  7 1808

IN THE TENNESSEE MILITIA, 1796-1811 63

Evans, James ............. Lieutenant 11th regiment ..April 2 1808
Houk, John ............... Captain 11th regiment .....April 2 1808
Lawson, Andrew ........... Lieutenant Light Infantry Company
                                11th regiment ...........July 8 1808
McCroskey, John .......... Ensign 11th regiment.......April 2 1808
Shields, William .......... Lieutenant 11th regiment ..April 2 1808
Stinson, Andrew ........... Cornet regiment of cavalry
                                2nd brigade ..........August 22 1808
Thomas, Ellis ............. Lieutenant 11th regiment ..May 7 1808
Thomas, Issac ............. Captain Volunteer Rifle Company
                                11th regiment ......December 9 1808
Toomy, John .............. First Major 11th regiment
                                February 24 1808
Walker, John .............. Ensign Volunteer Rifle Company
                                11th regiment ......December 9 1808
Williams, John ............ Second Major 11th
                                regiment ...........February 22 1808

*Smith County Regiments*

Birdwell, John ............. Lieutenant 16th regiment....May 7 1808
Debo, John A. ............. Lieutenant
                                16th regiment ......December 26 1808
Eoxun, William ............ Lieutenant 16th regiment....May 7 1808
Ferguson, William ......... Ensign 16th regiment..December 26 1808
French, Amos ............. Ensign 16th regiment.......May 7 1808
Henderson, William ........ Captain 16th regiment.December 26 1808
Johnston, James ........... Lieutenant
                                16th regiment ......December 26 1808
Lake, Daniel Thatcher ..... Ensign 16th regiment..December 26 1808
Madden, Joel ............. Lieutenant 16th regiment....May 7 1808
Maddon, Joel ............. Captain 16th regiment.December 26 1808
Martin, Brice ............. First Major
                                16th regiment ...........July 5 1808
Matlock, George .......... Lieutenant Colonel Commandant
                                16th regiment ...........July 5 1808
Pain, Thomas ............. Ensign 16th regiment.......May 7 1808
Reasonover, John ......... Captain 16th regiment......May 7 1808
Robertson, Moses ......... Lieutenant
                                16th regiment ......December 26 1808
Saunders, Adam ........... Ensign 16th regiment.......May 7 1808
Simmons, Joel ............ Ensign 16th regiment..December 26 1808
Strange, Beverly .......... Ensign 16th regiment..December 26 1808
Tate, Zachariah ........... Captain 16th regiment.December 26 1808
Turney, Henry ............ Captain 16th regiment......May 7 1808

*Sullivan County Regiments*

Coley, James .............. Ensign 2nd regiment.....August 11 1808
Fain, Nicholas ............. Adjutant regiment of cavalry
                                First Brigade .....September 5 1808

Jones, Samuel ............Captain 2nd regiment..December 26 1808
Looney, Joseph W. .........Captain regiment of cavalry
    First Brigade .........October 18 1808
Macey, Clement ...........Lieutenant 2nd regiment..August 11 1808
Magert, Henry ............Lieutenant 2nd regiment....May 30 1808
Royston, John .............Lieutenant
    2nd regiment .......December 26 1808
Shaver, David .............Captain 2nd regiment......May 30 1808
Slaughter, Abraham ........Ensign 2nd regiment ..September 28 1808
Stephens, Isaac ............Lieutenant Light Infantry Company
    2nd regiment ............May 30 1808
Stephens, Isaac ............Captain 2nd regiment..September 28 1808
Stephens, Peter ............Lieutenant
    2nd regiment .......September 28 1808
Waddell, George ...........Ensign 2nd regiment .......May 30 1808

*Sumner County Regiments*

Allen, Porter ..............Ensign 15th regiment.....March 5 1808
Baldridge, Stephen ........Lieutenant 15th regiment..August 11 1808
Ball, William ..............Ensign 15th regiment.....August 11 1808
Bates, Humphrey ..........Lieutenant Volunteer Rifle Company
    15th regiment .........August 11 1808
Black, George ............Lieutenant 15th regiment..August 11 1808
Black, George ............Captain 15th regiment...October 12 1808
Bledsoe, Henry ...........Lieutenant 15th regiment.October 12 1808
Bradley, John .............Lieutenant 15th regiment.October 12 1808
Bridges, Edmond .........Captain 15th regiment...October 12 1808
Brown, Samuel ...........Ensign 15th regiment....October 12 1808
Charlton, Edmund ........Lieutenant 15th regiment..March 5 1808
Cowden, James ...........Captain 15th regiment...October 12 1808
Cowden, Josiah ...........Lieutenant 15th regiment.October 12 1808
Cowden, William .........Ensign 15th regiment....October 12 1808
Cunningham, Alexander ....Ensign 15th regiment....October 12 1808
Dement, David ...........Captain 15th regiment....March 5 1808
Dickason, William .........Ensign 15th regiment....August 11 1808
Dobbins, Carson .........Lieutenant 15th regiment.October 12 1808
Ellis, Abraham ............Ensign 15th regiment.....March 5 1808
Farr, Robert .............Lieutenant 15th regiment..March 5 1808
Fellingin, John ...........Lieutenant 15th regiment..March 5 1808
Giles, Josiah E. ...........Captain Volunteer Rifle Company
    15th regiment .........August 11 1808
Hansbrough, Daniel .......Lieutenant 15th regiment..March 5 1808
Humphreys, David ........Adjutant 15th regiment...August 11 1808
Hunt, James ..............Lieutenant 15th regiment.October 12 1808
Lauderdale, Samuel D. ....Captain 15th regiment...October 12 1808
Lindsey, Isaac ............Ensign 15th regiment .....March 5 1808
McGuire, George .........Ensign 15th regiment....October 12 1808

IN THE TENNESSEE MILITIA, 1796-1811 65

McMurry, James .......... Captain 15th regiment... October 12 1808
Micklebury, Robert ....... Captain 15th regiment.... March 5 1808
Moffet, Robert ............ Lieutenant 15th regiment.. March 5 1808
Moore, Robert M. ......... Ensign Volunteer Rifle Company
                                       15th regiment.......... August 11 1808
Ozburn, Samuel ........... Ensign 15th regiment.... October 12 1808
Patton, David ............. Lieutenant 15th regiment. October 12 1808
Payton, William ........... Captain 15th regiment.... March 5 1808
Preston, Thomas .......... Captain 15th regiment.... March 5 1808
Price, William ............. Ensign 15th regiment..... March 5 1808
Sanders, Robert ........... Lieutenant 15th regiment. October 12 1808
Stone, William ............ Lieutenant 15th regiment.... May 21 1808
Tilmon, Haiden ............ Lieutenant 15th regiment.. March 5 1808
Turner, Samuel T. ......... Captain 15th regiment..... March 5 1808
Turner, William ........... Ensign 15th regiment..... March 5 1808
Walton, Josiah ............ Captain 15th regiment... October 12 1808
Watson, Samuel ........... Ensign 15th regiment.... October 12 1808

*Warren County Regiments*

Barns, Abraham ........... Ensign 29th regiment.. December 8 1808
Blanton, William .......... Lieutenant
                                   29th regiment ...... December 8 1808
Cunningham, John ........ Lieutenant
                                   29th regiment ...... December 8 1808
Denton, John ............. Captain 29th regiment. December 8 1808
Douglass, William ........ Captain 29th regiment. December 8 1808
Franklen, John ........... Lieutenant
                                   29th regiment ...... December 8 1808
Gailey, Moses ............. Lieutenant
                                   29th regiment ...... December 8 1808
Hammons, Leroy .......... Lieutenant Colonel Commandant
                                   29th regiment ........... May 21 1808
Koyl, Benjamin ........... Captain 29th regiment. December 8 1808
Lowrey, Granberry ........ Ensign 29th regiment.. December 8 1808
Lusk, William ............. Captain 29th regiment. December 8 1808
McDannold, William ....... Captain 29th regiment. December 8 1808
Rice, Archibald ............ Ensign 29th regiment.. December 8 1808
Scallions, Joab ............ Second Major 29th regiment. May 21 1808
Shults, Jacob ............. Ensign 29th regiment.. December 8 1808
Shults, John .............. Lieutenant
                                   29th regiment ...... December 8 1808
Simpson, David ........... Ensign 29th regiment.. December 8 1808
Smyly, Thomas ........... First Major 29th regiment... May 21 1808
Tate, James .............. Captain 29th regiment. December 8 1808
Vining, John .............. Lieutenant
                                   29th regiment ...... December 8 1808

Webb, Jacob ..............Ensign 29th regiment..December 8 1808
Webb, Jesse ...............Captain 29th regiment.December 8 1808
Webb, William ............Lieutenant
          29th regiment ......December 8 1808

## Washington County Regiments

Anderson, James ..........Second Major regiment of cavalry
          1st Brigade...........October 12 1808
Brown, George ............Lieutenant
          1st regiment........September 28 1808
Fain, William ............First Major regiment of cavalry
          1st Brigade...........October 12 1808
Felts, William .............Ensign 1st regiment...September 28 1808
Longmyer, George .........Ensign 1st regiment........July 23 1808
McCrackin, Samuel ........Lieutenant
          1st regiment........September 28 1808
Roadman, William C. ......Captain 1st regiment..September 28 1808
Snap, Laurence ............Ensign 1st regiment...September 28 1808
Vance, David G. ...........Captain of cavalry regiment
          1st Brigade............August 29 1808
Viney, Jesse ..............Captain 1st regiment........July 23 1808
Walker, John ..............Ensign 1st regiment........July 23 1808

## White County Regiments

Bryant, Wm. M. ...........Second Major
          34th regiment.......September 28 1808
Lourey, Alexander ........Lieutenant Colonel Commandant
          34th regiment...........May 7 1808
Neil, Arthur ..............Ensign ..................May 7 1808

## Williamson County Regiments

Aydelott, Thomas ..........Lieutenant
          21st regiment ......September 24 1808
Barnon, William ...........Lieutenant
          21st regiment ......September 24 1808
Brooks, Thomas ...........Ensign 21st regiment..September 24 1808
Casten, Robert ............Second Major
          21st regiment ...........May 21 1808
Clift, Daniel ..............Captain
          21st regiment ......September 24 1808
Cook, John ...............Captain
          21st regiment ......September 24 1808
Craig, Samuel ............Lieutenant
          21st regiment ......September 24 1808
Depriest, John ............Lieutenant 21st regiment...April 2 1808
Duffey, William ..........Ensign 21st regiment ..September 24 1808

IN THE TENNESSEE MILITIA, 1796-1811 67

| | | |
|---|---|---|
| Estes, Robert | Lieutenant 21st regiment | September 24 1808 |
| Gatland, Thomas | Lieutenant 21st regiment | April 2 1808 |
| Glover, Lancaster | Ensign 21st regiment | September 24 1808 |
| Haggard, Samuel | Ensign 21st regiment | September 24 1808 |
| Harden, Jacob | Ensign 21st regiment | September 24 1808 |
| Hill, William | Lieutenant 21st regiment | September 24 1808 |
| Johnson, Charles | Lieutenant 21st regiment | September 24 1808 |
| Laurence, John | Captain 21st regiment | September 24 1808 |
| Lock, Richard S. | Lieutenant 21st regiment | September 24 1808 |
| Long, Joseph | Ensign 21st regiment | September 24 1808 |
| McCretchen, James | Captain 21st regiment | September 24 1808 |
| McEwen, James | First Major 21st regiment | May 21 1808 |
| Mackey, William | Captain 21st regiment | April 2 1808 |
| Mebane, George | Captain 21st regiment | April 2 1808 |
| Neal, James | Captain 21st regiment | September 24 1808 |
| Patton, Isaac | Captain 21st regiment | September 24 1808 |
| Potters, Archibald | Captain 21st regiment | September 24 1808 |
| Shannon, Joseph | Captain 21st regiment | April 2 1808 |
| Simmons, Thomas | Captain 21st regiment | September 24 1808 |
| Tateham, Peter | Ensign 21st regiment | September 24 1808 |
| Thomas, James | Lieutenant 21st regiment | September 24 1808 |
| Walker, John | Lieutenant 21st regiment | April 2 1808 |
| Whitesitt, Joseph | Ensign 21st regiment | September 24 1808 |

*Wilson County Regiments*

| | | |
|---|---|---|
| Briant, Samuel | Lieutenant 17th regiment | August 8 1808 |
| Brooks, Henry | Second Major 17th regiment | August 11 1808 |
| Brown, John | Lieutenant 17th regiment | August 8 1808 |
| Cage, John | Captain 17th regiment | August 8 1808 |
| Caplinger, Samuel | Lieutenant 17th regiment | August 8 1808 |
| Carson, Thomas | Lieutenant 17th regiment | August 8 1808 |
| Chambers, Lewis | Ensign 17th regiment | August 8 1808 |
| Clifton, Joshua | Ensign 17th regiment | August 8 1808 |
| Cornelius, James | Lieutenant 17th regiment | August 8 1808 |

Cross, Samuel ............Captain 17th regiment....August 8 1808
Dunn, James .............Ensign 17th regiment.....August 8 1808
Gibson, John .............Ensign 17th regiment.....August 8 1808
Hallum, George ...........First Major
                          17th regiment ........August 11 1808
Henderson, John ..........Lieutenant 17th regiment..August 8 1808
Hill, John ................Captain 17th regiment....August 8 1808
Hodges, Josiah ............Lieutenant 17th regiment..August 8 1808
Hopson, Benjamin .......:..Ensign 17th regiment.....August 8 1808
Jones, Josiah .............Captain 17th regiment....August 8 1808
King, William .............Lieutenant 17th regiment..August 8 1808
Lawrence, Edward .........Ensign 17th regiment.....August 8 1808
Milligan, William ..........Ensign 17th regiment.....August 8 1808
Reaves, Drury .............Lieutenant 17th regiment..August 8 1808
Richards, John ............Captain 17th regiment....August 8 1808
Rogers, Peter .............Lieutenant 17th regiment..August 8 1808
Spinks, John ..............Captain 17th regiment....August 8 1808
Spradley, Tavenner ........Lieutenant 17th regiment..August 8 1808
Steel, John ................Captain 17th regiment....August 8 1808
Swingley, Nicholas .........Captain 17th regiment....August 8 1808
Walker, William ...........Lieutenant 17th regiment..August 8 1808
Williams, Beverly ..........Captain 17th regiment....August 8 1808
Woodward, William ........Lieutenant 17th regiment..August 8 1808

*Anderson County Regiments*

Davidson, Samuel ..........Captain 13th regiment ....October 4 1809
English, James ............Ensign 13th regiment ......May 12 1809
Griffith, Joseph ............Captain 13th regiment ......May 12 1809
Johnston, Samuel ..........Captain 13th regiment ......May 30 1809
Kirkpatrick, Charles .......Lieutenant 13th regiment ...May 30 1809
McAdoo, John, Junr. ......Cornet regiment of cavalry 3rd
                          brigade ................July 12 1809
McWhorter, Cyrus H. ......Lieutenant regiment of cavalry
                          3rd brigade ..............July 12 1809
Potter, Benjamin ..........Ensign 13th regiment ......May 30 1809
Scruggs, James ............Ensign 13th regiment ......May 30 1809
Sexton, William ...........Lieutenant 13th regiment ....May 12 1809
Sutherland, George ........Second Major 13th regiment .July 11 1809
Sutherland, George ........Second Major 13th
                          regiment .............October 17 1809
Thornberry, Martin ........Lieutenant 13th regiment....May 30 1809
Wright, Thomas ...........Ensign 13th regiment.......May 30 1809

*Bedford County Regiments*

Barton, William ...........Second Major 28th
                          regiment ............February 8 1809

IN THE TENNESSEE MILITIA, 1796-1811 69

| | | | |
|---|---|---|---|
| Blackwell, John | Lieutenant Colonel Commandant 28th regiment | February | 8 1809 |
| Burnham, Thomas | Cornet regiment of cavalry 5th brigade | December | 22 1809 |
| Floyd, David | Lieutenant Volunteer Rifle Company 28th regiment | December | 30 1809 |
| Gilbert, David | First Major 28th regiment | February | 8 1809 |
| Howel, Joseph B | First Major 28th regiment | October | 2 1809 |
| Prewet, Moses | Ensign Volunteer Rifle Company 28th regiment | December | 30 1809 |
| Shook, William | Captain Volunteer Rifle Company | December | 28 1809 |

### Bledsoe County Regiments

| | | | |
|---|---|---|---|
| Baker, Joseph | Ensign 31st regiment | August | 1 1809 |
| Clark, Charles | Lieutenant 31st regiment | August | 1 1809 |

### Blount County Regiments

| | | | |
|---|---|---|---|
| Bell, Thomas | Lieutenant 12th regiment | April | 3 1809 |
| Davis, William | Captain 12th regiment | April | 3 1809 |
| Fraizer, Samuel | Captain 12th regiment | October | 6 1809 |
| Henderson, Thomas | Captain 12th regiment | April | 3 1809 |
| Ingram, John | Lieutenant 12 regiment | October | 6 1809 |
| Johnson, Samuel | Lieutenant 12th regiment | October | 6 1809 |
| Panter, Joseph | Ensign 12th regiment | October | 6 1809 |
| Rhea, James | Ensign 12th regiment | April | 3 1809 |
| Rhea, James | Lieutenant 12th regiment | October | 6 1809 |
| Sherrill, Samuel | Ensign 12th regiment | October | 6 1809 |
| Tharp, Jonathan | Ensign 12th regiment | October | 6 1809 |
| Williams, James | Lieutenant 12 regiment | April | 3 1809 |
| Wright, Isaac | Captain 12th regiment | October | 6 1809 |

### Campbell County Regiments

| | | | |
|---|---|---|---|
| Baker, Samuel | Lieutenant 33rd regiment | October | 18 1809 |
| Brim, Henry | Lieutenant 33rd regiment | July | 28 1809 |
| Bumgarner, George | Captain 33rd regiment | July | 28 1809 |
| Bumgarner, George | Lieutenant Colonel Commandant | December | 16 1809 |
| Gardner, John | Ensign 33rd regiment | October | 18 1809 |

McBride, James ...........Lieutenant 33rd regiment....July 28 1809
Mayo, Valentine ..........Ensign 33rd regiment ......July 28 1809
Ridge, Robertson ..........Lieutenant 33rd regiment August 29 1809
Shelton, John .............Captain 33rd regiment ..October 18 1809
Walker, Samuel ...........Ensign 33rd regiment ....October 18 1809

### Carter County Regiments

Bolinger, Henry ...........Cornet regiment of cavalry
        1st brigade .............July 21 1809
Bradly, Daniel ............Captain 5th regiment ......July 21 1809
Carriger, John ............Captain 5th regiment......April 18 1809
Cartner, Jacob ............Lieutenant 5th regiment ....July 21 1809
Colvin, John .............Ensign 5th regiment ..November 10 1809
Craw (Crow) James .......Ensign 5th regiment ....August 25 1809
Doran, Robert Loury .....Lieutenant 5th regiment ...April 21 1809
Dugan, Abel ..............Captain 5th regiment ......April 18 1809
Dunlop, John .............Lieutenant 5th regiment ....July 21 1809
Emmert, Lewis ...........Ensign 5th regiment .......July 21 1809
Lacy, George ............Captain 5th regiment ......July 21 1809
Lovelace, Charles .........Ensign 5th regiment......April 18 1809
Millard, Nathaniel ........Lieutenant 5th regiment.....July 21 1809
Moreland, William ........Ensign 5th regiment ......April 18 1809
Peters, George Smith .....Lieutenant 5th regiment ..April 18 1809
Pratt, Barnard ............Lieutenant 5th regiment ..August 25 1809
Sloan, Joseph .............Ensign 5th regiment ......April 21 1809
Winsell, Adam ...........Captain 5th regiment ......April 21 1809

### Claiborne County Regiments

Anderson, Audley .........Lieutenant regiment of cavalry
        2nd brigade ..........March 8 1809
Barton, Elijah ............Lieutenant 9th regiment October 9 1809
Bradford, Robert .........Lieutenant Volunteer Rifle Com-
        pany 9th regiment ....March 28 1809
Greening, Thomas ........Lieutenant 9th regiment ....May 11 1809
Herbert, Nathaniel .......Captain regiment of cavalry 2nd
        brigade ...............March 8 1809
Hunter, Henry ...........Captain Volunteer Rifle Com-
        pany 9th regiment ....March 28 1809
Hunter, Joseph ...........Ensign Volunteer Rifle Com-
        pany 9th regiment......March 28 1809
Lee, John ................Captain 9th regiment ......May 11 1809
McCrany, John ..........Ensign 9th regiment ......May 11 1809
Norrell, Philip ............Cornet regiment cavalry 2nd
        brigade ...............March 8 1809
Posey, David Campbell ....Ensign 9th regiment ....October 9 1809

## Cocke County Regiments

| | | |
|---|---|---|
| Bigham, Josiah | Ensign 8th regiment | October 2 1809 |
| Campbell, David | Captain 8th regiment | October 2 1809 |
| Ginnings, James | Ensign 8th regiment | October 2 1809 |
| Ginnings, Thomas | Lieutenant 8th regiment | October 2 1809 |
| Jones, Branch | Captain 8th regiment | February 11 1809 |
| Keeny, Thomas | Captain 8th regiment | October 2 1809 |
| Lillard, John, Junr. | Lieutenant 8th regiment | October 2 1809 |
| McPherson, Bartlett | Lieutenant Volunteer Rifle Company 8th regiment | March 28 1809 |
| Mcrary, Benjamin | Ensign 8th regiment | October 2 1809 |
| Smith, Elias | Ensign 8th regiment | February 11 1809 |
| Solomon, James | Lieutenant 8th regiment | February 11 1809 |

## Davidson County Regiments

| | | |
|---|---|---|
| Anderson, B. C. | Lieutenant 19th regiment | November 10 1809 |
| Birdwell, Hugh | Lieutenant 20th regiment | February 11 1809 |
| Bishop, Collin | Lieutenant 19th regiment | April 25 1809 |
| Carter, James | Lieutenant 19th regiment | April 18 1809 |
| Cloyd, David | Captain 20th regiment | August 15 1809 |
| Creel, William | Captain 19th regiment | July 21 1809 |
| Curtis, James | Captain 20th regiment | August 15 1809 |
| Davy, Joseph | Captain 19th regiment | July 21 1809 |
| Gray, Benajah | Captain 19th regiment | April 25 1809 |
| Hall, John C. | Captain 19th regiment | April 18 1809 |
| Harris, William | Cornet regiment of cavalry 5th brigade | May 19 1809 |
| Higgins, William | Captain 19th regiment | April 18 1809 |
| Hooper, John | Lieutenant 19th regiment | August 1 1809 |
| Hooper, Thomas | Ensign 19th regiment | August 1 1809 |
| Hunter, Manuel | Ensign 20th regiment | August 15 1809 |
| Johnson, Robert | Ensign 19th regiment | April 18 1809 |
| Lassiter, Frederick | Cornet regiment of cavalry 5th brigade | July 21 1809 |
| Lenier, John | Ensign 20th regiment | August 15 1809 |
| Lintz, William | Lieutenant Independent Company 19th regiment | April 25 1809 |
| Lockhart, Hugh | Ensign 19th regiment | April 25 1809 |
| Lockhart, Hugh | Ensign 19th regiment | December 16 1809 |
| Lyle, Henry | Captain 19th regiment | July 21 1809 |
| McCutcheon, James | Cornet regiment of cavalry 5th brigade | July 21 1809 |
| Marshal, James | Ensign 20th regiment | August 15 1809 |
| Martin, James | Ensign 19th regiment | July 21 1809 |

Martin, William .......... Lieutenant 19th regiment .. April 25 1809
Morris, Dempsey .......... Captain 20th regiment .. August 15 1809
Morris, Dempsy ........... Captain 20th regiment .... July 21 1809
Morton, William .......... Lieutenant 19th regiment .............. December 16 1809
Motheral, James .......... Lieutenant 20th regiment August 15 1809
Motherall, James .......... Ensign 20th regiment... February 11 1809
Patterson, Mathew ........ Captain 20th regiment . February 11 1809
Piles, Leonard ............. Ensign 19th regiment .. November 10 1809
Robertson, Rhederick ...... Ensign 20th regiment .. February 11 1809
Roland, William ........... Lieutenant 20th regiment August 15 1809
Rowland, William ......... Lieutenant 20th regiment .. July 21 1809
Rutherford, William ....... Lieutenant regiment of cavalry 5th brigade ............. May 19 1809
Scruggs, Allen ............. Captain 20th regiment . February 11 1809
Spence, Lewis ............. Captain 19th regiment .... April 25 1809
Stewart, William .......... Lieutenant 19th regiment .. April 18 1809
Tull, Nicholas ............. Lieutenant 20th regiment August 15 1809
Tyrrel, Edmund ........... Captain 20th regiment.. February 11 1809
Waggoner, Jacob ......... Lieutenant 20th regiment ............... February 11 1809
Walker, John ............. Lieutenant 20th regiment ............... February 18 1809
Walker, Matthew P. ....... Second Major 20th regiment ................. August 1 1809
Walker, Nicholas T. ........ Ensign 19th regiment .... April 18 1809
Williamson, John .......... Captain of Independent Company 19th regiment .......... April 25 1809
Williamson, Joseph N. ...... Lieutenant 19th regiment .. April 18 1809
Wilson, Nicholas .......... Lieutenant 19th regiment .. July 21 1809
Woodard, Benjamin ....... Lieutenant 19th regiment .. July 21 1809

*Dickson County Regiments*

Allen, Barnabas .......... Lieutenant 25th regiment August 15 1809
Drake, Robert ........... Lieutenant regiment of cavalry 6th brigade ......... October 13 1809
Halleburton, William ...... Captain 25th regiment..... April 25 1809
Jarnegan, William ........ Lieutenant 25th regiment... April 25 1809
Jones, John .............. Ensign 25th regiment..... August 15 1809
McGraw, Cornelius ....... Captain 25th regiment.... August 15 1809
Molton, Michael ......... Captain regiment of cavalry 6th brigade ......... October 13 1809
Morris, William .......... Lieutenant 25th regiment .............. September 4 1809
Turner, Elisha ............ Ensign 25th regiment .... August 15 1809
Woods, James ............ Ensign 25th regiment ...... April 25 1809

## Franklin County Regiments

| | | |
|---|---|---|
| Arnold, Levy | Ensign 32nd regiment | ....April 15 1809 |
| Caperton, George | Captain 32nd regiment | ....April 15 1809 |
| Cartwright, Samuel | Lieutenant 32nd regiment | ..April 15 1809 |
| Cross, William | Captain 32nd regiment | ....April 15 1809 |
| David, Philip | Lieutenant 32nd regiment | ..April 15 1809 |
| Davidson, George | Captain 32nd regiment | ....April 15 1809 |
| Floyd, Elisha | Captain 32nd regiment | ....April 15 1809 |
| Gains, David | Ensign 32nd regiment | ....April 15 1809 |
| Gotcher, Samuel | Lieutenant 32nd regiment | ..April 15 1809 |
| Heryford, John | Lieutenant 32nd regiment | ..April 15 1809 |
| Johnson, Stephen | Ensign 32nd regiment | ....April 15 1809 |
| Killen, William | Captain 32nd regiment | ....April 15 1809 |
| McCrosky, Samuel | Ensign 32nd regiment | ......April 15 1809 |
| Martin, Daniel | Lieutenant 32nd regiment | ..April 15 1809 |
| Mattocks, Edward | Captain 32nd regiment | ....April 15 1809 |
| Moore, Alexander | Ensign 32nd regiment | ....April 15 1809 |
| Norman, William | Ensign 32nd regiment | ....April 15 1809 |
| Pharus, Hezekius | Ensign 32nd regiment | ....April 15 1809 |
| Roberts, Daniel | Lieutenant 32nd regiment | August 11 1809 |
| Rogers, Joseph | Captain 32nd regiment | ....April 15 1809 |
| Sweeten, Tesse | Lieutenant 32nd regiment | ..April 15 1809 |

## Grainger County Regiments

| | | |
|---|---|---|
| Atkins, Stephen | Lieutenant 7th regiment | October 10 1809 |
| Brewington, John | Ensign 7th regiment | ....October 10 1809 |
| Bryant, James | Lieutenant 7th regiment | October 10 1809 |
| Bull, John | Captain 7th regiment | ....October 10 1809 |
| Campbell, John | Lieutenant 7th regiment | ....May 30 1809 |
| Cocke, Sterling | Captain regiment of cavalry 2nd brigade | ..........January 17 1809 |
| Copeland, William | Captain 7th regiment | ......May 30 1809 |
| Cotner, John | Ensign 7th regiment | ....October 10 1809 |
| Countz, Nicholas, Junior | Cornet regiment of cavalry 2nd brigade | ..............August 25 1809 |
| Cox, Benjamin | Ensign 7th regiment | ......July 21 1809 |
| Cruize, William | Ensign 7th regiment | ......May 30 1809 |
| Daniel, Edward | Ensign 7th regiment | .....October 10 1809 |
| Hall, William | Captain 7th regiment | ...October 10 1809 |
| Harris, William | Captain 7th regiment | ......April 18 1809 |
| Ivy, John | Lieutenant 7th regiment | October 10 1809 |
| Mallacoat, Edmund | Lieutenant 7th regiment | ....May 30 1809 |
| Manroe, George | Lieutenant 7th regiment | ..October 10 1809 |
| Manrow, John | Lieutenant 7th regiment | October 10 1809 |
| Moony, William | Ensign 7th regiment | ......May 30 1809 |
| Morris, Shadrick | Lieutenant 7th regiment | ....July 21 1809 |

Morris, Thomas ...........Captain 7th regiment ....October 10 1809
Penn, Joseph .............Lieutenant 7th regiment October 10 1809
Peters, Brutin ...........Captain 7th regiment ....October 10 1809
Richardson, Samuel .......Captain 7th regiment ....October 10 1809
Shiply, Robert ...........Lieutenant 7th regiment ..April 18 1809
Turner, John .............Ensign 7th regiment ....October 10 1809
Williamson, Elisha .......Captain 7th regiment ......July 21 1809
Wirrick, Frederick .......Ensign 7th regiment ....October 10 1809

## Greene County Regiments

Baxtor, Levy .............Ensign 3rd regiment ....October 17 1809
Bell, James C. ...........Ensign 3rd regiment ....January 12 1809
Broyls, Jeremiah .........Lieutenant 3rd regiment .October 17 1809
Cathel, Elisha ...........Ensign 3rd regiment ....January 12 1809
Clark, Walter ............Captain 3rd regiment ......May 12 1809
Davis, Thomas ............Lieutenant 3rd regiment .October 17 1809
Fellis, Abraham ..........Captain 3rd regiment ......May 12 1809
Fox, Jerry ...............Ensign 3rd regiment ....October 17 1809
Gastin, Thomas ...........Lieutenant 3rd regiment ....May 12 1809
Golleher, Peter ..........Lieutenant 3rd regiment ....May 12 1809
Guinn, William ...........Lieutenant 3rd regiment .January 12 1809
Hays, Joseph .............Lieutenant 3rd regiment .October 17 1809
Hopper, Rolly ............Ensign 3rd regiment ....January 12 1809
Hoyl, Jacob ..............Captain 3rd regiment ...January 12 1809
Inglish, Alexander .......Lieutenant 3rd regiment .January 12 1809
Kelly, William ...........Captain 3rd regiment ...October 17 1809
Kerr, James ..............Lieutenant 3rd regiment .January 12 1809
Litnor, Christopher ......Lieutenant 3rd regiment ....May 12 1809
McBride, William .........First Major 3rd regiment January 12 1809
McNees, Samuel ...........Ensign 3rd regiment ....January 12 1809
Maye, Henry ..............Lieutenant 3rd regiment .October 17 1809
Nelson, George ...........Ensign 3rd regiment ......May 12 1809
Oldinger, John ...........Captain 3rd regiment ......May 12 1809
Rightsell, John ..........Ensign 3rd regiment .....October 17 1809
Russell, Hezekiah ........Ensign 3rd regiment ....January 12 1809
Samples, Robert ..........Ensign 3rd regiment ......May 12 1809
Smith, Thomas ............Ensign 3rd regiment ......May 12 1809
White, David .............Captain 3rd regiment ......May 12 1809
White, Frederick .........Lieutenant 3rd regiment .January 12 1809
Winkle, Frederick ........Ensign 3rd regiment Light
                          Infantry .............October 17 1809

## Hawkins County Regiments

Jones, Morton ............Lieutenant 4th regiment February 11 1809
Kearns, Jacob ............Lieutenant 4th regiment .October 7 1809
Loudeback, Isaac .........Captain 4th regiment ..February 11 1809

IN THE TENNESSEE MILITIA, 1796-1811 75

Lucas, John ............... Captain 4th regiment .. February 11 1809
Miller, Jacob ............. Lieutenant 4th regiment .... July 1 1809
Moore, Hugh G. ........... Captain 4th regiment ...... July 1 1809
Myers, Lewis ............. Captain 4th regiment .... October 7 1809
Oakwood, Henry ........... Ensign 4th regiment .... October 7 1809
Robinson, Thomas ......... Ensign 4th regiment ........ July 1 1809
Rowan, William ........... Ensign 4th regiment .... October 7 1809
Williams, Theophilus ..... Lieutenant 4th regiment . October 7 1809

### Hickman County Regiments

Alston, James ............. Captain 36th regiment .. October 2 1809
Carrithers, William ....... Captain 36th regiment .. October 2 1809
Copeland, John ............ Lieutenant 36th regiment October 2 1809
Faught, Samuel ............ Lieutenant 36th regiment October 2 1809
Haile, Joab ............... Ensign 36th regiment ... October 2 1809
Harris, John .............. Ensign 36th regiment ... October 2 1809
Harvey, Charles B. ........ Captain 36th regiment .. October 2 1809
Hassell, Silvenus ......... Ensign 36th regiment ... October 2 1809
Hawkins, Benjamin ........ Ensign 36th regiment ... October 2 1809
Hayly, William, Junr. ..... Captain 36th regiment .. October 2 1809
Humble, Jacob ............. Ensign 36th regiment ... October 2 1809
McCaleb, Epraim .......... Captain 36th regiment .. October 2 1809
Mayberry, Frederick ...... Lieutenant 36th regiment October 2 1809
Messor, Jones ............ Captain 36th regiment .. October 2 1809
Mitchell, John ............ Lieutenant 36th regiment October 2 1809
Mynett, William ........... Lieutenant 36th regiment October 2 1809
Owens, John ............... Lieutenant 36th regiment October 2 1809
Parker, Aaron ............. Lieutenant 36th regiment October 2 1809
Peery, John ............... Lieutenant 36th regiment October 2 1809
Philips, William .......... Captain 36th regiment .. October 2 1809
Snoddy, Samuel ........... Captain 36th regiment .. October 2 1809
Walker, John .............. Ensign 36th regiment ... October 2 1809

### Jackson County Regiments

Davidson, Andrew ......... Second Major 18th
                           regiment .............. August 15 1809
Lee, Ephraim ............. Lieutenant 18th regiment ... April 18 1809
Lock, Richard ............ Captain 18th regiment ..... April 18 1809
Maxwell, Samuel .......... Captain 18th regiment ..... April 18 1809
Morgan, Joseph ........... Lieutenant 18th regiment ... April 18 1809
Roulston, James .......... Lieutenant Colonel Commandant
                           18th regiment ....... February 18 1809
Spilman, Isaac ........... Ensign 18th regiment ...... April 18 1809
Spivy, James ............. Ensign 18th regiment ...... April 18 1809

### Jefferson County Regiments

Branson, Daniel .......... Ensign 6th regiment .... January 7 1809

Cannon, John .............. Ensign 6th regiment .. September 29 1809
Carry, Thomas ............ Ensign in Volunteer Rifle Com-
 pany 6th regiment ....... May 2 1809
Cofman, Samuel ........... Ensign 6th regiment ........ July 6 1809
Ellis, James ............... Lieutenant 6th regiment . January 7 1809
Ellis, James ............... Captain 6th regiment ...... July 3 1809
Franklin, Thomas .......... Lieutenant 6th regiment .... July 3 1809
Gregory, George ........... Captain 6th regiment ... January 16 1809
Hill, John ................. Lieutenant Light Infantry Com-
 pany 6th reg. ........ January 16 1809
Hill, William .............. Ensign 6th regiment .... January 16 1809
King, William ............. Lieutenant 6th regiment .... July 3 1809
McClenehan, John ......... Lieutenant 6th regiment . January 16 1809
McClister, Andrew ........ Ensign 6th regiment ........ May 2 1809
McFarland, John .......... Captain in Volunteer Rifle Com-
 pany 6th regiment ....... May 2 1809
McFarland, John .......... Captain regiment of cavalry
 2nd brigade ............. July 3 1809
McMins, Thomas .......... Captain Light Infantry Com-
 pany 6th regiment .... January 16 1809
McWilliams, Robert ....... Lieutenant in Volunteer Rifle
 Company 6th regiment ... May 2 1809
Nations, Thomas .......... Ensign 6th regiment ..... January 24 1809
Nelson, Thomas ........... Lieutenant 6th regiment . January 24 1809
Newman, Samuel .......... Lieutenant regiment of cavalry
 2nd brigade ............. July 3 1809
Snody, James ............. Lieutenant 6th regi-
 ment ............. September 29 1809
West, John B. ............. Lieutenant 6th regiment .... May 2 1809
Williams, William ............................... January 7 1809
Wilson, Abraham ......... Captain 6th regiment ...... May 2 1809

*Knox County Regiments*

Anthony, John ............ Cornet in Knoxville Volunteer Troop of
 Horse 3rd brigade ....... April 1 1809
Armstrong, Francis ....... Brigade Major
 3rd brigade ........ September 8 1809
Ault, Frederick ........... Ensign 10th regiment .... August 15 1809
Brannon, Edward ......... Ensign 10th regiment .. September 4 1809
Davis, George ............ Captain Volunteer Rifle Com-
 pany 10th regiment ...... May 30 1809
Dodd, James .............. Captain 10th regiment . September 4 1809
Dunnington, Reubin ....... Lieutenant 10th regiment ... July 21 1809
Fitzgerald, John .......... Lieutenant 10th regiment January 14 1809
Fristoe, Robert L. ......... Lieutenant 10th regiment ... May 6 1809
Gillespie, Thomas ......... Lieutenant Volunteer Rifle Com-
 pany 10th regiment ...... May 30 1809

Graves, Daniel ............Captain 10th regiment ..January 14 1809
Groves, Stephen ...........Ensign 10th regiment ......May  6 1809
Holstler, Adam ............Ensign 10th regiment .......July 21 1809
Hopkins, James P. .........Ensign 10th regiment ..February 27 1809
Hopkins, James P. .........Captain 10th regiment ......July  1 1809
Jackson, Joseph ...........Captain 10th regiment .November 10 1809
Kearns, Philip .............Captain 10th regiment .September  4 1809
Kelly, William ............Adjutant regiment of cavalry
                            3rd brigade ...............June  1 1809
McClintock, James .........Captain 10th regiment ......July 21 1809
McCorkle, Alexander .......Lieutenant 10th regiment ...July  1 1809
McDannel, John ...........Ensign 10th regiment .......July  1 1809
McEldry, John ............Ensign Volunteer Rifle Company
                            10th regiment ...........May 30 1809
Miller, John ...............Ensign 10th regiment ......July 21 1809
Morris, Andrew ...........Lieutenant 10th regiment ...July 21 1809
Price, Daniel ..............Lieutenant 10th regi-
                            ment ..............November 10 1809
Roach, Littleton ...........Ensign 10th regiment ....August 15 1809
Sevier, Robert .............Ensign 10th regiment .......July 21 1809
Shall, George ..............Lieutenant in Knoxville Vol-
                            unteer Troop of Horse
                            3rd brigade ............April  1 1809
Slaughter, Henry ..........Ensign 10th regiment ..November 10 1809
Stewart, James R. ..........Ensign 10th regiment ..September  4 1809
Underwood, William .......Lieutenant 10th regiment .March  8 1809
Walker, William ...........Ensign 10th regiment .....March  8 1809

*Maury County Regiments*

Alsup, Thomas ............Captain 27th regiment ...August  1 1809
Burns, Miles ..............Lieutenant 27th regiment .August  1 1809
Byas, James ...............Captain 27th regiment ....August  1 1809
Cockburn, George .........Ensign 27th regiment ....August  1 1809
Crowsby, Samuel .........Lieutenant 27th regiment October  2 1809
Davidson, Ephraim E. ......Lieutenant 27th regiment .August  1 1809
Ezell, Timothy ............Ensign 27th regiment ....August  1 1809
Fryerson, Moses G. .........Captain 27th regiment ....August  1 1809
Hamilton, Henry ..........Ensign 27th regiment ...August  1 1809
Henderson, Robert ........Lieutenant 27th regiment .August  1 1809
Howard, Shadrick .........Ensign 27th regiment ......April 18 1809
Isom, James ...............Captain 27th regiment ....August  1 1809
Kirk, Lewis ...............Captain 27th regiment ....August  1 1809
Lane, John ................Lieutenant 27th regiment October  2 1809
Lane, Joseph ..............Ensign 27th regiment ....October  2 1809
McVay, Jordan ............Lieutenant 27th regiment .August  1 1809
Morehead, John ...........Captain 27th regiment ...October  2 1809
Morrison, James ..........Cornet regiment of cavalry
                            5th brigade ........December 16 1809

Neely, John ............... Ensign 27th regiment .... August 1 1809
Reuby, Thomas ............ Lieutenant 27th regiment . August 1 1809
Reynolds, John ............ Lieutenant 27th regiment .. April 18 1809
Scott, Robert .............. Captain 27th regiment ... October 2 1809
Simmons, Flemmon R. ..... Ensign 27th regiment .... August 1 1809
Thompson, William W. ..... Captain regiment of cavalry
                        5th brigade ......... December 16 1809
Turner, Jesse .............. Ensign 27th regiment .... October 2 1809
White, James .............. Lieutenant regiment of cavalry
                        5th brigade ......... December 16 1809
Williams, James ........... Captain 27th regiment .... April 18 1809

### Montgomery County Regiments

Baker, Francis ............. Lieutenant 24th regiment ... May 19 1809
Brigham, James H. ........ Captain regiment of cavalry
                        6th brigade .......... August 15 1809
Brownson, Robert ......... Lieutenant regiment of cavalry
                        6th brigade .......... August 15 1809
Burtin, James A. ........... Captain 24th regiment ... August 15 1809
Dickson, Nathan ........... Ensign 24th regiment ...... May 25 1809
Ford, John P. .............. Captain 24th regiment .... August 1 1809
Ford, William ............. Lieutenant Light Infantry Com-
                        pany 24th regiment .... August 15 1809
Goodwin, William ......... Captain 24th regiment ..... May 19 1809
Hampton, John ............ Lieutenant 24th regiment ... May 25 1809
Haynes, William ........... Ensign 24th regiment ...... May 19 1809
Lister, James .............. Ensign Light Infantry Company
                        24th regiment ......... August 15 1809
Outlaw, Willie ............. Cornet regiment of cavalry
                        6th brigade .......... August 15 1809
Penny, William ............ Captain 24th regiment ...... May 19 1809
Poston, John H. ............ Captain Light Infantry Com-
                        pany 24th regiment .... August 15 1809
Robinson, John ............ Lieutenant 24th regiment . August 1 1809
Rook, John ................ Ensign 24th regiment .... August 15 1809
Temple, Robert ............ Lieutenant 24th regiment . August 15 1809
Trigg, William ............. Captain 24th regiment ..... May 25 1809

### Overton County Regiments

Armstrong, John .......... Lieutenant 35th regiment .. April 8 1809
Hudleston, Fielden ........ Ensign 35th regiment ...... April 8 1809

### Rhea County Regiments

Campbell, James ........... Ensign 30th regiment .. November 10 1809
Cozby, John ............... Cornet regiment of cavalry
                        3rd brigade ............ April 27 1809
Gale, Caleb ............... Ensign 30th regiment .. November 10 1809

Henry, Charles ............Lieutenant regiment of cavalry
 3rd brigade .............April 27 1809
Hunter, Jacob .............Ensign 30th regiment ..November 10 1809
Love, John ...............Quarter Master regiment of cavalry
 3rd brigade .............June  1 1809
Lyon, William .............Captain regiment of cavalry
 3rd brigade .............April 27 1809

### Roane County Regiments

Adams, Davis .............Ensign 14th regiment ....October 12 1809
Armstrong, Benjamin D. ....Lieutenant 14th regi-
 ment ..............September  4 1809
Bevins, Elisha.............Lieutenant 14th regi-
 ment ...............October 12 1809
Buckhannon, James .......Ensign 14th regiment .....March 28 1809
Campbell, Jefferson .......Captain 14th regiment ....August  7 1809
Cobb, Jesse ..............Captain 14th regiment ....August  7 1809
Cragg, John ..............Lieutenant 14th regiment .August  7 1809
Davis, James .............Ensign 14th regiment ....August  7 1809
Emery, Benjamin .........Lieutenant 14th regiment October 12 1809
Joine (Jones), Levy .......Lieutenant 14th regiment October 20 1809
Jones, Gabrail ............Ensign 14th regiment ....March 28 1809
Jones, Levy ..............Ensign 14th regiment ....March 28 1809
Lavender, Daniel S. .......Captain 14th regiment ...October 12 1809
Long, Joseph .............Ensign 14th regiment ....October 12 1809
Love, Richard H. .........Second Major 14th regi-
 ment .............September 29 1809
Matlock, Jason ...........Captain 14th regiment ...October 20 1809
Matlock, John ............Captain 14th regiment ..February  8 1809
Mitchell, Charles .........Ensign 14th regiment ..February  8 1809
Morrow, James ...........Lieutenant 14th regiment ..March 28 1809
Oden, John ...............Ensign 14th regiment ....October 12 1809
Owens, George H. .........Ensign 14th regiment ....March 28 1809
Percy, James .............Ensign 14th regiment ....August  7 1809
Richards, Tallepharo ......Lieutenant 14th regiment ..March 28 1809
Skillern, Isaac C. A. .......Captain 14th regiment ....August  7 1809
Smith, Drury ..:..........Captain 14th regiment ...October 12 1809
Smith, Merrewether .......First Major 14th regi-
 ment ..............September 29 1809
Thompson, Moses .........Captain 14th regiment ...October 12 1809
White, William ...........Captain 14th regiment ..October 12 1809
Winenger, Peter ..........Lieutenant 14th regiment February 8 1809
Young, Daniel ............Lieutenant 14th regiment .August  7 1809

### Robertson County Regiments

Ayers, Henry .............Lieutenant 23rd regiment ..April 25 1809
Brooks, John .............Captain 23rd regiment ......July 20 1809

Flewallen, William, Junr. ...Ensign 23rd regiment ......April 25 1809
Frye, Peter ................Lieutenant 23rd regiment ...July 20 1809
Gardner, Joshua ...........Lieutenant 23rd regiment ...July 21 1809
Houston, William ..........Captain 23rd regiment ....April 25 1809
Mastin, Gabriel ............Ensign 23rd regiment ....August 1 1809
Stoly, Henry ..............Ensign 23rd regiment ......July 20 1809
Walton, Meredith ..........Captain 23rd regiment .....April 18 1809
Young, Abrim .............Ensign 23rd regiment ......July 21 1809

*Rutherford County Regiments*

Arnold, William ...........Captain 22nd regiment .....May 19 1809
Banton, Joab ..............Ensign 22nd regiment .September 21 1809
Blair, John ................Captain 22nd regiment .....April 18 1809
Blair, Samuel .............Ensign 22nd regiment .November 10 1809
Boatwright, Daniel ........Lieutenant 22nd regiment
                          Rifle Company .....September 21 1809
Bowman, William ..........Captain of Rifle Company
                          22nd regiment .........April 18 1809
Canon, Robert .............Lieutenant 22nd regi-
                          ment .............November 10 1809
Chisom, Alexander ........Lieutenant 22nd regi-
                          ment .............September 21 1809
Crawford, John ............Ensign 22nd regiment .September 21 1809
Culbertson, Daniel ........Lieutenant 22nd regi-
                          ment .............September 21 1809
Davis, Willie J. ............Lieutenant 22nd regi-
                          ment .............November 10 1809
Douglass, George ..........Captain 22nd regiment November 10 1809
Fullerton, James ...........Lieutenant 22nd regi-
                          ment .............September 21 1809
Goodman, Claiborne .......Captain 22nd regiment .....April 18 1809
Harrison, Vinson ..........Ensign 22nd regiment .November 10 1809
Height, Sion H. ............Ensign 22nd regiment ......April 11 1809
Hunter, Edwin ............Lieutenant 22nd regi-
                          ment .............November 10 1809
Hunter, Ephraim ..........Ensign 22nd regiment .November 10 1809
Johnson, Mathew ..........Lieutenant 22nd regiment ..April 11 1809
Johnson, William ..........Captain 22nd regiment ....April 11 1809
Laughlin, William .........Lieutenant Light Infantry
                          22nd regiment .........April 18 1809
McClennahan, Mathew .....Captain Light Infantry
                          22nd regiment .........April 18 1809
McCree, James ............Ensign Rifle Company
                          22nd regiment .........April 18 1809
McRee, Lewis .............Ensign 22nd regiment .September 21 1809
Martin, William ...........Lieutenant 22nd regiment ..April 11 1809
Maxwell, John .............Ensign 22nd regiment .September 21 1809

Moore, Robert ............Lieutenant 22nd regi-
   ment ..............September 21 1809
Nash, George R. ...........Ensign Light Infantry
   22nd regiment ..........April 18 1809
Nash, John ................Ensign 22nd regiment ......May 19 1809
Puckett, Shiply A. .........Ensign 22nd regiment .September 21 1809
Richmond, John ...........Lieutenant of Rifle Company
   22nd regiment ..........April 18 1809
Smotherman, John .........Ensign 22nd regiment .September 21 1809
Wynn, Peter ..............Captain 22nd regiment September 21 1809

*Sevier County Regiments*

Armprester, John .........Captain 11th regiment ....March 28 1809
Bens, Matthias ...........Lieutenant 11th regiment October 2 1809
Black, John ..............Ensign 11th regiment ....October 2 1809
Davis, Parsons ...........Captain 11th regiment ....March 28 1809
Denton, David ...........Ensign 11th regiment ....March 28 1809
Gwin, William ............Lieutenant 11th regiment .March 28 1809
Huffacre, Peter ...........Ensign 11th regiment ....October 2 1809
Mitchell, John ...........Captain 11th regiment....March 28 1809
Sexton, Lewis ..............Lieutenant 11th regiment October 2 1809
Stephenson, Andrew .......Lieutenant regiment of cavalry
   3rd Brigade ..........August 15 1809

*Smith County Regiments*

Allen, George C. ...........Captain 16th regiment......April 25 1809
Beasby, Ephraim (Beasly)..Lieutenant 16th
   regiment ..........November 24 1809
Beasby, Henry (Beasly)....Ensign 16th regiment..November 24 1809
Burris, William ..........Ensign 16th regiment....August 25 1809
Campbell, John ............Lieutenant 16th regiment .August 25 1809
Collins, Joseph ............Captain regiment of cavalry
   4th brigade .............May 24 1809
Davis, Willie C. ............Lieutenant 16th regiment..April 25 1809
Duke, Matthew ...........Captain 16th regiment....August 25 1809
Durham, Nathaniel .......Lieutenant 16th regiment .August 25 1809
Ford, Andrew G. .........Captain 16th regiment....August 25 1809
Gray, Clifford ............Lieutenant 16th regiment ..April 25 1809
Herred, James ............Ensign 16th regiment ......April 25 1809
Johnson, Jesse ............Ensign 16th regiment ......April 25 1809
Jones, Thomas ...........Captain 16th regiment ..August 25 1809
Linch, John ..............Lieutenant 16th
   regiment ..........November 24 1809
Long, Samuel .............Lieutenant 16th
   regiment ..........November 24 1809
McBeard, Samuel .........Captain 16th regiment ...August 25 1809

McMillen, Malcom .........Lieutenant 16th regiment...April 25 1809
Mixson, William ...........Captain 16th regiment.November 24 1809
Moore, Shadrick ...........Captain 16th regiment ...August 25 1809
Patterson, Thomas .........Cornet regiment of cavalry
                           4th brigade .............May 24 1809
Pool, Jacob ................Captain 16th regiment ...August 25 1809
Sanderson, Edward .........Ensign 16th regiment ....August 25 1809
Scoby, John ...............Ensign 16th regiment ..November 24 1809
Thomas, Ichabud ..........Captain 16th regiment .November 24 1809
Ward, John ...............Lieutenant 16th
                           regiment ...........November 24 1809
Whitsett, James ...........Lieutenant regiment of cavalry
                           4th brigade .............May 24 1809
Wilkerson, Allen ...........Captain 16th regiment ....April 25 1809
Wilkerson, Daniel .........Ensign 16th regiment ......April 25 1809
Williams, James ...........Ensign 16th regiment ..November 24 1809
Wright, Claibourne ........Ensign 16th regiment ....August 25 1809

*Stewart County Regiments*

Allen, John ................Ensign 26th regiment ......May 25 1809
Allsup, William ...........Ensign 26th regiment ....August 1 1809
Atkins, Asa ...............Lieutenant 26th regiment .August 1 1809
Burton, John H. ...........Captain 26th regiment ......May 25 1809
Davidson, Hudson .........Lieutenant 26th regiment ...May 25 1809
Hall, Philip ...............Ensign 26th regiment ....August 1 1809
Jackson, John .............Lieutenant 26th regiment .August 1 1809
Kindall, Peter .............Captain 26th regiment ....August 1 1809
Lee, John .................Lieutenant 26th regiment .August 1 1809
Metheny, John ............Ensign 26th regiment ....August 1 1809
Olive, Joel ................Ensign 26th regiment ....August 1 1809
Ross, Nathan ..............Captain 26th regiment ....August 1 1809
Rushing, Elijah ............Captain 26th regiment ...August 1 1809
Walker, Robert ............Lieutenant 26th regiment .August 1 1809

*Sullivan County Regiments*

Bain, Owen ...............Ensign 2nd regiment ....October 13 1809
Blevins, David ............Lieutenant 2nd regiment .October 2 1809
Burkhart, Peter ............Lieutenant 2nd regi-
                           ment ..............September 4 1809
Cloud, Benjamin ..........Lieutenant 2nd regi-
                           ment ..............December 22 1809
Everett, Joseph ............Captain 2nd regiment ..December 22 1809
Faine, Nicholas ............First Major regiment of
                           cavalry 1st brigade ......July 21 1809
Gallaway, Thomas ........Cornet regiment of cavalry
                           1st brigade .............April 21 1809

IN THE TENNESSEE MILITIA, 1796-1811 83

Gallaway, Thomas ......... Cornet regiment of cavalry
 1st brigade .............. July 21 1809
Gammon, Richard ......... Lieutenant Rifle Company
 2nd regiment .......... August 1 1809
Harkbrode, Lawrence ....... Ensign 2nd regiment .. September 4 1809
Hicks, Jacob .............. Ensign 2nd regiment .. December 1 1809
Holeman, William ......... Ensign 2nd regiment .... October 6 1809
King, William ............. Captain Rifle Company
 2nd regiment .......... August 1 1809
Neal, Patrick ............. Lieutenant regiment of cavalry
 1st brigade ............. April 21 1809
Neil, Patrick ............. Lieutenant regiment of cavalry
 1st brigade .............. July 21 1809
Phagan, John ............. Second Major 2nd regiment .............. February 27 1809
Pryor, James .............. Ensign 2nd regiment .. December 22 1809
Rhea, Robert P. ........... Ensign Rifle Company
 2nd regiment .......... August 1 1809
Richards, Henry ........... Captain 2nd regiment . September 4 1809
Rogers, Jesse ............. Lieutenant 2nd regiment .............. December 1 1809
Scott, Joseph .............. Captain 2nd regiment ...... May 12 1809
Wallace, Robert B. ......... Ensign 2nd regiment .... October 13 1809

*Sumner County Regiments*

Allen, David .............. Captain 15th regiment September 23 1809
Aukerman (?), Jacob ....... Lieutenant 15th regiment .............. September 23 1809
Avint, Harris ............. Lieutenant 15th regiment .............. December 1 1809
Blackmore, James .......... Captain 15th regiment September 23 1809
Bradly, John D. ........... Captain 15th regiment . December 1 1809
Cathey, James ............ Ensign 15th regiment . September 23 1809
Cook, Henry .............. Captain 15th regiment September 23 1809
Gordon, Alexander B. ....... Ensign 15th regiment . September 23 1809
Guin, William, Junr. ....... Ensign 15th regiment . September 23 1809
Hall, William ............. Ensign 15th regiment . September 23 1809
Jones, William ............ Lieutenant 15th regiment .............. September 23 1809
Kelly, Edward ............ Ensign 15th regiment . September 23 1809
Kimbrough, M. D. ......... Lieutenant 15th regiment .............. September 23 1809
Lemmons, John ............ Lieutenant 15th regiment .. April 25 1809
Looney, Isaac ............. Ensign 15th regiment . September 23 1809
McDowell, John ........... Ensign 15th regiment .. December 1 1809
Mayo, Jacob .............. Ensign 15th regiment .. September 23 1809
Moore, John .............. Captain 15th regiment ..... April 25 1809

Payne, Sampson ........... Lieutenant 15th regiment .............. September 23 1809
Pitt, Stephen .............. Lieutenant 15th regiment .............. September 23 1809
Sarver, George ............. Captain 15th regiment . September 23 1809
Server, George ............. Ensign 15th regiment ...... April 25 1809
Shoulders, Solomon ........ Lieutenant 15th regiment .............. September 23 1809
Street, James .............. Ensign 15th regiment .. September 23 1809
Watkins, Charles .......... Captain 15th regiment September 23 1809
Wherry, Simeon ........... Lieutenant 15th regiment .............. September 23 1809
Wilson, Benjamin .......... Lieutenant 15th regiment .............. September 23 1809
Wilson, James ............. Lieutenant 15th regiment ... April 25 1809
Wilson, Moses ............. Ensign 15th regiment ...... April 25 1809

### Warren County Regiments

Bains, Abraham ........... Ensign 29th regiment .. November 16 1809
Campbell, William ......... Ensign 29th regiment .... August 25 1809
Devinny, John ............. Ensign 29th regiment .. November 10 1809
Duncan, William D. ....... Lieutenant 29th regiment .............. November 10 1809
Hill, James ................ Captain 29th regiment .... March 25 1809
Kenyon, Joseph ............ Lieutenant 29th regiment . August 25 1809
Koyl, Hiram ............... Lieutenant 29th regiment . March 25 1809
Perkins, John B. ........... Captain 29th regiment . November 16 1809
Rains, Asahel .............. Captain 29th regiment . November 10 1809
Ronly, George ............. Captain 29th regiment ... August 25 1809
Smartt, William C. ......... First Major 29th regiment .............. December 16 1809
Warren, Zachariah ......... Ensign 29th regiment ..... March 25 1809
Webb, Littleberry .......... Ensign 29th regiment .... August 25 1809
Weir, Merit ............... Lieutenant 29th regiment .............. November 16 1809

### Washington County Regiments

Acton, James .............. Lieutenant 1st regiment .... April 18 1809
Adair, James .............. Lieutenant 1st regiment .... May 19 1809
Andes, William ............ Ensign 1st regiment ........ April 18 1809
Booth, Joseph ............. Ensign 1st regiment ..... October 2 1809
Boring, Aman ............. Ensign 1st regiment ...... August 1 1809
Boring, Amon ............. Lieutenant 1st regiment . October 2 1809
Britton, Joseph ............ Ensign 1st regiment ...... August 1 1809
Brown, William ........... Lieutenant 1st regiment . October 2 1809
Clingon, John P. ........... Ensign 1st regiment ...... August 1 1809

IN THE TENNESSEE MILITIA, 1796-1811　85

Cox, George ............... Lieutenant 1st regiment .... April 18 1809
Davis, John ............... Captain 1st regiment ....... May 19 1809
Denneson, Robert .......... Captain 1st regiment ...... April 18 1809
Ellis, Jacob ............... Captain 1st regiment ...... April 18 1809
Heartsell, Jacob ........... Captain 1st regiment ...... April 18 1809
Henly, Isaac .............. Captain 1st regiment .... October 2 1809
Kirk, George .............. Ensign 1st regiment ....... May 19 1809
Mitchell, Samuel .......... Captain 1st regiment .... October 2 1809
Newman, Peter ............ Lieutenant 1st regiment .. August 1 1809
Vance, William K. ......... Cornet regiment of cavalry
　　　　　　　　　　　　　　1st brigade ........ September 4 1809

### White County Regiments

Austin, Saunders ........... Ensign 34th regiment ...... May 25 1809
Brock, John ............... Ensign 34th regiment ...... May 25 1809
Clement, Richard .......... Ensign 34th regiment .... August 1 1809
Cole, James ............... Captain 34th regiment ...... May 25 1809
Hill, William .............. Ensign 34th regiment .... August 1 1809
Isham, Charles ............ Lieutenant 34th regiment ... May 25 1809
McBride, Andrew .......... Captain 34th regiment ...... May 25 1809
Miller, Samuel ............ Ensign 34th regiment .... August 1 1809
Mitchell, Charles .......... Lieutenant 34th regiment .August 1 1809
Mitchell, John ............. Lieutenant 34th regiment .August 1 1809
Neill, Arthur .............. Lieutenant 34th regiment .August 1 1809
Nevill, Joseph ............. Captain 34th regiment .... August 1 1809
PettyJohn, Abraham ....... Lieutenant 34th regiment ... May 25 1809
Pruett, Isaac .............. Lieutenant 34th regiment ... May 25 1809
Shaw, William ............ Captain 34th regiment .... August 1 1809
Smith, Joseph ............. Captain 34th regiment ..... May 25 1809
Trap, John ................ Captain 34th regiment ..... May 25 1809

### Williamson County Regiments

Alexander, Thomas ......... Captain 21st regiment ... October 2 1809
Andrews, Taplet ........... Lieutenant 21st regiment .. May 30 1809
Andrews, Taply ............ Lieutenant 21st regiment .... July 21 1809
Bond, William ............. Ensign 21st regiment ...... April 25 1809
Bradshaw, Samuel ......... Ensign 21st regiment .... October 2 1809
Buchannan, John .......... Captain 21st regiment ...... May 30 1809
Campbell, John ............ Lieutenant 21st regiment ... May 30 1809
Campbell, John K. ......... Lieutenant 21st regiment ... July 21 1809
Collen, Thomas ............ Captain Volunteer Rifle Com-
　　　　　　　　　　　　　pany 21st regiment .. December 1 1809
Crawford, John ............ Captain 21st regiment ..... April 25 1809
Dickson, Josiah ........... Lieutenant 21st regiment .. May 30 1809
Dodson, Samuel H. ........ Captain 21st regiment ...... July 21 1809
Eastes, Robert ............. Captain 21st regiment ...... May 30 1809

Gardner, John .............Lieutenant Volunteer Rifle Company 21st regiment ..December 1 1809
Harden, Jacob .............Lieutenant 21st regiment ...May 30 1809
Hill, Green ................Ensign 21st regiment .......July 21 1809
Holloway, John ...........Lieutenant 21st regiment ....July 21 1809
Joab, Samuel .............Lieutenant 21st regiment ....July 21 1809
Jones, Quignal Martin ......Ensign 21st regiment ......May 30 1809
Kizler, John ...............Lieutenant 21st regiment ...May 30 1809
Mason, Abram ............Ensign Volunteer Rifle Company 21st regiment ..December 1 1809
Murry, Francis ............Lieutenant 21st regiment ...April 25 1809
Parks, John ...............Captain 21st regiment ......April 25 1809
Patton, George ............Ensign 21st regiment ......May 30 1809
Patton, John ..............Ensign 21st regiment ......May 30 1809
Roulston, Alexander ........Captain 21st regiment .....April 25 1809
Spral, John ................Ensign 21st regiment ......May 30 1809
Stobough, John C. .........Lieutenant 21st regiment .October 2 1809
Walker, Noah .............Ensign 21st regiment .......July 21 1809
Wright, Robert ............Lieutenant 21st regiment ...April 25 1809
Wright, William ...........Ensign 21st regiment ......April 25 1809

### Wilson County Regiments

Barns, Allen ..............Ensign 17th regiment ......May 19 1809
Bass, Ezekiel .............Captain 17th regiment ...August 25 1809
Bennet, Etheldred .........Ensign 17th regiment ......May 19 1809
Bond, Eli .................Ensign 17th regiment ...August 25 1809
Bonds, John ...............Lieutenant 17th regiment ...May 19 1809
Carter, James F. ...........Ensign 17th regiment ...August 25 1809
Davis, James E. ...........Ensign 17th regiment ...August 25 1809
Devault, Peter ............Ensign 17th regiment ...August 25 1809
Dillon, John ..............Lieutenant 17th regiment .August 25 1809
Drennan, James ..........Lieutenant 17th regiment .August 25 1809
Gibson, Jeremiah .........Ensign 17th regiment ...August 25 1809
Ginnings, Robt. L. .........Ensign 17th regiment ...August 25 1809
Hellum, George ..........First Major 17th regiment ..April 10 1809
Hellum, Morriss ..........Captain 17th regiment .....May 19 1809
Hodges, James C. .........Captain 17th regiment ...August 25 1809
Jackson, Jesse .............Ensign 17th regiment ......May 19 1809
Locksey, John T. ..........Lieutenant 17th regiment .August 25 1809
McCully, William .........Lieutenant 17th regiment ...May 19 1809
Martin, John ..............Captain 17th regiment .....May 19 1809
Poteet, Thomas ...........Lieutenant 17th regiment ...May 19 1809
Sherrill, Archibald .........Ensign 17th regiment ......May 19 1809
Smart, Philip .............Ensign 17th regiment ......May 19 1809
Smart, Philip .............Lieutenant 17th regiment .August 25 1809
Taylor, Solomon ..........Ensign 17th regiment ......May 19 1809
Tucker, Jeremiah .........Lieutenant 17th regiment .August 25 1809
Williamson, John .........Captain 17th regiment .....May 19 1809

## Anderson County Regiments

Breden, Andrew ..........Captain 13th regiment..February 13 1810
Campbell, Lewis ..........Lieutenant 13th regiment.August 29 1810
Keeny, Joseph, Junr........Lieutenant 13th
  regiment ..........February 13 1810
Scarborough, Robert ........Ensign 13th regiment.....August 29 1810

## Bedford County Regiments

Adams, James .............Lieutenant 28th regiment January 11 1810
Bassey, Washington ........Ensign 28th regiment..November 23 1810
Bell, William .............Captain 28th regiment.November 23 1810
Birdett, Jiles .............Captain 28th regiment.November 29 1810
Boilen, John .............Captain 28th regiment...January 11 1810
Bradford, John ............Captain regiment of cavalry
  5th brigade ........November 3 1810
Burnum, Samuel ..........Lieutenant 28th
  regiment ..........December 19 1810
Coats, John ...............Captain 28th regiment...January 11 1810
Couch, Thomas ............Ensign 28th regiment....January 11 1810
Ferrell, John ..............Ensign 28th regiment..November 29 1810
Findly, James .............Captain 28th regiment...January 11 1810
Fisher, Jacob .............Ensign 28th regiment..November 23 1810
Flemmin, Samuel ..........Captain 28th regiment...January 11 1810
Gaundell, Benjamin ........Lieutenant 28th
  regiment ..........November 29 1810
Gibson, Robert ............Ensign 28th regiment..December 27 1810
Haines, James ............Lieutenant 28th regiment January 11 1810
Haistings, Stephen .........Ensign 28th regiment..November 23 1810
Harrison, Thomas .........Captain 28th regiment...January 11 1810
Harrison, Thomas ........Captain 28th regiment.November 23 1810
Hewey, Samuel ...........Lieutenant 28th regiment January 11 1810
Hon, George .............Ensign 28th regiment....January 11 1810
Horner, Gideon ...........Ensign 28th regiment....January 11 1810
Houston, John ...........Captain 28th regiment.November 23 1810
Hubbard, Nathaniel ........Ensign 28th regiment....January 11 1810
Johnson, John ............Ensign 28th regiment....January 11 1810
King, Benjamin ...........Lieutenant 28th
  regiment ..........November 23 1810
Lakey, John ..............Ensign Light Infantry company
  28th regiment .........March 23 1810
Lee, John ...............Lieutenant 31st regiment.February 9 1810
Loe, David ...............Lieutenant Light Infantry company
  28th regiment .........March 23 1810
Longmire, William .........Captain 28th regiment...January 11 1810
Loyd, Jordan .............Ensign 28th regiment..November 23 1810
McCais, Thomas ..........Lieutenant 28th regiment January 11 1810

McCurdy, William ......... Lieutenant 28th
    regiment .......... November 23 1810
McCuestin, Thomas ........ Lieutenant 28th
    regiment .......... November 29 1810
McKinsey, Rowley ......... Lieutenant 28th regiment January 11 1810
McKisick, Joseph .......... Lieutenant 28th
    regiment .......... November 23 1810
McQuestion, Samuel ....... Ensign 28th regiment.... January 11 1810
Marberry, Isaac ........... Captain 28th regiment... January 11 1810
Medling, Lewis ............ Lieutenant 28th regiment January 11 1810
Murry, Francis ............ Captain 28th regiment. November 29 1810
Neely, Clement ............ Lieutenant 28th regiment January 11 1810
Neely, Richard ............ Captain 28th regiment...... July 23 1810
Patton, Francis ............ Captain 28th regiment... January 11 1810
Patton, John .............. Lieutenant 28th regiment January 11 1810
Peteet, James ............. Ensign 28th regiment.. November 23 1810
Rentfroe, Bartlet ......... Lieutenant 28th regiment January 11 1810
Roads, William ............ Ensign 28th regiment.... January 11 1810
Roberson, James ........... Captain 31st regiment.. February 9 1810
Roberts, John ............. Captain 28th regiment.. November 23 1810
Saunders, Isham ........... Ensign 28th regiment.. November 23 1810
Shinalt, James ............ Ensign 28th regiment.. December 19 1810
Shofner, John ............. Captain 28th regiment... January 11 1810
Smith, Thomas ............ Lieutenant 28th
    regiment .......... November 23 1810
Sutton, John .............. Captain 28th regiment. November 29 1810
Taylor, Michael ........... Ensign 31st regiment... February 9 1810
Townsen, Whitfield ....... Lieutenant 28th regiment January 11 1810
Wade, Edward ............ Lieutenant 28th
    regiment .......... November 23 1810
Walker, James ............ Captain 28th regiment... January 11 1810
Walker, Thomas ........... Ensign 28th regiment.... January 11 1810
Webster, Jonathan ......... Captain Light Infantry company
    28th regiment ......... March 23 1810
Wilson, James ............. Ensign 28th regiment.... January 11 1810
Worner, Gideon ........... Ensign 28th regiment.... January 11 1810
Yates, Elias ............... Ensign 28th regiment.... January 11 1810
Yell, James ............... Lieutenant 28th
    regiment .......... November 23 1810
Yell, James ............... Captain 28th regiment. December 27 1810
Young, Edmund ........... Ensign 28th regiment.. November 29 1810

### Bledsoe County Regiments

Anderson, John ............ Lieutenant Colonel Commandant
    31st regiment....... November 20 1810
Coulter, Thomas ........... Brigadier General
    8th brigade ............ May 8 1810

IN THE TENNESSEE MILITIA, 1796-1811 89

Looney, Peter ............. First Major
           31st regiment ....... November 20 1810
Roberts, Jesse ............. Second Major
           31st regiment ....... November 20 1810

## Blount County Regiments

Bain, Daniel ............... Ensign 12th regiment....... April 12 1810
Bain, Daniel ............... Lieutenant 12th
           regiment ........... November 23 1810
Beaty, James .............. Captain 12th regiment...... June 7 1810
Benson, Matthias .......... Ensign 12th regiment.. November 12 1810
Glass, John ................ Lieutenant 12th regiment... June 7 1810
Gould, John ............... Captain 12th regiment...... April 12 1810
Hood, Thomas ............. Lieutenant 12th regiment... June 7 1810
Houston, Samuel ........... Lieutenant 12th
           regiment ........... November 23 1810
Irvin, Alexander ........... Ensign 12th regiment....... June 7 1810
Skeets, John ............... Ensign 12th regiment.. November 23 1810
Taylor, William ............ Ensign 12th regiment....... June 7 1810
Wallace, William .......... Captain 12th regiment. November 23 1810
Williamson, William ....... Captain 12th regiment...... June 7 1810
Wright, John .............. Ensign 12th regiment.. November 23 1810

## Campbell County Regiments

Albright, John ............. Captain 33rd regiment...... May 16 1810
Allison, Benjamin .......... Captain 33rd regiment. November 23 1810
Baker, Samuel ............. Captain 33rd regiment...... May 16 1810
Bowlen, Abel .............. Ensign 33rd regiment....... May 16 1810
Branham, James ........... Ensign 33rd regiment.. November 23 1810
Branham, Martin .......... Lieutenant 33rd
           regiment ........... November 23 1810
Campbell, Joseph .......... Lieutenant 33rd
           regiment ........... November 23 1810
Cambers, Elijah ........... Ensign 33rd regiment....... May 16 1810
Cox, Joab ................. Ensign 33rd regiment.. November 23 1810
Cunningham, James ........ Captain 33rd regiment...... May 16 1810
Drake, George ............. Lieutenant 33rd regiment... May 16 1810
Grosse, Edmund ........... Captain 33rd regiment...... May 16 1810
Hoss, Thomas ............. Ensign 33rd regiment....... May 16 1810
Maho (Mayo), Valentine.... Lieutenant 33rd regiment... May 16 1810

## Carter County Regiments

Derrick, John ............. Lieutenant 5th regiment.. August 29 1810
Hampton, Johnson ......... Captain 5th regiment..... August 29 1810
Harris, Benjamin C. ....... Captain 5th regiment..... August 29 1810
Haun, John ............... Ensign 5th regiment........ June 2 1810

McIntiff, Samuel .......... Lieutenant 5th regiment ..... June 2 1810
Parkerson, Daniel ......... Lieutenant 5th
    regiment .......... November 29 1810
Peoples, William .......... Captain 5th regiment ....... June 2 1810
Warden, John ............. Ensign 5th regiment ...... August 29 1810

### Cocke County Regiments

Hern, Stephen B. W. ........ Ensign Rifle Company
    8th regiment .......... August 29 1810
Matthews, John ........... Cornet regiment of cavalry
    2nd brigade ......... October 15 1810
Rector, Presly ............ Lieutenant Volunteer Rifle Company 8th regiment .... February 20 1810
Smith, Alexander .......... First Major 8th regiment .... May 1810
Snodgrass, James ......... Lieutenant regiment of cavalry
    2nd brigade ........... March 14 1810

### Davidson County Regiments

Campbell, Philip .......... Captain 19th regiment .. February 20 1810
Cantrell, Stephen ......... Lieutenant 19th regiment ... July 23 1810
Cox, Benjamin ............ Ensign 19th regiment .. February 20 1810
Cragg, Alexander ......... Lieutenant 29th regiment. August 29 1810
Fraizer, John ............. Ensign 20th regiment ...... April 12 1810
Graham, William .......... Ensign 20th regiment ...... April 12 1810
Hays, O. B. ............... Captain 19th regiment ...... July 23 1810
Henny, William ........... Captain 19th regiment ... January 10 1810
Hickman, Edward ......... Lieutenant 19th regiment Cumberland College Company .... May 7 1810
Hover, Henry ............. Ensign 20th regiment ... February 20 1810
Johnston, Isaac ........... Captain 19th regiment Cumberland College Company .... May 7 1810
Kelly, Mordecai .......... Lieutenant 19th regiment ... July 23 1810
Kinkade, James .......... Captain 19th regiment ...... July 23 1810
Lanier, Buchannon ........ Captain 20th regiment .. February 20 1810
Lucas, John .............. Lieutenant 19th
    regiment ........... February 20 1810
Miers, Miles .............. Ensign 19th regiment ....... July 23 1810
Millen, William ........... Captain 29th regiment .... August 29 1810
Mitchell, Daniel .......... Ensign 19th regiment ....... July 23 1810
Napier, George F. .......... Ensign 19th regiment Cumberland College Company .. August 29 1810
Rogers, John ............. Lieutenant 20th regiment ... April 12 1810
Rogers, John ............. Lieutenant 19th regiment .... July 23 1810
Rogers, William .......... Lieutenant 20th
    regiment .......... February 20 1810
Rogers, William W. ........ Captain 20th regiment ...... April 12 1810

IN THE TENNESSEE MILITIA, 1796-1811 91

Smith, John ............... Ensign 19th regiment..November 14 1810
Smith, Willis R. ........... Ensign 19th regiment.......July 23 1810
Varner, Nathan ............ Ensign 19th regiment......June 5 1810
Williamson, Joseph N. ...... Captain 19th regiment......July 23 1810

### Dickson County Regiments

Adams, John .............. Lieutenant 25th
　　regiment ...........November 29 1810
Adams, William .......... Lieutenant 25th regiment...April 18 1810
Baker, Charles ........... Ensign 25th regiment..November 23 1810
Craig, John .............. Ensign 25th regiment.......April 18 1810
Devaul, Baily ............ Captain 25th regiment.....April 18 1810
Easly, Robert ............ Captain 25th regiment.....April 18 1810
Ellis, Francis S. .......... Lieutenant Light Infantry Company
　　25th regiment .......February 17 1810
Gunn, James ............. Lieutenant 25th
　　regiment ...........November 23 1810
Gunn, William ........... Ensign 25th regiment..November 23 1810
Hilliard, Needham ........ Lieutenant 25th
　　regiment ...........November 23 1810
Ragan, William .......... Ensign 25th regiment..November 23 1810
Russell, Lewis ............ Captain 25th regiment.November 23 1810
Shehon, Lewis ............ Ensign Light Infantry Company
　　25th regiment .......February 17 1810
Turner, William .......... Lieutenant 25th
　　regiment ...........November 23 1810
Walker, Archalas ......... Ensign 25th regiment..November 23 1810
Wright, John ............. Captain 25th regiment.November 23 1810

### Franklin County Regiments

Bean, Robert ............. Captain 32nd regiment......July 23 1810
Bradshaw, George ........ Ensign 32nd regiment.......May 16 1810
Burrows, Anthony ........ Captain 32nd regiment.....May 16 1810
Clark, Thomas ........... Ensign 32nd regiment
　　Rifle Company .........July 23 1810
Davis, James ............. Captain 32nd regiment
　　Rifle Company .........July 23 1810
Dougan, Sharp ........... Lieutenant 32nd regiment...July 23 1810
Drake, James ............ Lieutenant 32nd regiment...July 23 1810
Dun, William ............ Lieutenant 32nd regiment...May 16 1810
Elliot, Thomas ........... Ensign 32nd regiment..December 10 1810
Evans, Joseph ........... Captain 32nd regiment.....May 16 1810
Faris, Hezekiah .......... Lieutenant 32nd regiment...May 16 1810
Farris, Charles ........... Ensign 32nd regiment.......July 23 1810
Farriss, William .......... Captain 32nd regiment......July 23 1810
Harris, Samuel ........... Captain 32nd regiment.....May 16 1810
Hogue, James ............ Lieutenant 32nd regiment...July 23 1810

Jackson, Samuel, Junr. .....Ensign 32nd regiment.......May 16 1810
Jourdain, Elias ............Lieutenant 32nd regiment...July 23 1810
Keisy, Thomas ............Captain 32nd regiment......July 23 1810
King, John ...............Lieutenant 32nd regiment
                        Rifle Company .........July 23 1810
McGinniss, William .......Ensign 32nd regiment.......July 23 1810
Miller, John .............Lieutenant 32nd regiment...May 16 1810
Mors, John ...............Lieutenant 32nd regiment...May 16 1810
Neely, William ...........Ensign 32nd regiment.......May 16 1810
Pullen, Henry ............Ensign 32nd regiment.......May 16 1810
Roundtree, Thomas ........Captain 32nd regiment.....May 16 1810
Selman, Abner ............Ensign 32nd regiment.......July 23 1810
Townsen, William .........Lieutenant 32nd regiment...May 16 1810
Vanzant, Abraham .........Lieutenant 32nd regiment...May 16 1810
Williams, Charles ........Ensign 32nd regiment.......July 23 1810

*Giles County Regiments*

Benson, Eaity ............Captain 37th regiment.November 13 1810
Brown, Matthew ..........Lieutenant 37th
                        regiment ..........November 13 1810
Dodson, Reubin ..........Captain 37th regiment.November 13 1810
Dristall, Elias ............Ensign 37th regiment..November 13 1810
Easly, John ..............Captain 37th regiment.November 13 1810
Forgy, John ..............Captain 37th regiment.November 13 1810
Gordon, Thomas ..........Captain 37th regiment.November 13 1810
Gregory, John ............Lieutenant 37th
                        regiment ..........November 13 1810
Hauney, Thomas .........Lieutenant 37th
                        regiment ..........November 13 1810
Lamb, Isaac ..............Ensign 37th regiment..November 13 1810
Lemmins, John ...........Captain 37th regiment.November 13 1810
Love, Jonathan ...........Ensign 37th regiment..November 13 1810
Love, Joseph .............Lieutenant 37th
                        regiment ..........November 13 1810
McAnally, Charles ........Ensign 37th regiment..November 13 1810
McCullough, James .......Lieutenant 37th
                        regiment ..........November 13 1810
McVay, Jordan ...........First Major 37th regiment..April 18 1810
McVay, Kinson ...........Ensign 37th regiment..November 13 1810
Martin, Obediah .........Ensign 37th regiment..November 13 1810
Nuling, Henry ...........Captain 37th regiment.November 13 1810
Pickins, James ...........Lieutenant 37th
                        regiment ..........November 13 1810
Quinn, James ............Ensign 37th regiment..November 13 1810
Reid, Robert .............Lieutenant 37th
                        regiment ..........November 13 1810
Standford, Thomas ........Lieutenant 37th
                        regiment ..........November 13 1810

IN THE TENNESSEE MILITIA, 1796-1811    93

Steele, Robert .............Lieutenant Colonel Commandant
                           37th regiment...........April 18 1810
Tacker, Joshua ............Captain 37th regiment.November 13 1810
Watson, Thomas B. ........Ensign 37th regiment...November 13 1810
Wilson, John ..............Captain 37th regiment.November 13 1810
Woods, William ...........Second Major 37th regiment.April 18 1810

*Grainger County Regiments*

Broan, James .............Captain 7th regiment.......April 20 1810
Dyer, William .............Ensign 7th regiment........April 20 1810
Harl, John ................Lieutenant 7th regiment....April 20 1810
Holt, John, Junr. ..........Ensign 7th regiment........July 23 1810
McBroom, William ........Captain 7th regiment.......April 20 1810
Mann, Thomas ............Captain 7th regiment.......April 20 1810
Martin, William ..........Lieutenant 7th regiment....April 20 1810
Milligan, Alexander .......Lieutenant 7th regiment.....July 23 1810
Mitchell, Isaac ............Lieutenant 7th regiment.....July 23 1810
Reed, Thomas .............Ensign 7th regiment........April 20 1810
Rich, Joseph ..............Captain 7th regiment.......July 23 1810
Spoon, Abraham ..........Ensign 7th regiment........July 23 1810
Vandegriff, Gilbert, Junr. ...Ensign 7th regiment........April 20 1810

*Greene County Regiments*

Baily, John ...............Lieutenant 3rd
                           regiment ...........November 29 1810
Brown, John ..............Ensign 3d regiment....November 29 1810
Cook, Christopher ........Lieutenant 3rd
                           regiment ...........November 29 1810
Dyche, Jacob .............Lieutenant 3rd
                           regiment ...........November 29 1810
Flaker, Adam .............Ensign 3d regiment....November 29 1810
Grubb, William ...........Ensign 3d regiment....November 29 1810
Guin, William ............Captain 3d regiment...November 29 1810
Hancock, William M. ......Ensign 3d regiment....November 29 1810
Justice, Isaac .............Lieutenant 3rd
                           regiment ...........November 29 1810
Kilgore, John .............Captain 3d regiment...November 29 1810
Missmer, John ...........Ensign 3d regiment....November 29 1810
Parker, Benjamin .........Lieutenant 3rd
                           regiment ...........November 29 1810
Pooker, Jacob ............Lieutenant 3rd
                           regiment ...........November 29 1810
Price, Henry .............Ensign 3d regiment....November 29 1810
Woolsey, Israel ...........Ensign 3d regiment....November 29 1810

*Hawkins County Regiments*

Conner, Archibald ........Captain 4th regiment..November 21 1810
Conway, William .........Lieutenant 4th regiment....May 16 1810

Gaylard, James ............Ensign 4th regiment...November 23 1810
Griffin, James .............Captain 4th regiment..November 23 1810
Harman, David ...........Lieutenant 4th
    regiment ..........November 23 1810
Lane, Aquilla .............Ensign 4th regiment...November 23 1810
Lea, Edward ..............Lieutenant 4th
    regiment ..........November 23 1810
Lea, James ................Ensign 4th regiment...November 23 1810
McVaughn, John ..........Captain 4th regiment..November 23 1810
Miller, Jacob .............Lieutenant 4th
    regiment ..........November 23 1810
Roark, John ..............Lieutenant 4th
    regiment ..........November 23 1810
Smith, Jackson ...........Captain 4th regiment..November 23 1810

### Hickman County Regiments

Easly, Millington ..........Captain regiment of cavalry
    6th brigade ..........August 29 1810
Easly, Pleasant ...........Captain 36th regiment......June 7 1810
Hart, John ................Ensign 36th regiment......June 7 1810
Lomaxs, John .............Ensign 36th regiment......June 7 1810
Read, George .............Lieutenant 36th regiment....June 7 1810
Stewart, William ..........Cornet regiment of cavalry
    6th brigade ..........August 29 1810
Thomas, Tristram .........Lieutenant regiment of cavalry
    6th brigade ..........August 29 1810

### Humphreys County Regiments

Alston, John ..............First Major 38th regiment.March 14 1810
Arnold, Wyatt ............Lieutenant 38th regiment....May 29 1810
Brown, James .............Ensign 38th regiment......May 29 1810
Burton, John H. ..........Second Major
    38th regiment ........March 14 1810
Craig, James .............Lieutenant 38th regiment....May 29 1810
Craig, James .............Captain 38th regiment.November 14 1810
Craig, Robert ............Ensign 38th regiment......May 29 1810
Crow, Isaac L. ............Ensign 38th regiment......May 29 1810
Daverson, John ...........Lieutenant 38th regiment....May 29 1810
Ford, John ...............Captain 38th regiment......May 29 1810
Harris, David ............Lieutenant 38th
    regiment ..........November 14 1810
Holland, Hardy ...........Ensign 38th regiment......May 29 1810
Jarman, Robert ...........Lieutenant Colonel Commandant
    38th regiment ........March 14 1810
Langford, Thomas .........Captain 38th regiment......May 29 1810
Lewis, Samuel ............Ensign Volunteer Rifle Company
    38th regiment ..........June 20 1810

In the Tennessee Militia, 1796-1811    95

Lewis, William .............Captain Volunteer Rifle Company
                           38th regiment ..........June 20 1810
Medlock, Smith ...........Lieutenant Volunteer Rifle Company
                           38th regiment ..........June 20 1810
Powers, Lewis .............Captain 38th regiment......May 29 1810
Powers, Lewis .............First Major 38th
                           regiment ..........November 14 1810
Robbins, William ..........Lieutenant 38th regiment....May 29 1810
Simpson, Thomas ..........Captain 38th regiment......May 29 1810
Sparks, Isaac .............Lieutenant 38th regiment....May 29 1810
Traler, Hiram .............Captain 38th regiment......May 29 1810

### Jackson County Regiments

Butler, Baily ..............Lieutenant 18th
                           regiment ..........December 11 1810
Butler, Edmund ...........Ensign 18th regiment..December 11 1810
Butler, Thomas ............Captain 18th regiment.December 11 1810
Draper, James .............Captain 18th regiment.December 11 1810
Dudly, Abraham ..........Captain 18th regiment.December 11 1810

### Jefferson County Regiments

Denneson, John ...........Captain 6th regiment.......July  2 1810
Duke, Henry ..............Ensign 6th regiment......March 26 1810
Edgar, Alexander .........Captain regiment of cavalry
                           2nd regiment .........October 15 1810
Hill, William ..............Ensign Light Infantry Company
                           6th regiment .......November 14 1810
Humstead, Edward ........Captain Light Infantry 6th
                           regiment ..........November 14 1810
January, John .............Ensign 6th regiment........May 10 1810
Lock, John ................Lieutenant 6th regiment.....May 10 1810
Lyle, Daniel ...............Ensign 6th regiment...November 14 1810
Miller, John ...............Lieutenant Light Infantry Company
                           6th regiment .......November 14 1810
Pierce, Moses .............Lieutenant 6th regiment...March 26 1810
Roper, John ...............Captain 6th regiment.......June  5 1810
Tucker, James ............Captain 6th regiment......May 10 1810
White, William ............Captain 6th regiment....January  1 1810

### Knox County Regiments

Alston, John ..............Ensign 10th regiment.....August 29 1810
Armstrong, John ..........Captain 10th regiment.November 14 1810
Ault, Frederick ...........Lieutenant 10th
                           regiment ..........February 19 1810
Ayers, David .............Captain 10th regiment.November 14 1810
Blount, William G. .........Captain 10th regiment.....April 23 1810
Brannon, Edward .........Lieutenant 10th regiment January  4 1810

Byers, Cornelius ...........Ensign 10th regiment..November 14 1810
Carter, Richard ...........Lieutenant 10th regiment .August 29 1810
Fisher, William ...........Lieutenant 10th regiment...April  5 1810
Flint, Sims ...............Ensign 10th regiment....January  4 1810
Gibbs, Nicholas ............Captain 10th regiment......May 28 1810
Graves, George ............Ensign 10th regiment.......May 28 1810
Hankins, Absolom .........Ensign 10th regiment..November 14 1810
Hines, John H. ............Lieutenant 10th regiment...April  5 1810
King, Robert ..............Lieutenant 10th
                           regiment ...........November 14 1810
Lee, William ..............Lieutenant 10th regiment...May 28 1810
McLain, James ............Ensign 10th regiment.....August 29 1810
Martin, John ..............Ensign 10th regiment...February 19 1810
Miller, Thomas H. .........Ensign 10th regiment......April 23 1810
Monday, Reubin ..........Captain 10th regiment..January  4 1810
Morgan, Gideon ...........Lieutenant 10th regiment...April 23 1810
Mynett, Thomas ...........Ensign 10th regiment.......May 28 1810
Reynolds, John ............Second Major 10th
                           regiment ...........November 14 1810
Roach, Littleton ...........Lieutenant 10th
                           regiment ...........November 14 1810
Rogers, Thomas A. .........Ensign 10th regiment..November 14 1810
Sharp, John ...............Lieutenant 10th regiment...May 28 1810
Stewart, James ............Captain 10th regiment....August 29 1810
Tindall, Charles ..........Lieutenant 10th regiment January  4 1810
West, Henry ..............Ensign 10th regiment.......April  5 1810
Wolfe, Andrew ...........Ensign 10th regiment.......April  5 1810
Yarnell, Daniel ...........Captain 10th regiment...January  4 1810

*Lincoln County Regiments*

Higgins, William Y. ........First Major 39th regiment...May 26 1810
Moore, John ...............Second Major 39th regiment.May 26 1810
Williams, Wright .........Lieutenant Colonel Commandant
                           39th regiment ...........May 26 1810

*Maury County Regiments*

Ashmore, Samuel .........Lieutenant 27th regiment..August 29 1810
Bell, Stephenson ...........Ensign 27th regiment.......July 23 1810
Brooks, Isaac .............Captain 27th regiment:.....July 23 1810
Byers, James ..............Second Major 2nd regiment of
                           Maury County .....December 19 1810
Cannon, Burrell ...........Ensign 27th regiment.. February 20 1810
Craig, William ............Lieutenant 27th regiment....July 23 1810
Daimwood, Henry .........Captain 27th regiment..February 20 1810
Davis, Samuel .............Lieutenant 27th
                           regiment ...........November 14 1810
Dickey, George ............Ensign 27th regiment..November 14 1810

IN THE TENNESSEE MILITIA, 1796-1811 97

Emmerson, John ........... Lieutenant 27th regiment.... July 23 1810
Fitzpatrick, Morgan ....... Captain 27th regiment...... July 23 1810
Fryerson, Elias ............ First Major 27th
    regiment ........... November 14 1810
Goard, Robert ............. Ensign 27th regiment....... July 23 1810
Goforth, Andrew H. ........ Lieutenant 27th
    regiment ........... February 20 1810
Gurly, Jeremiah ........... Captain 27th regiment. November 14 1810
Hays, James .............. Ensign 27th regiment.. February 20 1810
Hilton, James ............. Ensign 27th regiment....... July 23 1810
Johnson, Robert ........... Lieutenant 27th regiment.... July 23 1810
Jones, Stephen ............ Captain 27th regiment...... July 23 1810
Kirkpatrick, Ebenezer ...... Captain 27th regiment... August 29 1810
McBride, William ......... Ensign 27th regiment.. November 14 1810
McCurdy, James .......... Ensign 27th regiment..... August 29 1810
McFall, Thomas ........... Ensign 27th regiment....... July 23 1810
McNair, Joseph ........... Ensign 27th regiment.. November 14 1810
Miller, Joseph H. .......... Ensign 27th regiment..... August 29 1810
Murphy, William ......... Ensign 27th regiment.. February 20 1810
Norris, Thomas ............ Ensign 27th regiment....... July 23 1810
Perkins, John ............. Ensign 27th regiment....... July 23 1810
Reynolds, Benjamin ........ Captain 27th regiment...... July 23 1810
Riding, Abijah ............ Lieutenant 27th regiment.... July 23 1810
Steel, Nathaniel Harrison ... Lieutenant 27th regiment.... July 23 1810
Taylor, Lewis ............. Ensign 27th regiment.. November 14 1810
Turner, Anthony J. ........ Lieutenant 27th regiment.. August 29 1810
Turner, Anthony J. ........ First Major 2nd regiment of
    Maury County ..... December 19 1810
Whitson, George ........... Captain 27th regiment.. February 20 1810
Wilkins, James ............ Lieutenant 27th
    regiment ........... November 14 1810
Williams, Samuel H. ....... Lieutenant Colonel Commandant 2nd
    regiment of Maury
    County ............ December 19 1810

*Montgomery County Regiments*

Allen, Abraham, Junr. ...... Captain 24th regiment. November 14 1810
Anderson, Richard ......... Lieutenant 24th
    regiment ........... November 14 1810
Blodgett, Beand ........... Captain 24th regiment.... March 16 1810
Boyd, John ............... Captain 24th regiment. November 14 1810
Corney, Christopher N. ..... Ensign Light Infantry Company
    24th regiment ...... November 14 1810
Gord, William ............. Lieutenant Rifle Company 24th
    regiment ........... November 14 1810
Grant, Zachariah ......... Lieutenant 24th
    regiment ........... November 14 1810

Hamilton, James ...........Captain Light Infantry Company 24th
                            regiment ...........November 14 1810
Handlin, William ..........Ensign 24th regiment.....March 16 1810
Haynes, William ...........Lieutenant Light Infantry 24th
                            regiment ...........November 24 1810
Lindsey, John .............Lieutenant 24th regiment..March 14 1810
Logans, William ...........Captain 24th regiment.November 14 1810
Love, Robert .............Ensign 24th regiment..November 14 1810
Noblett, Edward ..........Captain Volunteer Rifle Company 24th
                            regiment ...........November 14 1810
Rainey, Elisha ............Ensign 24th regiment..November 14 1810
Roberts, Collin ............Ensign 24th regiment..November 14 1810
Sommerville, Robert .......Captain 24th regiment.November 14 1810
Tompkins, John B. .........Lieutenant 24th regiment..March 16 1810
Webb, Ross ...............Lieutenant 24th
                            regiment ...........November 14 1810
Williams, James ...........Lieutenant regiment of cavalry 6th
                            brigade ...............April 12 1810

## Overton County Regiments

Berry, James .............Captain 35th regiment.November 29 1810
Clark, Branter ...........Lieutenant 35th
                            regiment ...........November 29 1810
Duncan, George ..........Lieutenant 35th
                            regiment ...........November 29 1810
Finley, James ............Captain 35th regiment.November 29 1810
Garner, John .............Ensign 35th regiment..November 29 1810
Sharp, Aaron .............Ensign 35th regiment..November 29 1810
Stewart, Samuel P. ........Ensign 35th regiment..November 29 1810

## Rhea County Regiments

Bird, John ...............Lieutenant 30th regiment.August 29 1810
Brazelton, Henry .........Lieutenant 30th regiment..March 28 1810
Goad, William ............Lieutenant 30th regiment...April  5 1810
Johnson, William .........Ensign 30th regiment....August 29 1810
Ledbetter, Ephraim .......Ensign 30th regiment.....March 28 1810
McClintock, Robert .......Captain 30th regiment....August 29 1810
Sands, Jacob .............Ensign 30th regiment.......April  5 1810
Washington, Frederick .....Captain 30th regiment....March 28 1810

## Roane County Regiments

Bacon, Allen S. ............Captain 14th regiment....August 29 1810
**Bevins,** Elijah .............Captain 14th regiment..February 20 1810
Childers, Thomas C........Lieutenant 14th regiment.August 29 1810
Clark, Thomas C. ..........Captain 14th regiment....August 29 1810
Crumby, Hugh ............Ensign 14th regiment.....August 29 1810
Griffith, Thomas ..........Lieutenant 14th
                            regiment ...........February 20 1810

IN THE TENNESSEE MILITIA, 1796-1811          99

Hankins, Gilbert .......... Lieutenant 14th
                            regiment ........... February 20 1810
Hendrick, Squire ........... Captain 14th regiment ...... May 29 1810
Hogwood, Jonathan ........ Lieutenant 14th regiment. August 29 1810
Phillips, Reubin ........... Ensign 14th regiment ... February 20 1810
Richards, William ......... Ensign 14th regiment ..... August 29 1810
Rogers, James R. .......... Captain 14th regiment .... August 29 1810
Timberlick, John C. ........ Lieutenant 14th regiment ... May 29 1810
Turner, Daniel ............ Lieutenant 14th regiment. August 29 1810
Walker, Thomas ........... Captain 14th regiment .... August 29 1810
Williams, Matthias ........ Ensign 14th regiment ....... May 29 1810

*Robertson County Regiments*

Ball, John, Junr. ........... Ensign 23d regiment ... December 11 1810
Benson, Richard .......... Captain 23d regiment .. December 11 1810
Braden, Robert ............ Captain 23d regiment ....... May 29 1810
Brewer, Edmund .......... Ensign 23d regiment ........ May 29 1810
Brewer, John ............. Lieutenant 23d regiment .... May 29 1810
Chapman, George ......... Captain 23d regiment .. December 11 1810
Cheatham, John B. ........ Captain regiment of cavalry
                            6th brigade ............. June 12 1810
Clark, Avery .............. Captain 23d regiment ... January  4 1810
Crunk, Richard ............ Lieutenant 23d regiment. January  4 1810
Elliot, Benjamin .......... Captain 23d regiment ...... April 24 1810
Faunt, William ............ Ensign 23d regiment ........ May  2 1810
Fox, Zenas ................ Captain 23d regiment .. December 11 1810
Fyne, Jacob ............... Lieutenant 23d regiment .... May 29 1810
Harwell, Richard M. ....... Captain 23d regiment ....... May 29 1810
Huddleston, Josiah D. ..... Lieutenant 23d regiment. January  4 1810
Johnson, James ........... Lieutenant 23d
                            regiment ........... December 11 1810
Martin, Gabriel ........... Captain 23d regiment .. December 11 1810
Menees, Benjamin W. ...... Ensign 23d regiment ........ May 29 1810
Morris, Hezekiah ......... Captain 23d regiment .. December 11 1810
Pace, Gideon ............. Lieutenant 23d
                            regiment ........... December 11 1810
Perry, Robert ............. Ensign 23d regiment ...... April 24 1810
Plummer, Richard ......... Cornet regiment of cavalry
                            6th brigade ............. June 12 1810
Redferren, Isaac .......... Ensign 23d regiment ... December 11 1810
Sanders, Daniel ........... Ensign 23d regiment ... December 11 1810
Sanders, Robert .......... Lieutenant 23d
                            regiment ........... December 11 1810
Smart, William ............ Ensign 23d regiment ..... January  4 1810
Spearman, Samuel ........ Lieutenant 23d
                            regiment ........... December 11 1810
Spence, Thomas .......... Ensign 23d regiment ... December 11 1810

Stringer, Gray .............. Ensign 23d regiment...December 11 1810
Strother, John .............. Captain 23d regiment..December 11 1810
Williams, Garland ......... Lieutenant 23d
    regiment ........... December 11 1810
Wynn, James ............. Lieutenant 23d regiment....April 24 1810

### Rutherford County Regiments

Abbott, David ............. Second Major 22nd
    regiment ........... December 27 1810
Carnahan, Thomas ......... Ensign 22d regiment....... April 23 1810
Dyer, Robert H. ........... Captain regiment of cavalry
    5th brigade ........... August 29 1810
Fuller, John ............... Lieutenant 22nd regiment...April 24 1810
Gilliam, John ............. Captain 22nd regiment..... April 24 1810
Gitton, John L. ............ Captain 22nd regiment..... April 24 1810
Griffin, John .............. Lieutenant regiment of cavalry
    5th brigade ........... August 29 1810
Hall, James ............... Lieutenant 22nd regiment...April 24 1810
Hall, John ................ Ensign 22nd regiment...... April 24 1810
Henderson, James ......... Lieutenant Colonel Commandant
    2nd regiment of Rutherford
    County .............. August 29 1810
Irvin, Samuel ............. Ensign 22nd regiment...... April 24 1810
Laughlin, James ........... First Major 2nd regiment of
    Rutherford County ....August 29 1810
McClannahan, Matthew ....First Major 22nd regiment..July 23 1810
McEwen, Alexander ........Second Major 2nd regiment
    Rutherford County ....August 29 1810
McEwen, James ........... Coronet regiment of cavalry
    5th brigade ........... August 29 1810
Orr, Alexander ............ Captain 22nd regiment..... April 24 1810
Searcy, William W. ........Lieutenant Colonel Commandant
    22nd regiment .......... July 23 1810
Seratt, Joseph ............. Ensign 22nd regiment...... April 24 1810
Smith, William ............ Captain 22nd regiment..... April 24 1810
Willeford, William ........ Lieutenant 22nd regiment...April 24 1810

### Sevier County Regiments

Clinkingbeard, Edward ..... Ensign 1th regiment...November 29 1810
Denton, David ............ Lieutenant 11th regiment.August 29 1810
Hargis, William ........... Ensign 11th regiment..... August 29 1810
McCrery, Benjamin ........ Lieutenant 11th regiment.August 29 1810
Pate, Charles .............. Ensign 11th regiment..... August 29 1810
Shahan, Thomas .......... Lieutenant 11th regiment.August 29 1810
Smith, William ............ Ensign 11th regiment..... August 29 1810
Snoddy, Samuel ........... Lieutenant 11th
    regiment ........... November 29 1810

IN THE TENNESSEE MILITIA, 1796-1811 101

## Smith County Regiments

| | | | |
|---|---|---|---|
| Cain, Cornelius | Lieutenant 16th regiment | April | 5 1810 |
| Carter, Beverly | Ensign 16th regiment | December | 27 1810 |
| Farly, Henry | Ensign 16th regiment | April | 5 1810 |
| Ferguson, William | Captain 16th regiment | December | 27 1810 |
| Goodall, Davis | Captain 16th regiment | December | 27 1810 |
| Griffin, John | Ensign 16th regiment | December | 27 1810 |
| Hayney, Elijah | Captain 16th regiment | April | 5 1810 |
| Lyon, John | Captain 16th regiment | December | 27 1810 |
| McKinniss, Hugh | Lieutenant 16th regiment | April | 5 1810 |
| Montgomery, James | Second Major 16th regiment | April | 5 1810 |
| Moores, Isaac | Second Major 2nd regiment Smith County | April | 12 1810 |
| Norton, Edward | Captain 16th regiment | April | 5 1810 |
| Pugh, Jesse | Ensign 16th regiment | April | 5 1810 |
| Read, John | Ensign 16th regiment | April | 5 1810 |
| Roads, John | Captain 16th regiment | April | 5 1810 |
| Robertson, Jonathan B. | Lieutenant Colonel Commandant 2nd regiment Smith County | April | 12 1810 |
| Robertson, William | Lieutenant 16th regiment | April | 5 1810 |
| Scott, John | Lieutenant 16th regiment | December | 27 1810 |
| Snider, Isaac | Captain 16th regiment | April | 5 1810 |
| Stiles, John | Lieutenant 16th regiment | April | 5 1810 |
| Strong, John | Ensign 16th regiment | April | 5 1810 |
| Strother, Robert | Ensign 16th regiment | April | 5 1810 |
| Sulvent, Edward | Ensign 16th regiment | December | 27 1810 |
| Thomas, Ichabud | First Major 2nd regiment Smith County | April | 12 1810 |
| Walker, Andrew | Lieutenant 16th regiment | April | 5 1810 |
| Waters, Thomas | Ensign 16th regiment | December | 27 1810 |
| York, Richard | Lieutenant 16th regiment | December | 27 1810 |

## Stewart County Regiments

| | | | |
|---|---|---|---|
| Denson, Jesse | Lieutenant Colonel Commandant 26th regiment | August | 29 1810 |
| Gray, Thomas | Captain 26th regiment | June | 26 1810 |
| Scarborough, John | Ensign 26th regiment | June | 26 1810 |

## Sullivan County Regiments

| | | | |
|---|---|---|---|
| Barrot, John | Ensign 2nd regiment | February | 14 1810 |
| Goodman, Andrew | Ensign 2nd regiment | July | 10 1810 |
| Johnson, Thomas | Lieutenant 2nd regiment | February | 14 1810 |
| King, Edward | Lieutenant 2nd regiment | July | 10 1810 |
| Royston, John | Captain 2nd regiment | August | 29 1810 |

## Sumner County Regiments

| | | |
|---|---|---|
| Barrett, James | Captain 15th regiment | July 23 1810 |
| Bennett, George | Ensign 15th regiment | May 8 1810 |
| Bradley, Edward | First Major 15th regiment | November 21 1810 |
| Brigan, William | Ensign 15th regiment | May 8 1810 |
| Buckham, Andrew | Cornet regiment of cavalry 4th brigade | May 8 1810 |
| Cantrell, Ota | Captain 15th regiment | May 8 1810 |
| Doherty, Mathew | Ensign 15th regiment | May 8 1810 |
| Durrin, Thomas | Ensign Rifle Company 15th regiment | July 23 1810 |
| Edwards, William, Junr. | Captain 15th regiment | May 8 1810 |
| Green, David | Captain 15th regiment | May 8 1810 |
| Green, Edmund | Lieutenant 15th regiment | May 8 1810 |
| Green, Michael | Lieutenant 15th regiment | July 23 1810 |
| Green, William | Ensign 15th regiment | July 23 1810 |
| Hamilton, Henry | Lieutenant 15th regiment | May 8 1810 |
| Hogan, Edmund | Lieutenant 15th regiment | May 8 1810 |
| Jones, John | Captain regiment of cavalry | |
| Leake, John | Ensign 15th regiment | July 23 1810 |
| Looney, Isaac | Lieutenant 15th regiment | May 8 1810 |
| | 4th brigade | May 8 1810 |
| McAdams, William R. | Ensign 15th regiment | May 8 1810 |
| Montgomery, William | Second Major 2nd regiment of Sumner County | November 21 1810 |
| Scurry, Thomas | Lieutenant regiment of cavalry 4th brigade | May 8 1810 |
| Sewell, Benjamin | Captain 15th regiment | May 8 1810 |
| Shaw, Thomas | Captain 15th regiment | May 8 1810 |
| Shippes, Archibald | Lieutenant 15th regiment | July 23 1810 |
| Shoulders, Solomon | Captain 15th regiment | May 8 1810 |
| Shoulders, William | Ensign 15th regiment | May 8 1810 |
| Shy, Robert | Captain 15th regiment | February 19 1810 |
| Simpson, Robert | Captain 15th regiment | May 8 1810 |
| Spradlen, Jesse | Lieutenant 15th regiment | February 19 1810 |
| Straton, Calvin | Captain 15th regiment | May 8 1810 |
| Taylor, Jacob | Ensign 15th regiment | February 19 1810 |
| Tollock, David | Ensign 15th regiment | May 8 1810 |
| Wallace, John | Lieutenant 15th regiment | May 8 1810 |
| Watkins, Charles | First Major 2nd regiment of Sumner County | November 21 1810 |
| Watson, Samuel | Lieutenant 15th regiment | May 8 1810 |
| Whitsell, Laurence | Lieutenant Colonel Commandant 2nd regiment of Sumner County | November 21 1810 |

## Warren County Regiments

| | | |
|---|---|---|
| Alexander, Silas | Ensign 29th regiment | June 22 1810 |
| Armstrong, William | Second Major 29th regiment | May 23 1810 |
| Barrett, Joseph W. | Lieutenant 29th regiment | November 14 1810 |
| Benton, David | Lieutenant 29th regiment | June 22 1810 |
| Dean, Michael | Captain 29th regiment | November 14 1810 |
| Franklen, John A. | Captain 29th regiment | November 14 1810 |
| Gibbs, George | Lieutenant 29th regiment | November 14 1810 |
| Hill, Alexander | Captain 29th regiment | June 22 1810 |
| Hill, Alexander | Captain 29th regiment | November 14 1810 |
| Kennedy, John | Captain 29th regiment | June 22 1810 |
| Looney, Stephen | Lieutenant 29th regiment | June 22 1810 |
| Martin, William | Ensign 29th regiment | November 14 1810 |
| Sellers, Drury | Ensign 29th regiment | June 22 1810 |
| Williams, James | Ensign 29th regiment | November 14 1810 |
| Withers, James | Lieutenant 29th regiment | November 14 1810 |

## Washington County Regiments

| | | |
|---|---|---|
| Bailis, Samuel | Lieutenant Colonel Commandant 1st regiment | November 29 1810 |
| Barran, Aman | Captain 1st regiment | March 14 1810 |
| Bayless, Hezekiah | Ensign 1st regiment | November 29 1810 |
| Brown, William | Captain 1st regiment | March 14 1810 |
| Gibson, David | Ensign 1st regiment | March 14 1810 |
| Gowers, William | Ensign 1st regiment | December 19 1810 |
| Hampton, John | Captain 1st regiment | December 19 1810 |
| Keener, Joseph | Lieutenant 1st regiment | March 14 1810 |
| McCray, Henry | Captain 1st regiment | November 29 1810 |
| McCray, Philip | Lieutenant 1st regiment | December 19 1810 |
| Parker, James | Second Major 1st regiment | November 29 1810 |
| Patton, Thomas C. | Lieutenant 1st regiment | November 29 1810 |
| Roadman, William C. | First Major 1st regiment | November 29 1810 |
| Tilson, John | Ensign 1st regiment | March 14 1810 |
| White, Richard | Lieutenant 1st regiment | March 14 1810 |

## White County Regiments

| | | |
|---|---|---|
| Atkinson, John | Ensign 34th regiment | November 27 1810 |
| Bryant, Morgan | Lieutenant 34th regiment | March 16 1810 |
| Bucher, David | Ensign 34th regiment | March 16 1810 |

Burton, Henry ............Ensign 34th regiment..November 29 1810
Deweese, Morgan ..........Ensign 34th regiment...February 20 1810
Fox, William ..............Lieutenant 34th
                          regiment ...........February 20 1810
Gillentine, Nicholas ........Lieutenant 27th
                          regiment ...........November 27 1810
Jones, Zachariah ...........Captain 34th regiment.November 29 1810
Lance, Samuel .............Lieutenant 34th
                          regiment ...........February 20 1810
Lewis, Elijah .............Lieutenant 34th
                          regiment ...........November 29 1810
Massey, Thomas ...........Ensign 34th regiment..November 29 1810
Rannolds, James ...........Captain 34th regiment....March 16 1810
Ridge, William ............Captain 34th regiment.November 29 1810
Rotton, Richard M. ........Captain 34th regiment.November 29 1810
Russell, George ............Ensign 34th regiment...February 20 1810
Smith, Andrew ...........Lieutenant 34th
                          regiment ...........November 29 1810
Smith, Bird ...............Brigadier General 7th
                          brigade ............November 24 1810
Smith, William ............Captain 34th regiment..February 20 1810
Warren, Bluford ...........Ensign 34th regiment..November 29 1810

*Williamson County Regiments*

Alexander, Aaron ..........Ensign 21st regiment.....March 20 1810
Burns, James ..............Ensign 21st regiment....January 15 1810
Callen, Thomas ............First Major 2nd regiment
                          Williamson County ....August 29 1810
Campbell, Hiram ..........Ensign 21st regiment....January 15 1810
Cannon, Newton ..........Lieutenant Colonel Commandant
                          2nd regiment .........August 29 1810
Crockett, Joseph ..........Captain 21st regiment....August 29 1810
Crucey, John ..............Cornet regiment of cavalry
                          5th brigade.........December 13 1810
Garret, Jacob .............Captain 21st regiment...January 15 1810
Giddens, James ...........Captain 21st regiment....March 20 1810
Holland, Thomas H. .......Captain 21st regiment....August 29 1810
Hungarford, Richard .......Lieutenant regiment of cavalry
                          5th brigade .........December 13 1810
Jackson, James ...........Lieutenant 21st regiment January 15 1810
Jossling, James ............Lieutenant 21st regiment..March 20 1810
Little, Neal ...............Lieutenant 21st regiment..August 29 1810
McCrakin, Joseph .........Captain 21st regiment....March 20 1810
Orton, Richard ............Captain regiment of cavalry
                          5th brigade ........December 13 1810
Roulston, Alexander ........Second Major 2nd
                          regiment ............August 29 1810

IN THE TENNESSEE MILITIA, 1796-1811     105

Saunders, Turner .......... Captain 21st regiment... January 15 1810
Stewart, Henry ............ Lieutenant 21st regiment January 15 1810
Tune, Lewis ............... Ensign 21st regiment.... January 15 1810
Walker, Hance ............ Lieutenant 21st regiment.. March 20 1810
Welks, Daniel ............ Lieutenant 21st regiment January 15 1810
Wells, Thomas ............ Captain 21st regiment... January 15 1810
Wilson, James, Junr. ....... Ensign 21st regiment.... January 15 1810
Wilson, John .............. Lieutenant 21st regiment January 15 1810

*Wilson County Regiments*

Alexander, Benjamin ....... Ensign 17th regiment.. September 12 1810
Bone, Eli ................. Captain 17th regiment..... April 12 1810
Boss, Sion ................ Ensign 17th regiment...... April 12 1810
Chastine, Elisha .......... Ensign 17th regiment...... April 12 1810
Davis, Thomas ............ Captain 17th regiment..... April 12 1810
Fletcher, Edmund ......... Ensign 17th regiment.. September 12 1810
Harris, Allen ............. Ensign 17th regiment...... April 12 1810
Lambert, Aaron ........... Lieutenant 17th regiment... April 12 1810
Lansden, Thomas ......... Lieutenant 17th regiment... April 12 1810
McCalpin, Thomas ........ Lieutenant regiment of cavalry
                            4th brigade.............. June  1 1810
McNeely, Alexander ....... Lieutenant 17th
                            regiment ........... September 12 1810
Meredith, Samuel .......... Cornet regiment of cavalry
                            4th brigade.............. June  1 1810
Perviance, Alexander ...... Captain 17th regiment.September 12 1810
Qualls, John .............. Lieutenant 17th regiment... April 12 1810
Robertson, John .......... Lieutenant 17th
                            regiment ........... September 12 1810
Stewart, Cirus ............ Ensign 17th regiment...... April 12 1810
Thompson, Neal .......... Captain 17th regiment..... April 12 1810
Vivrett, Lancelett ......... Lieutenant 17th regiment... April 12 1810
Walker, John B. ........... Captain regiment of cavalry
                            4th brigade.............. June  1 1810
Whittin, Robert .......... Lieutenant 17th regiment... April 12 1810

*Anderson County Regiments*

Chiles, Paul .............. Ensign 13th regiment...... April  8 1811
Clodfelter, Jacob ......... Ensign 13th regiment..... March 19 1811
Fry, John ................. Ensign 13th regiment..... March 19 1811
Hasler, Adam ............. Ensign 13th regiment..... August 13 1811
Horton, Isaac ............. Ensign 13th regiment..... March 19 1811
Leib, Daniel .............. Lieutenant 13th regiment.. March 19 1811
Marshal, Hardy ........... Ensign 13th regiment.. September  9 1811
Marshal, Richard ......... Captain 13th regiment.September  9 1811
Marshall, Richard ........ Lieutenant 13th regiment... April  8 1811
Martin, Nathaniel ........ Captain 13th regiment..... March 19 1811

Millican, Hugh ..........Lieutenant 13th regiment ..............September 9 1811
Parks, John ..............Second Major 13th regiment ................August 13 1811
Scruggs, James ............Captain 13th regiment....March 19 1811
Tunnell, James ............Captain 13th regiment....August 13 1811
Tunnell, William ..........First Major 13th regiment.August 13 1811

*Bedford County Regiments*

Burdett, Giles .............First Major 28th regiment ..............November 19 1811
Burns, John, Junior ........Ensign 28th regiment......April 19 1811
Enochs, Robert ...........Lieutenant 28th regiment.August 22 1811
Fitzpatrick, Joseph .......:Ensign 28th regiment.....August 22 1811
Gibson, John .............Lieutenant 28th regiment ..............February 21 1811
Hall, William .............Lieutenant 28th regiment..August 22 1811
Ham, John ................Ensign 28th regiment.......June 4 1811
Haynes, Robert ..........Lieutenant 28th regiment...June 4 1811
Huet, Benjamin ...........Captain 28th regiment....August 22 1811
Kennedy, Joseph .........Lieutenant 28th regiment..August 22 1811
Killengsworth, Henry ......Ensign 28th regiment....August 9 1811
McMurtry, John ..........Lieutenant 28th regiment..August 22 1811
Murray, Francis ...........Second Major 28th regiment ..............November 19 1811
Nail, James ...............Captain 28th regiment....August 9 1811
Payne, Sylvester ..........Ensign 28th regiment.....August 22 1811
Perry, Thomas ...........Ensign 28th regiment.......June 4 1811
Pots, John ................Lieutenant 28th regiment...April 19 1811
Ross, James ..............Lieutenant 28th regiment..August 9 1811
Shinalt, James ...........Captain 28th regiment....August 9 1811
Simmons, Benjamin .......Lieutenant 28th regiment..August 9 1811
Starrit, Joseph ............Ensign 28th regiment....August 22 1811
Tawnyhill, Benjamin Harris.Ensign 28th regiment.....August 9 1811
Venable, Richard ..........Ensign 28th regiment......April 19 1811
Wilson, Aaron, Junior .....Lieutenant 28th regiment...April 19 1811
Wortham, John ...........Captain 28th regiment......April 19 1811

*Bledsoe County Regiments*

Austin, Hezekiah ..........Lieutenant 31st regiment ..April 16 1811
Carlin, Joshua ...........Ensign 31st regiment.......July 13 1811
Dain, John ..............Lieutenant 31st regiment ..............February 21 1811
Graham, James ...........Ensign 31st regiment......April 16 1811
Hankins, John ...........Captain 31st regiment..February 21 1811
Hixon, John .............Lieutenant 31st regiment....April 16 1811
Kitchen, Joseph ..........Ensign 31st regiment...February 21 1811

IN THE TENNESSEE MILITIA, 1796-1811 107

Lamb, Adam ..............Captain 31st regiment......April 16 1811
Looney, David ...........Lieutenant 31st regi-
                          ment .................February 21 1811
Lowry, Andrew ...........Ensign 31st regiment...February 21 1811
Naramore, John, Junior ....Captain 31st regiment......April 16 1811
Rogers, John ............Lieutenant 31st regi-
                          ment ...................July 13 1811
Spears, John .............Ensign 31st regiment.......April 16 1811
Vernon, Miles ............Captain 31st regiment..February 21 1811
Williams, John ...........Ensign 31st regiment...February 21 1811

*Blount County Regiments*

Benson, Matthias .........Captain 12th regiment...October  7 1811
Biggs, Alexander .........Captain 12th regiment...October  7 1811
Bowerman, Michael .......Captain 12th regiment...October 16 1811
Campbell, Isaac ..........Captain 12th regiment....August 12 1811
Casteel, Moses ...........Ensign 12th regiment....October  7 1811
Cook, Joseph .............Ensign 12th regiment....October  7 1811
Duncan, Joseph ..........Captain 12th regiment...October  7 1811
Edmondson, William ......Lieutenant 12th regiment.October  7 1811
Guy, William .............Captain 12th regiment...October 16 1811
Harris, Samuel ...........Lieutenant 12th regiment.October 16 1811
Harris, William ..........First Major 12th regiment...July 30 1811
Henry, John ..............Ensign 12th regiment.....August 12 1811
Houston, John P. .........Second Major 12th regiment.July 30 1811
Houston, John P. .........Brigade Inspector for 3rd
                          brigade ............September 24 1811
Houston, Samuel .........Captain 12th regiment...October  7 1811
Lambert, Aaron ..........Lieutenant 12th regiment.October  7 1811
Legg, Samuel ............Lieutenant 12th regiment..August 12 1811
McGaughey, John ........Ensign 12th regiment....October  7 1811
McGinley, James .........Lieutenant Colonel Commandant
                          12th regiment ..........July 30 1811
McKinney, David ........Captain 12th regiment...October  7 1811
McNeely, James ..........Ensign 12th regiment....October  7 1811
Parsons, Joshua ..........Lieutenant 12th regiment.October  7 1811
Rhea, Samuel ............Ensign 12th regiment....October 16 1811
Rudd, William ...........Lieutenant 12th regiment.October 16 1811
Sheham, John ............Captain 12th regiment...October  7 1811
Simmons, William ........Lieutenant 12th regiment.October  7 1811
Taylor, James ............Lieutenant 12th regiment..August 12 1811
Walk, John ..............Ensign 12th regiment....October  7 1811
Walker, Thomas ..........Lieutenant 12th regiment.October  7 1811
Wear, Hugh ..............Lieutenant 12th regiment.October  7 1811

*Campbell County Regiments*

Doak, Robert ............Captain 33rd regiment.....April 20 1811

108   RECORD OF COMMISSIONS OF OFFICERS

Doak, Thomas ............Ensign 33rd regiment......April 20 1811
Fulkerson, John ..........Lieutenant 33rd regiment.October 2 1811
Grimes, George ...........Captain 33rd regiment......April 20 1811
Hail, James ..............Ensign 33rd regiment.....March 20 1811
Hayler, James ...........Ensign 33rd regiment....October 2 1811
Keck, Philip .............Captain 33rd regiment......April 20 1811
Moad, Ludwick ..........Lieutenant 33rd regiment...April 20 1811
Riley, Elisha .............Ensign 33rd regiment.....March 20 1811
Shelton, David ...........Captain 33rd regiment....March 20 1811
Stover, Joseph ...........Lieutenant 33rd regiment..March 20 1811

### Carter County Regiments

Baker, Thomas ...........Ensign 5th regiment...September 28 1811
Bowers, Henry ...........Lieutenant 5th regiment....June 3 1811
Boyd, Henry .............Ensign 5th regiment........June 3 1811
Buck, Ephraim ...........Lieutenant 5th regiment...March 21 1811
Emmert, John ...........Captain company of cavalry
                          1st brigade ........September 17 1811
Hendricks, Solomon .......Captain 5th regiment.....March 21 1811
Kelly, John ..............Ensign 5th regiment......March 21 1811
Sewell, John .............Lieutenant 5th regi-
                          ment .............September 28 1811

### Claiborne County Regiments

Anderson, David ..........Lieutenant 9th regiment..October 9 1811
Brock, John ..............Captain 9th regiment....October 9 1811
Gideon, Zepheniah ........Ensign 9th regiment......October 9 1811

### Cocke County Regiments

Allen, James .............Captain 8th regiment......April 9 1811
Allen, James .............Lieutenant 8th regiment..October 4 1811
Campbell, Russell ........Lieutenant Light Infantry Com-
                          pany 8th regiment.......April 9 1811
Coleman, Benjamin ........Ensign 8th regiment.......April 9 1811
Cunningham, David .......Captain 8th regiment...February 5 1811
Fugan, Evan .............Lieutenant 8th regiment..October 4 1811
Goodsey, Burley ..........Ensign 8th regiment.....October 4 1811
Grant, Richard ...........Lieutenant 8th regiment.February 5 1811
Gregg, John .............Ensign 8th regiment.....October 4 1811
Gregg, Samuel ...........Captain 8th regiment...February 5 1811
Hutson, John ............Ensign 8th regiment.....October 4 1811
Jackson, Robert ..........Lieutenant in Volunteer Rifle
                          Company 8th regiment...April 9 1811
Jennings, James ..........Lieutenant 8th regiment....April 9 1811
Jennings, William ........Ensign 8th regiment.......April 9 1811
Jones, Daniel ............Ensign 8th regiment.....October 16 1811

IN THE TENNESSEE MILITIA, 1796-1811 109

| | | | |
|---|---|---|---|
| Lillard, James | Captain Light Infantry Company 8th regiment............April | 9 | 1811 |
| Lillard, John | Ensign Light Infantry Company 8th regiment...........April | 9 | 1811 |
| Marberry, Leonard | Ensign 8th regiment....February | 5 | 1811 |
| Marberry, Leonard | Captain 8th regiment....October | 4 | 1811 |
| Milligan, Alexander | Lieutenant 8th regiment.February | 5 | 1811 |
| Moon, William | Lieutenant 8th regiment....April | 9 | 1811 |
| Morgan, Evan | Ensign 8th regiment.....October | 4 | 1811 |
| Ode, Nehemiah | Ensign 8th regiment .......May | 8 | 1811 |
| Ode, Solomon | Captain 8th regiment.......May | 8 | 1811 |
| Potter, William | Ensign 8th regiment....February | 5 | 1811 |
| Potter, Wilson | Lieutenant 8th regiment..October | 4 | 1811 |
| Strain, James | Lieutenant 8th regiment.February | 5 | 1811 |
| Ward, David | Captain 8th regiment.......April | 9 | 1811 |

*Davidson County Regiments*

| | | | |
|---|---|---|---|
| Allen, John | Ensign 19th regiment.......July | 17 | 1811 |
| Allen, Latten F. | Captain 19th regiment......May | 25 | 1811 |
| Allen, William | Lieutenant 19th regiment...July | 17 | 1811 |
| Allen, William S. | Captain 19th regiment......July | 17 | 1811 |
| Barnhart, John | Captain 19th regiment......May | 25 | 1811 |
| Bondurant, Edward | Captain in Volunteer Rifle Company 19th regiment..September | 17 | 1811 |
| Booth, James | Captain 20th regiment..February | 5 | 1811 |
| Bosly, James R. | Lieutenant in Volunteer Rifle Company 19th regiment..September | 17 | 1811 |
| Bradford, Thomas G. | First Major 19th regiment ...............January | 17 | 1811 |
| Butler, Isaac | Captain 20th regiment......June | 22 | 1811 |
| Carroll, William | Captain in the Independent Company (Blues) 19th regiment ...................May | 25 | 1811 |
| Davis, William J. | Ensign 20th regiment..November | 9 | 1811 |
| Dennis, Samuel | Ensign 19th regiment.......July | 17 | 1811 |
| Deval, Archibald | Ensign 19th regiment.......July | 17 | 1811 |
| Dickinson, Jacob | Lieutenant 20th regiment ..............November | 9 | 1811 |
| Dillahunt, Lewis | Ensign 19th regiment......April | 19 | 1811 |
| Drake, William | Captain 20th regiment.November | 9 | 1811 |
| Earkheart, Rodney | Lieutenant 29th regiment ..............November | 9 | 1811 |
| Foster, Anthony C. | Lieutenant 19th regiment....May | 25 | 1811 |
| Fowler, Moses | Ensign 20th regiment..November | 9 | 1811 |
| Fraizer, John | Lieutenant 20th regiment....June | 22 | 1811 |
| Freeland, James | Lieutenant 19th regiment ...July | 17 | 1811 |

Harris, Archibald H. .......Lieutenant 20th regi-
                             ment ..............November  9 1811
Hobbs, Edward D. ........Captain 19th regiment......July 17 1811
Horne, Etheldred ..........Captain 20th regiment.November  9 1811
Johnson, Robert ...........Second Major 19th regi-
                             ment ................January 17 1811
Lassesure, Littleberry ......Lieutenant 19th regiment ...July 17 1811
McAdams, William R. .....Captain 20th regiment.November  9 1811
McCormack, John ........Captain 20th regiment.November  9 1811
McElwain, John ..........Lieutenant 19th regiment..August 22 1811
Mitchell, James ...........Ensign 20th regiment.......June 22 1811
Murry, James .............Ensign 20th regiment..November  9 1811
Napier, John ..............Ensign 19th regiment........July 17 1811
Nelms, William ............Ensign 20th regiment..November  9 1811
Newton, Robert ...........Ensign 19th regiment......April 19 1811
Oar, John .................Lieutenant 20th regi-
                             ment ..............February  5 1811
Parker, John C. ...........Second Major 20th regiment.July 27 1811
Paxton, Joshua ............Lieutenant in the Independent
                             Company (Blues) 19th
                             regiment ................May 25 1811
Pipkin, Philip .............Lieutenant Colonel Commandant
                             19th regiment ........January 17 1811
Rogers, John ..............Ensign 19th regiment.......May 25 1811
Shepherd, Thomas ........Ensign in Volunteer Rifle Com-
                             pany 19th regiment..September 17 1811
Smith, Peton ..............Lieutenant 19th regiment...April 19 1811
Stump, John ..............Lieutenant Colonel Commandant
                             20th regiment ...........July 27 1811
Strungfellow, Robert .......Captain 19th regiment...August 22 1811
Tannihill, Wilkins ........Ensign in the Independent Com-
                             pany (Blues) 19th
                             regiment ................May 25 1811
Taylor, Samuel ............First Major 20th regiment...July 27 1811
Wade, Austin M. ..........Lieutenant 19th regiment...May 25 1811
Waggoner, George ........Lieutenant 20th regi-
                             ment ..............November  9 1811
White, Thomas B. .........Ensign 19th regiment....August 22 1811
Winfree, Valentine ........Captain 20th regiment.November  9 1811
Young, Nicholas ...........Lieutenant 20th regi-
                             ment ..............November  9 1811

*Dickson County Regiments*

Abney, John ...............Lieutenant 25th regiment..August 12 1811
Adams, Reeves ............Lieutenant 6th brigade.November 13 1811
Adkins, Drury .............Captain 25th regiment......May 25 1811
Amons, Michael ...........Ensign 25th regiment.....August 12 1811

In the Tennessee Militia, 1796-1811    111

Bothnot, John A. ..........Lieutenant 25th regiment...May 25 1811
Boyd, Jesse ...............Ensign 25th regiment.......May 25 1811
Duffil, Samuel ............Ensign 25th regiment.......May 25 1811
Ellis, Francis S. ............Captain 25th regiment......July 24 1811
Farmer, Stephen ..........Captain 25th regiment....August 12 1811
Hall, John ...............Cornet 6th brigade....November 13 1811
Hamilton, Andrew ........Lieutenant 25th regiment....July 24 1811
Hollen, Mark .............Ensign 25th regiment.....August 12 1811
Lacey, Abraham ..........Ensign 25th regiment.....August 12 1811
McHenry, Archibald .......Ensign in Volunteer Rifle
                          Company 25th regiment...May 25 1811
Moore, William ...........Ensign 25th regiment.......July 24 1811
Parmer, Martin ...........Captain in Volunteer Rifle
                          Company 25th regiment...May 25 1811
Peacock, William .........Captain regiment of cavalry 6th
                          brigade ............September 13 1811
Speight, William ..........Captain 25th regiment....August 12 1811
Teal, George .............Lieutenant in Volunteer Rifle
                          Company 25th regiment...May 25 1811

*Franklin County Regiments*

George, Solomon ..........Captain 32nd regiment......May 17 1811
Goodwin, Jesse ...........Lieutenant 32nd regi-
                          ment .............November 12 1811
Gray, William ............Captain 32nd regiment......May 12 1811
Haislep, Wallace ..........Ensign 32nd regiment......May 17 1811
Jackson, Samuel ..........Lieutenant 32nd regi-
                          ment .............November 12 1811
Kimbrel, John ............Ensign 32nd regiment......May 17 1811
Love, David ..............First Major 32nd regi-
                          ment .............December 17 1811
Miller, Garland ...........Lieutenant 32nd regi-
                          ment .............November 12 1811
Nelson, Preston ...........Captain 32nd regiment......May 17 1811
Powel, Obediah ...........Captain 32nd regiment......May 17 1811
Reed, Drury .............Lieutenant 32nd regi-
                          ment .............November 12 1811
Reed, Jesse ...............Ensign 32nd regiment..November 12 1811
Reed, William ............Ensign 32nd regiment..November 12 1811
Shankle, John ............Lieutenant 32nd regiment...May 17 1811
Stewart, William .........Lieutenant 32nd regiment...May 17 1811
Young, Jones ............Captain 32nd regiment......May 17 1811

## Giles County Regiments

Baily, Edmund J. ..........Lieutenant in Volunteer Rifle Company
    27th (37th) regiment[1]....June 22 1811
Baily, Edmund J. ..........Captain in Volunteer Rifle Company
    attached to 37th
    regiment ..........December 7 1811
Birns, Henry ..............Lieutenant 37th regiment....July 27 1811
Brown, Edward ............Lieutenant 37th regiment....June 22 1811
Buford, James .............Ensign in Volunteer Rifle Company
    27th (37th) regiment[2].....June 22 1811
Buford, James .............Lieutenant in Volunteer Rifle Company
    37th regiment ......December 7 1811
Crisp, John ................Lieutenant 37th regiment...April 19 1811
Cunningham, William ......Ensign 37th regiment.......April 19 1811
Farmer, Nathan ...........Captain in regiment of
    cavalry 5th brigade.......July 3 1811
Fitzpatrick, Morgan ........Captain 37th regiment......June 22 1811
Graves, Ralph .............Captain 37th regiment.....April 19 1811
Gregory, John .............Ensign in Volunteer Rifle Company
    37th regiment .......December 7 1811
Harwell, Buckner, Jr. .......Captain 37th regiment......June 22 1811
Harwell, Frederick .........Ensign 37th regiment.......June 22 1811
Henderson, William ........Captain 37th regiment......June 22 1811
Koher, George ............Ensign 37th regiment.......June 22 1811
McCullough, James .......Lieutenant regiment of cavalry
    5th brigade ..............July 3 1811
Marks, Thomas ...........Captain 37th regiment......July 27 1811
Patterson, Arthur .........Lieutenant 37th regiment.October 7 1811
Patterson, Banard M. ......Lieutenant 37th regiment...April 19 1811
Phillips, John .............Captain 37th regiment...October 7 1811
Prater, Andrew ...........Lieutenant 37th regiment ...June 22 1811
Scott, William ............Ensign 37th regiment.......June 22 1811
Simms, Robert ...........Lieutenant 37th regiment....June 22 1811
Smith, William ............Ensign 37th regiment........July 27 1811
Ward, Joseph J. ..........Ensign 37th regiment....October 7 1811
Westmoreland, Jesse .......Captain in Volunteer Company
    27th (37th) regiment[3].....June 22 1811
Woods, Israel .............Ensign 37th regiment.......June 22 1811
Young, Jarret ............Captain 37th regiment...October 7 1811

## Grainger County Regiments

Baily, John ...............Ensign 7th regiment........June 10 1811
Boatman, Ezekiel ..........Ensign 7th regiment.....October 22 1811

---

[1] Here 27th Regiment was written erroneously for 37th. The 27th was a Maury County regiment.
[2] *Idem.*
[3] *Idem.*

IN THE TENNESSEE MILITIA, 1796-1811   113

Branson, Nathaniel .......Lieutenant 7th regiment...March 12 1811
Campbell, John ...........Captain 7th regiment.......June 10 1811
Clark, Levy ..............Lieutenant in Volunteer Rifle
                          Company 7th regiment..August 22 1811
Cleveland, Martin ........Captain in Volunteer Rifle
                          Company 7th regiment..August 22 1811
Eaton, Robert D. .........Captain 7th regiment.......June 10 1811
Howell, John .............Captain 7th regiment.......June 10 1811
Jones, William ...........Lieutenant 7th regiment....June 10 1811
McAnally, David ..........Captain 7th regiment.....March 12 1811
Martin, Robert ...........Ensign in Volunteer Rifle
                          Company 7th regiment..August 22 1811
Mays, William ............Second Major 7th regiment..May 16 1811
Monroe, George ...........Captain 7th regiment.....March 12 1811
Paine, Charles ...........Ensign 7th regiment......March 12 1811
Read, Thomas .............Lieutenant 7th regiment..August 22 1811
Rhea, Thomas .............Lieutenant 7th regiment.....June 10 1811
Sands, Othnial ...........Captain 7th regiment.......June 10 1811
Shelton, Elijah ..........Lieutenant 7th regiment...March 12 1811
Shipley, Robert ..........Ensign 7th regiment......August 22 1811
Taylor, John .............Ensign 7th regiment......March 12 1811
Yoden, David .............Lieutenant 7th regiment....June 10 1811
Yoden, William P. ........Ensign 7th regiment........June 10 1811

*Greene County Regiments*

Bell, James C. ...........Lieutenant in Rifle Company
                          3rd regiment .......September 21 1811
Bibel, John ..............Lieutenant 3rd regiment..October 16 1811
Bright, Michael ..........Ensign in Rifle Company
                          3rd regiment .......September 21 1811
Coffman, Nicholas ........Ensign 3rd regiment.....October 16 1811
Cole, Philip .............Lieutenant in regiment of cavalry
                          1st brigade ............August  9 1811
Credick, William .........Ensign in Rifle Company
                          3rd regiment .......September 21 1811
Danley, Hezekiah .........Ensign in Rifle Company
                          3rd regiment .......September 21 1811
Hale, Joseph .............Captain in Rifle Company
                          3rd brigade ..:.....September 21 1811
Highberger, John .........Ensign in Rifle Company
                          3rd regiment .......September 21 1811
Johnson, Stephen .........Lieutenant in Rifle Company
                          3rd regiment .......September 21 1811
Murphy, Edward ...........Lieutenant in Rifle Company
                          3rd regiment .......September 21 1811
Neil, Hamilton ...........Captain in regiment of cavalry
                          1st brigade ............August  9 1811

Neilson, Joseph H. .........Lieutenant in Rifle Company
  3rd regiment .......September 21 1811
Porter, Stephen ............Cornet in regiment of Cavalry
  1st brigade ............August  9 1811
Smith, Beverly ............Lieutenant in Rifle Company
  3rd regiment .......September 21 1811
Smith, Thomas ............Captain in Rifle Company
  3rd regiment .......September 21 1811
Wilhite, John .............Ensign in Rifle Company
  3rd regiment .......September 21 1811
Wilson, David ............Ensign in Rifle Company
  3rd regiment .......September 21 1811

### Hawkins County Regiments

Bassel, Hugh ..............Ensign 4th regiment........May 17 1811
Davis, Silburn ............Ensign 4th regiment.....October 11 1811
Foster, Winkfield .........Ensign 4th regiment.....October 11 1811
Huffmaster, James ........Lieutenant 4th regiment..October 11 1811
Lockmiller, Frederick .....Lieutenant 4th regiment..October 11 1811
Lockmiller, Jonas .........Captain 4th regiment....October 11 1811
Luster, John .............Lieutenant 4th regiment..October 11 1811
Mills, Henry .............Lieutenant 4th regiment.....May 17 1811
Moore, Hugh G. ...........Second Major 4th regiment ..............September  7 1811
Powel, Benjamin .........Captain 4th regiment....October 11 1811
Smith, Nathaniel .........Captain 4th regiment.......May 17 1811

### Hickman County Regiments

Briggs, William ...........Lieutenant 36th regiment...May 16 1811
Carrithers, Samuel M. ......Captain 36th regiment.November 13 1811
Carrithers, William .......First Major 36th regiment ..............November 12 1811
Clark, James .............Lieutenant 36th regiment...May 16 1811
Easly, Pleasant ...........Captain 36th regiment.November 13 1811
Hannah, Josiah ...........Lieutenant 36th regiment ..............November 13 1811
Hassell, Silvanus .........Ensign 36th regiment.......May 16 1811
Holland, William .........Ensign 36th regiment.......May 16 1811
Humble, Jacob ...........Lieutenant 36th regiment ..............November 13 1811
Lewis, Obediah ...........Ensign 36th regiment.......June 10 1811
Mayberry, Henry .........Ensign 36th regiment.......June 10 1811
Muirheed, William ........Ensign 36th regiment ......May 16 1811
Obar, Daniel .............Captain 36th regiment.November 12 1811
Philips, William ..........Lieutenant Colonel Commandant
  36th regiment ......November 12 1811
Raynor, Aaron ............Lieutenant 36th regiment....June 10 1811
Reid, George .............Captain 36th regiment......May 16 1811

IN THE TENNESSEE MILITIA, 1796-1811 115

Searcy, Peter .............. Captain 36th regiment...... May 16 1811
Spencer, Charles, Junr. ..... Ensign 36th regiment.. November 13 1811
Twett, Henry M. .......... Lieutenant 36th regiment.... May 16 1811

### Humphreys County Regiments

Farmer, Conrod ........... Lieutenant 38th regiment.... July 17 1811
Farmer, John ............. Ensign 38th regiment....... July 17 1811
Simpson, Andrew .......... Ensign 38th regiment....... July 17 1811

### Jackson County Regiments

Apple, David .............. Lieutenant 18th regiment.... June 13 1811
Barger, Jasper ............. Captain 18th regiment...... June 13 1811
Bennett, James ............ Captain 18th regiment...... June 13 1811
Bradcut, Samuel ........... Captain 18th regiment...... June 13 1811
Brown, Hosea ............. Ensign 18th regiment....... June 13 1811
Clemmons, Christopher ..... Ensign 18th regiment....... June 13 1811
Cunningham, Samuel ....... Ensign 18th regiment....... June 13 1811
Grace, James .............. Captain 18th regiment...... June 13 1811
James, George ............. Ensign 18th regiment..... August 12 1811
Jared, William ............ Lieutenant 18th regiment.... June 13 1811
Keith, Daniel ............. Lieutenant 18th regiment.... June 13 1811
Kerby, William ............ Lieutenant 18th regiment.... June 13 1811
Moore, Achillis ............ Lieutenant 18th regiment.. August 12 1811
Reno, Jonathan ............ Captain 18th regiment...... June 13 1811
Studevent, Randolph ....... Ensign 18th regiment....... June 13 1811

### Jefferson County Regiments

Ahls, John ................ Lieutenant in Volunteer Rifle
                            Company 6th regiment.... May 25 1811
Ayers, John ............... Captain 6th regiment....... May 25 1811
Berry, Francis ............. Captain 6th regiment.... October 4 1811
Bishop, James ............. Ensign 6th regiment..... October 11 1811
Brown, John .............. Lieutenant 6th regiment..... May 25 1811
Carson, William ........... Ensign 6th regiment..... October 4 1811
Combs, Job ............... Ensign 6th regiment ....... May 25 1811
Denton, Joel .............. Second Major 6th regi-
                            ment ................ October 4 1811
Elder, Robert ............. Captain 6th regiment.... October 11 1811
Furman, John ............. Ensign 6th regiment..... October 4 1811
Haggard, Henry ........... Captain 6th regiment....... May 25 1811
Harmon, Jacob ............ First Major 6th regi-
                            ment ................ October 4 1811
Harrison, James ........... Lieutenant 6th regiment.... May 25 1811
Haun, John ............... Ensign 6th regiment..... October 4 1811
Hill, Thomas .............. Ensign 6th regiment........ May 25 1811
Koontz, Joseph ............ Lieutenant 6th regiment.. October 4 1811

## Record of Commissions of Officers

Layman, Jacob ............. Ensign 6th regiment...... October 4 1811
Leeth, James .............. Captain 6th regiment....... May 25 1811
McClennehan, Alexander ... Ensign in Volunteer Rifle Company
                              6th regiment ............ May 25 1811
McFarland, John .......... Second Major in regiment of
                              cavalry 2nd brigade ... January 22 1811
Markell, William .......... Lieutenant 6th regiment.. October 4 1811
Moon, Chaney ............. Lieutenant 6th regiment.. October 11 1811
Phayton, Evans ........... Ensign 6th regiment....... May 25 1811
Taffee, John .............. Lieutenant 6th regiment.. October 4 1811

### Knox County Regiments

Alexander, Joseph ......... Ensign 2nd regiment
                              (40th)[4] ............ September 21 1811
Bailess, Robert ........... Ensign 10th regiment..... August 9 1811
Beard, William ........... Ensign 10th regiment.... January 7 1811
Booth, Edwin E. .......... Lieutenant Colonel Commandant
                              2nd regiment (40th)[5].... March 18 1811
Burnett, Zachariah ........ Lieutenant 10th regiment.. August 9 1811
Campbell, Robert .......... Captain 10th regiment... January 7 1811
Edington, John ............ Captain 10th regiment... October 7 1811
Givens, William ........... First Major 2nd regiment
                              (40th)[6] ............... March 18 1811
Grant, Joshua ............. Ensign 10th regiment.... October 7 1811
Graves, Daniel ............ First Major 10th regiment.. April 2 1811
Grayson, Benjamin ........ Lieutenant 2nd regiment
                              (40th)[7] ............ September 24 1811
Huffacre, John ............ Captain 10th regiment.... August 9 1811
Lewis, John ............... Captain 2nd regiment
                              (40th)[8] ............ September 21 1811
Loness, George ............ Ensign 2nd regiment
                              (40th)[9] ............ September 21 1811
Love, Robert .............. Lieutenant 10th regiment. January 7 1811
McCauley, Edward ........ Lieutenant 10th regiment.... May 2 1811
McConnell, James ......... Ensign in Volunteer Rifle
                              Company 10th regiment. August 9 1811
McNaire, John ............ Captain in Volunteer Rifle
                              Company 10th regiment.. April 2 1811
Martin, John .............. Second Major 2nd regiment
                              (40th)[10] .............. March 18 1811

---

[4] Knox County had two regiments, First Regiment (the 10th Regiment as of June 11, 1792) and the Second Regiment (the 40th, same date).
[5] *Idem.*
[6] *Idem.*
[7] *Idem.*
[8] *Idem.*
[9] *Idem.*
[10] *Idem.*

Regens, William ........... Ensign 2nd regiment
　　　　　　　　　　　　(40th)[11] .......... September 24 1811
Scott, Arthur .............. Lieutenant 10th regiment.October　7 1811
Sharp, John ............... Captain 10th regiment.... August　9 1811
Simmons, Thomas ......... Captain 2nd regiment
　　　　　　　　　　　　(40th)[12] .............. August　9 1811
Taylor, Ezekiel ............ Captain 10th regiment..February 21 1811
Thompson, William ........ Lieutenant 2nd regiment
　　　　　　　　　　　　(40th)[13] .......... September 21 1811
Trout, Michael ............ Ensign 10th regiment ....... May　2 1811
Williams, John, Esquire .... Adjutant General of the Militia
　　　　　　　　　　　　of the State........ September 19 1811

### Lincoln County Regiments

Ball, John ................ Captain 39th regiment... January　4 1811
Bell, Hugh ................ Captain 39th regiment... January　4 1811
Bishop, Henry ............. Lieutenant 39th regiment.January　4 1811
Bishop, William ........... Lieutenant 39th regi-
　　　　　　　　　　　　ment .............. September　3 1811
Carney, David ............ Ensign Volunteer Rifle Company
　　　　　　　　　　　　39th regiment ...... September　3 1811
Covey, Joseph ............. Captain 39th regiment.November 12 1811
Davis, James .............. Captain 39th regiment... January　4 1811
Delaney, Thomas .......... Captain 39th regiment... January　4 1811
Dyer, Joel ................ Ensign 39th regiment.... January　4 1811
East, James ............... Lieutenant 39th regiment.January　4 1811
Elliot, Robert ............. Captain 39th regiment... January　4 1811
Haltshouzer, John ......... Captain 39th regiment... January　4 1811
Hargraves, John ........... Lieutenant 39th regiment
　　　　　　　　　　　　................... November 12 1811
Hicks, Charles ............. Ensign 39th regiment..September　3 1811
Hooker, Samuel B. ......... Lieutenant 39th regi-
　　　　　　　　　　　　ment .............. September　3 1811
Jones, Martin ............. Captain 39th regiment... January　4 1811
Jones, Martin ............. Captain 39th regiment.November 12 1811
Lee, Abel ................. Captain 39th regiment... January　4 1811
Lee, John ................. Lieutenant 39th regiment.January　4 1811
McAdams, John ........... Ensign 39th regiment.... January　4 1811
McAffie, James ............ Ensign 39th regiment.... January　4 1811
McCrary, Joel ............. Lieutenant 39th regiment
　　　　　　　　　　　　................... November 12 1811
McGeehee, William ........ Lieutenant 39th regiment.January　4 1811
Manship, George ........... Lieutenant 39th regiment.January　4 1811
Marshall, John ............ Ensign 39th regiment.... January　4 1811

---
[11] *Idem.*
[12] *Idem.*
[13] *Idem.*

| | | | |
|---|---|---|---|
| Maury, Riley | Ensign 39th regiment | January | 4 1811 |
| Maxwell, James | Captain 39th regiment | November | 12 1811 |
| Mitchell, George | Captain 39th regiment | September | 3 1811 |
| Mitchell, James | Captain 39th regiment | January | 4 1811 |
| Mitchell, James | Lieutenant 39th regiment | September | 3 1811 |
| Moore, John | Ensign 39th regiment | January | 4 1811 |
| Moore, William | Captain Volunteer Rifle Company 39th regiment | September | 3 1811 |
| Orrick, John | Lieutenant 39th regiment | January | 4 1811 |
| Parks, William | Lieutenant Volunteer Rifle Company 39th regiment | September | 3 1811 |
| Pennington, Joel | Ensign 39th regiment | January | 4 1811 |
| Porter, John | Captain 39th regiment | January | 4 1811 |
| Rolston, Samuel | Ensign 39th regiment | January | 4 1811 |
| Sewell, William | Lieutenant 39th regiment | January | 4 1811 |
| Shipmant, Jacob | Lieutenant 39th regiment | January | 4 1811 |
| Sitton, William | Captain 39th regiment | January | 4 1811 |
| Smith, David | Lieutenant 39th regiment | January | 4 1811 |
| Smith, David | Captain 39th regiment | January | 4 1811 |
| Smith, Jasper | Captain 39th regiment | January | 4 1811 |
| Tawnyhill, John | Ensign 39th regiment | January | 4 1811 |
| Taylor, David | Ensign 39th regiment | January | 4 1811 |
| Taylor, John C. | Lieutenant 39th regiment | January | 4 1811 |
| Waggoner, Jacob | Lieutenant 39th regiment | January | 4 1811 |
| White, Ewing | Lieutenant 39th regiment | January | 4 1811 |
| White, William | Captain 39th regiment | January | 4 1811 |
| Wilson, James | Captain 39th regiment | September | 3 1811 |
| Wiseman, John | Captain 39th regiment | September | 3 1811 |
| Woods, William G. | Ensign 39th regiment | January | 4 1811 |

## *Maury County Regiments*

| | | | |
|---|---|---|---|
| Alexander, Alexander B. | Ensign 27th regiment | August | 9 1811 |
| Allen, James | Lieutenant 27th regiment | August | 9 1811 |
| Anderson, Robert | Captain 27th regiment | August | 9 1811 |
| Ashmore, Samuel | Captain 27th regiment | August | 9 1811 |
| Baker, Andrew | Ensign 27th regiment | September | 4 1811 |
| Campbell, Robert | Captain 27th regiment | September | 4 1811 |
| Chisholm, John | Captain 27th regiment | September | 4 1811 |
| Copeland, Anthony | Captain 27th regiment | August | 9 1811 |
| Crawford, Samuel | Captain 27th regiment | September | 4 1811 |
| Darnel, John | Ensign 27th regiment | September | 4 1811 |
| Hays, George | Lieutenant 27th regiment | September | 4 1811 |
| Hays, Jonathan | Ensign 27th regiment | September | 4 1811 |
| Hogan, Isaiah | Lieutenant 27th regiment | September | 4 1811 |
| Hogan, John | Ensign 27th regiment | September | 4 1811 |

IN THE TENNESSEE MILITIA, 1796-1811      119

Hunter, Aaron ............Lieutenant 27th regi-
                             ment .............September  4 1811
Jarrel, David .............Lieutenant Company of cavalry
                             Fifth brigade ......September  3 1811
Jones, John ...............Ensign 27th regiment.....August  9 1811
Kirkpatrick, Ebenezer .....Captain 27th regiment.September  4 1811
Long, Matthew P. .........Lieutenant 27th regiment..August  9 1811
McCrackin, Ephraim ......Captain 27th regiment.September  4 1811
Miller, Joseph H. ..........Lieutenant 27th regi-
                             ment .............September  4 1811
Neely, James S. ............Captain 27th regiment....August  9 1811
Nicholson, John ...........Lieutenant 27th regi-
                             ment .............September  4 1811
Parr, William .............Lieutenant 27th regiment..August  9 1811
Polk, William .............Captain 27th regiment.September  4 1811
Russell, David ............Second Major 27th regi-
                             ment ................August 12 1811
Rutledge, William .........Captain 27th regiment....August  9 1811
Vashers, John .............Ensign 27th regiment..September  4 1811
Washington, Robert Gray ...Captain Company of cavalry
                             Fifth brigade ......September  3 1811
Winn, Philip P. ............Captain 27th regiment.September  4 1811

*Montgomery County Regiments*

Campbell, Charles L. .......Lieutenant 24th regi-
                             ment .............November 19 1811
Carney, Christopher W. ....Captain 24th regiment .....April  3 1811
Edgar, Zachariah ..........Ensign 24th regiment..November 19 1811
Gillespie, James ...........Cornet regiment of cavalry
                             Sixth brigade ......September 13 1811
Gold, David ...............Second Major 24th regiment.June  3 1811
Haynes, William ..........Captain 24th regiment .....April  3 1811
Holland, Andrew ..........Lieutenant 24th regi-
                             ment .............November 19 1811
Holloway, William .........Ensign 24th regiment..November 19 1811
Hutcheson, John ...........Ensign 24th regiment..November 19 1811
McCall, Henry ............Ensign 24th regiment..November 19 1811
McGall, Samuel ..........Lieutenant 24th regi-
                             ment .............November 19 1811
Outlaw, Right .............Captain 24th regiment.November 19 1811
Robinson, Israel ..........Lieutenant regiment of cavalry
                             Sixth brigade .......February 21 1811
Stanford, Hugh ...........Lieutenant 24th regi-
                             ment .............November 19 1811
Trice, James .............Lieutenant 24th regi-
                             ment .............November 19 1811
Whipple, Bray ............Captain 24th regiment.November 19 1811

Williams, James ...........Captain regiment of cavalry
                          Sixth brigade .......February 21 1811
Williams, Newton ..........Ensign 24th regiment..November 19 1811
Williams, William C. .......Captain 24th regiment.November 19 1811

### Overton County Regiments

Hill, Isaac ................Lieutenant 35th regiment..August  9 1811
Huddleston, Willie .........Captain 35th regiment....August  9 1811
Kennedy, Thomas ...........Captain 35th regiment....August  9 1811
Means, Andrew .............Ensign 35th regiment ....October 11 1811
Medlock, Mo ...............Captain 35th regiment...October 11 1811
Officer, Thomas ............Captain 35th regiment....August  9 1811
Parker, Robert ............Ensign 35th regiment.....August  9 1811
Parrott, Benjamin .........Lieutenant 35th regiment..August  9 1811
Sexton, Thomas ...........Lieutenant 35th regiment.October 11 1811
Shot, Caleb ................Ensign 35th regiment.....August  9 1811
Stewart, David ............Lieutenant 35th regiment..August  9 1811
Tindle, Samuel ............Captain 35th regiment....August  9 1811
Walker, Patterson ..........Ensign 35th regiment ....October 11 1811
Witt, Harman ..............Lieutenant 35th regiment..August  9 1811

### Rhea County Regiments

Berry, James ..............Captain 30th regiment......June 10 1811
Birdsong, William ..........Lieutenant 30th regiment....June 10 1811
Brazelton, Henry ..........Captain 30th regiment......June 10 1811
Brown, Thomas G. .........Captain 30th regiment......June 10 1811
Johnson, Abel .............Ensign 30th regiment.......June 10 1811
Lewis, Jesse ...............Ensign 30th regiment.......June 10 1811
Reigle, George W. ..........Captain 30th regiment......June 10 1811
Reigle, Jacob .............Ensign 30th regiment.......June 10 1811
Shoults, John .............Second Major 30th regiment.April  9 1811
Smith, John A. ............First Major 30th regiment..April  9 1811
Woodard, Charles ..........Lieutenant 30th regiment....June 10 1811
Woodard, William .........Ensign 30th regiment.......June 10 1811

### Roane County Regiments

Baily, Isaac ................Lieutenant 14th regiment...April 19 1811
Bryant, Little B. ...........Ensign 14th regiment........n. d.
Bryant, Little B. ...........Ensign 14th regiment.......April 19 1811
Duncan, Robert ...........Lieutenant 14th regiment...n. d.
Duncan, Robert ...........Lieutenant 14th regiment...April 19 1811
Fraizer, Harman ...........Captain 14th regiment....August 12 1811
Hall, Garret ...............Lieutenant 14th regiment.October 11 1811
Lane, Nathan G. ..........Lieutenant 14th regiment...n. d.
Lane, Nathan G. ..........Lieutenant 14th regiment...April 19 1811
Lavender, John ...........Captain 14th regiment....August 12 1811

IN THE TENNESSEE MILITIA, 1796-1811     121

McPherson, George ........Captain 14th regiment.....n. d.
Meek, Viven M. ...........Ensign 14th regiment.....August 12 1811
Owing, William ...........Lieutenant 14th regiment..August 12 1811
Ramsey, John .............Ensign 14th regiment....October 11 1811
Roberts, Joshua ..........Ensign 14th regiment.....August 12 1811
Scrivener, David .........Ensign 14th regiment.....August 12 1811
Stout, Abraham ...........Lieutenant 14th regiment.October 11 1811
Tuton, John ..............Lieutenant 14th regiment..August 12 1811
Tuton, Zacheus ...........Ensign 14th regiment.......April 19 1811
Wilkinson, Samuel ........Ensign 14th regiment.......n. d.
Wilkinson, Samuel ........Ensign 14th regiment.....August 19 1811

### Robertson County Regiments

Crunk, Richard ...........Captain 23rd regiment......May 25 1811
Dorris, Joseph ...........Ensign 23rd regiment.......April  9 1811
Elmore, Henry ............Ensign 23rd regiment.......April  9 1811
Flood, Seth ..............Ensign 23rd regiment.......June 22 1811
Heddleston, John .........Ensign 23rd regiment.......June 22 1811
Krisell, Andrew ..........Lieutenant 23rd regiment....June 22 1811
Lovell, Daniel ...........Ensign 23rd regiment....October  4 1811
Madox, Wilson ............Lieutenant 23rd regiment...April  9 1811
Matthews, Sampson ........Lieutenant 23rd regiment ...May 25 1811
Pinkley, Daniel ..........Captain 23rd regiment......May 25 1811
Pitts, Burwell ...........First Major 23rd regi-
                          ment ..............November 23 1811
Smart, William ...........Lieutenant 23rd regiment ...May 25 1811
Southerin, William .......Lieutenant 23rd regiment....June 22 1811
Steelee, Henry ...........Lieutenant 23rd regiment ...May 25 1811
Wilson, William ..........Ensign 23rd regiment.......May 25 1811

### Rutherford County Regiments

Allen, James .............Lieutenant Light Infantry Com-
                          pany 22nd regiment....August 22 1811
Anderson, William ........Ensign 2nd regiment (45th)*.July  3 1811
Bankhead, John ...........Ensign Volunteer Rifle Company
                          2nd regiment (45th)*..October  4 1811
Bankhead, Robert .........Lieutenant Volunteer Rifle Company
                          2nd regiment (45th)*..October  4 1811
Barckly, Henry ...........Ensign 2nd regiment (45th)*.April 17 1811
Bedford, George ..........Ensign 22nd regiment.......June  4 1811
Bishop, Sterling .........Ensign 2nd regiment (45th)*.May 24 1811
Bobbet, William ..........Ensign 2nd regiment (45th)*.July 24 1811
Borton, William ..........Lieutenant 2nd regiment
                          (45th)* .................July  3 1811
Bowman, John .............Ensign Light Infantry 2nd regi-
                          ment (45th)* ............July  3 1811
Bradly, Robert ...........Lieutenant 22nd regiment...June  4 1811

Brandon, George ...........Captain Volunteer Rifle Company
                           2nd regiment (45th)*..October 4 1811
Carson, Robert ............Captain 2nd regiment
                           (45th)* .................April 17 1811
Coldwell, William .........Ensign 2nd regiment (45th)*.May 24 1811
Crawford, John ............Captain 2nd regiment
                           (45th)* .................May 24 1811
Cummins, Richard W. ......Captain 22nd regiment .February 21 1811
Curle, Cullin .............Ensign 2nd regiment (45th)*.April 17 1811
Dixon, Don C. ............Captain 22nd regiment......June 4 1811
Eastwood, Daniel ..........Ensign 2nd regiment (45th)*.July 3 1811
Frederick, Hezekiah .......Ensign 22nd regiment....August 22 1811
Garner, Obediah ...........Ensign 22nd regiment..February 21 1811
Gooden, James ............Lieutenant 2nd regiment
                           (45th)* .................April 17 1811
Haily, Elijah .............Lieutenant 22nd regi-
                           ment ..............February 21 1811
Hand, Samuel ............Captain 2nd regiment.......July 24 1811
Hardgrove, Leroy .........Captain 2nd regiment.......May 24 1811
Howell, William ..........Captain 22nd regiment...August 22 1811
Jeton, Robert .............Captain 2nd regiment
                           (45th)* .................July 3 1811
Johnson, William .........Ensign 2nd regiment (45th)*.May 24 1811
Jones, William ............Ensign Light Infantry 22nd
                           regiment ..............August 22 1811
Kindel, William ..........Captain 2nd regiment
                           (45th)* .................July 3 1811
Laughlin, William .........Lieutenant 22nd regi-
                           ment ..............February 21 1811
Love, Philip S. ............Captain 22nd regiment..February 21 1811
McConnel, Moses .........Lieutenant 2nd regiment
                           (45th)* .................April 17 1811
McCoy, Amos A...........Lieutenant 2nd regiment
                           (45th)* .................May 24 1811
McCoy, Robert ...........Ensign 2nd regiment
                           (45th)* .................May 24 1811
McEwen, John ...........Ensign 2nd regiment
                           (45th)* .................July 13 1811
McFerren, James .........Captain 2nd regiment
                           (45th)* .................April 17 1811
McKee, William ..........Lieutenant 2nd regiment
                           (45th)* .................May 24 1811
Matthews, John ..........Ensign 22nd regiment ..February 21 1811
Mayberry, John ..........Lieutenant 2nd regiment
                           (45th)* .................May 24 1811
Mayfield, Solomon ........Ensign 2nd regiment
                           (45th)* .................June 10 1811

IN THE TENNESSEE MILITIA, 1796-1811   123

Miller, James ............Lieutenant 2nd regiment
  (45th)* .................July 24 1811
Nance, Bird ..............Captain 22nd regiment..February 21 1811
Nash, Travis C. ..........Captain 2nd regiment
  (45th)* .................May 24 1811
Overall, Nace ............Lieutenant 2nd regiment
  (45th)* .................July 13 1811
Parker, Daniel ...........Captain 2nd regiment
  (45th)* .................July 3 1811
Ramsey, William ..........Captain 2nd regiment
  (45th)* .................July 13 1811
Renshaw, Isaiah ..........Captain 2nd regiment
  (45th)* .................April 17 1811
Reynolds, John ...........Captain 2nd regiment
  (45th)* .................May 24 1811
Smotherman, John .........Lieutenant 2nd regiment
  (45th)* .................May 24 1811
Stephens, Henry ..........Lieutenant 22 regiment.....June 4 1811
Tacket, David ............Ensign 2nd regiment
  (45th)* .................April 17 1811
Thomas, Hamilton .........Captain 2nd regiment
  (45th)* .................June 10 1811
Vaughn, Peter ............Lieutenant 22nd regi-
  ment ...............February 21 1811
Ward, Burrel .............Ensign 22nd regiment ......June 4 1811
Welton, Samuel ...........Lieutenant 2nd regiment
  (45th)* .................June 10 1811
White, Stephen F. .........Ensign Light Infantry 2nd
  regiment (45th)* ........July 3 1811
White, William ...........Captain Light Infantry Company
  22nd regiment .........August 22 1811
Wood, John ...............Lieutenant 2nd regiment
  (45th)* .................April 17 1811
Wright, Jeremiah .........Lieutenant 2nd regiment
  (45th)* .................July 3 1811
Yardly, Thomas ...........Captain Light Infantry 2nd
  regiment (45th)* ........July 3 1811

*Sevier County Regiments*

Blakely, Jesse ............Lieutenant 11th regi-
  ment ..............September 30 1811
Campbell, John ...........Ensign 11th regiment..September 30 1811
Catlet, John .............Lieutenant Light Infantry 11th
  regiment ...............July 26 1811
Clenkingbeard, John .......Ensign 11th regiment..September 30 1811

---

*Rutherford County had two regiments: First regiment, the 22nd, as of October 25, 1803; Second regiment, the 45th, as of October 25, 1803.

Hickman, Thomas ........Lieutenant 11th regi-
　　　　　　　　　　　ment ...............February 14 1811
Hodges, Edmund .........Captain 11th regiment..February 14 1811
Holstonback, John ........Ensign 11th regiment...February 14 1811
Kerr, William .............Ensign Light Infantry Company
　　　　　　　　　　　11th regiment ..........July 26 1811
Lawson, Andrew ..........Captain Light Infantry Company
　　　　　　　　　　　11th regiment ......February 14 1811
McCane, John ............Captain 11th regiment......July 26 1811
Nicholas, John ...........Captain 11th regiment..February 14 1811
Ogle, William .............Lieutenant 11th regi-
　　　　　　　　　　　ment ...............February 14 1811
Rogers, George ...........Lieutenant 11th regi-
　　　　　　　　　　　ment ...............February 14 1811
Stephenson, James ........Ensign 11th regiment...February 14 1811
Vistol, Jeremiah ..........Lieutenant 11th regi-
　　　　　　　　　　　ment ..............September 30 1811
Waddle, David ............Captain 11th regiment......July 26 1811

*Smith County Regiments*

Bradley, Isaac .............Ensign 2nd regiment
　　　　　　　　　　　(41st)* .................June  3 1811
Bransford, William ........Ensign 16th regiment ......June 10 1811
Campbell, Alexander ......Lieutenant 16th regiment ...June 10 1811
Campbell, John ...........Lieutenant 2nd regiment
　　　　　　　　　　　(41st)* .................June  3 1811
Dallis, Stephen ...........Ensign 16th regiment ......June 10 1811
Dalton, William ..........Ensign 16th regiment ......June 10 1811
Dawson, John ............Captain 2nd regiment
　　　　　　　　　　　(41st)* .............January 24 1811
Debo, Stephen ............Captain 16th regiment ..February 25 1811
Fields, Jeremiah ..........Lieutenant 16th regiment...June 10 1811
Fite, Joseph ..............Lieutenant 2nd regiment
　　　　　　　　　　　(41st)* .................June  3 1811
French, Jeremiah .........Ensign 2nd regiment
　　　　　　　　　　　(41st)* .............January 24 1811
Gray, Alexander ..........Captain 16th regiment .....June 10 1811
Hodges, William ..........Captain 2nd regiment
　　　　　　　　　　　(41st)* .............January 24  1811
Hoss, Philip ..............Ensign 2nd regiment
　　　　　　　　　　　(41st)* .................June  3 1811
Legan, Masten ...........Ensign 16th regiment .......June 10 1811
Marsh, Henry ............Captain 16th regiment .....June 10 1811
Overall, Abraham .........Captain 2nd regiment
　　　　　　　　　　　(41st)* .................June  3 1811
Robertson, Thomas .......Lieutenant 2nd regiment
　　　　　　　　　　　(41st)* .............January 24 1811

IN THE TENNESSEE MILITIA, 1796-1811 125

Roe, Benjamin ............Captain 2nd regiment
                         (41st)* ...............January 24 1811
Roper, John ..............Lieutenant 16th regi-
                         ment ...............February 25 1811
Rowark, Reubin ...........Ensign 16th regiment ......June 10 1811
Sanderson, Edward ........Lieutenant 16th regiment ...June 10 1811
Strange, Beverly ..........Lieutenant 2nd regiment
                         (41st)* ...............January 24 1811
Tait, John ................Lieutenant 2nd regiment
                         (41st)* ...............January 24 1811
Thomas, James ............Lieutenant 2nd regiment
                         (41st)* ...............January 24 1811
Tubb, James ..............Lieutenant 2nd regiment
                         (41st)* ...............January 24 1811
Tubb, James ..............Captain 2nd regiment
                         (41st)* .................June 3 1811
Walker, Samuel ...........Ensign 2nd regiment (41st)*.June 3 1811
Ward, Dickson ............Ensign 2nd regiment
                         (41st)* ...............January 24 1811
Wilbourne, Robert ........Lieutenant 16th regiment ..June 10 1811

*Stewart County Regiments*

Acrey, John ..............Captain 26th regiment...January 22 1811
Andrews, Anderson ........Lieutenant 26th regiment ...June 10 1811
Askew, Josiah ............Captain 26th regiment .....June 10 1811
Atkins, Asa ..............Captain 26th regiment.September 3 1811
Curtes, William ..........Ensign 26th regiment .January...22 1811
Gatlet, Ephraim ..........Cornet regiment of cavalry
                         6th brigade .......September 13 1811
Gilbert, Jesse, Junior .....Ensign 26th regiment..November 13 1811
Gilbert, Stephen ..........Lieutenant 26th regi-
                         ment ..............November 13 1811
Jones, Robert ............Lieutenant 26th regiment ...June 10 1811
Kindall, Peter ............Second Major 26th regi-
                         ment ...............January 29 1811
Lewis, Thomas W. ........Lieutenant 26th regiment ...June 10 1811
McGinty, Alexander ......Lieutenant 26th regiment ...June 10 1811
Pearce, Abner ............Captain 26th regiment.November 13 1811
Sills, William ............Lieutenant 26th regi-
                         ment ..............June 10 1811
Smith, James .............Ensign 26th regiment....January 22 1811
Ussery, Richard ..........Lieutenant 26th regi-
                         ment ..............November 13 1811
Whitehurst, Pelatiah, .....Ensign 26th regiment.......June 10 1811

---

*Smith County had two regiments: First regiment, the 16th, as of October 26, 1799; Second regiment, the 41st, as of October 26, 1799.

Williams, James ...........Lieutenant 26th regi-
                                ment .............September 3 1811
Worden, John .............Captain 26th regiment...January 22 1811

### Sullivan County Regiments

Biffle, Valentine ...........Ensign Light Infantry Company
                                2nd regiment ........January 4 1811
Boudry, Samuel ...........Lieutenant 2nd regiment.January 19 1811
Branstrith, Daniel .........Lieutenant 2nd regiment....May 2 1811
Cross, Zachariah .........Captain regiment of cavalry
                                1st brigade ..........October 4 1811
Dixson, William ..........Cornet regiment of cavalry
                                1st brigade ..........March 25 1811
Gregg, Abraham ...........Ensign 2nd regiment ..September 14 1811
Johnson, Thomas ......:...Captain Light Infantry Company
                                2nd regiment ........January 4 1811
Kelly, Benjamin ...........Lieutenant Light Infantry Company
                                2nd regiment ........January 4 1811
Keys, George .............Ensign Volunteer Rifle Company
                                2nd regiment ........January 4 1811
King, William ............Captain Volunteer Rifle Company
                                2nd regiment ........January 4 1811
Newhouse, Isaac ..........Ensign 2nd regiment .....April 19 1811
Owens, Michael ...........Lieutenant Volunteer Rifle Company
                                2nd regiment ........January 4 1811
Plumly, Daniel ............Lieutenant 2nd regi-
                                ment .............September 14 1811
Scott, William ............Captain 2nd regiment..September 14 1811
Snodgrass, David ..........Captain 2nd regiment...January 19 1811

### Sumner County Regiments

Alexander, William, Junior..Captain 15th regiment.November 30 1811
Barker, Israel .............Lieutenant 2nd regiment
                                (43rd)* ................May 2 1811
Blackmore, John D. ........Lieutenant 15th regi-
                                ment .............November 30 1811
Bledsoe, Abraham .........Captain Volunteer Rifle Company
                                15th regiment .....September 23 1811
Blythe, Andrew ...........Captain 15th regiment.September 23 1811
Bradley, William ..........Ensign 2nd regiment
                                (43rd)* ................May 2 1811
Bruce, David .............Ensign 2nd regiment
                                (43rd)* ............October 7 1811
Crockett, William .........Captain 2nd regiment
                                (43rd)* ............October 2 1811
Cunningham, Alexander ....Ensign 2nd regiment
                                (43rd)* ................May 2 1811

IN THE TENNESSEE MILITIA, 1796-1811    127

Donoho, Thomas ..........Lieutenant 15th regi-
                          ment .............November 30 1811
Dotson, John .............Lieutenant 15th regi-
                          ment .............November 30 1811
Duren, Thomas ...........Lieutenant Volunteer Rifle Company
                          15th regiment ......September 23 1811
Ellis, Abraham ...........Lieutenant 2nd regiment
                          (43rd)* ................May  2 1811
Ellis, Simeon .............Ensign 2nd regiment
                          (43rd)* ................May  2 1811
Forrester, Isaac ..........Ensign 15th regiment..September 23 1811
Glover, William ..........Lieutenant 2nd regiment
                          (43rd)* ..............October  7 1811
Groves, Thomas ..........Captain 15th regiment.November 30 1811
Hamilton, Henry .........Captain 2nd regiment
                          (43rd)* .............October  7 1811
Lethum, John .............Ensign 15th regiment..November 30 1811
McCleary, Robert .........Ensign 15th regiment..September 23 1811
Markham, Jasper ..........Ensign Volunteer Rifle Company
                          15th regiment ......September 23 1811
Neal, Matthew ............Captain 15th regiment.September 23 1811
Reddick, David ...........Ensign 15th regiment..November 30 1811
Rice, Elijah ...............Ensign 2nd regiment
                          (43rd)* ............October  7 1811
Sanders, James ...........Lieutenant 15th regi-
                          ment .............November 30 1811
Saveley, John .............Lieutenant 2nd regiment
                          (43rd)* .................May  2 1811
Street, Lefever ...........Ensign 15th regiment..November 30 1811
Taylor, John ..............Lieutenant 15th regi-
                          ment .............November 30 1811
Yandell, John .............Ensign 15th regiment..November 30 1811

*Warren County Regiments*

Ballew, Flemming G. ......Lieutenant 29th regiment...April 19 1811
Blancit, Peter ............Ensign 29th regiment ......June 10 1811
Gibbs, Jesse ...............Captain 29th regiment......June 10 1811
Hubbard, Enos ............Captain 29th regiment......June 10 1811
Kain, James ..............Captain 29th regiment.....April 19 1811
Kitchen, George ..........Ensign 29th regiment ......April 19 1811
Little, Anthony ...........Ensign 29th regiment ......June 10 1811
Myers, Philip ............Captain 29th regiment.....April 19 1811
Smart, George B. .........Lieutenant 29th regiment...June 10 1811
Stone, William ...........Lieutenant 29th regiment...June 10 1811
Tate, Robert .............Ensign 29th regiment ......April 19 1811
Warren, Joseph ..........Ensign 29th regiment......June 10 1811

* Sumner County had two regiments: First regiment, the 15th, as of November 17, 1786; Second regiment, the 43rd, as of November 17, 1786.

## Washington County Regiments

Bacon, Joseph .............Ensign Volunteer Rifle Company
           1st regiment .......November 12 1811
Bayless, William ..........Adjutant of 1st regiment..March 15 1811
Bean, Russell .............Captain 1st regiment..November 9 1811
Bell, Joseph G. ...........Ensign 1st regiment...December 28 1811
Bell, Joseph H. ...........Lieutenant Volunteer Rifle Company
           1st regiment .......November 12 1811
Biddle, Samuel ............Ensign 1st regiment ........May 25 1811
Carrel, Luke ..............Lieutenant 1st regiment....May 2 1811
Carrithers, Samuel ........Captain 1st regiment......May 25 1811
Crawford, James ...........Captain 1st regiment ......April 24 1811
Gilworth, John ............Lieutenant 1st regiment ....May 25 1811
Gray, Robert ..............Lieutenant 1st regiment ....April 24 1811
Green, Ira ................Captain Mounted Infantry Company
           1st brigade ..........October 16 1811
Hoss, John ................Captain 1st regiment ......May 2 1811
Kelly, Joshua .............Ensign 1st regiment .......May 2 1811
Love, Samuel B. ...........Captain Volunteer Rifle Company
           1st regiment ......November 12 1811
McKee, Robert .............Lieutenant 1st regiment .............September 3 1811
McKie, William ............Lieutenant 1st regiment ..March 15 1811
McLin, William ............Captain 1st regiment ......May 2 1811
Malony, John ..............Lieutenant 1st regiment .............November 9 1811
Matthews, Ebenezer .......Ensign 1st regiment .......April 24 1811
Miller, Peter .............Lieutenant 1st regiment ....May 2 1811
Mitchell, Adam ...........Cornet in regiment of Cavalry
           1st brigade ..........January 23 1811
Mock, Joseph ..............Ensign 1st regiment ......March 15 1811
Nelson, John ..............Lieutenant Mounted Infantry
           Company 1st brigade..October 16 1811
Starns, Jacob .............Cornet in Mounted Infantry Company
           1st brigade ..........October 16 1811
Strain, Robert ............Ensign 1st regiment .......May 2 1811
Vance, William K. .........Lieutenant in regiment of Cavalry
           1st brigade ..........January 23 1811
Waddill, Jonathan .........Captain 1st regiment .....March 15 1811
Wheeler, Greenberry .......Ensign 1st regiment ..November 9 1811

## White County Regiments

Adkerson, John ............Lieutenant 34th regiment.August 9 1811
Carter, David .............Ensign 34th regiment..September 3 1811
Denton, Benjamin ..........Captain 34th regiment ...August 9 1811
Hawkins, William ..........Ensign 34th regiment ....August 9 1811
Justice, James ............Ensign 34th regiment..September 3 1811

In the Tennessee Militia, 1796-1811 129

| | | | |
|---|---|---|---|
| Kizar, Francis | Ensign 34th regiment..September | 3 | 1811 |
| Lawson, Thomas | Lieutenant 34th regiment.August | 9 | 1811 |
| Lundy, Richard | Ensign 34th regiment..September | 3 | 1811 |
| McCann, James | Ensign 34th regiment....August | 9 | 1811 |
| Mannefee, Willis | Lieutenant 34th regiment | September | 3 1811 |
| Miller, Joseph | Lieutenant 34th regiment | September | 3 1811 |
| Newman, Daniel | Captain 34th regiment...August | 9 | 1811 |
| Parkerson, Manuel | Captain 34th regiment.September | 3 | 1811 |
| Porter, Alexander | Ensign 34th regiment....August | 9 | 1811 |
| Prewett, Isaac | Captain 34th regiment....August | 9 | 1811 |
| Simpson, John W. | First Major 34th regiment..April | 19 | 1811 |
| Smith, David | Captain 34th regiment...August | 9 | 1811 |
| Smith, Joseph | Second Major 34th regiment | April | 19 1811 |
| Templeton, John | Lieutenant 34th regiment.August | 9 | 1811 |
| Thomas, Nevill | Ensign 34th regiment....August | 9 | 1811 |
| Townsend, John | Captain 34th regiment...August | 9 | 1811 |
| Warren, Bluford | Lieutenant 34th regiment.August | 9 | 1811 |
| Weaver, Benjamin | Lieutenant 34th regiment.August | 9 | 1811 |
| Williams, William | Captain 34th regiment...August | 9 | 1811 |
| Winkle, Jeremiah | Ensign 34th regiment....August | 9 | 1811 |

*Williamson County Regiments*

| | | | |
|---|---|---|---|
| Barns, George | Captain 2nd regiment (44th)* | April | 15 1811 |
| Bridges, John | Lieutenant 2nd regiment (44th)* | April | 15 1811 |
| Bugg, Ephraim M. | Lieutenant 2nd regiment (44th)* | April | 15 1811 |
| Campbell, Daniel | Lieutenant 21st regiment | September | 9 1811 |
| Cannon, Robert | Captain 2nd regiment (44th)* | September | 17 1811 |
| Carlton, Thomas | Ensign 2nd regiment (44th)* | November | 13 1811 |
| Carrithers, John | Ensign 21st regiment | April | 24 1811 |
| Coldwell, David | Lieutenant 21st regiment | September | 9 1811 |
| Crunk, John W. | Lieutenant regiment of Cavalry 5th brigade | November | 12 1811 |
| Dalton, John | Captain 2nd regiment (44th)* | April | 15 1811 |
| Davis, John | Ensign 21st regiment..September | 9 | 1811 |

*Williamson County had two regiments: First, the 21st, as of October 26, 1799; Second, the 44th, as of October 26, 1799.

Dillard, Nicholas .......... Captain 2nd regiment
  (44th)* ................ April 15 1811
Dunn, David .............. Captain 21st regiment. September 21 1811
Elliot, Andrew ............ Ensign 21st regiment...... April 24 1811
Estis, Samuel ............. Lieutenant regiment of Cavalry
  9th brigade ........ December 28 1811
Fitzpatrick, Andrew ........ Lieutenant 2nd regiment
  (44th)* ................ April 15 1811
Gault, James ............. Captain 2nd regiment
  (44th)* ................ April 15 1811
Germain, Zacheus ......... Cornet regiment of Cavalry
  5th brigade ........ December 28 1811
Guttery, William F. ........ Ensign 21st regiment.. September 9 1811
Hickman, William ......... Captain 2nd regiment
  (44th)* ................ April 15 1811
Hooker, William ........... Captain 2nd regiment
  (44th)* ................ July 3 1811
Johnson, Charles .......... Captain 2nd regiment
  (44th)* ................ April 15 1811
Lowry, David ............. Lieutenant 2nd regiment
  (44th)* ................ April 15 1811
McKnight, William ........ Ensign 2nd regiment
  (44th)* ................ April 15 1811
McMurtry, Joseph ......... Ensign 21st regiment.. September 9 1811
McNair, Thomas .......... Lieutenant 2nd regiment
  (44th)* ................ April 15 1811
McRory, Thomas, Junior ... Lieutenant 21st regiment... April 24 1811
Mason, Isaac .............. Ensign Volunteer Rifle Company
  2nd regiment (44th)*. September 17 1811
Mason, David ............ Lieutenant Light Infantry
  21st regiment ........ October 7 1811
Mason, Joseph ............ Lieutenant 2nd regiment
  (44th)* .......... September 17 1811
Oslin, John ............... Ensign 2nd regiment
  (44th)* ................ April 15 1811
Pate, Kinchen ............. Lieutenant 2nd regiment
  (44th)* .......... November 13 1811
Pettice, Horatio ........... Lieutenant 2nd regiment
  (44th)* .......... September 21 1811
Powers, Robert ........... Lieutenant regiment of Cavalry
  5th brigade ............ April 24 1811
Ragsdale, Lancaster ....... Ensign 2nd regiment
  (44th)* .......... September 21 1811
Reynolds, Reubin ......... Lieutenant 2nd regiment
  (44th)* ................ July 3 1811
Ridley, James ............. Captain 2nd regiment
  (44th)* ................ April 15 1811
Rivers, Joel T. ............ Captain 21st regiment. September 9 1811

IN THE TENNESSEE MILITIA, 1796-1811   131

Sims, James ...............Lieutenant 21st regiment...April 24 1811
Smith, Weeks .............Ensign 2nd regiment
                          (44th)* ................April 15 1811
Stewart, James ...........Ensign Light Infantry
                          21st regiment .........October  7 1811
Thompson, Leonard .......Ensign 2nd regiment
                          (44th)* ................April 15 1811
Waters, John .............Lieutenant 2nd regiment
                          (44th)* ................April 15 1811
Wilson, Jason .............Cornet regiment Cavalry
                          5th brigade ........November 12 1811
Wisener, Henry ...........Lieutenant 2nd regiment
                          (44th)* ................April 15 1811
Wisener, James ...........Ensign 2nd regiment
                          (44th)* ................April 15 1811

## *Wilson County Regiments*

Alexander, Benjamin ......Lieutenant 17th regi-
                          ment .............September 28 1811
Barksdale, David ........Captain 17th regiment.November 19 1811
Black, James .............Captain 2nd regiment
                          (42nd)* ................June  1 1811
Boon, Jesse ..............Ensign Light Infantry Company
                          17th regiment ......September 28 1811
Brown, Joshua ............Ensign 2nd regiment
                          (42nd)* ................June  1 1811
Cartwright, John ..........Ensign 2nd regiment
                          (42nd)* ................June  1 1811
Citton, James ............Ensign 2nd regiment
                          (42nd)* ................June  1 1811
Cooper, Abraham .........Lieutenant 2nd regiment
                          (42nd)* ................June  1 1811
Estes (Esters) John .......Captain 2nd regiment
                          (42nd)* ................June  1 1811
Farrington, Jehne ........Lieutenant 2nd regiment
                          (42nd)* ................June  1 1811
Fisher, Philip ............Lieutenant 2nd regiment
                          (42nd)* ................June  1 1811
Garrison, Benjamin .......Lieutenant 17th regi-
                          ment .............September 28 1811
Gray, James ..............Lieutenant 17th regi-
                          ment .............September 28 1811
Harrel, Eli ...............Lieutenant 2nd regiment
                          (42nd)* ................June  1 1811
Henderson, John ..........Captain 2nd regiment
                          (42nd)* ................June  1 1811
Hicks, Richard ...........Ensign 17th regiment..September 28 1811

Higgins, William .......... Lieutenant 2nd regiment
 (42nd)* ................ June 1 1811
Hight, Robert ............. Ensign 2nd regiment
 (42nd)* ................ June 1 1811
Howard, Bradford ......... Captain 2nd regiment
 (42nd)* ................ June 1 1811
Jadwin, Joseph ............ Lieutenant 17th regi-
 ment .............. September 28 1811
Kirkpatrick, Joseph ........ Captain 17th regiment. September 28 1811
Landson, Eli M. ........... Ensign 2nd regiment
 (42nd)* ................ June 1 1811
Lester, Presly ............. Lieutenant 2nd regiment
 (42nd)* ................ June 1 1811
Lockhart, James B. ........ Captain 17th regiment. September 28 1811
McAdams, Samuel ......... Captain Light Infantry
 17th regiment ...... September 28 1811
McWherter, George ....... Lieutenant Light Infantry
 17th regiment ...... September 28 1811
Macklin, William A. ....... Lieutenant 2nd regiment
 (42nd)* ................ June 1 1811
Palmer, Isham ............. Captain 17th regiment. September 28 1811
Quarles, John ............. Captain 2nd regiment
 (42nd)* ................ June 1 1811
Robertson, John ........... Captain 17th regiment. September 28 1811
Smith, Bird ............... Captain 2nd regiment
 (42nd)* ................ June 1 1811
Smith, Charles ............ Ensign 2nd regiment
 (42nd)* ................ June 1 1811
Stacy, William ............ Lieutenant 2nd regiment
 (42nd)* ................ June 1 1811
Stewart, Aaron ............ Ensign 2nd regiment
 (42nd)* ................ June 1 1811
Thompson, Moses ......... Captain 2nd regiment
 (42nd)* ................ June 1 1811
Williams, Coleman ......... Ensign 17th regiment. November 19 1811
Williams, Green ........... Lieutenant 17th regi-
 ment .............. November 19 1811
Williams, Isaac ............ Ensign 2nd regiment
 (42nd)* ................ June 1 1811
Young, Baxter ............ Ensign 17th regiment. . September 28 1811

---

*Wilson County had two regiments: First, the 17th, as of October 26, 1799; Second, the 42nd, as of October 26, 1799.

# Index

Abbot, David, 62.
Abbott, David, 100.
Able, Ezekiel, 8.
Abney, John, 110.
Acrey, John, 125.
Acton, James, 84.
Acuff, Isaac, 47.
Adair, James, 84.
Adams, Davis, 79.
Adams, James, 87.
Adams, John, 34, 93.
Adams, Reeves, 110.
Adams, Thomas, 4.
Adams, William, 7, 91.
Adkerson, John, 128.
Adkins, Drury, 110.
Adkins, James, 12.
Ahls, John, 115.
Aike, Joseph, 21.
Aiken, Matthew, 34 (2).
Albright, John, 89.
Aldridg, William, 21.
Alexander, Aaron, 104.
Alexander, Alexander B., 118.
Alexander, Archibald, 28.
Alexander, Benjamin, 105, 131.
Alexander, John, 4 (2).
Alexander, Joseph, 4, 116.
Alexander, Joshua, 50.
Alexander, Robert, 50.
Alexander, Silas, 32, 103.
Alexander, Thomas, 85.
Alexander, William, Junior, 126.
Allan, Reuben, 19.
Allen, Abraham, Junior, 97.
Allen, Barnabas, 72.
Allen, Carter, 54.
Allen, Charles, 49.
Allen, Daniel, 30.
Allen, David, 83.
Allen, Edwin, 51.
Allen, George C., 81.
Allen, Isaac, 7, 39.
Allen, James, 108 (2), 118, 121.
Allen, John, 82, 109.
Allen, Latten F., 109.
Allen, Porter, 64.
Allen, Reuben, 7.
Allen, Theophilus, 37.
Allen, William, 109.
Allen, William S., 109.
Allison, Benjamin, 89.
Allison, Ewen, 14.
Allison, John, 4, 30, 40.

Allison, Robert, 34.
Allred, Eli, 58.
Allsup, William, 82.
Alston, James, 75.
Alston, John, 40, 94, 95.
Alsup, Thomas, 77.
Amons, Michael, 110.
Anderson, Audley, 70.
Anderson, B. C., 71.
Anderson, David, 108.
Anderson, James, 37, 66.
Anderson, John, 51, 88.
Anderson, Joseph, 48.
Anderson, Richard, 97.
Anderson, Robert, 118.
Anderson, Robert, G., 48.
Anderson, Thomas, 6, 21, 57.
Anderson, William, 121.
Andes, William, 84.
Andrews, Anderson, 125.
Andrews, Taplet, 85,
Andrews, Taply, 85.
Anthony, John, 76.
Apple, David, 115.
Argenbright, George, 56.
Armprester, John, 81.
Armstrong, Benjamin D., 79.
Armstrong, Frencis, 58, 76.
Armstrong, James L., 45.
Armstrong, John, 21 (3), 43, 78, 95.
Armstrong, Robert, 21.
Armstrong, William, 103.
Arnold, James, 50.
Arnold, Levy, 73.
Arnold, Thomas, 53.
Arnold, William, 19, 80.
Arnold, Wyatt, 94.
Arrendell, James, 38.
Ashmore, Samuel, 96, 118.
Ashworth, John, 42.
Askew, Josiah, 125.
Atkins, Asa, 82, 125.
Atkins, James, 44.
Atkins, Stephen, 73.
Atkinson, John, 103.
Atkinson, William, 21.
August, John, 12.
Aukerman, Jacob, 83.
Ault, Frederick, 76, 95.
Austin, Hezekiah, 106.
Austin, Saunders, 85.
Avery, John, 61.
Avint, Harris, 83.
Aydelott, Thomas, 66.

Ayers, David, 95.
Ayers, Henry, 79.
Ayers, John, 115.
Ayers, Jonathan, 58.
Babb, Matthew, 60.
Bacon, Allen S., 98.
Bacon, Joseph, 128.
Badget, Jonathan, 32.
Bailess, Robert, 116.
Bailey, Britan, 17.
Bailey, Britton, 17.
Bailey, David, 21.
Bailey, Samuel, 32.
Bailey, Thomas, 17.
Bailey, William, 17.
Bailis, Samuel, 103.
Baily, Edmund J., 112 (2).
Baily, Isaac, 120.
Baily, John, 93, 112.
Bain, Daniel, 89 (2).
Bain, Owen, 82.
Bains, Abraham, 84.
Baker, Abraham B., 46.
Baker, Andrew, 118.
Baker, Charles, 91.
Baker, Endemion, 47.
Baker, Francis, 78.
Baker, George, 42.
Baker, Jacob, 56.
Baker, Joseph, 69.
Baker, Nathaniel M., 8.
Baker, Samuel 12, 69, 89
Baker, Thomas, 108.
Baker, William, 54, 56.
Baker, Zacheus, 8.
Baldridge, Stephen, 64.
Ball, Amous, 34.
Ball, John, 117.
Ball, John, Junior, 99.
Ball, William, 64.
Ballew, Flemming G., 127.
Ballow, James, 29, 32.
Ballow, William, 54.
Bankhead, John, 121.
Bankhead, Robert, 121.
Banton, Joab, 80.
Barckly, Henry, 121.
Barefield, James, 62.
Barger, Jasper, 115.
Barker, Israel, 126.
Barksdale, David, 131.
Barnet, Gilbert, 17.
Barnett, Elijah, 41.
Barnett, William, 54.
Barnhart, John, 109.
Barnon, William, 66.
Barns, Abraham, 65.
Barns, Allen, 86.
Barns, George, 129.

Barns, Jeremiah, 28.
Barns, Solomon, 32.
Barr, Constant O., 51.
Barr, Daniel, 61.
Barr, Silas, 62.
Barran, Aman, 103.
Barrett, James, 102.
Barrett, Joseph W., 103.
Barrot, John, 101.
Bartlet, Joseph, 21.
Bartlett, Joseph, 17.
Barton, Elijah, 70.
Barton, Hugh, 30, 50.
Barton, William, 68.
Bass, Ezekiel, 86.
Bassel, Hugh, 114.
Bassey, Washington, 87.
Bates, Humphrey, 64.
Bates, Matthew, 19.
Batie, Andrew, 43.
Baxter, Alexander, 43.
Baxter, James, 43.
Baxter, Robert, 49.
Baxter, Levy, 74.
Bay, John, 49.
Bayles, William, 34.
Bayless, Hezekiah, 21, 103.
Bayless, William, 128.
Bean, Edmund, 34.
Bean, Ellis, 12.
Bean, George, 12.
Bean, Robert, 91.
Bean, Russell, 128.
Beard, William, 116.
Beasby, (Beasly), Ephraim, 81.
Beasby, (Beasly), Henry, 81.
Beaty, Aaron, 38.
Beaty, James, 89.
Beaty, John, 25, (2).
Beaty, Samuel, 25.
Bedford, George, 121.
Beeasun, William, 25.
Beevers, James, 8.
Bell, Hugh, 117.
Bell, James C., 74, 113.
Bell, John, 8, 41.
Bell, Joseph G., 128.
Bell, Joseph H., 128.
Bell, Robert, 54.
Bell, Stephenson, 96.
Bell, Thomas, 69.
Bell, William, 25, 54, 87.
Benge, Obediah M., 8.
Bennet, Etheldred, 86.
Bennett, George, 102.
Bennett, James, 115.
Bens, Matthias, 81.
Benson, Eaity, 92.
Benson, Matthias, 89, 107.

Benson, Richard, 99.
Benton, David, 103.
Benton, James, 49.
Benton, Samuel, 62.
Berry, Francis, 30, 115.
Berry, James, 17, 98, 120.
Berry, Thomas, 17.
Berton, John, 12.
Bevely, John, 61.
Bevins, Elijah, 98.
Bevins, Elisha, 79.
Bibel, John, 113.
Bible, Adam, 56.
Bice, Jonathan, 4.
Biddle, Samuel, 128.
Biddle, Thomas, 34.
Biffle, Valentine, 126.
Biggs, Alexander, 107.
Bigham, Andrew, 14, (2).
Bigham, Josiah, 71.
Bigham, Nathaniel, 4.
Bills, Isaac, 58.
Bird, Abraham, 19.
Bird, John, 12, 98.
Bird, Stephen, 21.
Birden, Hawkins, 51.
Birden, William, 21.
Birdett, Jiles, 87.
Birdsong, William, 120.
Birdwell, Hugh, 71.
Birdwell, John, 63.
Birdwell, William, 30.
Birns, Henry, 112.
Bishop, Collin, 71.
Bishop, David, 21.
Bishop, Henry, 117.
Bishop, Jacob, 42.
Bishop, James, 115.
Bishop, Jones, 32, 37.
Bishop, Joseph, 32, 37.
Bishop, Sterling, 121.
Bishop, William, 117.
Black, Gabriel, 32.
Black, George, 64, (2).
Black, Given, 4.
Black, James, 131.
Black, John, 81.
Black, Josiah, 29.
Black, Peter, 43.
Blackely, Alexander, 21.
Blackley, Alexander, 21.
Blackmore, James, 83.
Blackmore, John D., 126.
Blackmore, William, 8.
Blackston, Youngue, 39.
Blackwell, James, 26, 44.
Blackwell, John, 69.
Blair, Brice, 34.
Blair, James, 12.

Blair, James, Jr., 12.
Blair, John, 80.
Blair, Samuel, 8, 28, 80.
Blair, Solomon, 46.
Blakely, Jesse, 123.
Blancit, Peter, 127.
Blanton, Thomas, 61.
Blanton, William, 65.
Bledsoe, Abraham, 126.
Bledsoe, Henry, 64.
Blevins, David, 82.
Blodgett, Beand, 97.
Blount, Benjamin, 45, 62.
Blount, William G., 95.
Blythe, Andrew, 126.
Boatman, Ezekiel, 112.
Boatwright, Daniel, 80.
Bobbet, William, 121.
Bockman, Nathaniel, 30.
Bogle, Hugh, 4.
Bogle, Samuel, 4.
Boilen, John, 87.
Bolinger, Henry, 70.
Boman, Elisha, 55.
Boman, William, 12.
Bond, Eli, 86.
Bond, Isaac, 42.
Bond, William, 85.
Bonds, John, 86.
Bondurant, Edward, 109.
Bone, Eli, 105.
Booher, John, 30.
Booker, John, 58.
Boon, Jesse, 131.
Booth, Edwin E., 42, 116.
Booth, James, 54, 109.
Booth, Joseph, 84.
Boring, Absolom, 34.
Boring, Aman, 84.
Boring, Amon, 84.
Borough, Valentine, 6.
Borton, William, 121.
Bosly, James R., 109.
Boss, Sion, 105.
Bothnot, John A., 111.
Boudry, Samuel, 126.
Bounds, Thomas, 26.
Bowan, Randal, 58.
Bowen, James, 12.
Bowen, John, 12, 21, (2).
Bowerman, Michael, 107.
Bowers, Henry, 108.
Bowlen, Abel, 89.
Bowling, Larkin, 50.
Bowman, Abraham, 58.
Bowman, John, 30, 42, 121.
Bowman, William, 80.
Boyd, Harrison, 8.
Boyd, Henry, 108.

Boyd, Jesse, 111.
Boyd, John, 8, 97.
Boyd, John, Jr., 8.
Boyd, Robert, 4, 12.
Boyles, James, 39.
Bradcut, Samuel, 115.
Braden, Robert, 99.
Bradford, Hamilton, 42.
Bradford, Henry 42, 57
Bradford, John, 87.
Bradford, Robert, 70.
Bradford, Thomas G., 109.
Bradley, Edward, 102.
Bradley, Isaac, 124.
Bradley, John, 4, 64.
Bradley, William, 126.
Bradly, Daniel, 70.
Bradly, Isua, 32.
Bradly, John D., 83.
Bradly, Robert, 121.
Bradly, Thomas, 32.
Bradshaw, George, 91.
Bradshaw, John C., 39.
Bradshaw, Samuel, 85.
Brady, Alexander, 48.
Brag, Hugh, 53.
Bragg, William, 7.
Brandon, George, 122.
Branham, Ephraim, 50.
Branham, James, 89.
Branham, Martin, 89.
Brannon, Edward, 76, 95.
Bransford, William, 124.
Branson, Daniel, 75.
Branson, Nathaniel, 55, 113.
Branstrith, Daniel, 126.
Brantley, Charles, 25.
Brantstter, Peter, 6.
Braselton, William, 19.
Brasheers, Sampson, 47.
Brazeal, Valentine, 21.
Brazelton, Henry, 98, 120.
Breatherton, William, 14.
Breden, Andrew, 87.
Brendley, Frazer, 19.
Bresheers, Samuel, 30.
Brewer, Edmund, 99.
Brewer, John, 99.
Brewer, Samuel, 14.
Brewington, John, 73.
Briant, Samuel, 67.
Bridges, Edmond, 64.
Bridges, John, 129.
Brigan, William, 102.
Briggance, George S., 32.
Briggance, William, 32.
Briggs, William, 114.
Brigham, David, 30.
Brigham, James H., 78.

Bright, John, 58.
Bright, Michael, 113.
Brim, Henry, 69.
Briscoe, John, 26.
Brittain, Abraham, 30.
Britten, Richard, 32.
Britton, Joseph, 84.
Broan, James, 93.
Brock, John, 85, 108.
Brock, Joshua, 38.
Brooks, Henry, 67.
Brooks, Isaac, 96.
Brooks, John, 79.
Brooks, Thomas, 66.
Brooks, Thomas, Sr., 49.
Brown, Benjamin, 34, (2).
Brown, Daniel, 60, (2).
Brown, Darden, 25.
Brown, Edward, 112.
Brown, George, 66.
Brown, Hosea, 115.
Brown, Hugh, 14.
Brown, Jacob, 34.
Brown, James, 94.
Brown, Jesse, 38.
Brown, John, 12, 34, 61, 67, 93, 115.
Brown, Joseph, 8, (2).
Brown, Joshua, 62, 131.
Brown, Jothan, 56.
Brown, Matthew, 92.
Brown, Samuel, 64.
Brown, Thomas, 14, 21.
Brown, Thomas G., 120.
Brown, William, 17, 42, 48, 84, 103.
Browner, Thomas, 32.
Brownson, Robert, 78.
Broyls, George, 4.
Broyls, Jeremiah, 74.
Bruce, David, 126.
Brunk, Solomon, 49.
Bruten, Samuel, 12.
Bruton, John, 52.
Bryan, Henry H., 59, (2).
Bryan, Joseph, 17.
Bryan, Peter, 28.
Bryan, Thomas, 62.
Bryant, Andrew, 14.
Bryant, James, 73.
Bryant, John, 26.
Bryant, Joseph, 55.
Bryant, Little B., 120, (2).
Bryant, Morgan, 103.
Bryant, William, 59.
Bryant, William, M., 66.
Buchannan, John, 85.
Buchannon, Edward, 51.
Bucher, David, 103.
Buck, Abraham, 6.

Buck, Ephraim, 108.
Buckham, Andrew, 102.
Buckhannon, James, 79.
Buckly, Joab, 49.
Buford, James, 112 (2).
Bugg, Ephraim M., 129.
Buland, John, 14.
Bull, John, 73.
Bullard, Christopher, 14.
Bumgarner, George, 69, (2).
Burdett, Giles, 106.
Burdon, William, 21.
Burkhart, Peter, 82.
Burlesson, Joseph, 48.
Burnett, Zachariah, 116.
Burnham, John, 39.
Burnham, Thomas, 69.
Burns, James, 104.
Burns, John, Junior, 106.
Burns, Miles, 77.
Burnum, Samuel, 87.
Burras, John, 17.
Burress, William, 51.
Burris, William, 81.
Burrows, Anthony, 91.
Burtin, James, A., 78.
Burton, Henry, 104.
Burton, John H. 82, 94
Butler, Baily, 95.
Butler, Colier, 57.
Butler, Edmund, 95.
Butler, Isaac, 109.
Butler, James, 21.
Butler, Thomas, 95.
Byas, James, 77.
Byers, Cornelius, 96.
Byers, James, 96.
Byrd, John, 17.
Caffee, William, 39.
Cage, John, 67.
Cage, Wilson, 32.
Cain, Cornelius, 101.
Callahan, William, 60.
Callen, Thomas, 104.
Calvert, William, 34.
Cambers, Elijah, 89.
Camp, Thomas, 54, (2).
Campbell, Alexander 21, 124
Campbell, Charles L., 119.
Campbell, Daniel, 129.
Campbell, David, 8, 21, (2), 71.
Campbell, Hiram, 104.
Campbell, Isaac, 6, 107.
Campbell, James, 25, 61, 78.
Campbell, Jefferson, 79.
Campbell, John, 21, 28, 73, 81, 85, 113, 123, 124.
Campbell, John K., 85.
Campbell, Joseph, 89.

Campbell, Lewis, 87.
Campbell, Patrick, 36.
Campbell, Philip, 39, 90.
Campbell, Ralph, 28.
Campbell, Richard, 21, 34.
Campbell, Robert, 42, 116, 118.
Campbell, Russell, 108.
Campbell, William, 6, (2), 7, 84.
Camron, Ezra, 12.
Cannon, Benjamin, 43.
Cannon, Burrell, 96.
Cannon, John, 76.
Cannon, Newton, 104.
Canon, Robert, 80.
Canon, Robert, 79.
Cantabury, John, 12.
Canter, Zachariah, 46.
Canterberry, Zachariah, 38.
Cantrell, Ota, 102.
Cantrell, Stephen, 32, 90.
Caperton, George, 73.
Caplinger, Samuel, 67.
Carithers, Jonathan, 34.
Carithers, Samuel, 30, (2).
Carlin, Joshua, 106.
Carlock, Abraham, 19.
Carlton, Thomas, 129.
Carmack, John, 17.
Carmicle, Alexander, 22.
Carnahan, Thomas, 100.
Carney, Christopher W., 119.
Carney, David, 117.
Carns, Alexander, 25.
Carr, Andrew, 19.
Carr, Benjamin, 45.
Carr, James, 14.
Carr, John, 32.
Carr, Lawrence, 26.
Carrel, Luke, 128.
Carrigar, Christian, 53.
Carriger, Godfrey, 6.
Carriger, John, 70.
Carrithers, John, 129.
Carrithers, Samuel, 128.
Carrithers, Samuel M., 114.
Carrithers, William, 75, 114.
Carrol, Stephen, 45.
Carroll, William, 109.
Carry, Thomas, 76.
Carson, Adam, 19.
Carson, Robert 19, 122
Carson, Thomas, 67.
Carson, William, 115.
Carter, Beverly, 101.
Carter, David, 128.
Carter, Ezekiel, 14.
Carter, James, 71.
Carter, James F., 86.
Carter, Jesse, 14.

Carter, John, 6.
Carter, Landon, 6.
Carter, Richard, 96.
Carthey, George, 19.
Cartner, Jacob, 70.
Cartwright, John, 131.
Cartwright, Joshua, 48.
Cartwright, Samuel, 73.
Cartwright, Thomas, 8.
Carty, John, 62.
Casady, James, 48.
Casey, Levi, 29.
Casteel, Moses, 107.
Casteele, Edmond, 4.
Casten, Robert, 66.
Castleman, John, 8.
Cate, John, 42.
Cathel, Elisha, 74.
Cathey, James, 83.
Catlet, John, 123.
Caughran, John, 26.
Cavanaugh, Charles, 37.
Cavett, Joseph, 32.
Cavett, Richard, 22.
Center, Willes Stephen 17
Chambers, Alexander, 8.
Chambers, John, 36.
Chambers, Lewis, 67.
Chapman, Asahel, 22.
Chapman, George, 99.
Charlton, Edmund, 64.
Chastine, Elisha, 105.
Cheatham, John B., 99.
Cheatham, Peter, 44.
Cheatham, Thomas, 44.
Cheathem, Edward, 26.
Chestnut, Henry, 17.
Childers, Thomas C., 98.
Childress, Stephen, 8.
Chiles, Paul, 105.
Chilton, Thomas, 51.
Chilton, William, 12.
Chisholm, John, 118.
Chisolm, James, 22.
Chisom, Alexander, 80.
Chisum, James, 12.
Choat, Aaron, 25.
Choat, Joseph, 25.
Christian, William, 30.
Churchman, Edward, 12.
Citton, James, 131.
Clabough, William, 62.
Clap, Adam, 26.
Clap, Ludwick, 38.
Clark, Avery, 99.
Clark, Branter, 98.
Clark, Charles, 69.
Clark, James, 114.
Clark, John, 34, 49.

Clark, Levy, 113.
Clark, Thomas, 7, 91.
Clark, Thomas C., 98.
Clark, Walter, 74.
Clark, William, 48.
Clarke, Isaac, Jr., 28.
Clement, Richard, 85.
Clemmons, Christopher, 115.
Clemons, Isaac, 54.
Clenkingbeard, John, 123.
Cleveland, Martin, 113.
Clevengher, Richard, 7.
Clift, Daniel, 66.
Clift, Henry, 42.
Clifton, Joshua, 67.
Clingon, John P., 84.
Clinkingbeard, Edward, 100.
Clodfelter, Jacob, 105.
Cloud, Benjamin, 17, 82.
Cloud, Jeremiah, 30.
Cloyd, David, 71.
Coapland, Joseph, 29.
Coats, John, 87.
Coats, Richard, 55.
Cobb, Asa, 22.
Cobb, Jesse, 79.
Cochran, James, 4, 46.
Cockburn, George, 77.
Cocke, John, 12, 25, 59.
Cocke, Richard, 26.
Cocke, Sterling, 73.
Cocke, William, 59.
Coffman, Nicholas, 113.
Cofman, Samuel, 76.
Coke, Richard, 17.
Coldwell, Amos, 58.
Coldwell, David, 4, 129.
Coldwell, William, 122.
Cole, James, 85.
Cole, Jesse, 38.
Cole, Philip, 113.
Coleman, Benjamin, 108.
Coleman, John, 61.
Coley, James, 63.
Colgan, Charles, 26.
Colker, William, 22.
Collen, Thomas, 85.
Collins, Joseph, 81.
Collinsworth, James 9
Collum, Jonathan, 34.
Collums, George, 34.
Colvill, Joseph, 4.
Colvin, John, 70.
Combs, George, 13.
Combs, Job, 115.
Condray, James, 14.
Conger, John, 39.
Conly, David, 34.
Conn, James, 55.

Conner, Archibald, 93.
Conner, William, 51.
Connoly, Andrew, 9.
Conway, Charles, 22.
Conway, Christopher, 14.
Conway, George, 14.
Conway, William, 14, 93.
Cook, Christopher, 93.
Cook, George, 61.
Cook, Henry, 83.
Cook, James, 57.
Cook, John, 66.
Cook, Joseph, 107.
Cook, Mathias, 51.
Cook, William, 52.
Cooke, Markes, 13.
Cooper, Abraham, 49, 131.
Cooper, Joel, 7, 19.
Cooper, John, 17.
Cooper, Zacheus, 45.
Copeland, Anthony, 118.
Copeland, James, 49.
Copeland, John, 43, 75.
Copeland, Richard, Jr., 43.
Copeland, Stephen, 43.
Copeland, William, 60, 73.
Copland, Zachariah, 20.
Copus, John, 47.
Corder, Jesse, 57.
Cornelius, James, 67.
Corney, Christopher N., 97.
Corum, Robert, 46.
Cotner, John, 73.
Cotton, Allen, 29.
Cotton, James, 9.
Couch, George, 14.
Couch, Jonathan, 58.
Couch, Thomas, 87.
Coulter, Thomas, 51, 88.
Country, George, 45.
Country, Isaac, 45.
Counts, David, 40.
Countz, Michael, 62.
Countz, Nicholas, Jr., 73.
Covey, Joseph, 117.
Cowan, Andrew, 28.
Cowan, James, 20.
Cowan, John, 4.
Cowan, Samuel, 52.
Cowan, Wallace, 22.
Cowan, William W., 58.
Cowden, James, 64.
Cowden, Josiah, 64.
Cowden, William, 64.
Cowser, Freeland, 49.
Cox, Benjamin, 73, 90.
Cox, Daniel, 17.
Cox, George 52, 85
Cox, Joab, 89.

Cox, John, 47.
Cox, Nathaniel, 61.
Cox, Samuel, 22.
Cox, Thomas, 9, 13.
Cozby, John, 78.
Crabtree, Barnet, 34.
Craft, Jacob, 17.
Craft, Thomas, 30.
Cragg, Alexander, 90.
Cragg, John, 79.
Craig, David, 4.
Craig, James, 94, (2).
Craig, John, 49, 91.
Craig, Robert, 94.
Craig, Samuel, 66.
Craig, William, 49, 96.
Crain, Benjamin, 22.
Craw (Crow), James, 70.
Crawford, James, 128.
Crawford, John, 22, 80, 85, 122.
Crawford, Samuel, 58, 118.
Crawford, Sebret, 40.
Crawford, William, 15.
Creaton, James, 28.
Credick, William, 113.
Creel, William, 71.
Crelly, William, 22.
Crisp, John, 112.
Crocket, Samuel 36
Crockett, Joseph, 104.
Crockett, William, 126.
Crombwell, Dawsey, 26.
Croslin, Samuel, 7.
Cross, Elijah, 30.
Cross, John, 9.
Cross, John B., 9, 43.
Cross, Joseph, 17.
Cross, Maclin, 9.
Cross, Samuel, 68.
Cross, William, 73.
Cross, Zachariah, 126.
Crossen, Asa (?), 6.
Crossen, Samuel, 6.
Crow, Benjamin, 15.
Crow, Isaac L., 94.
Crowford, English, 22.
Crowsby, Samuel, 77.
Crowson, Richard, 28.
Crozier, Arthur, 22, (2).
Crozier, John, 22, (3),
Crucey, John, 104.
Cruize, William, 73.
Crumby, Hugh, 98.
Crunk, John W., 129.
Crunk, Richard, 99, 121.
Culbertson, Daniel, 80.
Cummins, Richard W., 122.
Cunningham, Aaron, 6.
Cunningham, Alexander, 64, 126.

Cunningham, David, 108.
Cunningham, James, 4, 20, 38, 89.
Cunningham, John, 6, 48, 65.
Cunningham, Samuel, 115.
Cunningham, William, 112.
Cupper, James, 39.
Curle, Cullin, 122.
Curtes, William, 125.
Curtis, James, 71.
Curry, Robert B., 26.
Curry, Samuel, 9.
Daimwood, Henry, 96.
Dain, John, 106.
Dakerson, Nathaniel, 26.
Dale, John, 41.
Dale, Thomas, 60.
Dallis, Stephen, 124.
Dalton, John, 129.
Dalton, William, 124.
Dalzall, Francis, 41.
Damran, Joseph, 20.
Daniel, Edward, 73.
Daniel, William, 49, 58, 60.
Danley, Hezekiah, 113.
Dardin, Jonathan, 27.
Dardis, James, 17, (2).
Darnel, John, 118.
Darnell, David, 58.
Darr, Henry, 44.
Daverson, John, 94.
David, Philip, 73.
Davidson, Andrew, 75.
Davidson, Ephraim E., 77.
Davidson, George, 73.
Davidson, Hudson, 82.
Davidson, John, 46.
Davidson, John E., 59.
Davidson, Samuel, 68.
Davies, John, 17.
Davis, Cadwalader, 57.
Davis, Clayton, 42.
Davis, George, 34, 76.
Davis, James, 79, 91, 117.
Davis, James E., 86.
Davis, John, 48, 85, 129.
Davis, Moses, 53.
Davis, Nathaniel, 22.
Davis, Nathaniel, Jr., 34.
Davis, Parsons, 81.
Davis, Samuel, 96.
Davis, Silburn, 114.
Davis, Thomas, 13, 22, 74, 105.
Davis, William, 15, 69.
Davis, William J., 109.
Davis, Willie C., 81.
Davis, Willie J., 80.
Davis, Wilson, 22.
Davy, Joseph, 71.
Dawson, John, 124.

Deakins, John, 34.
Dean, Michael, 103.
Dearmond, Richard, 4, (3).
Debo, John A. 63
Debo, Stephen, 124.
Delaney, Thomas, 117.
Dement, David, 64.
Demose, James, 9.
Demoss, John, 39.
Demwood, Henry, 59.
Denneson, John, 95.
Denneson, Robert, 85.
Dennis, John, 49.
Dennis, Samuel, 109.
Denniston, John, 58.
Denson, Jesse, 101.
Denton, Benjamin, 128.
Denton, David, 81, 100.
Denton, George, 62.
Denton, Joel, 42, 115.
Denton, John 7, 65
Denton,Thomas, 45.
Depriest, John, 66.
Derham, Josiah, 43.
Deroset, Samuel, 20.
Derrick, John, 89.
Deval, Archibald, 109.
Devald, Henerey, 53.
Devaul, Baily, 91.
Devault, Peter, 86.
Devinny, John, 84.
Deweese, Morgan, 104.
Dickason, William, 64.
Dickey, George, 96.
Dickinson, Jacob, 109.
Dickson, Eli, 52.
Dickson, Joseph, 28.
Dickson, Josiah, 85.
Dickson, Molton, 40.
Dickson, Nathan, 78.
Dill, Leonard, 15, (2).
Dillahunt, Lewis, 109.
Dillard, Elisha, 37.
Dillard, John, 48.
Dillard, Nicholas, 130.
Dillehunty, William, 9.
Dillingham, Absalom, 22.
Dillon, John, 86.
Dixon, Don C., 122.
Dixson, William, 126.
Doak, John, 39.
Doak, Robert, 50, 107.
Doak, Thomas 108
Doake, Robert, 45.
Dobbins, Carson, 64.
Dodd, James, 76.
Dodd, John, 15.
Dodson, Oliver, 17, (2).
Dodson, Reuben, 92.

Dodson, Rolley, 17.
Dodson, Samuel H., 85.
Doherty, George, 20.
Doherty, James, 20.
Doherty, Mathew, 102.
Donaldson, Robert, 4.
Donoho, Patrick, 29.
Donoho, Thomas, 127.
Dooley, William, 36.
Doran, Robert Loury 70
Dorris, John, 27.
Dorris, Joseph, 121.
Dortch, Isaac, 27.
Doss, John, 58.
Dosset, Moses, 52.
Dotson, John, 127.
Dougan, Sharp, 91.
Dougherty, Andrew, 38.
Douglass, James 22
Douglass, Edward, 32.
Douglass, George, 80.
Douglass, Reuben, 32.
Douglass, William, 65.
Dowler, Francis, 43.
Downs, Benjamin, 30.
Drake, George, 89.
Drake, James, 91.
Drake, Robert, 72.
Drake, William, 109.
Draper, James, 95.
Draper, Thomas, 29.
Dredin, David, 30.
Dreneron, Robert, 39.
Drennan, James, 86.
Drenon, Robert, 54.
Dristall, Elias, 92.
Dudly, Abraham, 95.
Duff, Barney, 43, 59.
Duffey, William, 66.
Duffil, Samuel, 111.
Dugan, Abel, 70.
Duggan, Daniel, 28.
Dugger, Julius, 6.
Duke, Henry, 95.
Duke, John, 13.
Duke, Matthew, 81.
Dullany, Elkanah, 30.
Dun, William, 91.
Duncan, Benjamin, 56.
Duncan, George, 98.
Duncan, Joseph, 22, 34, 107.
Duncan, Martin, 27.
Duncan, Robert, 120, (2).
Duncan, William, D., 84.
Dunlop, John, 70.
Dunlop, Samuel, 58.
Dunn, David, 130.
Dunn, James, 68.
Dunn, Jonathan, 43.

Dunnington, Reuben, 76.
Dunsmore, Samuel, 30.
Duren, Thomas, 127.
Durham, Nathaniel, 81.
Durham, William, 4, (2).
Durrin, Thomas, 102.
Duvall, Moilmore, 59.
Dyche, Jacob, 93.
Dyer, Henry, 17.
Dyer, Joel, 17, 117.
Dyer, Robert H., 100.
Dyer, Robert Henry, 45.
Dyer, William, 93.
Eames, Jonathan, 49.
Earheart, David, 9.
Earkheart, Rodney, 109.
Early, Michael, 60.
Earnest, Henry, 56.
Easly, John, 92.
Easly, Millington, 94.
Easly, Pleasant, 94, 114.
Easly, Robert 91
East, James, 117.
East, Mathew, 41.
Easterly, Cunrod, 15.
Easterly, John, 56.
Eastes, Robert, 85.
Eastwood, Daniel, 122.
Eaton, Robert D., 113.
Eddington, Luke, 61.
Edgar, Alexander 95
Edgar, John, 59.
Edgar, Zachariah, 119.
Edington, John, 116.
Edmondson, Samuel, 15, 58.
Edmondson, William, 107.
Edmonston, John, 26.
Edwards, John, 34.
Edwards, Jonathan, 34.
Edwards, Owen, 9.
Edwards, Thomas, 41.
Edwards, William, Junior, 102.
Eikols, John, 37.
Eikols, Kanah, 37.
Elder, John, 62.
Elder, Robert, 115.
Elder, Samuel, 58.
Eldridge, Nathan, 22.
Eldridge, Simion, 20.
Elliot, Andrew, 130.
Elliot, Benjamin, 99.
Elliot, John, 48.
Elliot, Robert, 117.
Elliot, Thomas, 91.
Elliott, John 26
Ellis, Abraham, 64, 127.
Ellis, Francis, S., 91, 111.
Ellis, Jacob, 85.
Ellis, James, 42, 76 (2).

Ellis, John, 45.
Ellis, Simeon, 127.
Elmore, Henry, 121.
Elsey, John, 60.
Emery, Benjamin, 79.
Emmerson, John, 97.
Emmert, George, 53.
Emmert, John, 53, 108.
Emmert, Lewis, 70.
England, John, 22, 62.
English, James, 13, 68.
Enochs Isaac, 9 (2).
Enochs, Robert, 106.
Eoxun, William, 63.
Ervin, William 48, 54
Estes (Esters), John, 131.
Estes, Robert, 67.
Estis, Samuel, 130.
Etter, George H., 17.
Evans, James, 63.
Evans, Joseph, 28, (2), 91.
Evans, Robert, 9.
Evans, William, 39, 60.
Evens, Even, 56.
Everett, Joseph, 82.
Ewing, William 9
Ezell, Timothy, 77.
Fain, John, 34.
Fain, Nicholas, 63.
Fain, William, 48, 66.
Faine, Nicholas, 82.
Fambrow, Stewart, 9.
Fannon, Middleton, 60.
Fansher, James, 20.
Faris, Hezekiah, 91.
Farly, Henry, 101.
Farmer, Conrod, 115.
Farmer, John, 115.
Farmer, Nathan, 112.
Farmer, Stephen, 111.
Farr, Robert, 64.
Farrington, Jehne, 131.
Farris, Charles, 91.
Farriss, William, 91.
Faught, Samuel, 75.
Faunt, William, 99.
Fearnsworth, George, 15.
Fears, James, 55.
Fellingin, John, 64.
Fellis, Abraham, 74.
Felts, William, 66.
Fenley, James, 52.
Ferguson, William, 54, 63, 101.
Ferrel, Charles, 22.
Ferrell, John, 87.
Ferrill, Charles, 48.
Fields, Jeremiah, 124.
Fikes, Nathan 44
Findly, James, 87.

Fine, David, 39.
Fine, Ledgerd, 7.
Fine, Peter, 7.
Finley, James, 98.
Fisher, Jacob, 87.
Fisher, Philip, 131.
Fisher, William, 96.
Fite, Joseph, 124.
Fitzgerald, John, 76.
Fitzpatrick, Andrew, 130.
Fitzpatrick, Joseph, 106.
Fitzpatrick, Morgan, 97, 112.
Flaker, Adam, 93.
Flemmin, Samuel, 87.
Flenniken, James Wallace, 22.
Fletcher, Edmund, 105.
Flewallen, William, Jr., 80.
Flint, Sims, 96.
Flood, Seth, 121.
Floyd, David, 69.
Floyd, Elisha, 73.
Follet, David, 51.
Ford, Andrew G., 81.
Ford, Jacob, 6.
Ford, James, 26.
Ford, John, 94.
Ford, John P., 78.
Ford, Joseph, 6, (2).
Ford, William, 78.
Ford, Zachary, 22.
Forgy, John, 92.
Forrester, Isaac, 127.
Forrester, William, 38.
Fort, Josiah, 27.
Fost, Adam, 28.
Foster, Anthony C., 109.
Foster, Winkfield, 114.
Fowler, Jacob, 17.
Fowler, Moses, 109.
Fowler, Thomas, 39.
Fox, Jerry, 74.
Fox, William, 104.
Fox, Zenas, 99.
Fraizer, Harman, 120.
Fraizer, John, 90, 109.
Frazier, Samuel, 69.
Franklen, John, 65.
Franklen, John A. 103
Franklin, John, 32.
Franklin, Thomas, 76.
Franks, Samuel, 38.
Frazer, Daniel, 9.
Frazor, Daniel, 9.
Frazor, James, 32.
Frazor, Julian, 22.
Frederick, Hezekiah, 122.
Freeland, James, 109.
Freeman, James, 62.
Frenary, Richard 15

French, Amos, 63.
French, Jeremiah, 124.
Frierson, Elias, 59.
Friley, Caleb, 48.
Friley, Martin, 22.
Fristoe, Robert L., 76.
Fristoe, William, 22.
Fronier, N. H. S., 22.
Frost, Ebenezer, 60.
Frost, Edward, 22.
Frost, Samuel, 22.
Fry, John, 105.
Fryas, William, 43.
Frye, Peter, 80.
Fryerson, Elias, 97.
Fryerson, Moses G., 77.
Fugan, Evan, 108.
Fulkerson, John, 108.
Fuller, John, 100.
Fullerton, James, 80.
Fulton, Thomas, 22.
Furlong, Martin, 46.
Furman, John, 115.
Fuston, John, 34.
Fyne, Jacob, 99.
Gailey, James, 4.
Gailey, Moses, 65.
Gains, Ambrose, 30.
Gains, David, 73.
Gains, Edmond, 30.
Gale, Caleb, 78.
Gallaher, James, 4.
Gallahor, William, 34.
Gallaway, Thomas, 82, 83.
Gallian, George, 30.
Gamble, Andrew, 4.
Gamble, Charles, 61.
Gamble, John, 22, (2).
Gammon, Richard, 83.
Gann, Nathan, 34, (2).
Garagas, John, 59.
Gardinhire, William, 22.
Gardner, Jesse, 44.
Gardner, John, 69, 86.
Gardner, Joshua, 44, 80.
Gardner, William, 52.
Garner, John, 98.
Garner, Obediah, 122.
Garret, George, 32.
Garret, Jacob, 104.
Garrison, Benjamin, 131.
Gast, Moses, 17.
Gastin, Thomas, 74.
Gates, Jacob, 34.
Gatland, Thomas, 67.
Gatlet, Ephraim, 125.
Gault, James, 130.
Gaundell, Benjamin, 87.
Gaylard, James, 94.

Geerin, John, 22.
Gennings, William, 53.
Gentry, George, 36.
Gentry, Jesse, 22.
George, Edward, 20.
George, Solomon, 111.
Gerin, Solomon, 23.
Germain, Zacheus, 130.
Gholston, John, 59.
Gibbons, Epps, 56.
Gibbs, George, 103.
Gibbs, Jesse, 127.
Gibbs, John, 23.
Gibbs, Nicholas, 96.
Gibson, David, 103.
Gibson, Jeremiah, 86.
Gibson, John, 15, (2), 32, 68, 106.
Gibson, Joseph, 32.
Gibson, Robert, 87.
Gibson, Witson, 26.
Giddens, James, 104.
Gideon, Zepheniah, 108.
Giffard, George, 55.
Gifford, George, 55.
Gifford, Gibbs, 46.
Gifford, Jabes, 32.
Gifford, Jabues, 29.
Gifford, Jabus, 30.
Gilbert, David, 69.
Gilbert, Jesse Junior, 125.
Gilbert, Stephen, 125.
Giles, Josiah E., 64.
Gillaspie, Thomas, 43.
Gillentine, Nichols, 104.
Gillenwaters, William, 57.
Gillespie, Alexander, 49.
Gillespie, Allen, 34, (2).
Gillespie, George, 35.
Gillespie, James 4 (2), 35, 119
Gillespie, Thomas, 76.
Gilliam, John, 100.
Gilliland, James, 60.
Gillingwaters, Thomas, 17.
Gilmore, Mathew, 55.
Gilworth, John, 128.
Ginens, Ryal, 13.
Ginkins, William, 32.
Ginnings, James, 71.
Ginnings, Robert L., 86.
Ginnings, Thomas, 71.
Gitton, John, 62.
Gitton, John L., 100.
Givens, William, 116.
Glascock, Archibald, 35.
Glass, John, 89.
Glasscock, Archibald, 35.
Glover, Lancaster, 67.
Glover, William, 127.
Goad, William, 98.

Goard, Robert, 97.
Goens, Mashack, 42.
Goens, Shadrick 42
Goforth, Andrew H., 97.
Going, William, 9.
Gold, David, 119.
Golden, William, 17.
Goldman, John, 15.
Golleher, Peter, 74.
Goodall, Davis, 101.
Gooden, James, 122.
Goodman, Andrew, 101.
Goodman, Claiborne, 80.
Goodpasture, James, 43.
Goodrey, George, 17.
Goodrich, Samuel E., 49.
Goodsey, Burley, 108.
Goodson, John, 30.
Goodwin, Jesse, 111.
Goodwin, William, 78.
Gord, Samuel, 39.
Gord, William, 97.
Gordon, Alexander B., 83.
Gordon, Thomas, 92.
Goshue, Jacob, 47.
Gosuage, William, 53.
Gotcher, Samuel, 73.
Gott, Lott, 35.
Gould, John, 89.
Gowers, William, 103.
Grace, James, 115.
Gragg, John, 15.
Graham, James, 106.
Graham, Nimrod, 59.
Graham, Spencer, 13.
Graham, William, 41, 42, 90.
Grant, James, 52.
Grant, James, Jr., 52.
Grant, Joshua, 116.
Grant, Richard, 108.
Grant, Zachariah, 97.
Graves, Daniel, 77, 116.
Graves, George, 96.
Graves, Ralph, 112.
Gray, Alexander, 124.
Gray, Benajah, 71.
Gray, Clifford, 81.
Gray, Frederick, 46.
Gray, James, 35, 131.
Gray, Joseph, 37, 52.
Gray, Robert, 128.
Gray, Thomas, 101.
Gray, William, 111.
Grayson, Benjamin, 116.
Green, David, 102.
Green, Edmund, 102.
Green, Ira, 128.
Green, Jesse, 23.
Green, Joseph, 23.

Green, Michael, 102.
Green, William 38, 102
Green, Zachariah, 32.
Greening, Thomas, 70.
Greer, Alexander, 6.
Greer, Andrew, 29.
Gregg, Abraham, 126.
Gregg, John, 108.
Gregg, Samuel, 15, 39, 108.
Gregory, George, 58, 76.
Gregory, John, 57, 92, 112.
Gregory, Laben, 46.
Greson, William 26
Griffin, James, 94.
Griffin, John, 100, 101.
Griffin, Solomon, 6.
Griffit, Griffe, 55.
Griffith, Joseph, 68.
Griffith, Thomas, 98.
Griffiths, Eli, 5.
Grills, Elliott, 23.
Grimes, George, 13, 108.
Grimes, William, 27.
Gristham, John, 35.
Grizard, William, 39.
Groger, Spencer, 43.
Groom, Valentine, 27.
Grosse, Edmund, 89.
Groves, Stephen, 77.
Groves, Thomas, 127.
Grubb, William, 93.
Guardner, Conrad, 41.
Guin, John, 32.
Guin, Norton, 5.
Guin, William 32, 93
Guin, William, Jr., 83.
Guinn, Alexander, 32.
Guinn, Bartholomew, 54.
Guinn, William, 74.
Gullick, Reese, 15.
Gunn, James, 91.
Gunn, William, 91.
Gunter, Francis, 49.
Gurly, Jeremiah, 97.
Guthrey, Francis, 17.
Guttary, James, 15.
Guttery, William F., 130.
Guy, William, 107.
Gwin, William, 81.
Hackney, William, 54.
Haffacker, Peter, 13.
Haggard, Henry, 115.
Haggard, Samuel, 67.
Haggard, William, 27.
Hail, George, 54.
Hail, James, 108.
Hail, Nathan, 23.
Haile, Joab 75
Haile, Thomas, 35.

Haily, Elijah, 122.
Haily, Thomas, 40.
Haines, James, 87.
Haines, John, 17.
Hair, Jacob, 15.
Haislep, Wallace, 111.
Haistings, Stephen, 87.
Hale, Alexander, 31.
Hale, John, 57.
Hale, Joseph, 113.
Hale, Nathan, 23.
Hale, Shadrack, 35.
Halffaker, Peter, 13.
Hall, Garret, 120.
Hall, James, 100.
Hall, John, 17, 100, 111.
Hall, John, C., 71.
Hall, Luke, 5.
Hall, Philip, 81.
Hall, Samuel, 23, 62.
Hall, William, 32, 73, 83, 106.
Halleburton, William, 72.
Hallum, George, 68.
Haltshouzer, John, 117.
Ham, Jacob, 43.
Ham, John, 106.
Hambleton, Alexander, 26.
Hambright, John, 23.
Hamilton, Andrew, 111.
Hamilton, Henry, 77, 102, 127.
Hamilton, Isaiah, 27.
Hamilton, James, 18, 98.
Hamilton, John, 18.
Hamilton, Johnston, 18.
Hamilton, William, 13.
Hamlinton, Robert, 32.
Hammons, Leroy, 48, 65.
Hammons, Thomas, 18.
Hampelton, David 27
Hampton, John, 78, 103.
Hampton, Johnson, 89.
Hancock, William M., 93.
Hand, Samuel, 122.
Handlin, William, 98.
Handly, John, 35.
Handy, James, 28.
Hanes, John, 20.
Haney, Jesse, 32.
Haney, Spencer, 18.
Hankins, Absolom, 96.
Hankins, Gilbert, 99.
Hankins, John, 23, 51, 106.
Hankins, William, 32, (2).
Hannah, Andrew, 5, 31, 35.
Hannah, Josiah, 114.
Hansborough, Smith, 32.
Hansbrough, Daniel, 64.
Harden, Jacob, 67, 86.
Hardgrove, Leroy, 122.

Hardin, James, 23.
Hargis, William, 100.
Hargiss, William 29
Hargraves, John, 117.
Harkbrode, Lawrence 83
Harl, John, 93.
Harle, Baldwin, 7, 35.
Harlson, John, 23.
Harlson, Paul, 23.
Harman, Adam, Jr., 60.
Harman, David, 94.
Harman, George, 15.
Harman, Jacob, 20.
Harman, Peter, 56.
Harmon, Jacob, 115.
Harmon, John, 15.
Harmon, Thomas, 57.
Harney, Thomas, 9, (2).
Harper, Mathew, 46.
Harpole, Martin, 37.
Harpole, Solomon, 32, 37.
Harrel, Eli, 131.
Harrelson, John, 13.
Harrington, Whitmill, 44.
Harris, Alexander, 52.
Harris, Allen, 105.
Harris, Archibald H., 110.
Harris, Benjamin C., 89.
Harris, David, 94.
Harris, John, 26, 75.
Harris, Samuel, 91, 107.
Harris, William, 71, 73, 107.
Harrison, Edmund, 15.
Harrison, Isaiah, 15.
Harrison, James, 115.
Harrison, James Junior, 44.
Harrison, John, 18.
Harrison, Michael, 35.
Harrison, Nathaniel, 32.
Harrison, Solomon, 13.
Harrison, Thomas, 87, (2).
Harrison, Vinson, 80.
Harriss, Thompson, 26.
Harrold, John, 35.
Hart, Alexander, 52.
Hart, John, 94.
Hart, Moris, 29.
Harvey, Charles B., 75.
Harwell, Buckner, Jr., 112.
Harwell, Frederick, 112.
Harwell, James, 39.
Harwell, Richard M., 99.
Hasler, Adam, 105.
Hassell, Silvanus, 114.
Hassell, Silvenus, 75.
Hatgrove, James, 49.
Haun, John, 89, 115.
Hauney, Thomas, 92.
Havens, William, 23.

Hawkins, Benjamin, 75.
Hawkins, Samuel C., 60.
Hawkins, William, 128.
Hawn, Abraham, 6.
Hay, David, 9.
Hay, Joseph, 9.
Hayler, James, 108.
Hayley, David, 13.
Hayly, William, Jr., 75.
Haynes, Christopher, 18.
Haynes, James, 27.
Haynes, Michael, 53.
Haynes, Robert, 106.
Haynes, William, 78, 98, 119.
Hayney, Elijah, 101.
Hays, George, 118.
Hays, James, 97.
Hays, Jonathan, 118.
Hays, Joseph, 74.
Hays, Nathaniel, 23.
Hays, O. B., 90.
Hays, Robert, 9.
Heard, Stephen, 50.
Heartsell, Jacob, 85.
Heaton, Enoch, 9.
Heaton, John, 6.
Heddleston, John, 121.
Height, Sion H., 80.
Hellum, George, 86.
Hellum, Morriss, 86.
Helton, Abraham, 49.
Hemby, Dennis, 43.
Henderson, Daniel, 15.
Henderson, James, 45, (2), 100.
Henderson, John, 68, 131.
Henderson, Robert, 28, (2), 77.
Henderson, Thomas, 69.
Henderson, William, 13, 18, 28, 63, 112.
Henderson, William, Jr., 28.
Hendrick, Squire, 99.
Hendricks, Abner, 59.
Hendricks, Solomon, 108.
Hendrex, Luke 23
Hendrix, Nathan, 53.
Henly, Isaac, 85.
Henninger, Jacob, 15.
Henny, William, 90.
Henry, Charles, 79.
Henry, George, 7.
Henry, Hugh, 27.
Henry, John, 107.
Henry, Thomas, 27.
Herbert, Nathaniel, 70.
Hern, Stephen, B. W., 90.
Herred, James, 81.
Heryford, John, 73.
Hess, John, 5.
Hewey, Samuel, 87.
Hewit, Robert, 9.

Hickey, John, 18.
Hickey, Michael, 44.
Hickman, Edward, 90.
Hickman, Thomas, 124.
Hickman, William, 130.
Hicks, Charles, 117.
Hicks, Jacob, 83.
Hicks, Richard, 131.
Hickson, Andrew, 15.
Hickson, Ephraim, 15.
Higens, Philemon, 28.
Higginbotham, William, 45.
Higgins, William, 71, 132.
Higgins, William, Y., 96.
Highberger, John, 113.
Hight, Robert, 132.
Hill, Alexander, 103, (2).
Hill, Green, 86.
Hill, Isaac, 120.
Hill, James, 9, 84.
Hill, Joab, 13.
Hill, John, 20, 36, 43, (2), 68, 76.
Hill, Samuel, 20.
Hill, Thomas, 44, 115.
Hill, William, 67, 76, 85, 95.
Hilliard, Needham, 91.
Hilton, James, 97.
Hinch, John, 49.
Hindman, John, 42.
Hines, John H., 96.
Hines, Levi, 23.
Hinnegan, James, 59.
Hinson, John, 6.
Hinton, Jeremiah, 9.
Hixon, Ephraim, 51.
Hixon, John, 106.
Hobbs, Edward D., 110.
Hobbs, James, 23.
Hobbs, Joel, 23.
Hoddge, John, 13.
Hodge, Moses, 13.
Hodges, Charles, 20.
Hodges, Edmund, 124.
Hodges, James C., 86.
Hodges, Josiah, 68.
Hodges, Moses, 55.
Hodges, William, 124.
Hogan, David, 55.
Hogan, Edmund, 102.
Hogan, Isaiah, 118.
Hogan, James, 18.
Hogan, John, 118.
Hoge, Samuel, 5.
Hogue, James, 91.
Hogun, William, 46.
Hogwood, Jonathan, 99.
Holaday, Peter, 49.
Holeman, James, 41.
Holeman, William, 83.

Holland, Andrew, 119.
Holland, Hardy, 94.
Holland, John, 57.
Holland, Thomas, 7.
Holland, Thomas, H., 104.
Holland, William, 114.
Hollen, Mark, 111.
Hollis, James, 26.
Holloday, William, 5.
Holloway, John 49, 86
Holloway, William, 119.
Holly, William Tyrrel, 62.
Holms, Drury, 39.
Holms, Simon, 60.
Holster, Adam, 77.
Holstonback, John, 124.
Holt, John Junr., 93.
Hon, George, 87.
Hood, Thomas, 89.
Hooker, Samuel B., 117.
Hooker, William, 130.
Hooper, Ennis, 10.
Hooper, John, 71.
Hooper, Thomas, 71.
Hopkins, James P., 77 (2).
Hopper, Rolly, 74.
Hopson, Benjamin, 68.
Hord, William, 18.
Horncock, John, 53.
Horne, Etheldred, 110.
Horner, Gideon, 87.
Horner, John, 13.
Horton, Isaac, 105.
Horton, John, 50.
Hoss, John, 128.
Hoss, Philip, 124.
Hoss, Thomas, 89.
Houk, John, 63.
House, Gabrial, 42.
Housley, Robert, 31 (2).
Houstion, John, 45.
Houston, John, 87.
Hopston, John P., 52, 107, (2).
Houston, Robert, 52.
Houston, Samuel, 89, 107.
Houston, William, 80.
Hover, Henry, 90.
Howard, Bradford, 132.
Howard, John, 44.
Howard, Johnson, 53.
Howard, Shadrick, 77.
Howard, Stephen, 53.
Howard, William, 13, 15.
Howel, Joseph, B., 69.
Howell, Caleb, 13.
Howell, Henry, 13.
Howell, John, 113.
Howell, Malachia 13
Howell, William, 122.

Howerd, John, 6.
Hoyl, Jacob, 74.
Hubbard, Enos, 127.
Hubbard, Nathaniel, 87.
Huddleston, Josiah D., 99.
Huddleston, Willie, 120.
Hudleston, Fielden 78
Hudspeath, William, 60.
Hues, Moses, 5.
Huet, Benjamin, 106.
Huett, Robert, 62.
Huffacre, John, 116.
Huffacre, Michael, 38.
Huffacre, Peter, 81.
Huffmaster, James, 114.
Hughes, Robert, 39.
Humble, Jacob, 75, 114.
Humphreys, David, 64.
Humphreys, William, 62.
Humphries, John, 48.
Humstead, Edward, 95.
Hungarford, Richard, 104.
Hunt, James, 55, 64.
Hunt, Uriah, 35.
Hunter, Aaron, 119.
Hunter, Edwin, 80.
Hunter, Ephraim, 80.
Hunter, Henry, 70.
Hunter, Jacob, 79.
Hunter, James A., 50.
Hunter, Joseph, 70.
Hunter, Manuel, 54, 71.
Hurcherson, William, 18.
Hurd, James, 23.
Hutchans, Smith, 7.
Hutchens, Smith, 23.
Hutcheson, John, 119.
Hutcheson, Thomas, 26.
Hutchison, Thomas, 27.
Hutson, John, 108.
Ice, Frederick, 18.
Inglish, Alexander, 74.
Inglish, James, 13.
Ingram, John, 69.
Inman, Daniel, 7, 20.
Inman, David, 20.
Inman, Ezekiel, 42.
Inman, James, 20.
Inman, John, 7.
Inman, Joseph, 57.
Irvin, Alexander, 89.
Irvin, Samuel, 100.
Irvine, David, 40.
Irwin, David, 55.
Irwin, Francis, 23.
Isbels, Zachariah, 48.
Isbells, James, 48.
Ish, John, 38.
Isham, Charles, 85.

148  RECORD OF COMMISSIONS OF OFFICERS

Isom, James, 77.
Ivey, Henry, 13.
Ivy, John, 73.
Jack, John F., 40.
Jack, William, 7.
Jackson, Brice, 60.
Jackson, James, 104.
Jackson, Jesse, 86.
Jackson, John, 82.
Jackson, Joseph, 77.
Jackson, Robert, 108.
Jackson, Samuel, 111.
Jackson, Samuel Junr., 92.
Jadwin, Joseph, 132.
James, George, 115.
James, John, 27, 41.
James, Joseph, 53.
James, Joshua, 39.
James, Thomas, 55.
James, Walten, 31.
Jamison, Robert W., 56.
January, John, 95.
Jared, William, 115.
Jarman, Robert, 94.
Jarnegan, William, 72.
Jarrel, David, 119.
Jefferey, Jeremiah, 23.
Jeffers, William, 41.
Jennings, James, 108.
Jennings, John, 47.
Jennings, Thomas, 54.
Jennings, William, 108.
Jentry, Martin, 20.
Jermin, Robert, 40.
Jeton, Robert, 122.
Jinkins, John, 46.
Jinkins, William, 6.
Joab, Samuel, 86.
Job, James, 59.
Jobe, Abraham, 35.
Johnson, Abel, 120.
Johnson, Charles, 67, 130.
Johnson, James, 99.
Johnson, Jesse, 81.
Johnson, John, 27, 53, 87.
Johnson, Mathew, 80.
Johnson, Peter, 10.
Johnson, Robert, 71, 97, 110.
Johnson, Samuel 69.
Johnson, Stephen, 73, 113.
Johnson, Thomas, 27, 101, 126.
Johnson, William, 18, 23, 27, (2), 51, 61, 80, 98, 122.
Johnson, Zaphre, 15.
Johnston, Isaac, 90.
Johnston, James, 63.
Johnston, John, 10.
Johnston, John, Jr., 35.
Johnston, Robert, 39.

Johnston Samuel, 68.
Joine (Jones) Levy, 79.
Joiner, Cornelius, 50.
Jones, Aquilla, 55.
Jones, Azor, 36.
Jones, Branch, 71.
Jones, Daniel, 40, 110.
Jones, Eli, 27.
Jones, Gabrail, 79.
Jones, Jesse, 27.
Jones, John, 15, 44, 62, 72, 102, 119.
Jones, Josiah, 68.
Jones, Levy, 79.
Jones, Lewis, 49.
Jones, Martin, 117, (2).
Jones, Morton, 74.
Jones, Prettyman, 5.
Jones, Quignal Martin, 86.
Jones, Nathaniel, 35.
Jones, Robert, 125.
Jones, Samuel, 64.
Jones, Stephen, 97.
Jones, Sugar, 50.
Jones, Thomas, 7, 40, 81.
Jones, William, 83, 113, 122.
Jones, William D., 54.
Jones, Zachariah, 104.
Josseling, Benjamin, 10.
Jossling, James, 104.
Jourdain, Elias 92
Joy, John, 55.
Justice, Isaac, 93.
Justice, James, 128.
Justice, Thomas, 41.
Kain, James, 127.
Kane, James, 48.
Karbrough, John, 41.
Kasterson, John, 15.
Katron, Charles, 60.
Kearns, Jacob, 74.
Kearns, James, 44.
Kearns, Philip, 43, 77.
Keck, Philip, 53, 108.
Keef, John, 13.
Keen (Kun) Enoch, 47.
Keen, Harper, 47.
Keener, Joseph, 103.
Keeny, Joseph Junr., 87.
Keeny, Thomas, 71.
Keisy, Thomas, 92.
Keith, Daniel, 115.
Kelley, John, 5.
Kelley, William, 15 (2).
Kellensworth, John, 18.
Kelly, Benjamin, 126.
Kelly, Edward, 83.
Kelly, John 5, 108
Kelly, Joshua, 128.
Kelly, Mordecai, 90.

Kelly, William, 74, 77.
Kelso, Alexander, 20, (2).
Kelso, Hugh, 20.
Kelson, John, 35.
Kennedy, John, 103.
Kennedy, Joseph, 106.
Kennedy, Thomas, 120.
Kenney, James, 53.
Kenyon, Joseph, 84.
Kerby, William, 115.
Kerr, Benjamin, 62.
Kerr, James, 74.
Kerr, Samuel, 10.
Kerr, William, 124.
Kettwell, John, 13.
Keys, George, 126.
Keys, James, 38.
Kilday, Henry, 41.
Kilgore, John, 93.
Killen, William, 73.
Killengsworth, Henry, 106.
Killgore, Charles, 27.
Killgore, Thomas, 27.
Kimbrel, John, 111.
Kimbrough, M. D., 83.
Kincheloe, Elijah, 35.
Kindall, Peter, 82, 125.
Kindel, William, 122.
King, Benjamin, 87.
King, Edward, 101.
King, Harvey, 47.
King, Isaac, 31.
King, John, 15, 31, 92.
King, Phillip, 31.
King, Robert, 62, 96.
King, William, 15, (2), 68, 76, 83, 126.
Kinkade, James, 90.
Kirby, Caleb, 46.
Kirk, George, 85.
Kirk, Lewis, 77.
Kirby, William, 59.
Kirkpatrick, Charles, 68.
Kirkpatrick, David, 32.
Kirkpatrick, Ebenezer, 97, 119.
Kirkpatrick, Hugh, 20.
Kirkpatrick, James, 33, (2), 37.
Kirkpatrick, John, 37.
Kirkpatrick, Joseph, 132.
Kitchen, George, 127.
Kitchen, Jesse, 13.
Kitchen, John, 13.
Kitchen, Joseph, 106.
Kizar, Francis, 129.
Kizler, John, 86.
Knidever, Jacob, 31.
Koher, George, 112.
Koontz, Joseph, 115.
Koyl, Benjamin, 65.
Koyl, Hiram, 84.

Koyle, William, 18.
Krisel, John, 27, (2).
Krisell, Andrew, 121.
Lacey, Abraham, 111.
Lacky, Archibald, 5.
Lacy, Amos, 33.
Lacy, George, 70.
Lacy, James, 6.
Ladderdale, John, 61.
Laderdale, James, 15.
Ladey, Henry, 47.
Lady, John, 47.
Lain, Isaac, 13.
Lake, Daniel Thatcher, 63.
Lakey, John, 87.
Lamb, Adam, 107.
Lamb, Isaac, 92.
Lamb, John, 54.
Lamberson, John, 46.
Lambert, Aaron, 105, 107.
Lammons, Samuel, 7.
Lancaster, Robert, 27.
Lancaster, William, 37.
Lance, Samuel, 104.
Landrum, Younger, 15.
Landson, Eli M., 132.
Lane, Aquilla, 94.
Lane, John, 77.
Lane, Jorden, 62.
Lane, Joseph, 77.
Lane, Nathan G., 120, (2).
Lane, Tidance, 35.
Lane, Tidence, 20.
Lane, William, 18.
Langford, Thomas, 94.
Langham, Abel, 13.
Lanier, Buchannon, 90.
Lansden, Thomas, 105.
Large, Samuel, 39.
Larkin, Henry S., 57.
Lassesure, Littleberry, 110.
Lassiter, Frederick, 71.
Latimer, Griswold, 33.
Latimore, Griswold, 33.
Lattimer, Joseph, 33.
Lauderdale, Samuel D., 64.
Laughlin, James, 45, 100.
Laughlin, William, 80, 122.
Laurence, John, 67.
Lavender, Daniel, 62.
Lavender, Daniel S., 79.
Lavender, John, 23, (2), 120.
Lawrance, Randolph, 41.
Lawrence, Edward, 68.
Lawson, Andrew 63, 124
Lawson, Epephoditus, 27.
Lawson, Eppaphroditus, 44.
Lawson, Isham, 18.
Lawson, Jacob, 18, (2).

Lawson, Thomas, 129.
Lax, Solomon, 39.
Layman, Jacob, 28, 116.
Lea, Edward, 94.
Lea, James, 94.
Lea, John, 13, 51.
Lea, Joseph, 23.
Lea, Zachariah, 23.
Leake, John, 102.
Lebow, Daniel, 53.
Lebow, John, 18, 53.
Ledbetter, Ephraim, 98.
Lee, Abel, 117.
Lee, Braxton, 40.
Lee, Cader, 18.
Lee, Edward, 41.
Lee, Ephraim, 75.
Lee, John, 70, 82, 87, 117.
Lee, Needam, 18.
Lee, Needham, 18.
Lee, William, 96.
Leeth, James, 42, 116.
Leeth, George, 20.
Legan, Masten, 124.
Legg, Samuel, 107.
Leib, Daniel, 105.
Leich, George, 61.
Leister, William, 61.
Lemmins, John, 92.
Lemmons, John, 83.
Lemon, Daniel, 28.
Lenier, John, 71.
Lentz, William, 40.
Lester, Presly, 132.
Lethum, John, 127.
Lettrell, John, 15.
Leture, Christohper, 47.
Levingston, William, 44.
Lewis, Benjamin, 48.
Lewis, Elijah, 104.
Lewis, James, 40.
Lewis, Jesse, 120.
Lewis, John, 7, 61, 116.
Lewis, Obediah, 114.
Lewis, Samuel, 94.
Lewis, Thomas, 6.
Lewis, Thomas W., 125.
Lewis, William, 31, (2), 95.
Lieuney, Peter, 33.
Lillard, James, 7, 20, 109.
Lillard, John, 7, 109.
Lillard, John Junr., 71.
Lillard, William, 7.
Lilly, Noah, 29, 33.
Linch, John, 81.
Lindsey, Issac, 64.
Lindsey, John, 98.
Lindville, Warley, 49.
Lines, Jacob, 18.

Lintz, William, 71.
Lister, James, 78.
Litnor, Christopher, 74.
Little, Anthony, 127.
Little, Neal, 104.
Litton, James, 45.
Lock, John, 95.
Lock, Richard, 75.
Lock, Richard S., 67.
Lockhart, Hugh, 71, (2).
Lockhart, James, 27.
Lockhart, James B., 132.
Lockmiller, Frederick, 114.
Lockmiller, Jonas, 114.
Locksey, John T., 86.
Loe, David, 87.
Logan, David, 41.
Logans, William, 98.
Lomaxs, John, 94.
Lonas, Jacob, 23.
London, William, 10.
Loness, George, 116.
Long, Joseph, 67, 79.
Long, Matthew P., 119.
Long, Samuel, 81.
Long, William, 23, 43.
Longacre, Andrew, 42.
Longacre, Benjamin, 20.
Longmire, William, 87.
Longmires, John, 35.
Longmyer, George, 66.
Looney, Absolom, 57.
Looney, David, 107.
Looney, Isaac, 83, 102.
Looney, John, 46.
Looney, Joseph W., 64.
Looney, Peter, 23, 51, 89.
Looney, Robert, 18.
Looney, Stephen, 103.
Loudeback, Isaac, 74.
Lourey, Alexander, 66.
Love, David, 33, 111.
Love, John, 6, 23, 49, 79.
Love, Jonathan, 92.
Love, Joseph, 92.
Love, Philip S., 122.
Love, Richard H., 79.
Love, Robert, 98, 116.
Love, Samuel B., 128.
Lovelace, Charles, 70.
Lovelady, Jesse, 28.
Lovelady, John, 51.
Lovelady, Stephen, 28.
Lovelice, David, 5.
Lovell, Daniel, 121.
Low, Aquala, 23.
Low, Aquila, 23.
Low, John, 23, (3).

IN THE TENNESSEE MILITIA, 1796-1811   151

Lourey, John Junior, 47.
Lowrey, Alexander 29
Lowrey, Granberry 65
Lowry, Adam, 35, (2).
Lowry, Alexander, 15.
Lowry, Andrew, 107.
Lowry, David, 130.
Lowry, James, 20.
Loy, John, 50.
Loy, William, 51.
Loyd, John, 56.
Loyd, Jordan, 87.
Luburn, John, 20.
Lucas, John, 75, 90.
Lundy, Richard, 129.
Lusk, William, 65.
Luster, John, 114.
Lyle, Daniel, 95.
Lyle, Henry, 71.
Lyon, John, 33, 101.
Lyon, William, 79.
McAdams, Hugh, 35.
McAdams, John, 117.
McAdams, Samuel, 132.
McAdams, William R., 102, 110.
McAdoo, John Junr., 68.
McAffie, James, 117.
McAffry, Terence, 23.
McAllister, John, 35.
McAnally, Charles, 92.
McAnally, David, 113.
McAnally, Jesse, 55.
McAnier, David, 23.
McBeard, Samuel, 81.
McBeth, Robert, 23.
McBride, Andrew, 85.
McBride, Francis, 45, 62.
McBride, James, 70.
McBride, John, 47.
McBride, Samuel, 45.
McBride, William, 74, 97.
McBroom, William, 93.
McCais, Thomas, 87.
McCaleb, Epraim, 75.
McCall, Henry, 119.
McCalpin, Thomas, 105.
McCamey, David, 52.
McCampbell, Solomon, 5, (2).
McCampbell, William, 23.
McCamy, John, 23, (2).
McCane, John, 124.
McCann, James, 129.
McCans, James, 57.
McCarty, Thomas, 53.
McCauley, Edward, 116.
McClanahan, Matthew, 5.
McClannahan, Matthew, 100.
McCleary, Robert, 127.
McClellan, Abraham, 23.

McClellan, David, 62.
McClellan, John, 24.
McClellan, Samuel, 24 (2).
McClenahan, Matthew, 5.
McClenehan, John, 76.
McClennahan, Mathew, 80.
McClennehan, Alexander, 116.
McClennehan, Joshua, 54.
McClennehan, William, 42.
McClintock, James, 77.
McClintock, Robert, 58, 98.
McClister, Andrew, 76.
McClung, Charles, 24.
McClung, John, 29.
McCollister, John Jr., 35.
McCollough, William, 18.
McCollum, Hugh, 26.
McConnel, Moses, 122.
McConnel, Samuel, 40.
McConnell, James, 116.
McConnell, John P., 40.
McConnell, Montgomery, 33.
McCopen, Alexander, 15.
McCord, William, 60.
McCorkle, Alexander, 77.
McCormack, John, 110.
McCorry, Thomas, 24.
McCoy, Amos A., 122.
McCoy, Moses, 20.
McCoy, Robert, 122.
McCoy, William, 51.
McCoy, William (McCag), 38.
McCrabb, Alexander, 31.
McCrackin, Ephraim, 119.
McCrackin, Samuel, 66.
McCrady, Alexander, 49.
McCrakin, Joseph, 104.
McCrany, John, 70.
McCrary, Joel, 117.
McCraw, Dancey, 18.
McCraw, Gabriel, 57.
McCray, Henry, 103.
McCray, Philip, 103.
McCree, James, 80.
McCrery, Benjamin, 100.
McCretchen, James, 67.
McCrory, Thomas, 10, 36.
McCroskey, John, 63.
McCrocky, Samuel 73
McCuestin, Thomas, 88.
McCuistion, James, 20.
McCuiston, Thomas, 58.
McCullough, James, 92, 112.
McCully, William, 86.
McCurdy, James, 97.
McCurdy, William, 88.
McCutcheon, James, 71.
McDaniel, David, 29.
McDaniel, John, 77.

McDannell, John, 20.
McDannold, William, 49, 57, 65.
McDonald, James 20
McDonel, James, 20.
McDonel, John, 20.
McDonold, Daniel, 24.
McDonold, Randolph, 18.
McDowell, James, 33.
McDowell, John, 83.
McEldry, John, 77.
McElwain, John, 110.
McEwen, Alexander, 45, 100.
McEwen, James, 67, 100.
McEwen, John, 122.
McEwing, David, 10.
McFall, Thomas, 97.
McFarland, John, 76, (2), 116.
McFarland, Robert, 20.
McFerren, James, 122.
McGall, Samuel, 119.
McGaugh, John, 10.
McGaughey, John, 107.
McGaughey, George W., 59.
McGaughy, James, 29.
McGee, George, 35.
McGee, James, 37.
McGee, William, 49.
McGeehee, William, 18, 117.
McGill, Hugh, 15.
McGill, Robert, 29.
McGinley, James, 5, 52, 107.
McGinniss, William, 92.
McGinty, Alexander, 125.
McGlaughlin, Samuel, 54.
McGlolen, John, 7.
McGowan, James, 60.
McGowan, William, 60.
McGraw, Cornelius, 72.
McGuire, George, 64.
McHenry, Archibald, 111.
McIntiff, Samuel, 90.
McIntirff, David, 38.
McKain, Robert, 18, (3).
McKamy, William, 24.
McKee, John, 33.
McKee, Matheia, 13.
McKee, Mathew, 13.
McKee, Robert, 128.
McKee, William, 122.
McKie, William, 128.
McKinney, David, 107.
McKinney, Henry, 33.
McKinney, John, 36.
McKinniss, Hugh, 101.
McKinsey, Rowley, 88.
McKisick, Joseph, 88.
McKnight, John, 10.
McKnight, William, 130.
McKorkle, Robert, 24.

McKorkle, William, 33.
McLain, James, 96.
McLaughlin, Alexander, 29.
McLin, William, 128.
McMahan, John, 52.
McMahan, Michael, 31.
McMeans, Thomas, 42.
McMicken, Andrew, 62.
McMillen, Malcom, 82.
McMillen, William, 36.
McMinn, Joseph, 18.
McMins, Thomas, 76.
McMullen, James, 62.
McMullin, Samuel, 7.
McMurrey, David, 33.
McMurry, Charles, 29.
McMurry, James, 65.
McMurtry, John, 106.
McMurtry, Joseph, 15, (2), 130.
McNabb, Absolom, 6.
McNabb, Baptiste, 6, (2).
McNair, Joseph, 97.
McNair, Thomas, 130.
McNaire, John, 116.
McNeely, Alexander, 105.
McNeely, James, 107.
McNees, Samuel, 74.
McNight, Alexander, 33.
McNutt, William, 24.
McPherron, William, 43.
McPherson, Bartlett, 71.
McPherson, George, 121.
McPherson, Henry, 7.
McPherson, Joseph, 7.
McQuestion, Samuel, 88.
McRandels, John, 5.
Mcrary, Benjamin, 71.
McRee, Lewis, 80.
McRee, William, 24.
McRory, Thomas, Junior, 130.
McSpaden, John, 58.
McSpaden, Samuel, 20.
McVaughan, John, 47.
McVaughn, John, 94.
McVay, James, 57.
McVay, Jordan, 77, 92.
McVay, Kinson, 92.
McWherter, George, 132.
McWhorter, Cyrus H., 68.
McWilliams, Andrew, 41.
McWilliams, Robert, 76.
Macey, Charles, 37.
Macey, Clement, 64.
**Mackey, William, 10, 49, 67.**
Macklin, William A., 132.
Madden, Champ, 33.
Madden, Joel, 63.
Maddon, Joel, 63.
Maddy, James, 53.

Maclin, James C. 10
Madox, Wilson, 121.
Magee, James C., 53.
Magert, Henry, 31, 64.
Mahan, James, 15.
Mahan, John, 29.
Maho (Mayo) Valentine, 89.
Mahon, John, 29.
Maines, Thomas, 35.
Malcolm, Robert, 42.
Mallacoat, Edmund, 73.
Malony, John, 128.
Manifee, Nimrod, 10, (2).
Mann, Thomas, 93.
Mannefee, Willis, 129.
Manroe, George, 73.
Manrow, John, 73.
Manship, George, 117.
Marberry, Isaac, 88.
Marberry, Leonard, 109, (2).
Margin, Solomon, 31.
Markell, William, 116.
Markham, Jasper, 127.
Markham, Josiah, 18.
Marks, David, 35.
Marks, Thomas, 112.
Marsh, Henry, 124.
Marshal, Hardy, 105.
Marshal, James, 71.
Marshal, Richard, 105.
Marshall, John, 117.
Marshall, Richard, 105.
Martin, Brice, 63.
Martin, Daniel, 73.
Martin, Gabriel, 99.
Martin, Hugh, 47.
Martin, James, 24, 71.
Martin, Joel, 55.
Martin, John, 86, 96, 116.
Martin, Menai, 44.
Martin, Nathaniel, 38, 105.
Martin, Obediah, 92.
Martin, Robert, 55, 113.
Martin, William, 72, 80, 93, 103.
Mason, Abram, 86.
Mason, David, 130.
Mason, Isaac, 130.
Mason, Joseph, 6, 130.
Massengale, Robert, 55.
Massey, Thomas, 104.
Masterson, Aaron, 24.
Mastin, Gabriel, 80.
Mathews, James, 44.
Mathews, Obediah, 29.
Mathews, Sampson, 27.
Matlock, Charles, 44.
Matlock, George, 63.
Matlock, Jason, 79.

Matlock, John, 79.
Matthews, Ebenezer, 128.
Matthews, John, 90, 122.
Matthews, Obediah, 8.
Matthews, Sampson, 27, 121.
Mattocks, Edward, 73.
Maury, Riley, 118.
Maxwell, James, 118.
Maxwell, James M., 44.
Maxwell, John, 80.
Maxwell, Samuel, 75.
Maxwell, Thomas, 6.
May, James, 49.
Maybary, Frederick, 8.
Mayberry, Frederick, 75.
Mayberry, Henry, 114.
Mayberry, Jacob, 60.
Mayberry, John, 122.
Maye, Henry, 74.
Mayfield, Solomon, 122.
Mayo, Jacob, 83.
Mayo, Valentine, 70.
Mays, William, 113.
Means, Andrew, 120.
Means, William, 52.
Mebane, George, 67.
Medling, Lewis, 88.
Medlock, Mo, 120.
Medlock, Smith, 95.
Meek, Viven M. 121
Meeole, James, 57.
Melone, Jesse, 47.
Melvin, Thomas, 35.
Mendinhall, Martin, 20.
Menees, Benjamin, Jr., 27.
Menees, Benjamin W., 99.
Menees, Isaac, 27.
Mercer, Jones, 35.
Meredith, Samuel, 105.
Merrow, Richard, 24.
Messer, John, 27.
Messor, Jones, 75.
Metcalf, William, 55.
Metheny, John, 82.
Micklebury, Robert, 65.
Miers, Miles, 90.
Milburn, Jonathan, 15.
Miles, Richard, 26.
Miles, William, 27.
Millard, Nathaniel, 70.
Millen, William, 90.
Miller, Garland, 111.
Miller, Jacob, 18, 75, 94.
Miller, James, 123.
Miller, John, 10, 24, 31, 43, 77, 92, 95.
Miller, Joseph, 129.
Miller, Joseph H. 97, 119

Miller, Michael, 57.
Miller, Peter, 128.
Miller, Robert, 24.
Miller, Samuel, 85.
Miller, Thomas, 58.
Miller, Thomas H., 96.
Miller, William, Jr., 29.
Millican, Hugh, 106.
Milligan, Alexander, 93, 109.
Milligan, William, 68.
Mills, David, 54.
Mills, Henry, 114.
Milton, Joel, 49.
Missmer, John, 93.
Mitcalf, Anthony, 46.
Mitchell, Adam, 128.
Mitchell, Charles, 79, 85.
Mitchell, Daniel, 90.
Mitchell, Edward, 18, 37.
Mitchell, George, 118.
Mitchell, Hiram, 58.
Mitchell, Isaac, 93.
Mitchell, James, 61, 110, 118 (2).
Mitchell, John, 40, 75, 81, 85.
Mitchell, Nathaniel, 8.
Mitchell, Samuel, 85.
Mitchell, Spencer, 49.
Mitchell, Thomas, 13, 54.
Mitchell, William, 18, 35.
Mitcheson, William, 26.
Mixson, William, 82.
Moad, Ludwick, 108.
Mock, Joseph, 128.
Moffet, Robert, 65.
Molton, Michael, 72.
Monday, Reubin, 96.
Monroe, George, 113.
Montgomery, Alexander, 5, 49.
Montgomery, James, 46, 101.
Montgomery, Murphrey, 5.
Montgomery, William, 48, 102.
Moody, Martin, 55.
Moon, Chaney, 116.
Moon, William, 39, 109.
Moony, William, 73.
Moore, Achillis, 115.
Moore, Alexander, 10, 35, 73.
Moore, Edward, 45.
Moore, Edwin S., 54.
Moore, Hugh G., 75, 114.
Moore, James, 5.
Moore, John, 56, 83, 96, 118.
Moore, Robert, 81.
Moore, Robert M., 65.
Moore, Samuel, 31.
Moore, Shadrick, 82.
Moore, William, 50, 111, 118.
Moores, Isaac, 101.

Morehead, John, 77.
Moreland, William, 70.
Morgan, Evan, 109.
Morgan, Gideon, 96.
Morgan, James, 18.
Morgan, Joseph, 75.
Morrel, Thomas, 31, (2).
Morris, Andrew, 77.
Morris, Dempsey, 72.
Morris, Dempsy, 72.
Morris, Demsey, 54.
Morris, Hezekiah, 99.
Morris, Shadrach, 15.
Morris, Shadrick, 73.
Morris, Thomas, 74.
Morris, William, 72.
Morrison, James, 77.
Morriss, John, 44.
Morriss, Shadrach, 13.
Morrisson, Thomas, 5.
Morrouson, Joseph, 35.
Morrow, George, 56.
Morrow, James, 79.
Morrow, William, 45.
Mors, John, 92.
Morse, George, 41.
Morton, James, 45.
Morton, Quin, 50.
Morton, William, 72.
Moseley, James, 40.
Motheral, James, 72.
Motherall, James, 72.
Motherall, John, 10.
Motherel, John, 10.
Mount, Humphrey, 58.
Muirheed, William, 114.
Mulendore, Abraham, 29.
Mullindore, Abraham, 46.
Murphey, David, 20.
Murphey, Samuel, 46.
Murphey, William, 53.
Murphy, Edward, 113.
Murphy, William, 97.
Murray, Francis, 106.
Murray, William, 33.
Murrey, Jacob, 38.
Murry, Francis, 86, 88.
Murry, James, 110.
Myers, Jacob, 41.
Myers, James, 20.
Myers, John, 48.
Myers, Lewis, 75.
Myers, Phillip, 127.
Mynett, Thomas, 96.
Mynett, William, 75.
Myres, David, 20.
Nail, James, 106.
Nance, Bird, 10, 123.
Napier, George F., 90.

Napier, John, 110.
Naramore, John, Junior, 107.
Nash, George R., 81.
Nash, John, 81.
Nash, Travis C., 123.
Nations, Nathaniel, 49.
Nations, Thomas, 76.
Neal, James, 67.
Neal, Matthew, 127.
Neal, Patrick, 83.
Neal, Peter, 53.
Neal, William, 35.
Neel, Benjamin 41
Neel, David, 54.
Neeley, Joseph, 33.
Neeley, William, 10.
Neely, Clement, 88.
Neely, George, 10.
Neely, James, 58.
Neely, James S., 119.
Neely, John, 49, 78.
Neely, Richard, 88.
Neely, William, 10, 92.
Neely, William Washington, 8.
Neil, Arthur, 66.
Neil, Hamilton, 41, 113.
Neil, Patrick, 47, 83.
Neill, Arthur, 85.
Neilson, Joseph H., 114.
Nelms, William, 110.
Nelson, Alexander, 18 (2), 19.
Nelson, David, 24.
Nelson, George, 74.
Nelson, John, 58, 128.
Nelson, Lewis, 5.
Nelson, Preston, 111.
Nelson, Samuel, 36.
Nelson, Thomas, 76.
Nevill, Joseph, 85.
Newel, William, 60.
Newhouse, Isaac, 126.
Newland, Thomas, 39.
Newman, Daniel, 129.
Newman, John, 16.
Newman, Peter, 85.
Newman, Samuel, 76.
Newton, Robert, 110.
Niblet, Edward, 60.
Nichol, John, 52.
Nicholas, Flail, 29.
Nicholas, John, 124.
Nicholson, Jeremiah, 20.
Nicholson, John, 119.
Nicholson, Joseph, 21.
Nicholson, Richard, 16.
Noblett, Edward, 98.
Nolen, Berry, 36.
Nolen, Robert, 10.
Norfleet, James, 27.

Norman, Joseph, 44.
Norman, William, 73.
Norrell, Philip, 70.
Norris, Thomas, 97.
Norton, Edward, 101.
Norward, John, 36.
Norwood, Samuel, 5.
Nuling Henry, 92.
Nusbell, John, 40.
Oaks, Isaac, 61.
Oakwood, Henry, 75.
Oar, John, 110.
Obar, Daniel, 114.
Ode, Nehemiah, 109.
Ode, Solomon, 109.
Odell, Nehemiah, 54.
Oden, John, 79.
Officer, Thomas, 120.
Ogdon, John, 8.
Ogle, William, 124.
Ogwin, Stephen, 43.
Oldinger, John, 74.
Olive, Joel, 82.
Oliver, Durrett 51
Oliver, Lunsford, 50
Oliver, Richard, 24 (2).
Oneal, James, 51.
Oneal, John, 56.
Oneal, Robert, 44.
Ore, James, 13.
Orr, Alexander, 100.
Orrick, John, 118.
Orsbon, Icabud, 10.
Orton, Richard, 104.
Orton, William, 10.
Osborn, Icabud, 27.
Oslin, John, 130.
Outlaw, Right, 119.
Outlaw, Willie, 78.
Overall, Abraham, 124.
Overall, Nace, 123.
Owen, John, 47.
Owen, William, 47.
Owens, Benjamin, 27.
Owens, Edward, 24.
Owens George, H., 79.
Owens, John, 75.
Owens, Michael, 126.
Owing, William, 121.
Oyler, Jonathan, 27.
Ozburn, Michael, 29.
Ozburn, Samuel, 65.
Pace, Gideon, 99.
Pain, Thomas, 63.
Paine, Charles, 113.
Pale, (Pate), Stephen, 29.
Pale, (Pate), Willecoy, 29.
Palmer, Isham, 132.
Pangle, Frederick, 21.

Pangle, Isaac, 42.
Panter, Joseph, 69.
Parker, Aaron, 75.
Parker, Benjamin, 93.
Parker, Benjamin C., 24.
Parker, Daniel, 123.
Parker, David, 10.
Parker, Isaac, 33.
Parker, James, 103.
Parker, John, 61.
Parker, John C., 110.
Parker, Josiah, 36.
Parker, Robert, 120.
Parker, William, 40.
Parkerson, Daniel, 90.
Parkerson, Manuel, 129.
Parks, John, 10, 50, 86, 106.
Parks, William, 118.
Parmer, Martin, 111.
Parr, William, 119.
Parrott, Benjamin, 120.
Parson, George, 16.
Parsons, Joshua, 107.
Parsons, Robert, 5.
Pate, Charles, 100.
Pate, Kinchen, 130.
Pate, Stephen, 29, 58.
Pate, Thomas, 29.
Pate, Willecoy, 29.
Patterson, Arthur, 112.
Patterson, Banard M., 112.
Patterson, David, 27.
Patterson, John, 29.
Patterson, Mathew 72
Patterson, Robert, 19.
Patterson, Thomas, 82.
Patterson, William, 16.
Patton, Alexander, 10.
Patton, David, 65.
Patton, Francis, 88.
Patton, George, 86.
Patton, Isaac, 67.
Patton, John, 86, 88.
Patton, Thomas C., 103.
Paty, Jesse, 47.
Paxton, Joshua, 110.
Payne, George, 10.
Payne, Matthew, 10.
Payne, Sampson, 84.
Payne, Sylvester, 106.
Payton, William, 65.
Peacock, William, 111.
Peake, John M., 62.
Pearce, Abner, 125.
Pearce, Isaac, 33.
Pearsall, Edward, 40.
Pearson, Abel, 6.
Peck, Jacob, 21.
Peery, John, 75.

Penell, (Perrel), George, 54.
Penn, Joseph, 74.
Penney, James, 16.
Pennington, Joel, 118.
Penny, William, 78.
Peoples, William, 90.
Percy, James, 79.
Perkins, John, 97.
Perkins, John B., 84.
Perriman, James, 19.
Perrin, Joel, 14.
Perry, Robert, 28, 99.
Perry, Samuel, 14.
Perry, Thomas, 106.
Perviance, Alexander, 105.
Peteet, James, 88.
Peters, Brewton, 56.
Peters, Brutin, 74.
Peters, George Smith, 70.
Peterson, Isaac, 26.
Pettet, Nehemiah, 16.
Pettice, Horatio, 130.
PettyJohn, Abraham, 85.
Phagan, John, 83.
Pharus, Hezekius, 73.
Phayton, Evans, 116.
Phelen, Richard C., 54.
Phenix, Henry, 10.
Philips, William 49, 75, 114
Phillips, Isaac, 28.
Phillips, John, 112.
Phillips, Jonathan, 10.
Phillips, Merrel, 54.
Phillips, Reubin, 99.
Phillips, Samuel, 10.
Pickins, James, 92.
Pierce, Moses, 95.
Piles, Leonard, 72.
Pillow, Gideon, 11.
Pillow, William 11 (2), 59
Pinkley, Daniel, 121.
Piper, John, 30, 47.
Pipkin, Philip, 11, 110.
Pipkin, Phillip, 11.
Pirtle, Nathaniel, 48.
Pitt, Stephen, 84.
Pittman, William, 50.
Pitts, Burwell, 121.
Plumly, Daniel, 126.
Plummer, Richard, 99.
Poils, Conrath, 14.
Polk, William, 59, 119.
Polly, Elijah, 53.
Pooker, Jacob, 93.
Pool, Jacob, 82.
Porter, Alexander, 129.
Porter, John, 118.
Porter, Joseph, 36.
Porter, Stephen, 114.

Porter, William, 60.
Posey, David, Campbell, 70.
Poston, John H., 78.
Poteet, Squire, 61.
Poteet, Thomas, 86.
Pots, John, 106.
Potter, Benjamin, 68.
Potter, William, 109.
Potter, Wilson, 109.
Potters, Archibald, 67.
Powel, Benjamin, 114.
Powel, Obediah, 111.
Powell, Samuel, 57.
Powers, Lewis, 95 (2).
Powers, Robert, 130.
Prater, Andrew, 112.
Pratt, Barnard, 70.
Prentice, Robert, 29.
Preston, Alexander, 46.
Preston, George, 24 (2).
Preston, James, 24 (2).
Preston, Thomas, 65.
Prewet, Moses, 69.
Prewet, William, 30.
Prewett, Isaac, 129.
Prewett, Jacob, 24.
Price, Daniel, 77.
Price, Henry, 93.
Price, Reuben, 24.
Price, William, 65.
Pride, Benjamin, 24.
Profit, Pleasant, 53.
Profit, Robert, 56.
Profitt, Pleasant, 38.
Prothro, David, 31.
Pruet, Jacob, 24.
Pruett, Isaac, 85.
Pryar, Jonathan, 41.
Pryer, William, 21.
Pryor, James, 83.
Pucket, Lewis, 43.
Puckett, Shiply A., 81.
Pugh, Jesse, 101.
Pullen, Henry, 92.
Punch, John, 31.
Pursley, David, 11.
Qualls, John, 105.
Quarles, John, 132.
Quin, Morton, 37.
Quinn, James, 92.
Radford, Edward, 11.
Ragan, William, 91.
Ragsdale, Lancaster, 130.
Rainey, Elisha, 98.
Rains, Asahel, 84.
Rains, John, 11.
Rains, William, 11.
Rallings, Moses, 36.
Ramsey, John, 121.

Ramsey, Joshua, 59.
Ramsey, Robert, 45.
Ramsey, William, 45, 123.
Rankin, James, 21.
Rankin, Samuel S., 42.
Rannolds, James, 104.
Ratherford, Thomas 21
Rawles, Abel, 44.
Rawlings, John, 61.
Rawls, Shadrack, 28.
Ray, William, 11.
Raynor, Aaron, 114.
Read, George, 94.
Read, John, 101.
Read, Thomas, 113.
Reader, Jacob, 11.
Reagan, Ahimaaz, 5.
Reasonover, John, 63.
Reaves, Drury, 68.
Rector, John, 8.
Rector, Presly, 90.
Reddick, David, 127.
Redferren, Isaac, 99.
Reed, Drury, 111.
Reed, James, 16.
Reed, Jesse, 111.
Reed, John, 38.
Reed, Joseph, 49.
Reed, Robert, 16, 42.
Reed, Thomas, 93.
Reed, William, 33, 111.
Reeder, Jacob, 11.
Reeves, James, 16, 54.
Regens, William, 117.
Reid, George, 114.
Reid, Robert, 92.
Reid, William, 36.
Reigle, George, 61.
Reigle, George W., 120.
Reigle, Jacob, 120.
Renney, Jesse, 53.
Reno, Jonathan, 115.
Reno, Thomas, 21.
Renshaw, Isaiah, 123.
Rentfroe, Bartlet, 88.
Resterson, John, 16.
Reuby, Thomas, 78.
Reves, Moses, 5.
Reynolds, Benjamin, 59, 97.
Reynolds, George, 41.
Reynolds, John, 78, 96, 123.
Reynolds, Moses, 6.
Reynolds, Reubin, 130.
Reynolds, Robert, 24, (3).
Rhea, George, 47.
Rhea, James, 52, 69, (2).
Rhea, John, 52.
Rhea, Joseph, 31,
Rhea, Robert, 5.

Rhea, Robert P., 83.
Rhea, Samuel, 107.
Rhea, Thomas, 113.
Rice, Archibald, 65.
Rice, David, 16.
Rice, Elijah, 48, 127.
Rice, John, 39.
Rich, Joseph, 93.
Richards, Henry, 83.
Richards, John, 68.
Richards, Tallepharo, 79.
Richards, William, 99.
Richardson, Samuel, 74.
Richardson, William, 29.
Richmond, John, 81.
Rickett, Jonathan, 50.
Ricks, Sandrus, 14.
Riddle, John, 19.
Ridge, Robertson, 70.
Ridge, William, 104.
Riding, Abijah, 97.
Ridley, James, 130.
Right, William, 38.
Rightsell, John, 74.
Riley, Andrew, 59.
Riley, Elisha, 108.
Rivers, Joel T., 130.
Roach, Littleton, 58, 77, 96.
Roadman, William C., 66, 103.
Roads, John, 101.
Roads, William, 88.
Roark, John, 94.
Robbins, William, 95.
Roberson, James, 88.
Roberts, Collin 98
Roberts, Daniel, 73.
Roberts, George, 19.
Roberts, Isaac, 11.
Roberts, Jesse, 89.
Roberts, John, 16, 88.
Roberts, Joshua, 121.
Roberts, Nathan, 24.
Robertson, Andrew, 58.
Robertson, Charles, 36, 48.
Robertson, Christopher, 40.
Robertson, Hughes, 14.
Robertson, James, 51.
Robertson, John, 16, (2), 105, 132.
Robertson, Jonathan B., 47, 101.
Robertson, Jonathan F., 11.
Robertson, Michael, 38.
Robertson, Moses, 63.
Robertson, Rhederick, 72.
Robertson, Thomas, 124.
Robertson, William, 101.
Robinson, Israel, 119.
Robinson, John, 78.
Robinson, Thomas, 75.
Rochel, Amos, 60.

Rock, John, 57.
Roddy, James, 52.
Rodgers, Josiah, 29.
Roe, Benjamin, 125.
Rogers, Elisha, 51.
Rogers, George, 29, 124.
Rogers, James R., 99.
Rogers, Jeremiah, 24.
Rogers, Jesse, 83.
Rogers, John 51, 55, 90 (2), 107, 110
Rogers, Joseph, 47, 51, 73.
Rogers, Larkin, 26.
Rogers, Peter, 68.
Rogers, Reuben, 5, (2).
Rogers, Thomas A., 96.
Rogers, William, 90.
Rogers, William W., 90.
Roland, William, 72.
Rolston, Samuel, 118.
Ronly, George, 84.
Rook, John, 78.
Roper, John, 95, 125.
Ross, James, 106.
Ross, Nathan, 82.
Rotton, Richard M., 104.
Roulston, Alexander, 86, 104.
Roulston, James, 75.
Roulston, John, 54.
Roundtree, Thomas, 92.
Rowan, William, 75.
Rowark, Reubin, 125.
Rowland, William, 72.
Royston, John, 64, 101.
Ruble, Jacob, 48.
Rucker, James, 62.
Rudd, William, 107.
Rushing, Elijah, 82.
Rushing, John, 60.
Russell, David, 119.
Russell, George, 104.
Russell, Hezekiah, 74.
Russell, John, 16.
Russell, Lewis, 91.
Russell, William, 30.
Ruth, John, 46.
Rutherford, William, 72.
Rutledg, Robert, 31.
Rutledge, George, 31.
Rutledge, James, 59.
Rutledge, William, 37, 41, 119.
Ryborne, Thomas, 60.
Sample, Samuel, 24.
Samples, Robert, 74.
Sanders, Daniel, 99.
Sanders, James, 127.
Sanders, Robert 65, 99
Sanders, William, 30.
Sanderson, Edward, 82, 125.
Sands, Jacob, 98.

Sands, Othnial, 113.
Sandusky, Emanually, 39.
Sargant, John H., 62.
Sarver, George, 84.
Saunders, Adam, 63.
Saunders, Isham, 88.
Saunders, John, 19.
Saunders, Turner, 105.
Saveley, John, 127.
Sawyers, John, 24.
Scaggs, Elie, 24.
Scallions, Joab, 65.
Scarborough, John, 101.
Scarborough, Robert, 87.
Scoby, John, 82.
Scoby, Matthew, 33.
Scott, Andrew, 41.
Scott, Arthur, 117.
Scott, James, 5.
Scott, John, 31, 101.
Scott, Joseph, 83.
Scott, Laurence, 25.
Scott, Robert, 78.
Scott, William, 8, 11, 112, 126.
Scrivener, David, 121.
Scruggs, Allen, 72.
Scruggs, James, 50, 68, 106.
Scurry, Thomas, 102.
Searcy, Peter, 115.
Searcy, William W., 45, 100.
Seduskes, James, 8.
Seehorn, John, 30.
Self, Thomas, 16.
Sellards, Samuel, 21.
Sellers, Drury, 103.
Sellers, Lard, 59.
Selman, Abner, 92.
Senter, Talbert, 19.
Seratt, John, 49.
Seratt, Joseph, 100.
Server, George, 84.
Settle, Edward, 30.
Sevier, Charles, 44.
Sevier, Robert, 77.
Sevier, Valentine, 36.
Sewell, Benjamin, 102.
Sewell, George, 58.
Sewell, John, 108.
Sewell, William, 118.
Sexton, Lewis, 81.
Sexton, Thomas, 120.
Sexton, William, 68.
Shahan, Thomas, 100.
Shall, George, 77.
Shankle, John, 111.
Shannon, David, 11.
Shannon, Joseph, 67.
Shannon, Thomas, 11.
Sharp, Aaron, 98.

Sharp, Isaac, 53.
Sharp, James, 45.
Sharp, John, 96, 117.
Sharp, Joseph, 38.
Sharp, Marcus, 45.
Sharp, Thomas, 56.
Shaver, David, 64.
Shaw, Hugh, 11.
Shaw, Robert, 33.
Shaw, Thomas, 102.
Shaw, William, 85.
Sheham, John, 107.
Shehon, Lewis, 91.
Shelby, Isaac, 60.
Shell, Frederick, 31.
Shelly, John, 6.
Shelton, Cutburd, 14.
Shelton, David, 14, 108.
Shelton Elijah, 113.
Shelton, John, 70.
Shepherd, Thomas 110
Sherrell, John, 5.
Sherrill, Archibald, 86.
Sherrill, John, 5.
Sherrill, Samuel, 69.
Shield, William, 21.
Shields, Henry, 36.
Shields, James, 29.
Shields, Joseph, 36.
Shields, William, 63.
Shinalt, James, 88, 106.
Shipley, Nathan, 36.
Shipley, Robert, 113.
Shiply, Robert, 74.
Shipmant, Jacob, 118.
Shippes, Archibald, 102.
Shoemaker, Leonard Clabourne, 16.
Shofner, John, 88.
Shook, William, 69.
Shot, Caleb, 120.
Shote, John, 25.
Shoulders, Solomon, 84, 102.
Shoulders, William, 102.
Shoults, John, 120.
Shous, John, 11.
Shults, Jacob, 65.
Shults, John, 65.
Shy, Robert, 102.
Sicks, John, 19.
Sidner, Martin, 36.
Sidnor, Martin, 36.
Sills, William, 125.
Simmons, Benjamin, 106.
Simmons, Charles, 28.
Simmons, Flemmon R., 78.
Simmons, Henry, 29.
Simmons, Joel, 63.
Simmons, Thomas, 49, 67, 117.
Simmons, William, 107.

Simms, Robert, 112.
Simpson, Andrew, 115.
Simpson, David, 65.
Simpson, John W., 129.
Simpson, Robert, 102.
Simpson, Thomas, 95.
Simpson, William, 59.
Sims, James, 131.
Sims, Mathew, 14.
Singleton, John, 5.
Sitton, William, 118.
Sively, Jacob, 21.
Skeets, John, 89.
Skidmore, Henry, 14.
Skillern, Isaac C. A., 79.
Skippeth, Needham, 6.
Slaughter, Abraham, 64.
Slaughter, Henry, 77.
Sloan, Joseph, 70.
Sloan, William, 5.
Smart, George B., 127.
Smart, Philip, 86, (2).
Smart, William, 99, 121.
Smartt, William C., 84.
Smith, Alexander, 19, 90.
Smith, Allan, 19.
Smith, Andrew, 104.
Smith, Beverly, 114.
Smith, Bird, 104, 132.
Smith, Charles, 132.
Smith, Cornelious, 16.
Smith, Cornelius, 16.
Smith, Daniel, 7.
Smith, David, 118, (2), 129.
Smith, Drury, 79.
Smith, Ebenezer, 49.
Smith, Elias, 71.
Smith, Ezekiel, 14.
Smith, Iri, 61.
Smith, Jackson, 94.
Smith, James, 38, 125.
Smith, Jasper, 118.
Smith, John, 5, 19, 33, 91.
Smith, John A., 61, 120.
Smith, Joseph, 19, 25, 85, 129.
Smith, Josiah, 50.
Smith, Merrewether, 79.
Smith, Moses, 59.
Smith, Nathaniel 45, 114
Smith, Patrick, 38.
Smith, Peton, 110.
Smith, Reuben, 25.
Smith, Robert, 37, 53, 60.
Smith, Samuel, 19.
Smith, Thomas, 56, 74, 88, 114.
Smith, Weeks, 131.
Smith, William, 11, 100, (2), 104, 112.
Smith, William J., 43.
Smith, Willis R., 91.

Smotherman, John, 81, 123.
Smyly, Thomas, 65.
Snap, Laurence, 66.
Snelson, James, 8.
Snider, George, 5.
Snider, Isaac, 101.
Snider, Peter, 5.
Snody, James, 76.
Snoddy, James, 58.
Snoddy, Samuel, 75, 100.
Snoddy, William, 33.
Snodgrass, David, 126.
Snodgrass, James, 8, 90.
Snodgrass, William, 31, (2), 43.
Snyder, Henry, 47.
Solomon, James, 71.
Sommers, Abraham, 37.
Sommerville, Robert, 98.
Southerin, William, 121.
Sparks, Isaac, 95.
Spearman, Samuel, 99.
Spears, John, 107.
Speight, William, 111.
Spence, Lewis, 72.
Spence, Thomas, 99.
Spencer, Charles, Jr., 115.
Spickant, Jacob, 37.
Spilman, Isaac, 75.
Spinks, John, 68.
Spivy, James, 75.
Spoon, Abraham, 93.
Spradlen, Jesse, 102.
Spradley, Tavenner, 68.
Spral, John, 86.
Spring, Valentine, 51.
Spurgin, John, 61.
Squibb, John, 36.
Srigly, Samuel, 59.
Stacy, Mashak, 19.
Stacy, William, 132.
Stanburg, William, 16.
Standefer, Samuel 25
Standefor, Samuel, 25.
Standford, Thomas, 92.
Stanfield, John, 16.
Stanford, Hugh, 119.
Stanley, Rodes, 25.
Starns, Jacob, 128.
Starns, Jesse, 48.
Starrit, Joseph, 106.
Steal, Andrew, 16.
Steel, John, 68.
Steel, Joseph, 33.
Steel, Nathaniel Harrison 97
Steele, Robert, 59, 93.
Steele, Samuel, 37.
Steele, William, 37.
Steelee, Henry, 121.
Stephens, Henry, 123.

Stephens, Isaac, 51, 64, (2).
Stephens, Peter, 64.
Stephenson, Andrew, 81.
Stephenson, James, 16, 124.
Stephenson, Moore, 33.
Stepherson, Matthew, 36.
Sterns, Jacob, 58, (2).
Sterns, John, 16, 33.
Stewart, Aaron, 132.
Stewart, Cirus, 105.
Stewart, David, 120.
Stewart, Henry, 105.
Stewart, James, 96, 131.
Stewart, James R., 77.
Stewart, John, 33.
Stewart, Samuel P., 98.
Stewart, William, 72, 94, 111.
Stiles, John, 101.
Still, Daniel, 49.
Stinnet, William, 8.
Stinson, Andrew, 63.
Stobough, John C., 86.
Stokes, Benjamin, 44.
Stoly, Henry, 80.
Stone, John, 25.
Stone, Eusebius, 33.
Stone, William 65, 127
Storm, John, 7.
Stout, Abraham, 121.
Stover, Joseph, 108.
Stoydell, John, 38.
Strain, James, 109.
Strain, Robert, 128.
Stramler, George, 11.
Strange, Beverly, 63, 125.
Straton, Calvin, 102.
Street, James, 84.
Street, Lefever, 127.
Stringer, Gray, 100.
Strong, John, 101.
Strother, John, 100.
Strother, Robert, 101.
Stroud, Isaac, 14.
Strungfellow, Robert, 110.
Stubbelfield, George 33
Stubblefield, William, 19.
Studevent, Randolph, 115.
Stump, John, 11, (2), 55, 110.
Stump, Jonathan, 11.
Styers, Henry, 8.
Sulvent, Edward, 101.
Sumpter, John, 19.
Surguine, James, 19.
Sutherland, George, 68, (2).
Sutton, John, 88.
Sutton, Joseph, 39, 54.
Swallow, Jacob, 44.
Swan, Thomas, 44.
Sweeten, Tesse, 73.

Swingley, Nicholas, 68.
Sysemore, Edward, 57.
Tacker, Joshua, 93.
Tacket, David, 123.
Taffee, John, 116.
Tait, John, 125.
Talbert, Frederick, 14.
Tannihill, Wilkins, 110.
Tarben, John, 41.
Tarkinton, Jesse, 11.
Tate, David, 16, (2).
Tate, Edward, 16.
Tate, James, 65.
Tate, Robert, 127.
Tate, William, 42.
Tate, Zachariah, 63.
Tateham, Peter, 67.
Tatum, James, 40.
Tawnyhill, Benjamin Harris, 106.
Tawnyhill, John, 118.
Taylor, Argyle, 42.
Taylor, Daniel, 14.
Taylor, David, 118.
Taylor, Ezekiel, 117.
Taylor, Henry, 36, 43.
Taylor, Jacob, 102.
Taylor, James, 5, 107.
Taylor, John, 11, 19, 31, 50, 52, 113, 127.
Taylor, John C., 118.
Taylor Joseph, 25.
Taylor, Lewis, 97.
Taylor, Michael, 88.
Taylor, Nathaniel, 7.
Taylor, Samuel, 55, 110.
Taylor, Solomon, 86.
Taylor, Walter, 50.
Taylor, William, 36, 89.
Taylor, William S., 52.
Teal, George, 111.
Teas, William, 26.
Tedford, George, 5.
Tedford, Hugh, 37.
Tempel, William, 25.
Temple, James, 16, (2).
Temple, Robert, 78.
Temple, Thomas, 16.
Templeton, John, 129.
Tenen, Thomas, 26.
Terrel, Laten, 41.
Terry, Jesse, 25.
Terry, Richard, 14.
Terry, Samuel, 25.
Tharp, Jonathan, 69.
Tharp, Levi, 51.
Thomas, Benjamin, 26.
Thomas, David, 47.
Thomas, Ellis, 63.
Thomas, Ephraim, 57.
Thomas, Grant (?), 43.

Thomas, Grieph, 29.
Thomas, Hamilton, 123.
Thomas, Ichabud, 82, 101.
Thomas, Isaac, 63.
Thomas, James, 67, 125.
Thomas, Nathaniel, 40.
Thomas, Nevill, 129.
Thomas, Tristram, 94.
Thompson, David, 58.
Thompson, Jacob, 40.
Thompson, James, 11.
Thompson, John, 19, (2).
Thompson, Leonard, 131.
Thompson, Lyle, 43.
Thompson, Moses, 79, 132.
Thompson, Neal, 105.
Thompson, Robert, 25.
Thompson, Samuel, 11, 52.
Thompson, Thomas, 11, (2).
Thompson, William 11, 117
Thompson, William W., 78.
Thorlaton, Robert, 16, (2).
Thornberry, Martin, 68.
Thurman, Eli, 51.
Tilley, John, 11.
Tilmon, Haiden, 65.
Tilson, John, 103.
Timberlick, John C., 99.
Tindall, Charles, 96.
Tindle, Samuel, 120.
Tinnen, Alexander, 43.
Tippet, James, 62.
Tipton, James, 52.
Tipton, John, 31, 52, (2).
Tipton, Jonathan, 7.
Tipton, Thomas, 7.
Tollock, David, 102.
Tompkins, James, 7.
Tompkins, John B., 98.
Toomy, John, 63.
Touson, William J., 47.
Townsen, Whitfield, 88.
Townsen, William, 92.
Townsend, John, 129.
Tracey, Evan, 12.
Traler, Hiram, 95.
Trap, John, 85.
Trice, James, 119.
Trigg, William, 78.
Trotter, John, 21, 60.
Trousdale, Alexander, 26.
Trout, Michael, 117.
Tubb, James, 125, (2).
Tucker, James, 95.
Tucker, Jeremiah, 86.
Tull, Nicholas, 72.
Tune, Lewis, 105.
Tunnell, James, 37, 106.
Tunnell, William, 106.

Turner, Anthony, J., 97, (2).
Turner, Daniel, 99.
Turner, Elisha, 72.
Turner, James, 21, 44.
Turner, Jesse, 78.
Turner, Jirasha, 30.
Turner, John, 74.
Turner, Samuel T., 65.
Turner, William, 65, 91.
Turney, Henry, 63.
Tuton, John, 121.
Tuton, Zacheus, 121.
Twett, Henry M., 115.
Tyner, Lewis, 31.
Tyrrel, Edmund, 72.
Underwood, John, 37.
Underwood, William, 77.
Ussery, Richard, 125.
Ussery, William, 25.
Vanbibber, John, 14.
Vance, David G., 66.
Vance, John, 21.
Vance, Samuel, 43.
Vance, William K. 85, 128
Vandegriff, Gilbert, Jr. 93
Vanhoozer, Valentine, 58.
Vannoy, William, 7.
Vanzant, Abraham, 92.
Varner, Nathan, 91.
Varnille, Joseph, 46.
Vashers, John, 119.
Vaughn, Peter, 123.
Veech, Elijah, 21.
Venable, Richard, 106.
Venbeber, Peter, 14.
Vernon, Miles, 107.
Viney, Jesse, 66.
Vineyard, John, Jr., 56.
Vining, John, 65.
Vinson, James, 33.
Vistol, Jeremiah, 124.
Vivrett, Lancelett, 105.
Voden, William, 47.
Wade, Austin M., 110.
Wade, Edward, 88.
Waddell, George, 64.
Waddle, David, 46, 124.
Waddill, Charles, 36, (2).
Waddill, Jonathan, 128.
Waggoner, George, 110.
Waggoner, Jacob, 72, 118.
Walk, John, 107.
Walker, Abraham, 12.
Walker, Andrew, 101.
Walker, Archalas, 91.
Walker, Hance, 105.
Walker, James, 31, 88.
Walker, John, 5, 50, 61, 63, 66, 67, 72, 75.
Walker, John B., 105.

Walker Matthew P., 72.
Walker, Nicholas T., 72.
Walker, Noah, 86.
Walker, Patterson, 120.
Walker, Robert, 82.
Walker, Samuel, 70, 125.
Walker, Thomas, 88, 99, 107.
Walker, William, 5, 52, 61, 68, 77.
Wall, Daniel, 50.
Wallace, Joel, 5.
Wallace, John, 102.
Wallace, Oliver, 62.
Wallace, Robert B., 83.
Wallace, William, 89.
Wallen, Stephen, 31.
Wallice, Thomas, 36.
Walling, James, 19.
Walroud, William, 29.
Walters, John, 21.
Walton, Isaac, 33.
Walton, Josiah, 48, 65.
Walton, Meredith, 28, 80.
Ward, Burrel, 45, 123.
Ward, David, 109.
Ward, Dickson, 125.
Ward, John, 12, 82.
Ward, Joseph J., 112.
Warden, John, 90.
Ware, James, 31.
Warnar, Stephen, 25.
Warner, John, 50.
Warnock, William, 50.
Warren, Bluford, 104, 129.
Warren, Joseph, 127.
Warren, Zachariah, 84.
Washington, Frederick, 98.
Washington, Robert Gray, 119.
Waters, John, 131.
Waters, Thomas, 101.
Watkins, Charles, 84, 102.
Watkins, Daniel, 50.
Watson, John, 25.
Watson, Samuel, 65, 102.
Watson, Thomas B., 93.
Watson, William, 53.
Wattson, James, 5.
Weakley Benjamin, 28.
Weakley, David, 28.
Weakley, John, 60.
Weakley, Robert, 12.
Wear, George, 36.
Wear, Hugh, 52, (2), 107.
Wear, James, 6.
Wear, Samuel, 29.
Weaver, Benjamin, 129.
Weaver, Christian, 40.
Weaver, Elijah, 61.
Webb, Aaron, 31.
Webb, Abel, 31.

Webb, Able, 37.
Webb, Benjamin, 31, (2).
Webb, Jacob, 66.
Webb, Jesse, 66.
Webb, Littleberry, 84.
Webb, Ross, 98.
Webb, William, 66.
Webster, John, 19.
Webster, Jonathan, 88.
Weir, James, 6.
Weir, Merit, 84.
Welch, James, 59.
Weldon, John, 52.
Welks, Daniel, 105.
Wells, Archelas, 26.
Wells, Archelus, 26.
Wells, Archibald, 26.
Wells, Thomas, 105.
Welton, Samuel, 123.
West, Henry, 96.
West, John B., 76.
West, William, 39.
Western, William, 7.
Westmoreland, Jesse, 112.
Wetzel, John H., 25.
Wetzell, John H., 25.
Wever, Benjamin, 14.
Wheeler, Greenberry, 128.
Wheeler, John, 25.
Wherry, Simeon, 84.
Whipple, Bray, 119.
Whitacer, John, Junior, 50.
Whitacer, John, Senior, 50.
White, Andrew, 25.
White, David, 33, (2), 74.
White, Ewing, 118.
White, Frederick, 74.
White, Jacob, 12.
White, James, 25, 78.
White, Moses, 25.
White, Richard, 103.
White, Robert, 33.
White, Samuel, 30.
White, Stephen F., 50, 123.
White, Thomas, 48.
White, Thomas B., 110.
White, William, 16, 62, 79, 95, 118, 123.
Whitehurst, Pelatiah, 125.
Whiteside, Abraham, 25.
Whitesitt, Joseph, 67.
Whitfield, Needham, 60.
Whithead, John, 16.
Whitnell, Josiah, 31.
Whitsell, Laurence, 102.
Whitsett, James, 33, 82.
Whitson, George, 97.
Whitson, Isaac, 7.
Whitten, Archibald, 48.
Whittin, Robert, 105.

Whittle, Robert, 14.
Whittsets, Lawrence, 33.
Whitworth, Philman, 60.
Wilbourne, James, 45.
Wilbourne, Robert, 125.
Wilhite, John, 114.
Wilkerson, Allen, 82.
Wilkerson, Daniel, 82.
Wilkins, James, 97.
Wilkinson, Samuel, 121, (2).
Willeford, William, 100.
William, John, 43, 50.
Williams, Archibald, 7.
Williams, Beverly, 68.
Williams, Charles, 92.
Williams, Coleman, 132.
Williams, David, 61.
Williams, Elijah, 48.
Williams, Garland, 100.
Williams, Green, 132.
Williams, Henry, 26.
Williams, Isaac, 46, 56, 132.
Williams, James, 19, 69, 78, 82, 98, 103, 120, 126.
Williams, John, 6, 29, 61, 63, 107.
Williams, John, Esquire, 117.
Williams, Joseph, 19.
Williams, Joshua, 50.
Williams, Matthias, 99.
Williams, Newton, 120.
Williams, Peter, 44, (2).
Williams, Pierce, 28.
Williams, Rite, 12.
Williams, Sampson, 33.
Williams, Samuel H., 97.
Williams, Silas, 14.
Williams, Theophilus, 75.
Williams, Thomas, 8.
Williams, William, 14, 76, 129.
Williams, William C., 120.
Williams, Wright, 96.
Williamson, Elisha, 74.
Williamson, John, 12, 72, 86.
Williamson, John S., 40.
Williamson, Joseph N., 72, 91.
Williamson, Thomas, 12, (2).
Williamson, William, 89.
Willis, Abel, 61.
Willis, Henry, 61.
Willis, Richard, 33.
Willoughby, Elijah, 16.
Wills, James, 12.
Wills, Peter, 7.
Willson, Michael, 19.
Wilson, Aaron, Junior, 106.
Wilson, Abraham, 56, 76.
Wilson, Benjamin, 25, 84.
Wilson, David, 114.
Wilson, James, 33, 84, 88, 118.

Wilson, James, Jr., 105.
Wilson, Jason, 131.
Wilson, John, 93, 105.
Wilson, Joseph, 57.
Wilson, Michael, 19.
Wilson, Moses, 84.
Wilson, Nicholas, 72.
Wilson, Stephen, 62.
Wilson, Tapley, 38.
Wilson, Thomas, 56.
Wilson, William, 33, 50, 121.
Winchester, James, 33.
Windell, Joseph Hawkins, 61.
Windham, William, 40.
Winenger, Peter, 79.
Winfree, Valentine, 110.
Winfrey, Valentine, 55.
Winkle, Frederick, 74.
Winkle, Jeremiah, 129.
Winn, Philip P., 119.
Winsell, Adam, 70.
Winters, Christopher 41
Winton, William, 21.
Wirrick, Frederick, 74.
Wiseman, John, 118.
Wisener, Henry, 131.
Wisener, James, 131.
Witcher, Lay, 47.
Withers, James, 103.
Witson, Stephen, 39.
Witt, Harman, 120.
Witt, James, 44.
Woldridge, Edmond, 29.
Wolfe, Andrew, 96.
Wombill, Readin, 37.
Wood, James, 36.
Wood, John, 123.
Wood, William, 36.
Woodard, Benjamin, 55, 72.
Woodard, Charles, 120.
Woodard, William, 120.
Woodfork, William, 41.
Woodrich, Josiah, 50.
Woods, Daniel T., 50.
Woods, Israel, 112.
Woods, James, 72.
Woods, John, 6.
Woods, Richard M., 56.
Woods, William, 93.
Woods, William G., 118.
Woodward, Thomas, 25.
Woodward, William, 68.
Woolse, Stephen, 16.
Woolsey, Israel, 93.
Worden, John, 126.
Work, Jacob, 31.
Worley, George, 61.
Worner, Gideon, 88.
Wortham, John, 40, 106.

Wright, Claibourne, 82.
Wright, Isaac, 36, 69.
Wright, Jeremiah, 123.
Wright, John, 48, 89, 91.
Wright, Richard, 45.
Wright, Robert, 86.
Wright, Thomas, 68.
Wright, William, 86.
Wyatt, John, 50.
Wyatt, Samuel, 50.
Wynn, James, 100.
Wynn, Peter, 81.
Wynne, John, 37.
Yandell, Henry, 38.
Yandell, John, 127.
Yardly, Thomas, 123.
Yarnell, Daniel, 96.
Yates, Elias, 88.
Yell, James, 88, (2).
Yoacham, Solomon, 8.

Yoden, David, 113.
Yoden, William P., 113.
York, Richard, 101.
York, William, 14, 36.
Young, Abraham, 28.
Young, Abrim, 80.
Young, Baxter, 132.
Young, Daniel, 79.
Young, Edmund, 88.
Young, Francis, 56.
Young, James, 57.
Young, Jarret, 112.
Young, John, 28.
Young, Jones, 111.
Young, Joseph, 36.
Young, Milton, 47.
Young, Nicholas, 110.
Young, Samuel, 30.
Young, William, 19, 44.

# PART II

# RECORD OF COMMISSIONS OF OFFICERS IN THE TENNESSEE MILITIA, 1812-1815

# RECORD OF COMMISSIONS OF OFFICERS IN THE TENNESSEE MILITIA, 1812

### Compiled by Mrs. John Trotwood Moore

Correction:

In the Williamson County regiments listed in this periodical Vol. VI No. 1 March, 1947, Page 67, the brigade numbers in the records of Samuel Estis and Zacheus Germain should have been nine instead of five.

*Anderson County Regiments*

Anderson, James ..........Captain regiment of Cavalry
                                    3rd brigade ..............July 13 1812
Bledsoe, David ............Ensign 13th regiment .......July 28 1812
Davidson, William, Jr. ......Ensign 13th regiment ......July 1 1812
Dixon, Thomas ............Ensign 13th regiment ......July 1 1812
Dunn, Samuel .............Lieutenant 13th regiment ...July 1 1812
King, James ..............Ensign 13th regiment ......July 1 1812
Kirkpatrick, James ........Lieutenant 13th regiment ...July 1 1812
Leatch, James ............Lieutenant 13th regiment ...July 28 1812
McCampbell, William A. ....Lieutenant regiment of Cavalry
                          L   3rd brigade ..............July 13 1812
Oliver, Lunesford .........First Major 13th regiment ..July 28 1812
Pursley, James ............Cornet regiment of Cavalry
                          L | 3rd brigade ..............July 13 1812
Russell, Thomas ..........Lieutenant 13th regiment ...July 1 1812
Taylor, Samuel ............Lieutenant 13th regiment ...July 1 1812
Tunnell, William, Jr. .......Lieutenant Colonel Commandant
                                13th regiment ..........April 13 1812
Wilson, John ..............Lieutenant 13th regiment ...July 28 1812

*Bedford County Regiments*

Allen, Valentine ..........Lieutenant 28th regiment .March 14 1812
Barrett, Isaac ............Lieutenant Volunteer Rifle
                                Company attached to 28th
                                regiment ............January 14 1812
Blackwell, Nathan ........Lieutenant 28th regiment .March 14 1812
Bradford, John ...........First Major regiment of Cavalry
                                5th brigade .............July 24 1812
Burges, John ..............Ensign Light Infantry Company
                                attached to 28th regiment March 11 1812
Burnon, Jesse .............Ensign Volunteer Rifle Company
                                attached to 47th regiment ...July 24 1812
Cage, Edward ............Captain 47th regiment ......July 24 1812
Coats, John ..............Captain Light Infantry Company
                                attached to 28th regiment .March 11 1812

RECORD OF COMMISSIONS OF OFFICERS

Coats, John ...............First Major 28th regiment ..Dec. 21 1812
Couch, Thomas ............Captain Volunteer Rifle Company
 attached to 47th regiment ...July 24 1812
Crain, Newel ..............Ensign 28th regiment ....March 14 1812
Crump, George ............Ensign 47th regiment .......July 24 1812
Crump, George ............Lieutenant 47th regiment ...July 24 1812
Demsey, John B. ..........Captain 28th regiment ....March 14 1812
*Doherty, Robert ..........Ensign Volunteer Company of
 infantry ................July 3 1812
Fisher, Jacob ..............Lieutenant 28th regiment January 11 1812
Fulton, James C. ...........Lieutenant 28th regiment .August 1 1812
*Gambrell, James H. .......Lieutenant Volunteer Company of
 Infantry ................July 3 1812
Gibson, Thomas ...........Ensign 28th regiment ....March 14 1812
Hamilton, John ............Lieutenant 47th regiment ...July 24 1812
*Hewett, Benjamin ........Captain Volunteer Company of
 Infantry ................July 3 1812
Holt, Michael .............Ensign Volunteer Rifle Company
 attached to 28th regiment .July 14 1812
Irvine, Josephus ...........Lieutenant 47th regiment ...July 24 1812
Jackson, John .............Captain Light Infantry Company
 attached to 47th regiment .July 24 1812
Kelly, Alfred ..............Ensign 28th regiment ....March 14 1812
Kelly, William .............Ensign 47th regiment ......July 24 1812
Larrimer, James ...........Ensign 47th regiment ......July 24 1812
Lovins, Hugh G. ...........Ensign 28th regiment ....August 1 1812
Loyd, Jordan .............Lieutenant 47th regiment ...July 24 1812
McBride, John ............Lieutenant Light Infantry Company
 attached to 28th regiment March 11 1812
McWilliams, John ........Captain 28th regiment ....March 14 1812
Medlin, Lewis ............Captain 28th regiment ....March 14 1812
Milton, Michael ...........Ensign 47th regiment ......July 24 1812
Murphy, Stephen ..........Captain 47th regiment ......July 24 1812
Patterson, Andrew ........Captain 28th regiment ....March 14 1812
Perry, William ...........Lieutenant 28th regiment .March 14 1812
Phillips, Samuel ...........Captain 47th regiment ......July 24 1812
Pickens, Joseph ...........Second Major regiment Cavalry
 5th brigade ..............July 24 1812
Prewet, Moses H. ..........Lieutenant 28th regiment .March 14 1812
Starrot, Joseph ...........Lieutenant Light Infantry Company
 attached to 47th regiment ..July 24 1812
Tolliver, Charles ...........Ensign 47th regiment ......July 24 1812
Wamock, Josiah ...........Ensign Volunteer Rifle Company
 attached to 28th regiment January 14 1812
White, George ............Lieutenant Volunteer Rifle Company
 attached to 47th regiment ...July 24 1812

---

*Voluntary Company of Infantry raised in conformity with the provisions of an act of Congress of the United States passed February 6, 1812.

Williams, James ...........Ensign 28th regiment ...January 11 1812
Winston, John .............Captain 47th regiment ......July 24 1812
Woodrow, Joel ............Ensign Light Infantry Company
                          attached to 47th regiment ...July 24 1812

*Bledsoe County Regiments*

Anderson, Audley .........Captain 31st regiment ..January 11 1812
Brown, Jesse ..............Lieutenant 31st regiment January 11 1812
Bush, John ................Lieutenant 31st regiment January 11 1812
Childers, Joseph ..........Lieutenant 31st regiment ...May 8 1812
Cowan, Samuel ...........Ensign 31st regiment ...February 24 1812
Gilbreath, David ..........Lieutenant 31st regiment ....Feb. 24 1812
Hogan, Richard ...........Ensign Volunteer Rifle Company
                          attached to 31st regiment ..Sept. 11 1812
Holt, Irby ................Captain 31st regiment ..January 11 1812
Jones, John ..............Lieutenant Volunteer Rifle Company
                          attached to 31st regiment ..Sept. 11 1812
Osborn, George ...........Ensign 31st regiment .......May 8 1812
Owens, William ..........Ensign 31st regiment ...January 11 1812
Roberson, James ..........Second Major 31st regiment .Sept. 11 1812
Rogers, Elisha ............Cornet regiment Cavalry
                          8th brigade ..............July 1 1812
Rogers, John .............Captain 31st regiment ...January 11 1812
Rogers, Joseph ...........Captain regiment Cavalry
                          8th brigade ..............July 1 1812
Scott, Hercules ...........Lieutenant 31st regiment ...Nov. 23 1812
Self, Jesse ................Lieutenant 31st regiment ...Feb. 24 1812
Self, Levy ................Ensign 31st regiment ...February 24 1812
Skillern, Anderson ........Lieutenant regiment cavalry
                          8th brigade ..............July 14 1812
Spring, John .............Lieutenant 31st regiment ....Jan. 11 1812
Standifer, James, Jr. .......Captain Volunteer Rifle Company
                          attached to 31st regiment ...Sept. 11 1812
Tallet, Henry .............Ensign 31st regiment ....January 11 1812
White, Silas ..............Captain 31st regiment ....August 5 1812

*Blount County Regiments*

Benson, Matthias .........Lieutenant 12th regiment October 8 1812
Black, George ............Lieutenant 12th regiment .August 6 1812
Cox, John ................Ensign 12th regiment ....October 8 1812
Critenton, Henry .........Ensign 12th regiment ....August 6 1812
Davidson, Samuel C. ......Captain 12th regiment ...August 6 1812
Dearmond, Thomas .......Lieutenant 12th regiment October 8 1812
Dillard, George ...........Lieutenant 12th regiment .August 6 1812
Fusher, Henry ............Ensign 12th regiment ....August 6 1812
Gold, John ...............Lieutenant 12th regiment .August 6 1812
Hanson, William ..........Ensign 12th regiment ....August 6 1812

## RECORD OF COMMISSIONS OF OFFICERS

Harris, Joseph ............. Ensign 12th regiment .... August 6 1812
Holladay, Elliott .......... Ensign 12th regiment .... October 8 1812
Johnson, John ............. Ensign 12th regiment .... August 6 1812
Love, James ............... Lieutenant 12th regiment . August 6 1812
McCartney, James ......... Ensign 12th regiment ...... April 3 1812
McClung, James ........... Lieutenant 12th regiment . August 6 1812
McGhauy, John ........... Lieutenant 12th regiment ... April 3 1812
McKee, Alexander ......... Captain 12th regiment .... August 6 1812
McKercle, Joel ............ Lieutenant 12th regiment . August 6 1812
Orre, Francis ............. Captain 12th regiment ... August 6 1812
Ray, Samuel .............. Ensign 12th regiment .... August 6 1812
Regan, John .............. Captain 12th regiment ... August 6 1812
Rider, Alexander .......... Ensign 12th regiment .... August 6 1812
Stephens, John ........... Captain 12th regiment ... October 8 1812
Strain, John .............. Ensign 12th regiment ... August 6 1812
Thompson, Samuel ........ Captain 12th regiment ... August 6 1812
Trimble, John ............ Captain Volunteer Rifle Company
                                  attached to 12th regiment ... Aug. 6 1812

### Campbell County Regiments

Chambers, Thomas ........ Captain 33rd regiment .... April 29 1812
Dagley, Elias, Sr. ......... Captain 33rd regiment ...... Feb. 27 1812
Gififes, James ............. Ensign 33rd regiment ...... April 29 1812
James, William ........... Captain 33rd regiment ...... July 14 1812
Longimiers, John ......... Captain 33rd regiment ..... Feb. 27 1812
Newman, James .......... Lieutenant 33rd regiment .. April 29 1812
Sharp, Henry ............. Ensign 33rd regiment ...... April 29 1812
Trammel, David .......... Ensign 33rd regiment ...... April 29 1812
Wallen, Evan ............. Lieutenant 33rd regiment .. April 29 1812
Warriner, Thomas ........ Ensign 33rd regiment ...... April 29 1812

### Carter County Regiments

Campbell, John ........... Ensign 5th regiment ........ July 14 1812
McPharson, James ........ Lieutenant 5th regiment . October 14 1812
Moreland, John ........... Ensign 5th regiment .... February 12 1812
Palmer, Anthony ......... Brigade Major 1st brigade .. Aug. 5 1812
Smith, Ezekiel ............ Lieutenant 5th regiment .... Feb. 5 1812
Winant, Vanderpool ....... Lieutenant 5th regiment .... July 14 1812

### Claiborne County Regiments

Blank, Christian .......... Captain 9th regiment ..... March 24 1812
Burges, William .......... Lieutenant 9th regiment .... July 14 1812
Chapman, John ........... Ensign 9th regiment ...... March 24 1812
Davis, Aaron ............. Captain 9th regiment ...... May 21 1812
Dobbs, John .............. Lieutenant 9th regiment .... June 9 1812
Ealey, Barton ............ Ensign 9th regiment ........ May 21 1812

Ealey, William ............Lieutenant 9th regiment ....May 21 1812
Evans, Cornelius ...........Ensign 9th regiment ........July 14 1812
Gomes, Isaiah .............Lieutenant 9th regiment ..March 24 1812
Harper, Joseph ............Lieutenant 9th regiment ....June  9 1812
Hill, Joab ................Lieutenant Colonel Commandant
                            9th regiment .......September  9 1812
Hopson, James ............Ensign 9th regiment ........June  9 1812
McReynolds, James ........Captain 9th regiment ......June  9 1812
McVey, Thomas ...........Lieutenant 9th regiment ....May 21 1812
Moss, Reuben .............Lieutenant Volunteer Rifle Company
                            attached to 9th regiment ...Sept. 11 1812
Ostin, Benjamin ...........Ensign 9th regiment ........May 21 1812
Person, George ...........Captain 9th regiment ......June  9 1812
Rogers, John ..............Captain 9th regiment ......July 14 1812
Sowder, Jacob ............Lieutenant 9th regiment ....June  9 1812
White, William ............Ensign 9th regiment .......May 21 1812

*Cocke County Regiments*

Dunn, William ............Ensign 8th regiment ........July 24 1812
Easterly, Jacob ............Ensign 8th regiment ........July 24 1812
Gilliland, William .........Lieutenant 8th regiment ....July 24 1812
Irvin, Joseph ..............Ensign 8th regiment ........July 24 1812
Jackson, John .............Lieutenant 8th regiment ....July 24 1812
Jackson, Robert ...........Captain 8th regiment ....October  8 1812
Maughan, James ..........Captain 8th regiment ......July 24 1812

*Davidson County Regiments*

Baker, William ...........Lieutenant of cavalry
                            9th brigade ..........March 14, 1812
Benning, James ..........Captain 19th regiment .February 11, 1812
Birdwell, Hugh ............Captain 20th regiment ....April 29, 1812
Boyd, Richard ............Captain 19th regiment....March 24, 1812
Deaderick, David S. ........Lieutenant in company of
                            Republican
                            Blues attached to
                              19th regiment ......December  3, 1812
Dotson, Allen .............Lieutenant 19th regiment ..April 16, 1812
Drury, John ...............Lieutenant 19th regiment .March 24, 1812
Edmiston, Thomas .........Lieutenant of cavalry
                            9th brigade ........December 18, 1812
Edmuston, Andrew J. .......Cornet of cavalry
                            9th brigade .............July 12, 1812
Gwin, John ...............Lieutenant
                            19th regiment ......September 12, 1812
Hobbs, Collin S. ...........Ensign 19th regiment.September 12, 1812

| | | |
|---|---|---|
| Hooper, Absolom | Lieutenant in Capt. Stump's Volunteer troop of cavalry 9th brigade | August 1, 1812 |
| Johnston, Charles | Ensign 19th regiment | July 1, 1812 |
| Kent, William | Lieutenant 19th regiment | February 11, 1812 |
| Lanier, Buchannon | Ensign in Capt. Stump's company of Mounted Infantry attached to 20th regiment | September 15, 1812 |
| Long, John B. | Major of 7th brigade | September 18, 1812 |
| McAdams, William | Lieutenant 20th regiment | April 29, 1812 |
| McCutcheon, James | Captain regiment of cavalry 9th brigade | July 1, 1812 |
| McMurry, William | Ensign 19th regiment | March 24, 1812 |
| Martin, George J. | Ensign 19th regiment | July 1, 1812 |
| Moore, John | Ensign 19th regiment | July 13, 1812 |
| Pipkin, Thomas B. | Ensign 19th regiment | December 3, 1812 |
| Ragan, Benjamin | Ensign 20th regiment | May 26, 1812 |
| Richardson, David | Captain 19th regiment | April 16, 1812 |
| Rogers, John | Lieutenant 19th regiment | July 13, 1812 |
| Rutherford, Thomas | First Major of cavalry 9th brigade | April 3, 1812 |
| Sitler, James | Ensign in company of Republican Blues attached to 19th regiment | December 12, 1812 |
| Stringfellow, Richard | Ensign 19th regiment | April 16, 1812 |
| Thomas, Jesse W. | Captain 19th regiment | March 24, 1812 |
| Traylor, James | Ensign 19th regiment | February 11, 1812 |
| Vaulx, William | Ensign 19th regiment | July 13, 1812 |
| Whetson, George | Lieutenant 19th regiment | March 24, 1812 |
| Wolf, George W. | Lieutenant 19th regiment | July 1, 1812 |
| Wright, Peter | Captain 19th regiment | March 24, 1812 |

*Dickson County Regiments*

| | | |
|---|---|---|
| Dickson, Robert | Captain 25th regiment | November 26, 1812 |
| Hames, Simon | Ensign 25th regiment | November 26, 1812 |
| Moore, William | Lieutenant 25th regiment | May 21, 1812 |
| Nall, William | Captain 25th regiment | July 13, 1812 |
| Nesbitt, Thomas | Ensign 25th regiment | May 21, 1812 |
| Powel, Osborn | Ensign 25th regiment | July 13, 1812 |
| Shropshire, Joel | Ensign 25th regiment | November 26, 1812 |
| Story, Henry | Ensign 25th regiment | November 26, 1812 |
| Story, Samuel | Lieutenant 25th regiment | November 26, 1812 |
| Taylor, Samuel | Lieutenant 25th regiment | July 13, 1812 |

IN THE TENNESSEE MILITIA, 1812          175

Williams, Daniel .......... Lieutenant
                           25th regiment ...... November 26, 1812

### Franklin County Regiments

Black, George G. .......... Captain 32nd regiment..... July 1, 1812
Brown, Thomas .......... Lieutenant Volunteer Company
                           of Infantry ............. July 1, 1812
Hunt, Nathaniel .......... Captain Volunteer Company of
                           Infantry ................ July 1, 1812
Jordan, Levy ............. Ensign 32nd regiment...... July 1, 1812
Jorden, John ............. Captain
                           32nd regiment ..... November 26, 1812
Lane, Roling ............. Lieutenant
                           32nd regiment ..... November 26, 1812
McAllister, William ....... Ensign 32nd regiment...... April 9, 1812
McBride, Patrick .......... Ensign 32nd regiment. November 26, 1812
McCliskey, William ....... Ensign 32nd regiment...... July 1, 1812
Montgomery, John ......... Captain 32nd regiment..... July 1, 1812
Neighbours, Francis ...... Lieutenant 32nd regiment... July 1, 1812
Norman, John ............. Lieutenant 32nd regiment... July 1, 1812
Parish, John G. ........... Lieutenant 32nd regiment.. April 9, 1812
Sharpe, Richard .......... Captain 32nd regiment..... July 1, 1812
Smith, Francis ........... Ensign 32nd regiment...... July 1, 1812
Smith, James ............. Ensign Volunteer Company
                           of Infantry ............. July 1, 1812
Taylor, Harden .......... Lieutenant 32nd regiment.. July 1, 1812
Townsen, William ........ Captain 32nd regiment.... April 9, 1812
Witt, William ............ Lieutenant 32nd regiment... July 1, 1812

### Giles County Regiments

Alexander, Archibald ....... Ensign 37th regiment... January 1, 1812
Blue, Moses .............. Lieutenant
                           37th regiment ....... January 1, 1812
Crowson, Jacob ........... Lieutenant 37th regiment... July 1, 1812
Davis, Nathan ........... Lieutenant Volunteer Rifle
                           Company attached to
                           37th regiment ........ October 8, 1812
Dement, Thomas M. ....... Lieutenant
                           37th regiment ........ October 8, 1812
Ezell, Timothy ........... Lieutenant 37th regiment... July 1, 1812
Griffath, Anderson ........ Ensign 37th regiment... January 1, 1812
Lindsay, Samuel .......... Ensign 37th regiment...... April 29, 1812
Lyon, Peter, Jr. .......... Ensign 37th regiment.. November 23, 1812
McVay, Kinson .......... Ensign 37th regiment.... October 8, 1812
McVerminch, Absolem ..... Lieutenant 37th regiment.. April 29, 1812
Nations, Nathaniel ....... Lieutenant 37th regiment... July 1, 1812

Osburn, James ............ Lieutenant 37th regiment...July 24, 1812
Pickens, William .......... Captain 37th regiment.....April 29, 1812
Powers, Robert ............ Cornet of cavalry
                                     5th brigade ........February 29, 1812
Simmons, James ........... Lieutenant
                                     37th regiment .....November 23, 1812
Smith, John ............... Ensign 37th regiment....October 8, 1812
Smith, Thomas ............ Captain 37th regiment..October 8, 1812
Stark, James .............. Captain 37th regiment..January 1, 1812
Stone, John ............... Ensign 37th regiment...January 1, 1812
Williams, Thomas ......... Ensign 37th regiment....October 8, 1812
Wisdom, William .......... Lieutenant
                                     37th regiment .......October 8, 1812
York, Jonathan ........... Ensign 37th regiment..November 23, 1812

*Grainger County Regiments*

Baker, Martin ............. Lieutenant 7th regiment..March 19, 1812
Blackbourn, John .......... Ensign 7th regiment..September 11, 1812
Boatright, William ........ Lieutenant 7th regiment..March 19, 1812
Cameron, Samuel .......... Ensign 7th regiment..September 8, 1812
Cuff, William A. ........... Ensign 7th regiment ..September 8, 1812
Ivy, John ................. Lieutenant 7th regiment....June 23, 1812
McMillin, Thomas ......... Ensign 7th regiment......March 19, 1812
Mayes, John .............. Ensign 7th regiment.......June 23, 1812
Moore, John .............. Captain 7th regiment.....March 19, 1812
Moses, Peter .............. Ensign 7th regiment.......June 23, 1812
Moyers, Henry ............ Lieutenant
                                     7th regiment ......September 11, 1812
Mumpower, Benjamin ...... Ensign 7th regiment......March 19, 1812
Ritcheson, James .......... Lieutenant
                                     7th regiment ......September 8, 1812
Rook, Aaron .............. Lieutenant
                                     7th regiment ......September 8, 1812
Taylor, Daniel, Jr. ......... Ensign 7th regiment..September 11, 1812
Wolfenbarger, Phillip ...... Ensign 7th regiment......March 19, 1812
Wyrick, Frederick ......... Lieutenant 7th regiment..March 19, 1812

*Greene County Regiments*

Blanton, James ............ Ensign 3rd regiment.....August 3, 1812
Bruntson, Daniel .......... Lieutenant 3rd regiment..August 3, 1812
Dyche, Jacob ............. Captain Volunteer Rifle Company
                                     attached to
                                     3rd regiment .........August 3, 1812
Gillespie, Allen ............ Major 1st brigade.........April 4, 1812
Highbarger, John ......... Lieutenant Volunteer Rifle
                                     Company attached to
                                     3rd regiment .........August 3, 1812

IN THE TENNESSEE MILITIA, 1812    177

Justice, Janathan .......... Ensign 3rd regiment ..... August 3, 1812
Reaves, George ............ Ensign Volunteer Rifle
                            Company attached to
                            3rd regiment ........ August 3, 1812
Ross, John ................ Lieutenant 3rd regiment .. August 3, 1812
Russell, John .............. Major 1st brigade ..... February 10, 1812
Wagg, John ................ Ensign 3rd regiment ..... August 3, 1812

*Hawkins County Regiments*

Argentright, George ........ Captain Volunteer Rifle
                            Company attached to
                            4th regiment ........ October 8, 1812
Finly, William ............. Lieutenant Volunteer Rifle
                            Company attached to
                            4th regiment ........ October 8, 1812
Young, Francis ............. Ensign Volunteer Rifle
                            Company attached to
                            4th regiment ........ October 8, 1812

*Hickman County Regiments*

Alston, James ............. Captain 36th regiment . November 26, 1812
Easley, Drury ............. Ensgin 36th regiment . November 26, 1812
Easley, Washam ........... Ensign 36th regiment ...... July 13, 1812
Gee, Edmond ............. Lieutenant 36th regiment .. April 29, 1812
Greggs, Thomas ........... Captain 36th regiment .. January 22, 1812
Hornback, Eliot ........... Lieutenant 36th Regiment .. July 13, 1812
McCaleb, Ephraim ........ Captain
                          36th regiment ..... September 8, 1812
Malugin, William .......... Ensign 36th regiment ...... July 24, 1812
Miller, John .............. Lieutenant 36th regiment ... May 21, 1812
Miller, Loan .............. Captain 36th regiment ..... May 21, 1812
Patton, Tilman ............ Ensign 36th regiment ...... May 21, 1812
Scott, John ............... Lieutenant 36th regiment ... July 13, 1812
Simpson, Nathaniel ........ Captain 36th regiment ... March 24, 1812
Thomas, Tristram B. ....... Lieutenant
                          36th regiment ..... November 26, 1812
Walker, Elisha ............ Ensign 36th regiment ...... April 3, 1812

*Humphreys County Regiments*

Barnade, John ............ Lieutenant 38th regiment .. April 3, 1812
Bohannon, John ........... Ensign 38th regiment ... January 11, 1812
Carley, John .............. Captain 38th regiment ..... April 3, 1812
Harrison, Daniel .......... Lieutenant
                          38th regiment ...... December 2, 1812
Peoples, William .......... Captain 38th regiment .. January 11, 1812

178  RECORD OF COMMISSIONS OF OFFICERS

Suton, William ............ Lieutenant
         38th regiment ....... January 11, 1812
Williams, Joshua .......... Ensign 38th regiment.. December 2, 1812

### Jackson County Regiments

Bennet, Noah ............. Ensign 18th regiment...... April 1, 1812
Gilbreath, William ........ Captain 18th regiment..... April 1, 1812
Halfacre, Jacob ........... Ensign 18th regiment...... April 1, 1812
Holonsworth, Abraham ..... Captain 18th regiment..... April 1, 1812
Sutton, John .............. Lieutenant 18th regiment.. April 1, 1812

### Jefferson County Regiments

Arms, Edward ............. Ensign 6th regiment... February 8, 1812
Barton, William ........... Lieutenant 6th regiment.. October 8, 1812
Campbell, William ........ Lieutenant Volunteer troop
         of cavalry attached to
         regiment of cavalry
         3rd brigade .......... August 1, 1812
Churchman, James ........ Captain 6th regiment...... May 21, 1812
Dogget, Thomas ........... Lieutenant
         6th regiment ........ January 7, 1812
Goodson, Joseph .......... Captain 6th regiment... January 7, 1812
Goodson, Joseph .......... Captain 6th regiment...... May 21, 1812
Gorgas, Charles ........... Ensign Light Infantry
         Company attached to
         6th regiment ............ June 7, 1812
Hankins, James ........... Lieutenant
         6th regiment ....... February 8, 1812
Lane, Joseph .............. Lieutenant
         6th regiment ....... December 2, 1812
Longacre, Richard ......... Lieutenant 6th regiment.... May 21, 1812
Lyle, Daniel .............. Captain 6th regiment.. December 2, 1812
McFarland, Robert ........ Captain 6th regiment.... October 8, 1812
Miller, John .............. Captain Light Infantry
         Company attached to
         6th regiment .......... June 9, 1812
Milliken, Elihu ............ Captain 6th regiment... January 7, 1812
Pearce, Moses ............. Captain 6th regiment.. February 8, 1812
Peck, Moses Looney ....... Lieutenant 6th regiment... May 21, 1812
Perrin, Matthew ........... Ensign 6th regiment....... May 21, 1812
Rankin, David ........... Lieutenant
         6th regiment ....... December 2, 1812
Rankin, John .............. Ensign 6th regiment... December 2, 1812
Ray, George W. .......... Ensign 6th regiment.... January 7, 1812
Slover, John .............. Ensign 6th regiment.... October 8, 1812
Tinman, John ............. Ensign 6th regiment.... October 8, 1812
Wilkerson, Povy .......... Lieutenant 6th regiment.... July 1, 1812

Anthony, John ............Captain Volunteer troop
                         cavalry attached to
                         regiment of cavalry
                         3rd brigade ..........August  1, 1812
Armstrong, Josiah ........Cornet regiment of
                         cavalry 3rd brigade .....July 28, 1812
Ayres, David .............Captain regiment cavalry
                         3rd brigade .............July 28, 1812
Cavitt, Thomas ...........Lieutenant 40th regiment.August  3, 1812
Edmonson, John ...........Ensign 40th regiment......July 28, 1812
Farquaharson, Robert .....Ensign 40th regiment......April 16, 1812
French, Joseph ...........Captain 40th regiment....March 24, 1812
Gains, John S. ...........Ensign 10th regiment....August  3, 1812
George, Reuben ...........Lieutenant 10th regiment..April 29, 1812
Gilbreath, Thomas ........Lieutenant 10th regiment...July  1, 1812
Hagard, James ............Ensign 40th regiment..November 26, 1812
Herrelson, William .......Lieutenant 10th regiment.August  3, 1812
Howell, William S. .......Captain 40th regiment.....April 16, 1812
Hudeburgh, Lewis .........Lieutenant regiment of
                         cavalry 3rd brigade......July 28, 1812
Johnston, Christopher ....Ensign 10th regiment....August  3, 1812
Keas, James ..............Ensign 10th regiment......July  1, 1812
Kelly, Nathan ............Lieutenant 10th regiment...May 28, 1812
McNutt, James ............Captain 10th regiment.....May 21, 1812
Morrice, Joseph ..........Ensign 40th regiment......June 23, 1812
Morrice, William .........Lieutenant 40th regiment...June 23, 1812
Patton, Robert ...........Ensign 10th regiment......April 29, 1812
Rogers, William ..........Ensign 40th regiment....August  3, 1812
Russell, Andrew ..........Ensign 40th regiment....August  3, 1812
Smith, Isaac .............Ensign 40th regiment....March 24, 1812
Thatch, Thomas ...........Lieutenant 40th regiment..April 16, 1812
Tipton, Reuben ...........Captain 40th regiment.....June 23, 1812
Wright, Thomas ...........Ensign 10th regiment......April 29, 1812

*Lincoln County Regiments*

Armstrong, David .........Captain 49th regiment......June  9, 1812
Armstrong, William .......Ensign 49th regiment......June  9, 1812
Asten, James .............Ensign 39th regiment..November 23, 1812
Astin, Samuel G. .........Lieutenant
                         39th regiment ......November 23, 1812
Bird, Janathan ...........Captain 49th regiment......June  9, 1812
Burgess, William .........Lieutenant
                         39th regiment ......November 23, 1812
Burton, John .............Lieutenant 49th regiment...June  9, 1812
Carrathers, William ......First Major 39th regiment..June  9, 1812

## RECORD OF COMMISSIONS OF OFFICERS

Chitwood, John ........... Captain 39th regiment..November 23, 1812
Clayton, Charles C. ........ Lieutenant 49th regiment...June 9, 1812
Collins, William ........... Lieutenant
                          39th regiment ...... November 23, 1812
Craze, John ............... Ensign 39th regiment..November 23, 1812
Crittenton, Thomas W. ..... Captain 39th regiment.November 23, 1812
Cross, William ............ Ensign 39th regiment..November 23, 1812
Davis, John ............... Captain 49th regiment...... July 24, 1812
Grant, James .............. Lieutenant 49th regiment...June 9, 1812
Guess, William ............ Lieutenant 49th regiment...July 24, 1812
Hanby, John ............... Captain 49th regiment...... July 24, 1812
Harkins, Joseph ........... Lieutenant 49th regiment...June 9, 1812
Henderson, William ........ Ensign 49th regiment...... June 24, 1812
Henry, Andrew ............ Captain 39th regiment.November 23, 1812
Higgins, William Y. ........ Lieutenant-colonel com-
                          mandant 49th regiment..April 1, 1812
Hunter, Sherid ............ Ensign Volunteer Rifle
                          Company attached to
                          39th regiment ........ October 8, 1812
Isaacs, Abraham ........... Captain 39th regiment.November 23, 1812
Lee, John ................. Captain 49th regiment..... June 9, 1812
Lewis, John ............... Ensign 49th regiment...... June 9, 1812
Luna, Robert ............. Lieutenant Volunteer Rifle
                          Company attached to
                          39th regiment ........ October 8, 1812
McCown, Francis .......... Captain 39th regiment.November 23, 1812
McKamey, D. ............. Lieutenant Light Infantry
                          Company attached to
                          49th regiment .......... June 9, 1812
McKinney, John V. ........ Second Major
                          49th regiment .......... June 9, 1812
McMahan, Abraham ....... Ensign 49th regiment...... June 9, 1812
Menefee, Reuben .......... Ensign Light Infantry
                          Company attached to
                          49th regiment .......... June 9, 1812
Milligan, Samuel D. ........ Ensign 39th regiment.November 23, 1812
Moore, Reuben ............ Ensign 39th regiment.November 23, 1812
Moore, Samuel ............ Ensign 39th regiment.November 23, 1812
Northcutt, William ........ Ensign 39th regiment.November 23, 1812
Odean, John .............. Ensign 49th regiment....... July 24, 1812
Owens, William ........... Lieutenant
                          39th regiment ...... November 23, 1812
Philpot, Horatio ........... Lieutenant
                          39th regiment ...... November 23, 1812
Pinson, Nathan G. ......... Second Major
                          39th regiment .......... June 9, 1812
Porter, Joseph ............. Captain 39th regiment..November 23, 1812

IN THE TENNESSEE MILITIA, 1812　　　　181

Prewd, John ............... Captain 49th regiment ..... June 9, 1812
Rogers, Edmund ........... Lieutenant 49th regiment ... July 24, 1812
Sebastian, Isaac ........... Lieutenant 49th regiment ... July 24, 1812
Smith, Jasper ............. First Major
　　　　　　　　　　　　　　49th regiment .......... June 9, 1812
Smith, Jesse .............. Ensign 39th regiment .. November 23, 1812
Smith, William ............ Captain
　　　　　　　　　　　　　　39th regiment ...... November 23, 1812
Tate, Zedekiah ............ Captain Light Infantry
　　　　　　　　　　　　　　Company attached to
　　　　　　　　　　　　　　49th regiment .......... June 9, 1812
Tatum, Nathaniel .......... Ensign 49th regiment ....... July 24, 1812
Waggoner, Jacob .......... Captain 49th regiment ...... July 24, 1812
Waller, Obediah .......... Captain 39th regiment. November 23, 1812
Walt, John A. ............. Lieutenant 49th regiment ... June 9, 1812
Ward, Presley ............ Lieutenant
　　　　　　　　　　　　　　39th regiment ...... November 23, 1812
Watkins, Isaac ........... Ensign 49th regiment ...... June 9, 1812
Watt, Samuel ............. Captain 49th regiment ...... July 24, 1812
Wilson, John ............. Lieutenant
　　　　　　　　　　　　　　39th regiment ...... November 23, 1812

*Maury County Regiments*

Balch, Amos P. ............ Lieutenant 27th regiment. March 14, 1812
Barr, John W. ............. Ensign 27th regiment. September 11, 1812
Beaty, John .............. Ensign 27th regiment. September 11, 1812
Blockner, Elijah .......... Captain 27th regiment ..... July 24, 1812
Boyd, James .............. Lieutenant 27th regiment. March 14, 1812
Bradshaw, John ........... Ensign 27th regiment ...... July 24, 1812
Bullock, Jonathan ........ Lieutenant 27th regiment ... July 24, 1812
Byers, William ............ Cornet cavalry regiment
　　　　　　　　　　　　　　5th brigade ............ May 21, 1812
Byers, William ............ Lieutenant cavalry regiment
　　　　　　　　　　　　　　5th brigade .......... October 6, 1812
Caldwell, Thomas ......... Ensign Light Infantry
　　　　　　　　　　　　　　Company attached to
　　　　　　　　　　　　　　27th regiment .......... May 8, 1812
Craig, David ............. Lieutenant Volunteer Rifle
　　　　　　　　　　　　　　Company attached to
　　　　　　　　　　　　　　27th regiment ........ March 14, 1812
Crawford, Samuel ......... Second Major 46th regiment. July 24, 1812
Creasy, John ............. Lieutenant 27th regiment ... July 24, 1812
Daniel, William .......... Captain Volunteer Rifle
　　　　　　　　　　　　　　Company attached to
　　　　　　　　　　　　　　27th regiment ........ March 14, 1812

Dill, John ............... Ensign Volunteer Rifle
                          Company attached to
                          27th regiment ......... March 14, 1812
Elliot, John .............. Lieutenant
                          27th regiment ..... September 11, 1812
Gholson, John ............. Ensign 27th regiment...... July 24, 1812
Gordon, William ........... Ensign 27th regiment. September 11, 1812
Gray, Curtis G. ............ Ensign 27th regiment...... July 24, 1812
Hamilton, Thomas ......... Lieutenant cavalry
                          5th brigade ........... May 21, 1812
Hughs, Buddet ........... Lieutenant* Volunteer
                          Company of Infantry.... July 24, 1812
Hurt, Bird J. .............. Captain 27th regiment..... July 24, 1812
Johnson, Thomas ......... Lieutenant 27th regiment. March 14, 1812
Johnston, Robert ......... Lieutenant 27th regiment... July 24, 1812
Kilcrist, John ............ Lieutenant Light Infantry
                          attached to
                          27th regiment .......... May 8, 1812
Leach, David ............. Ensign 27th regiment..... March 14, 1812
Lynch, James ............. Lieutenant 27th regiment... July 24, 1812
McCarley, Andrew ........ Captain 27th regiment.... March 14, 1812
McClean, James D. ....... Captain 46th regiment...... July 24, 1812
McKnitt, Joseph .......... Lieutenant
                          27th regiment ..... September 11, 1812
Mathews, Abner .......... Ensign 27th regiment.... March 14, 1812
May, Charles P. .......... Lieutenant
                          27th regiment ..... September 11, 1812
Mayfield, A. B. ........... Captain cavalry regiment
                          5th brigade ......... October 6, 1812
Moore, Bennet ........... Lieutenant 46th regiment... July 24, 1812
Neelly, Robert ........... Captain
                          27th regiment ...... September 11, 1812
Neilly, Charles ........... Captain cavalry
                          5th brigade ........... May 21, 1812
Norvel, John P. .......... Captain* Volunteer
                          Company of Infantry.... July 24, 1812
Porter, William .......... Lieutenant
                          27th regiment ...... September 11, 1812
Scott, Nathaniel .......... Ensign 46th regiment...... July 24, 1812
Sims, John ............... Captain
                          27th regiment ...... September 11, 1812
Taylor, Thomas .......... Ensign 46th regiment...... July 24, 1812

---

* Volunteer Company of Infantry raised in conformity with the provisions of an Act of Congress of the United States passed February 6, 1812.

# RECORD OF COMMISSIONS OF OFFICERS IN THE TENNESSEE MILITIA 1812

COMPILED BY MRS. JOHN TROTWOOD MOORE

*Maury County Regiments*

Thompson, William W. .....Lieutenant-colonel commandant cavalry regiment
 5th brigade .............July 24, 1812
Toones, John ..............Ensign 46th regiment......July 24, 1812
Tuttle, David .............Ensign 27th regiment.September 11, 1812
Wade, Dabney ............Cornet cavalry regiment
 5th brigade .............July 1, 1812
Wade, William J. ..........Captain Light Infantry
 attached to
 27th regiment ..........May 8, 1812
White, Alfred .............Ensign 27th regiment.......July 24, 1812
Wilson, Hardin ............Captain 46th regiment.....June 9, 1812

*Montgomery County Regiments*

Anderson, Richard ........Captain 50th regiment......July 1, 1812
Blair, William ............Lieutenant
 24th regiment .....September 19, 1812
Bowen, Charles ...........Lieutenant cavalry regiment
 6th brigade .......September 20, 1812
Boyers, David .............Lieutenant
 50th regiment .....September 19, 1812
Bryan, Henry H. ..........Lieutenant-colonel commandant 50th regiment..April 1, 1812
Cocke, James W. ..........Lieutenant
 24th regiment .....September 19, 1812
Cocke, William B. .........Ensign 24th regiment.September 19, 1812
Dennis, Zebedee ..........Captain 50th regiment......July 1, 1812
Ford, Moses ..............Ensign 50th regiment.September 19, 1812
Frost, Ebenezer ..........First Major
 24th regiment .....September 19, 1812
Horn, Thomas .............Lieutenant
 24th regiment .....September 19, 1812
Hutchins, Joseph ..........Lieutenant
 50th regiment .....September 19, 1812
Lynes, William J. ..........Second Major
 50th regiment ..........April 1, 1812
Jones, Charles .............Captain 50th regiment......July 1, 1812
Mitchell, Michael ..........Captain 24th regiment.September 19, 1812

Mitchell, Samuel .......... Ensign 24th regiment. September 19, 1812
Searcy, Robert ............ First Major
    50th regiment .......... April 1, 1812
Smith, Aaron .............. Ensign 24th regiment. September 19, 1812
Stewart, Bartholemew G. ... Captain cavalry regiment
    6th brigade ....... September 20, 1812
Stuart, Andrew ............ Cornet cavalry regiment
    6th brigade ........ September 20, 1812
Wall, Charles ............. Ensign 50th regiment....... July 1, 1812
Whiliss, Herbert .......... Lieutenant
    50th regiment ...... September 19, 1812
Willis, Elishs ............ Captain 24th regiment. September 19, 1812

## Overton County Regiments

Beaty, John ............... Ensign 35th regiment...... June 9, 1812
Beuford, Thomas ........... Lieutenant 35th regiment... June 9, 1812
Carpenter, James .......... Ensign 35th regiment...... June 9, 1812
Collier, David ............ Ensign* Volunteer
    Company Infantry ...... June 26, 1812
Hearn, George ............. Ensign 35th regiment...... June 9, 1812
Jones, Jesse .............. Ensign 35th regiment...... June 9, 1812
Kee, Benjamin ............. Ensign 35th regiment...... June 9, 1812
Kennedy, John ............. Captain*
    Volunteer Infantry ...... June 6, 1812
Livingston, Thomas ........ Captain 35th regiment..... June 9, 1812
Matlock, Charles .......... Lieutenant*
    Volunteer Infantry ...... June 26, 1812
Mitchell, Arthur .......... Lieutenant 35th regiment... June 9, 1812
Miller, John .............. Lieutenant 35th regiment... June 9, 1812
Paris, Joel ............... Lieutenant 35th regiment... June 9, 1812
Sevier, Archibald ......... Ensign 35th regiment...... June 9, 1812
Smith, John ............... Ensign 35th regiment...... June 9, 1812
Smith, Richard ............ Lieutenant 35th regiment... June 9, 1812
Stogdon, John ............. Lieutenant 35th regiment... June 9, 1812
Stogdon, John ............. Captain 35th regiment..... June 24, 1812

## Rhea County Regiments

Alexander, William ........ Captain 30th regiment... March 5, 1812
Anderson, Thomas .......... Ensign 30th regiment...... July 24, 1812
Goad, William ............. Captain 30th regiment.... March 5, 1812
Horton, Archibald ......... Lieutenant 30th regiment... July 24, 1812
Howerton, Jackson ......... Ensign 30th regiment....... July 24, 1812
Mars, Benjamin ............ Ensign 30th regiment..... March 5, 1812
Owens, William ............ Lieutenant 30th regiment. March 5, 1812

---

* Volunteer Company of Infantry raised in conformity with the provisions of an Act of Congress of the United States passed February 6, 1812.

# IN THE TENNESSEE MILITIA, 1812    185

Ragsdale, David ..........Lieutenant 30th regiment.March 5, 1812
Reigle, Jacob .............Lieutenant 30th regiment...July 24, 1812
Smith, Randolph ..........Ensign 30th regiment.......July 24, 1812
Upton, James ............Captain 30th regiment....March 5, 1812
Williams, John ...........Ensign 30th regiment....March 5, 1812
Winton, George W. ........Captain 30th regiment......July 24, 1812
Woodward, William .......Lieutenant 30th regiment.March 5, 1812

## *Roane County Regiments*

Adams, David ............Ensign 14th regiment......June 9, 1812
Brown, Thomas ..........Second Major cavalry
                              regiment 8th brigade.....May 28, 1812
Cox, Joshua ..............Captain Light Infantry
                              Company attached to
                              14th regiment ..........July 28, 1812
Eldridge, Benjamin .......Lieutenant 14th regiment...July 28, 1812
Evans, Evan .............Captain Volunteer Rifle
                              Company attached to
                              14th regiment ........August 3, 1812
Kannon, Thomas .........Lieutenant 14th regiment..April 29, 1812
Luttrell, Mason ...........Ensign 14th regiment......July 28, 1812
McKamy, John ...........Lieutenant 14th regiment...June 9, 1812
McKorkel, Henry .........Ensign 14th regiment......May 26, 1812
McMeans, Isaac S. .......First Major cavalry
                              regiment 8th brigade.....May 28, 1812
Neilson, William D. ........Captain 14th regiment.....May 8, 1812
Prigmore, Thomas ........Lieutenant Light Infantry
                              attached to
                              14th regiment ..........June 26, 1812
Rogers, Patterson .........Ensign 14th regiment.November 23, 1812
Rogers, William ..........Ensign Volunteer Rifle
                              Company attached to
                              14th regiment ........August 3, 1812
Standifer, James ..........Lieutenant colonel com-
                              mandant cavalry regiment
                              8th brigade ............May 28, **1812**
Stone, Abraham ..........Lieutenant Volunteer Rifle
                              Company attached to
                              14th regiment ........August 3, 1812
Turner, Nathan ..........Lieutenant
                              14th regiment ......November 23, 1812
Underwood, John .........Captain 14th regiment.....April 29, 1812
Vaun, Achiles ............Ensign 14th regiment......May 26, 1812
Warren, Edward ..........Ensign Light Infantry
                              Company attached to
                              14th regiment ..........June 26, 1812

RECORD OF COMMISSIONS OF OFFICERS

## Robertson County Regiments

Daimwood, Henry .........Ensign 23rd regiment..September 17, 1812
Darr, Henry .............Lieutenant
    23rd regiment ......January 18, 1812
Dunkin, John ............Lieutenant
    23rd regiment .....September 17, 1812
Elliott, Benjamin ..........Second Major
    23rd regiment ......November 16, 1812
Flood, Seth ...............Ensign 23rd regiment.November 16, 1812
Gardner, John ............Lieutenant
    23rd regiment .....September 17, 1812
Gardner, John ............Captain
    23rd regiment .....November 26, 1812
Grimes, Jacob ............Ensign 23rd regiment...January 18, 1812
Holland, John ...........Lieutenant
    23rd regiment ......January 18, 1812
Lovell, Daniel ............Ensign 23rd regiment.November 16, 1812
More, Joel ...............Captain 23rd regiment...January 18, 1812
Mosley, Thomas .........Cornet cavalry regiment
    6th brigade ............May 21, 1812
Sanders, Robert ..........Captain
    23rd regiment ......January 18, 1812
Swann, Burch ............Ensign 23rd regiment...January 18, 1812
Wair, George T. ..........Ensign 23rd regiment.September 17, 1812
Webb, John ..............Ensign 23rd regiment.November 16, 1812
Williams, Samuel .........Ensign 23rd regiment.September 17, 1812
Yeates, James, Jr. ........Lieutenant
    23rd regiment ......January 18, 1812
Yeates, William ..........Lieutenant
    23rd regiment ......January 18, 1812

## Rutherford County Regiments

Alford, William ..........Lieutenant
    22nd regiment .....November 26, 1812
Arnold, William ..........Ensign 22nd regiment....March 24, 1812
Arnold, William ..........Lieutenant 22nd regiment...July 24, 1812
Barkly, William K. ........Ensign 45th regiment......April 29, 1812
Byford, John .............Ensign 45th regiment.....March 11, 1812
Caldwell, William ........Lieutenant 45th regiment.March 11, 1812
Clark, John ..............Lieutenant 45th regiment..April 29, 1812
Cooper, Wells ............Ensign 45th regiment....March 11, 1812
Davis, John ..............Ensign 45th regiment....March 11, 1812
Doak, John ...............Lieutenant 45th regiment..April 29, 1812
Elder, William ...........Lieutenant
    22nd regiment .....September 11, 1812
Espey, William ...........Ensign 22nd regiment.September 11, 1812

## IN THE TENNESSEE MILITIA, 1812

Gannaway, Walker ........Lieutenant cavalry regiment
                                  9th brigade ............July 24, 1812
Gilleland, James ...........Ensign 45th regiment......July 24, 1812
Harris, Archibald ..........Captain 22nd regiment..October 8, 1812
Harris, William G. .........Captain 45th regiment....April 29, 1812
Higgins, William ..........Ensign 22nd regiment....March 24, 1812
Hunter, Ephraim ..........Lieutenant 22nd regiment...June 9, 1812
Jett, Murphrey ............Ensign 45th regiment......July 24, 1812
Latty, Eli ................Ensign 45th regiment......July 24, 1812
McClain, Charles ..........Ensign 45th regiment......April 29, 1812
McCrackin, George ........Captain 45th regiment.....April 29, 1812
McQuaig, John ............Ensign Light Infantry
                                  Company attached to
                                  22nd regiment ........March 24, 1812
Maberry, John ............Captain 45th regiment.....July 24, 1812
Millekin, Isaac ............Ensign 45th regiment......April 29, 1812
Miller, James .............Ensign 45th regiment......July 24, 1812
Moore, James ............Ensign 45th regiment......April 29, 1812
Nance, Isaac ..............Captain 22nd regiment...March 24, 1812
Pace, James ...............Lieutenant 45th regiment..April 29, 1812
Patton, David .............Captain Light Infantry
                                  Company attached to
                                  22nd regiment ........March 24, 1812
Sanford, Robert ...........Ensign 22nd regiment....March 24, 1812
Shanks, Archibald .........Lieutenant 45th regiment...July 24, 1812
Sharpe, Alfred ............Lieutenant 22nd regiment.March 24, 1812
Sharpe, Cyrus ............Lieutenant 22nd regiment...July 24, 1812
Stricklin, Barnabas ........Ensign 45th regiment.......July 24, 1812
Todd, William ............Lieutenant 45th regiment...July 24, 1812
Uselton, Samuel ..........Captain 45th regiment......July 24, 1812
Ward, Burrell .............Ensign 22nd regiment...October 8, 1812
Watkins, Henry ...........Lieutenant 22nd regiment.March 24, 1812
Wills, Archibald ...........Ensign 22nd regiment......June 9, 1812
Woote, Daniel ............Ensign 45th regiment......April 29, 1812

*Sevier County Regiments*

Armbrister, Henry .........Ensign 11th regiment......May 26, 1812
Blair, Samuel, Jr. ..........Lieutenant 11th regiment.August 3, 1812
Bryan, Allen ..............Ensign Volunteer Rifle
                                  Companp attached to
                                  11th regiment ........August 6, 1812
Bryan, Thomas ...........Captain Volunteer Rifle
                                  Company attached to
                                  11th regiment ........August 6, 1812
Evens, James .............Cornet cavalry regiment
                                  3rd brigade ..........August 8, 1812
Guin, John ...............Lieutenant 11th regiment.August 3, 1812

Henderson, Samuel ........Captain 11th regiment...August 3, 1812
Hubbard, Benneman .......Lieutenant Volunteer Rifle
                         Company attached to
                         11th regiment ........August 6, 1812
Jones, William ............Ensign 11th regiment....August 3, 1812
Langley, Jonathan ........Lieutenant 11th regiment...May 26, 1812
Maples, Wilson ...........Captain 11th regiment.....May 26, 1812
Mitchell, William ..........Captain cavalry regiment
                         3rd brigade ............June 15, 1812
Pope, Jacob ..............Ensign 11th regiment....August 3, 1812
Preston, Alexander ........First Major
                         11th regiment ......February 24, 1812
Shahan, Thomas ..........Lieutenant
                         11th regiment ........October 8, 1812
Shields, Robert ............Captain 11th regiment.....May 26, 1812
Stephenson, Andrew .......Lieutenant cavalry regiment
                         3rd brigade ..........August 8, 1812
Thomas, Isaac, Jr. ........Second Major
                         11th regiment ......February 24, 1812
Wear, John ..............Lieutenant 11th regiment.August 3, 1812

*Smith County Regiments*

Baker, John E. ............Lieutenant
                         16th regiment .....September 19, 1812
Black, Robert ............Lieutenant
                         16th regiment .....November 23, 1812
Bradley, Charles ..........Ensign 16th regiment.September 19, 1812
Bratton, David ...........Ensign 16th regiment.November 23, 1812
Brewer, Daniel ...........Ensign 16th regiment.September 19, 1812
Cauley, George ...........Ensign 41st regiment...January 11, 1812
Dolton, William ..........Lieutenant
                         16th regiment .....September 19, 1812
Driver, Thomas ..........Ensign 41st regiment...January 11, 1812
Farrier, Nathaniel ........Ensign 41st regiment.September 18, 1812
Ford, Andrew G. ..........Captain
                         16th regiment ......November 23, 1812
Foster, John .............Ensign 16th regiment.September 19, 1812
Gibbons, Samuel ..........Lieutenant
                         41st regiment .....September 18, 1812
Giffard, Giddeon .........Ensign 16th regiment.November 23, 1812
Green, Thomas S. .........Captain 41st regiment..January 11, 1812
McCalister, Garland .......Lieutenant
                         41st regiment ......September 18, 1812
McGee, William ..........Ensign 16th regiment.September 19, 1812
Martin, William ..........First Major
                         41st regiment .........April 1, 1812

IN THE TENNESSEE MILITIA, 1812  189

Murry, Bland ............. Lieutenant
                           16th regiment ..... September 19, 1812
Overall, Abraham ......... Second Major
                           41st regiment ...... September 19, 1812
Patterson, Thomas ......... Captain
                           41st regiment ...... September 18, 1812
Plover, Edward ........... Lieutenant
                           41st regiment ....... January 11, 1812
Reynolds, William ......... Captain
                           41st regiment ........ January 11, 1812
Roads, Moses ............. Captain
                           16th regiment ..... September 19, 1812
Roberts, Robert W. ........ First Major
                           41st regiment ..... September 19, 1812
Robertson, Christopher ..... Lieutenant
                           41st regiment ........ January 11, 1812
Shaw, Josiah ............. Captain
                           16th regiment ..... September 19, 1812
Spurlock, Josiah .......... Ensign 41st regiment.. September 18, 1812
Sullivan, Lee ............. Lieutenant colonel com-
                           mandant 41st regiment... May 21, 1812
Temples, John ............ Ensign 16th regiment. September 19, 1812
Tittle, Samuel ............ Captain
                           41st regiment ...... September 18, 1812
Turney, George ........... Lieutenant
                           41st regiment ..... September 18, 1812
Vanhook, Loyd ............ Ensign 41st regiment. September 18, 1812
Ward, Anthony .......... Lieutenant
                           Captain 41st regiment.. January 11, 1812
Watkins, Joel M. .......... Lieutenant
                           16th regiment ..... September 19, 1812
Watson, George .......... Lieutenant
                           41st regiment ....... January 11, 1812
Weeks, Solomon .......... Ensign 16th regiment. November 23, 1812
Williams, Henry .......... Ensign 41st regiment... January 11, 1812

*Stewart County Regiments*

Crosswell, Nelson ......... Lieutenant
                           26th regiment ....... January  1, 1812
Gray, James ............. Captain Volunteer Company
                           Light Infantry attached
                           to 26th regiment...... January  1, 1812
Griffy, William ........... Ensign Volunteer Light
                           Infantry Company attached
                           to 26th regiment.... February 24, 1812
Grimmer, Henry ......... Ensign 26th regiment.... October  8, 1812
Jackson, Hugh ........... Ensign 26th regiment... January  1, 1812

Lewis, John ............... Captain
                          26th regiment .......January  1, 1812
Moore, Travers ........... Lieutenant Volunteer Light
                          Infantry Company attached
                          to 26th regiment....February 24, 1812
Polk, Andrew ............. Captain 26th regiment...August  1, 1812
Polk, William ............ Ensign 26th regiment....August  1, 1812
Ross, Samuel ............. Ensign 26th regiment...January  1, 1812
Rushing, Abraham ........ Ensign 26th regiment...January  1, 1812

*Sullivan County Regiments*

Booker, Jacob ............. Captain 2nd regiment......July 27, 1812
Brown, John .............. Ensign 2nd regiment.....March 17, 1812
Chester, John ............ Lieutenant
                          2nd regiment ......November 16, 1812
Dixon, William ........... Lieutenant
                          2nd regiment ...........July 27, 1812
Gallaway, John ........... Lieutenant
                          2nd regiment ...........May 21, 1812
Hommell, Daniel ......... Ensign 2nd regiment....October  8, 1812
Hulse, William ........... Captain 2nd regiment......July  1, 1812
Keys, Washington ........ Captain 2nd regiment......July 27, 1812
Landen, James ............ Captain 2nd regiment......July  1, 1812
Melone, Michael ......... Ensign 2nd regiment.......July  1, 1812
Neuton, Henry ........... Ensign 2nd regiment.......May 21, 1812
Newton, Kennerry ........ Ensign 2nd regiment.......July  1, 1812
Offill, James .............. Ensign 2nd regiment.......July  1, 1812
Rogers, Joseph ........... Captain 2nd regiment......May 21, 1812
Shaw, Robert ............. Ensign 2nd regiment.......July 27, 1812
Smith, William ........... Lieutenant
                          2nd regiment ........October  8, 1812
Suckler, Jacob ............ Ensign 2nd regiment.......July  1, 1812
Wassom, Jonathan ........ Lieutenant 2nd regiment..March 17, 1812
White, Thomas ........... Lieutenant 2nd regiment....July  1, 1812

*Sumner County Regiments*

Anthony, William ......... Lieutenant 15th regiment...July 13, 1812
Barns, Bright ............. Ensign 43rd regiment...October  8, 1812
Bradley, Edward ......... Lieutenant colonel com-
                          mandant 15th regiment...July 24, 1812
Brigance, William ........ Ensign 43rd regiment...October  8, 1812
Brown, Hardy ............. Lieutenant
                          43rd regiment ........October  8, 1812
Brown, Joseph ............ Ensign 43rd regiment......July 13, 1812
Edwards, William ......... Captain 43rd regiment..October  8, 1812
Ellis, Samuel ............. Ensign 43rd regiment....October  8, 1812
Green, Lewis ............. Captain 43rd regiment..October  8, 1812

IN THE TENNESSEE MILITIA, 1812      191

Hall, John ................Lieutenant 43rd regiment...July 13, 1812
Hall, William .............Brigadier General
                          4th brigade ............June 19, 1812
Johnston, George ..........Ensign 15th regiment.September 22, 1812
Lauderdale, Samuel ........First Major
                          15th regiment ...........July 24, 1812
Lauderdale, William .......Captain
                          15th regiment .....September 22, 1812
Leath, Isaac ..............Ensign 15th regiment......July 13, 1812
Looney, Isaac .............Lieutenant
                          43rd regiment ........October 8, 1812
Martin, James L. ..........Captain 15th regiment.....July 13, 1812
Norman, Ezekiel ...........Lieutenant
                          43rd regiment ........October 8, 1812
Ross, Ezekiel .............Lieutenant
                          15th regiment ......September 22, 1812
Spooner, Jonathan .........Ensign 43rd regiment......July 13, 1812
Stratton, James ...........Lieutenant
                          43rd regiment ........October 8, 1812
Summers, Levy .............Ensign 43rd regiment......July 13, 1812
Summers, William ..........Lieutenant 43rd regiment...July 13, 1812
Truett, John B. ...........Ensign Light Infantry
                          Company attached to
                          15th regiment ........October 8, 1812
Tyree, Richmond C. ........Lieutenant Light Infantry
                          Company attached to
                          15th regiment ........October 8, 1812
Wallace, John .............Captain 43rd regiment..October 8, 1812

*Warren County Regiments*

Cain, James ...............Second Major
                          29th regiment ...........July 1, 1812
Crabtree, James ...........Ensign 29th regiment.....March 5, 1812
Dodson, Elisha ............Lieutenant 29th regiment.March 5, 1812
Duncan, William ...........Lieutenant 29th regiment.March 5, 1812
Forrest, Richard ..........Ensign 29th regiment....March 5, 1812
Jones, Nathaniel ..........Lieutenant
                          29th regiment ......November 23, 1812
McReynolds, William .......Captain
                          29th regiment ......November 23, 1812
Mitchell, David ...........Lieutenant
                          29th regiment ........October 8, 1812
Robertson, Isaac ..........Ensign 29th regiment..November 23, 1812
Smith, Amos ...............Lieutenant
                          29th regiment ......November 23, 1812
Tittle, James .............Ensign 29th regiment.....March 5, 1812
Williams, David ...........Ensign 29th regiment.....March 5, 1812

## Washington County Regiments

| | | |
|---|---|---|
| Baker, Robert | Ensign 1st regiment | July 24, 1812 |
| Collom, John | Ensign 1st regiment | February 17, 1812 |
| Copas, John | Captain 1st regiment | April 29, 1812 |
| Cosson, John | Ensign 1st regiment | October 8, 1812 |
| Doke, John | Lieutenant 1st regiment | April 29, 1812 |
| Dunwody, Patrick M. | Lieutenant 1st regiment | March 29, 1812 |
| Gray, Robert | Lieutenant 1st regiment | October 8, 1812 |
| Humphreys, Lasley | Lieutenant 1st regiment | March 5, 1812 |
| Jameson, Samuel | Ensign 1st regiment | March 29, 1812 |
| Lain, Samuel | Ensign 1st regiment | March 5, 1812 |
| McCray, Elisha | Ensign 1st regiment | March 5, 1812 |
| McRaken, Samuel | Captain 1st regiment | July 24, 1812 |
| McSpadden, Thomas | Captain 1st regiment | March 29, 1812 |
| Melony, Robert | Captain Light Infantry Company attached to 1st regiment | March 29, 1812 |
| Patton, John | Lieutenant 1st regiment | July 24, 1812 |
| Russell, Alexander | Ensign Light Infantry Company attached to 1st regiment | March 29, 1812 |
| Stuart, Thomas | Second Major Cavalry regiment 1st brigade | July 4, 1812 |
| Winkle, Frederick F. | Lieutenant Light Infantry Company attached to 1st regiment | March 29, 1812 |
| Yeager, James | Ensign 1st regiment | October 8, 1812 |

## White County Regiments

| | | |
|---|---|---|
| Branson, Thomas | Lieutenant 34th regiment | May 26, 1812 |
| Crane, Jobson | Ensign 34th regiment | May 26, 1812 |
| Cummings, John | Captain 34th regiment | December 28, 1812 |
| Fox, William | Ensign 34th regiment | May 26, 1812 |
| Hamblet, George | Ensign 34th regiment | December 28, 1812 |
| Keathly, Jesse | Ensign 34th regiment | May 26, 1812 |
| McLane, Benjamin | Lieutenant 34th regiment | December 28, 1812 |
| Miller, Charles | Ensign 34th regiment | May 26, 1812 |
| Norris, Absolem | Ensign 34th regiment | December 28, 1812 |
| O'Daniel, John | Ensign 34th regiment | May 26, 1812 |
| Parkison, Daniel | Lieutenant 34th regiment | December 28, 1812 |
| Potts, Jeremiah | Ensign 34th regiment | December 28, 1812 |
| Smith, William J. | Captain 34th regiment | December 28, 1812 |

## IN THE TENNESSEE MILITIA, 1812

Anglan, James ............Captain 21st regiment.....April 29, 1812
Armstrong, John M. ........Ensign
    Company of Rangers*....June 1, 1812
Bateman, William ........Ensign 21st regiment......April 29, 1812
Benton, Nathaniel .........Ensign Volunteer Infantry
    Company attached to
    21st regiment ..........April 29, 1812
Benton, Thomas H. ........Captain Volunteer Infantry
    Company attached to
    21st regiment ..........April 29, 1812
Caruthers, John ..........Lieutenant 21st regiment..April 29, 1812
Coffer, Reuben ............Ensign 21st regiment....October 7, 1812
Crafton, John B. ..........Ensign Light Infantry
    Company attached to
    44th regiment ......September 8, 1812
Crawford, John ...........Captain Volunteer Rifle
    Company attached to
    21st regiment ...........July 1, 1812
Criddle, Edward .........Lieutenant Volunteer Rifle
    Company attached to
    21st regiment ...........July 1, 1812
Currin, Jonathan ..........Second lieutenant
    Company of* Rangers ...June 1, 1812
Curtis, Joshua ............Lieutenant
    21st regiment ......February 24, 1812
Duncan, James ............Ensign 21st regiment......April 29, 1812
Eaton, William B. .........First lieutenant
    *Company of Rangers....June 1, 1812
Gholson, Benjamin ........Ensign 21st regiment....October 7, 1812
Hall, Allen ...............Lieutenant
    21st regiment ........October 7, 1812
Harden, Jeremiah .........Captain Light Infantry
    Company attached to
    44th regiment ......September 8, 1812
Harden, Jeremiah, Jr. ......Lieutenant Light Infantry
    Company attached to
    44th regiment ......September 8, 1812
House, James .............Ensign 44th regiment......July 4, 1812
Kavanaugh, Charles .......Captain
    **Volunteer Cavalry .....July 3, 1812
Kavanaugh, Lot ...........Second Lieutenant
    **Volunteer Cavalry ....July 3, 1812
McCrory, Thomas, Jr. ......Captain 21st regiment.....April 29, 1812

---

*Company of Rangers in conformity of an Act in Congress of the United States for that purpose January 2, 1812.

McEwen, James .......... Lieutenant Volunteer
Infantry attached to
21st regiment .......... April 29, 1812
McGhan, Eli ............. Ensign 21st regiment.. February 24, 1812
Maden, Elisha ........... Ensign 21st regiment.. February 24, 1812
Marshal, Gilbert ......... Lieutenant
44th regiment ...... February 24, 1812
Mason, David ............ Captain
*Company of Rangers.... June 1, 1812
May, Benjamin .......... Lieutenant 21st regiment.. April 29, 1812
Perkins, William O. ....... Lieutenant 21st regiment.. April 29, 1812
Ragsdale, Edward ........ First Lieutenant **Cavalry. July 3, 1812
Ragsdale, John ........... Cornet **Volunteer Cavalry. July 3, 1812
Shelton, John P. .......... Lieutenant 44th regiment... July 4, 1812
Sims, James .............. Captain
21st regiment ...... February 24, 1812
Sims, Robert ............. Ensign 21st regiment.... October 7, 1812
Slater, Henry ............ Ensign 21st regiment...... April 29, 1812
Staggs, Felix ............. Ensign 21st regiment.... October 7, 1812
Staggs, Flemmon ......... Ensign 21st regiment.. February 24, 1812
Stanley, Wright .......... Ensign 21st regiment...... April 29, 1812
Swanson, Richard ........ Lieutenant Ensign
21st regiment ...... February 24, 1812
Threat, Howard D. ....... Ensign 21st regiment.... October 7, 1812
Wait, William ............ Ensign Volunteer Rifle
Company attached to
21st regiment .......... July 1, 1812
Walker, Elisha ........... Ensign 44th regiment.. February 29, 1812
Warren, Edward .......... Lieutenant
21st regiment ........ October 7, 1812
Wills, Edward ............ Ensign 21st regiment... February 24, 1812

*Wilson County Regiments*

Alexander, Joshia ......... Captain 42nd regiment..... July 24, 1812
Alexander, Robert ........ First Major
42nd regiment .......... July 24, 1812
Allen, William ............ Ensign 17th regiment... October 19, 1812
Anderson, James ......... Second Major
17th regiment .......... July 24, 1812
Armstrong, James ........ Lieutenant 42nd regiment... July 24, 1812
Avery, William ........... Ensign 17th regiment.... October 19, 1812
Bone, Henry ............. Ensign 42nd regiment.. December 31, 1812

---

** Troop of Cavalry raised in conformity with the provisions of an Act of the Congress of the United States February 2, 1812.

* Company raised in conformity with the provisions of an Act of Congress of the United States January 2, 1812.

## IN THE TENNESSEE MILITIA, 1812

Branch, Robert ............ Captain Light Infantry
Company attached to
42nd regiment .......... July 24, 1812
Byrne, Rezen ............. Captain
42nd regiment ...... December 31, 1812
Campbell, William ........ Lieutenant Light Infantry
Company attached to
42nd regiment .......... July 24, 1812
Carr, Walter .............. Ensign 17th regiment.... October 19, 1812
Clark, David .............. Lieutenant 17th regiment... June 9, 1812
Coplinger, Samuel ........ Lieutenant
42nd regiment ...... December 1, 1812
Doake, John .............. Lieutenant Colonel Commandant 42nd regiment.. June 9, 1812
Douglass, Harry L. ........ Captain 17th regiment..... June 9, 1812
Elles, John ............... Ensign 17th regiment.... October 19, 1812
Fisher, Phillip ............ Captain
42nd regiment ..... December 1, 1812
Hardrige, Zachariah ....... Ensign Light Infantry
Company attached to
42nd regiment .......... July 24, 1812
Harris, Edward ........... Captain 17th regiment.. October 19, 1812
Hill, Samuel .............. Lieutenant
42nd regiment ..... December 31, 1812
Hill, Thomas .............. Ensign 42nd regiment...... July 24, 1812
Hodges, James C. .......... Second Major
42nd regiment .......... July 24, 1812
Kelly, David .............. Ensign 42nd regiment. December 31, 1812
McDermott, Jacob ......... Ensign 17th regiment...... June 9, 1812
Marshall, Robert .......... Ensign 17th regiment...... June 9, 1812
Marshall, Robert .......... Lieutenant
17th regiment ........ October 19, 1812
Richmond, Alexander P. .... Ensign 17th regiment.... October 19, 1812
Roan, James .............. Ensign 17th regiment...... June 9, 1812
Wade, Charles ............ Captain 17th regiment..... June 9, 1812

# RECORD OF COMMISSIONS OF OFFICERS IN THE TENNESSEE MILITIA, 1813

COMPILED BY MRS. JOHN TROTWOOD MOORE

*Anderson County Commissions*

| | | |
|---|---|---|
| Butcher, Daniel | Ensign 13th regiment.... October | 1, 1813 |
| Durret, J. G. | Lieutenant 13th regiment ....... October | 1, 1813 |
| Foster, Enoch | Captain 13th regiment... October | 1, 1813 |
| Griffith, Jacob | Ensign 13th regiment.... October | 1, 1813 |
| Haskell, Charles | Lieutenant 13th regiment........ October | 1, 1813 |
| Kirkpatrick, James | Captain in Volunteer Rifle Company attached to 13th regiment..... October | 1, 1813 |
| Lewellen, Charles | Lieutenant in Volunteer Rifle Company attached to 13th regiment...... October | 1, 1813 |
| McAdoe, John | Lieutenant 13th regiment........ October | 1, 1813 |
| Miller, John | Captain 13th regiment..... April 27, | 1813 |

*Bedford County Commissions*

| | | |
|---|---|---|
| Allison, William | Lieutenant 28th regiment.. April 27, | 1813 |
| Atkinson, John | Captain Volunteer Company of men not subject to militia duty........... July 7, | 1813 |
| Barecraft, Daniel | Captain Volunteer Company attached to 28th regiment ............. April 27, | 1813 |
| Bell, Samuel | Captain 28th regiment..... April 27, | 1813 |
| Brittain, Joseph | Lieutenant Volunteer Company of men not subject to militia duty........... July 7, | 1813 |
| Burdet, Giles | Lieutenant Colonel Commandant 28th regiment...... September 28, | 1813 |
| Burnam, Samuel | Ensign Volunteer Rifle Company attached to 47th regiment...... November 8, | 1813 |
| Busby, Thomas | Captain 47th regiment..... June 14, | 1813 |
| Calhoun, John | Lieutenant 47th regiment....... November 8, | 1813 |
| Carothers, William | Captain 47th regiment... August 13, | 1813 |
| Christian, William | Ensign 47th regiment.... August 13, | 1813 |
| Dandy, Elancer | Ensign 47th regiment...... June 14, | 1813 |

IN THE TENNESSEE MILITIA, 1813        197

Dixon, James ............Ensign Volunteer Company
                          of men not subject
                          to militia duty ..........July 7, 1813
Fleming, Samuel .........Captain 28th regiment...August 7, 1813
Hall, Elisha .............Captain 28th regiment.February 11, 1813
Hall, John ...............Captain 47th regiment.....June 14, 1813
Harris, James ............Captain Company Light
                          Infantry attached to
                          28th regiment..........April 27, 1813
Kelly, Alfred ............Ensign 28th regiment..February 11, 1813
Kerr, James ..............Lieutenant
                          28th regiment.......February 11, 1813
King, Jacob ..............Ensign 28th regiment..February 11, 1813
McCrory, John ............Ensign 47th regiment..November 8, 1813
McGill, James ............Captain 47th regiment.November 8, 1813
Marshall, Leven ..........Lieutenant 47th regiment...June 14, 1813
Medaris, Washington D. ...Captain 28th regiment.February 11, 1813
Miller, William ..........Ensign 28th regiment..February 11, 1813
Neil, John ...............Captain 28th regiment.February 11, 1813
Norman, Thomas ..........Lieutenant 47th regiment..June 14, 1813
Orr, John ................Lieutenant
                          28th regiment.......February 11, 1813
Orr, Robert ..............Ensign 28th regiment..February 11, 1813
Parker, Noah .............Ensign 47th regiment......June 14, 1813
Parker, Samuel ...........Captain 47th regiment....June 14, 1814
Paterson, Andrew ........Lieutenant regiment of cavalry
                          in 6th brigade.....September 27, 1813
Patterson, Andrew .......Captain 28th regiment.February 11, 1813
Patton, Samuel B. ........Captain Volunteer Rifle
                          Company attached to
                          47th regiment......November 8, 1813
Perry, William ...........Lieutenant
                          28th regiment.......February 11, 1813
Ragsdale, John, Senr. ......Captain regiment of
                          cavalry 5th brigade.September 27, 1813
Saling, Peter ............Lieutenant 47th regiment...June 14, 1813
Shinault, Walter .........Lieutenant 47th regiment...June 14, 1813
Thompson, Reuben ........Ensign 28th regiment......April 27, 1813
Yates, Thomas ...........Lieutenant 47th regiment.August 13, 1813

*Bledsoe County Commissions*

Cherry, Benjamin ........Ensign 31st regiment..November 8, 1813
Hoge, Joseph ............Lieutenant Volunteer Company
                          of men not subject
                          to militia duty..........May 3, 1813
Jones, John ..............Captain Volunteer Rifle
                          Company attached to
                          31st regiment......November 8, 1813

# RECORD OF COMMISSIONS OF OFFICERS

Lewis, Jesse ..............Lieutenant Volunteer Rifle
Company attached to
31st regiment......November 8, 1813
Rainey, John ..............Ensign 31st regiment..November 8, 1813
Rany, William ............Captain Volunteer Company
of men not subject
to militia duty..........May 3, 1813
Roberson, William .........Ensign Volunteer Company
of men not subject
to militia duty ..........May 3, 1813

## Blount County Commissions

Campbell, Arthur .........Ensign 12th regiment.November 8, 1813
Gamble, James ............Ensign 12th regiment.November 8, 1813
Gardiner, James ..........Lieutenant 12th regiment..April 27, 1813
Hamble, Robert ..........Lieutenant 12th regiment..April 27, 1813
Houston, Samuel ..........Second Major
12th regiment..........May 19, 1813
Jones, Robert ............Lieutenant
12th regiment......November 8, 1813
McCartney, James ........Lieutenant
12th regiment......November 8, 1813
Megill, William ..........Ensign 12th regiment.....April 27, 1813
Strain, John .............Lieutenant
12th regiment......November 8, 1813
Tedford, James ..........Ensign 12th regiment.November 8, 1813
Thornberry, John .........Captain 12th regiment.....April 27, 1813
Wallace, Benjamin ........Ensign 12th regiment.November 8, 1813
Wallace, William ..........Captain
12th regiment......November 8, 1813
Whittenbarger, Mathew ....Lieutenant
12th regiment......November 8, 1813
Woods, Joseph B. ..........Ensign 12th regiment.....April 27, 1813
Young, Robert ............Lieutenant
12th regiment......November 8, 1813

## Campbell County Commissions

Brien, Henry .............Captain 33rd regiment.....April 27, 1813
Camron, Elisha ..........Captain 33rd regiment...August 7, 1813
Jackson, Thomas ..........Lieutenant
33rd regiment........October 2, 1813
Lek, Mathew H. ...........Ensign 33rd regiment...October 2, 1813
Perkins, Edward .........Captain 33rd regiment...August 7, 1813
Pierfelt, Jeremiah ........Lieutenant
33rd regiment........October 2, 1813
Smith, Thomas ............First Major
33rd regiment.........August 7, 1813

IN THE TENNESSEE MILITIA, 1813      199

Whilams, James ..........Captain 33rd regiment...August 7, 1813

### Carter County Commissions

Bogart, Samuel ............Captain 5th regiment......July 7, 1813
Boring, Greenberry ........Lieutenant 5th regiment....July 7, 1813
Boyd, Bartley ............Lieutenant 5th regiment....June 14, 1813
Boyd, Bartley ............Captain
         5th regiment.........October 1, 1813
Gourley, Robert ..........Ensign 5th regiment.......July 7, 1813
Reese, Isaac .............Ensign 5th regiment.......June 14, 1813
Smith, Daniel, Jr. .........Captain 5th regiment.February 11, 1813

### Claiborne County Commissions

Bales, Alexander ..........Cornet regiment of cavalry
         2nd brigade..........January 28, 1813
Bobbs, Seth ...............Captain 9th regiment.....April 27, 1813
Brock, George ............Lieutenant 9th regiment...April 27, 1813
Dobbs, William ..........Captain 9th regiment .....April 27, 1813
Gosage, William ..........Lieutenant 9th regiment...April 27, 1813
Huston, William ..........Captain regiment of cavalry
         2nd Brigade.........January 28, 1813
Neil, Grimes .............Lieutenant regiment of
         cavalry 2nd Brigade..January 28, 1813
Onsley, Stephen ..........Ensign 9th regiment.......April 27, 1813
Osly, Nathan .............Ensign 9th regiment.......April 27, 1813
York, William ............Lieutenant 9th regiment...April 27, 1813

### Cocke County Commissions

Derrett, John H. ..........Lieutenant regiment of
         cavalry 8th regiment.February 11, 1813
Fine, L. .................Captain 8th regiment..February 11, 1813
Goan, Shadrick ..........Lieutenant
         8th regiment........February 11, 1813
Hill, Jesse ...............Lieutenant 8th regiment..August 31, 1813
Irwin, Joseph, Junr. .......Captain 8th regiment....August 31, 1813
Jack, Samuel ............Captain 8th regiment....August 31, 1813
Jackson, Robert ..........Captain 8th regiment..February 11, 1813
McMillan, Daniel ........Captain 8th regiment....August 31, 1813
Nave, Henry .............Ensign 8th regiment.....August 31, 1813
Nelson, John ............Lieutenant
         8th regiment.......November 8, 1813
Sisk, Elias ...............Ensign 8th regiment.....August 31, 1813
White, John ..............Cornet regiment of cavalry
         8th regiment........February 11, 1813
White, William ..........Captain regiment of cavalry
         8th regiment........February 11, 1813

# RECORD OF COMMISSIONS OF OFFICERS

## Davidson County Commissions

| | | |
|---|---|---|
| Ballow, William | Captain 20th regiment | December 21, 1813 |
| Campbell, Phillip | First Major 19th Brigade | April 7, 1813 |
| Childress, Nathaniel G. | Ensign 20th regiment | May 3, 1813 |
| Clanton, Drury | Lieutenant 19th regiment | August 7, 1813 |
| Cobler, John | Ensign 19th regiment | June 14, 1813 |
| Critz, George F. | Lieutenant 19th regiment | June 14, 1813 |
| Demoss, John | Captain 19th regiment | August 31, 1813 |
| Drake, John, Junr. | Lieutenant 20th regiment | May 3, 1813 |
| Fotherage, David | Ensign 20th regiment | May 3, 1813 |
| Hardgrave, Shelton | Lieutenant 19th regiment | January 28, 1813 |
| Herbet, Nathaniel | Ensign 19th regiment | August 7, 1813 |
| Hicks, James G. | Captain 19th regiment | August 31, 1813 |
| Hicks, John C. | Lieutenant 19th regiment | August 31, 1813 |
| Hobbs, Edward D. | Second Major 19th regiment | April 7, 1813 |
| Hooper, John | Lieutenant 20th regiment | May 3, 1813 |
| Howell, James | Lieutenant 19th regiment | March 6, 1813 |
| Kennedy, Lemuel | Lieutenant 20th regiment | May 3, 1813 |
| McCutcheon, William | Ensign 19th regiment | August 7, 1813 |
| Maxey, Bennet | Lieutenant 20th regiment | December 21, 1813 |
| Miller, William S. | Ensign 19th regiment | August 7, 1813 |
| Moore, John | Lieutenant 19th regiment | June 14, 1813 |
| Osborn, Thompson | Ensign 19th regiment | March 6, 1813 |
| Payne, Greenwood | Lieutenant 20th regiment | September 24, 1813 |
| Pierce, Jeremiah | Captain 20th regiment | May 3, 1813 |
| Pipkin, Thomas B. | Captain 19th regiment | June 14, 1813 |
| Scott, George | Ensign 19th regiment | March 6, 1813 |
| Sitler, James W. | Captain Company of Republican Blues attached to 19th regiment | August 7, 1813 |
| Stull, Samuel | Ensign 20th regiment | December 21, 1813 |
| Thompson, Allen | Captain 19th regiment | March 6, 1813 |
| White, Thomas | Lieutenant in Captain Frederick Stump's Company of Mounted infantry attached to 20th regiment | September 24, 1813 |
| Williams, James | Ensign 20th regiment | May 3, 1813 |

## Dickson County Commissions

| | | |
|---|---|---|
| Bibb, Minor | Lieutenant 25th regiment | February 20, 1813 |

# IN THE TENNESSEE MILITIA, 1813

Fish, James ...............Ensign 25th regiment......July 7, 1813
Gallion, George ..........Captain 25th regiment.....July 7, 1813
Green, Elisha ............Ensign 25th regiment......April 27, 1813
Horner, George ...........Captain 25th regiment.February 20, 1813
King, Jonathan ...........Ensign 25th regiment......July 7, 1813
McCawley, James .........Lieutenant 25th regiment...July 7, 1813
Shelby, William ..........Captain 25th regiment.....July 7, 1813

### Franklin County Commissions

Armstrong, William .......Ensign 32nd regiment.September 30, 1813
Atwood, Peter B. ..........Captain 32nd regiment...March 22, 1813
Ayres, Moses .............Captain 32nd regiment.....June 14, 1813
Collins, Barbe ............Captain 32nd regiment...March 22, 1813
Covey, Joseph ............Captain
 32nd regiment......September 30, 1813
Cowan, James ............Captain 32nd regiment...March 22, 1813
Estes, Andrew ............Lieutenant 32nd regiment March 22, 1813
Estes, John ...............Ensign 32nd regiment....March 22, 1813
Doddy, Alfred ............Ensign 32nd regiment.....June 14, 1813
Dougan, Sharp ...........Ensign 32nd regiment....March 22, 1813
Faris, Absolam ...........Lieutenant 32nd regiment..June 14, 1813
Farris, Absolam ..........Lieutenant
 32nd regiment......September 30, 1813
Farris, Joseph ............Ensign 32nd regiment.September 30, 1813
Foreman, Wilson .........Ensign 32nd regiment.September 30, 1813
Gilliam, Thomas .........Captain 32nd regiment.....June 14, 1813
Gooden, Jesse ............Captain
 32nd regiment.........March 22, 1813
Greenlee, James ..........Ensign 32nd regiment.September 30, 1813
Holmes, Josiah L. .........Lieutenant
 32nd regiment........March 22, 1813
Hunt, Henry .............Captain 32nd regiment.....June 14, 1813
Jordan, John .............Ensign 32nd regiment.....June 14, 1813
Jordan, John .............Lieutenant
 32nd regiment.....September 30, 1813
Kuykindale, James ........Lieutenant 32nd regiment..June 14, 1813
Lassiter, Abner ...........Ensign 32nd regiment....March 22, 1813
Neighbours, Francis .......Captain
 32nd regiment.....September 30, 1813
Nichols, Solomon .........Ensign 32nd regiment.....June 14, 1813
Robertson, John ..........Lieutenant 32nd regiment.March 22, 1813
Scandling, William ........Ensign 32nd regiment......June 14, 1813
Sisk, James ...............Ensign 32nd regiment......June 14, 1813
Tarrant, John ............Captain
 32nd regiment......September 30, 1813
Taylor, James ............Lieutenant
 32nd regiment......September 30, 1813

Walker, Andrew ...........Lieutenant 32nd regiment..June 14, 1813
Woods, Peter ..............Lieutenant 32nd regiment..June 14, 1813

*Giles County Commissions*

Bentley, Richard ..........Ensign 37th regiment......June 14, 1813
Biles, Stephen .............Lieutenant regiment of cavalry
                                            5th Brigade........September 7, 1813
Brown, George ............Lieutenant 37th regiment.August 2, 1813
Brownlow, William ........Lieutenant Light Infantry
                                            attached to 37th regiment.June 14, 1813
Campbell, George .........Captain 37th regiment....April 27, 1813
Clark, Thomas ............Lieutenant
                                            37th regiment.......February 11, 1813
Carrell, Clemment ........Ensign 37th regiment......June 14, 1813
Forrest, Nathan ...........Cornet regiment of
                                            cavalry 5th brigade.September 7, 1813
Gordin, John .............Cornet regiment of
                                            cavalry 5th brigade..February 23, 1813
Harrelson, Thomas ........Lieutenant
                                            37th regiment.......February 11, 1813
Hill, Caleb ...............Captain 37th regiment...August 2, 1813
McLaughlin Elijah .......Ensign Light Infantry attached
                                            to 37th regiment........June 14, 1813
Malton, Elijah ............Ensign 37th regiment....August 31, 1813
Mayfield, Campbell .......Ensign 37th regiment......June 14, 1813
Mitchell, Marcus ..........Lieutenant 37th regiment..June 14, 1813
Paxton, James ............Captain 37th regiment...August 31, 1813
Phillips, Thomas ..........Captain 37th regiment...August 31, 1813
Pickens, James ...........Captain Light Infantry
                                            Company attached to
                                            37th regiment..........April 27, 1813
Pickens, Robert ...........Ensign 37th regiment......April 27, 1813
Quinn, James .............Lieutenant 37th regiment..April 27, 1813
Read, Robert .............Captain
                                            37th regiment.......February 11, 1813
Samuel, John .............Ensign 37th regiment..February 11, 1813
Thompson, John ..........Lieutenant 37th regiment..June 14, 1813
Tinnen, John .............Lieutenant 37th regiment..June 14, 1813
Turner, William ..........Ensign 37th regiment....August 31, 1813
Wilkerson, Thomas ........Lieutenant 37th regiment..June 14, 1813
Williams, James H. ........Captain Volunteer Rifle
                                            Company attached to
                                            37th regiment..........June 14, 1813
Young, Nathaniel .........Lieutenant 37th regiment.August 31, 1813

*Grainger County Commissions*

Arwine, John .............Captain 7th regiment......July 24, 1813
Clingan, Thomas ..........Lieutenant 7th regiment....July 24, 1813

IN THE TENNESSEE MILITIA, 1813 203

*Greene County Commissions*

Adams, David ............Ensign 3rd regiment....October 1, 1813
Bibb, George .............Ensign 3rd regiment...December 21, 1813
Bibb, John ...............Lieutenant
                          3rd regiment.......December 21, 1813
Blevins, George ...........Ensign 3rd regiment.....October 1, 1813
Bowman, Henry ..........Captain 3rd regiment...October 1, 1813
Farrensworth, David ......Lieutenant
                          3rd regiment.........October 1, 1813
Greeham, Joseph ..........Lieutenant
                          3rd regiment.........October 1, 1813
Harmon, Peter ...........Lieutenant Light Infantry attached
                          to 3rd regiment......October 1, 1813
Johnston, Stephen .........Captain 3rd regiment...October 1, 1813
McCalpin, Robert .........Captain 3rd regiment...October 1, 1813
Meroney, Phillip D. .......Captain 3rd regiment...October 1, 1813
Reeves, George ...........Lieutenant Volunteer Rifle
                          Company attached to
                          3rd regiment.........October 1, 1813
Robertson, James .........Ensign 3rd regiment....October 1, 1813
Scrugs, James ...........Ensign 3rd regiment....October 1, 1813
Smith, William ...........Lieutenant
                          3rd regiment.........October 1, 1813
Smith, William ...........Captain 3rd regiment..December 21, 1813

*Hawkins County Commissions*

Balden, Nicholas ..........Lieutenant
                          4th regiment.......September 27, 1813
Barnard, Jonathan ........Captain
                          4th regiment.......September 27, 1813
Burton, Robert ...........Ensign
                          4th regiment.......September 27, 1813
Cruise, Jacob ............Captain
                          4th regiment.......September 27, 1813
Cumins, James ...........Captain
                          4th regiment.......September 27, 1813
Foster, Winkfield .........Lieutenant
                          4th regiment.......September 27, 1813
Gillenwaters, William T. ...Ensign
                          4th regiment.......September 27, 1813
Hainey, Daniel ...........Ensign
                          4th regiment.......December 21, 1813
Hale, George ............Lieutenant Colonel Commandant
                          4th regiment........February 19, 1813
Hale, John ..............Lieutenant
                          4th regiment.......September 27, 1813

McVeil, Neil ............. Captain
    4th regiment....... September 27, 1813
Mann, William ........... Ensign
    4th regiment....... September 27, 1813
Martin, James ........... Lieutenant
    4th regiment....... September 27, 1813
Moore, Cleon ............ Lieutenant
    4th regiment....... September 27, 1813
Owen, Fain .............. Ensign
    4th regiment....... September 27, 1813
Slaten, John ............. Captain
    4th regiment....... December 21, 1813

### Hickman County Commissions

Bowen, Robert G. ......... Lieutennat
    36th regiment...... December 21, 1813
Copeland, Ripley .......... Ensign 36th regiment.... August 2, 1813
Easley, Stephen ........... Ensign 36th regiment...... June 14, 1813
Flin, John .............. Ensign 36th regiment...... April 27, 1813
Higgenbotham, Alexander .. Captain 36th regiment... August 2, 1813
Jones, Harvey ........... Captain 36th regiment..... April 27, 1813
Lane, Garret ............. Captain 36th regiment.. January 28, 1813
McSwiney, Alexander ..... Captain 36th regiment..... June 14, 1813
Tolly, Barnard ........... Lieutenant
    36th regiment...... December 21, 1813
Walker, Richard ......... Lieutenant
    36th regiment......... August 2, 1813

### Humphreys County Commissions

Barker, Allen ............. Ensign 38th regiment... August 17, 1813
Burton, Samuel H. ........ Captain 38th regiment.. August 17, 1813
Hildreth, Reuben ......... Ensign 38th regiment... October 1, 1813
Hudson, Edward G. ....... Ensign 38th regiment...... June 7, 1813
Lattimore, James ......... Lieutenant
    38th regiment...... November 8, 1813
McFall, Samuel P. ........ Lieutenant
    38th regiment......... August 17, 1813
Moore, James ............ Lieutenant 38th regiment... June 7, 1813
Vinson, George ........... Captain 38th regiment.. October 1, 1813

### Jackson County Commissions

Butler, Thomas ........... First Major
    48th regiment....... January 28, 1813
Montgomery, Alexander .... Second Major
    48th regiment........ January 28, 1813

IN THE TENNESSEE MILITIA, 1813          205

Scanland, William ........Lieutenant Colonel Commandant
                         48th regiment........January 28, 1813
Smith, Samuel, G. .........Second Major
                         48th regiment........March 29, 1813

*Jefferson County Commissions*

Baker, John ..............Lieutenant 6th regiment....June 14, 1813
Bradford, James .........Lieutenant Colonel Commandant
                         6th regiment.......November 8, 1813
Carbet, James ...........Lieutenant 6th regiment..August 17, 1813
Doherty, George .........Second Major
                         6th regiment.......November 8, 1813
Hill, James ..............Ensign 6th regiment..November 8, 1813
Horner, Isaac ............Lieutenant
                         6th regiment.......November 8, 1813
Jarnagan, Preston B. ......Captain 6th regiment......June 14, 1813
Johnson, Joseph ..........Captain Volunteer Rifle
                         Company attached to
                         6th regiment.......November 8, 1813
McCeustian, Thomas ......Captain 6th regiment......June 14, 1813
McClanahan, Alexander ...Lieutenant Volunteer Rifle
                         Company attached to
                         6th regiment.......November 8, 1813
McDonald, William .......Lieutenant
                         6th regiment.......November 8, 1813
McGee, Bartley ..........Ensign 6th regiment..November 8, 1813
Meales, Lewis ...........Ensign 6th regiment..November 8, 1813
Moreland, William ........Ensign 6th regiment.......June 14, 1813
Reaves, Samuel ..........Ensign 6th regiment.....August 17, 1813
Riche, James ............Ensign Volunteer Rifle
                         Company attached to
                         6th regiment.......November 8, 1813
Ropper, John ............Captain 6th regiment......June 14, 1813
Slover, John .............Lieutenant
                         6th regiment.......November 8, 1813
Snoddy, James ...........Lieutenant
                         6th regiment.......November 8, 1813
Toff, John ..............Captain
                         6th regiment.......November 8, 1813

*Knox County Commissions*

Armstrong, Aaron ........Lieutenant 10th regiment.August 7, 1813
Birdwell, George .........Ensign Volunteer Rifle
                         Company attached to
                         40th regiment........January 28, 1813
Bond, Stephen ...........Captain Volunteer Rifle
                         Company attached to
                         40th regiment........January 28, 1813

Boyd, James ..............Lieutenant 40th regiment..April 27, 1813
Boyd, James ..............Lieutenant 40th regiment...May 19, 1813
Breedlove, Charles ........Lieutenant 10th regiment.August 7, 1813
Chumneigh, John ..........Ensign 10th regiment....August 7, 1813
Crawford, Samuel .........Ensign 10th regiment...January 28, 1813
Douglas, Alexander ........Captain 10th regiment...August 7, 1813
Graves, Henry ............Captain 10th regiment...August 7, 1813
Hansard, John ............Ensign 10th regiment....October 1, 1813
Hood, John ...............Lieutenant 40th regiment..June 14, 1813
Hood, Luke ...............Ensign 40th regiment......June 14, 1813
Lonas, Henry .............Lieutenant 40th regiment..April 27, 1813
Lonas, Jacob .............Lieutenant 40th regiment...May 19, 1813
McLemore, Areabel .......Ensign 10th regiment..January 28, 1813
Mulvaney, Henry .........Lieutenant 10th regiment.August 7, 1813
Parsons, Enoch ............Brigadier Major
                              1st brigade...........August 17, 1813
Pew, Daniel ..............Ensign 10th regiment....August 7, 1813
Swan, John ...............Lieutenant Volunteer Rifle
                              Company attached to
                              40th regiment........January 28, 1813
Trout, Michael ............Lieutenant
                              10th regiment........January 28, 1813
Turner, Jesse .............Ensign 10th regiment...January 28, 1813
Whitson, John ............Ensign 40th regiment......May 19, 1813
Whitson, William ........Ensign 40th regiment......April 27, 1813

*Lincoln County Commissions*

Adkins, Thomas ..........Ensign 49th regiment..February 23, 1813
Awalt, Michael ...........Captain
                              49th regiment......November 8, 1813
Buchannan, John B. .......Cornet regiment of cavalry
                              5th brigade..........October 1, 1813
Chapman, Robert ........Lieutenant
                              39th regiment........January 28, 1813
Cox, Adam ...............Lieutenant
                              49th regiment.......February 23, 1813
Cuningham, Robert .......Lieutenant
                              49th regiment......November 8, 1813
Floyd, Jonathan ..........Lieutenant
                              49th regiment......November 8, 1813
George, John .............Lieutenant
                              49th regiment......November 8, 1813
Humphreys, John ........Captain
                              39th regiment.........January 8, 1813
Irvine, Robert ............Captain
                              39th regiment.........August 31, 1813
McDowell, Benjamin ......Lieutenant
                              49th regiment......November 8, 1813

Morgan, John ............Ensign 49th regiment. November 8, 1813
Mucbery, Archibald ......Lieutenant regiment of cavalry
                          5th brigade..........October 1, 1813
Murphy, John ............Captain regiment of cavalry
                          5th brigade..........October 1, 1813
Nail, Samuel ............Ensign 39th regiment....August 31, 1813
Norton, John ............Lieutenant 39th regiment. August 31, 1813
O'Callahan, Patrick .......Captain Light Infantry
                          Company attached to
                          49th regiment......November 8, 1813
Osburn, John .............Lieutenant Volunteer
                          Company attached to
                          39th regiment.........August 31, 1813
Payne, Joel ...............Ensign Light Infantry
                          Company attached to
                          49th regiment......November 8, 1813
Pulloum, William .........Lieutenant
                          49th regiment........January 23, 1813
Rapier, John ............Captain
                          49th regiment......November 8, 1813
Reid, Clement ............Lieutenant 39th regiment. August 31, 1813
Scales, Robert ...........Ensign 39th regiment....August 31, 1813
Simms, Bartlett ..........Ensign 49th regiment..February 23, 1813
Simms, James ............Captain 49th regiment. February 23, 1813
Small, George ............Ensign 49th regiment..February 23, 1813
Smith, Joel ..............Ensign 39th regiment....August 31, 1813
Sumner, Isaac ............Ensign Volunteer Rifle Company
                          attached to
                          39th regiment.........August 31, 1813
White, Robert ............Captain 39th regiment...August 31, 1813
Wilson, William ..........Captain Volunteer Rifle
                          Company attached to
                          39th regiment.........August 31, 1813
Woodward, German .......Ensign 39th regiment....August 31, 1813

*Maury County Commissions*

Alexander, Adam R. .......Second Major
                          27th regiment......September 10, 1813
Allen, Henry D. ..........Captain
                          27th regiment........January 28, 1813
Arnold, Robert ...........Lieutenant
                          27th regiment........January 28, 1813
Aydolott, Thomas W. ......Ensign 46th regiment......May 14, 1815
Bankhead, George ........Lieutenant 27th regiment..July 10, 1813
Brown, Joseph ...........Lieutenant Colonel Commandant
                          27th regiment......September 10, 1813
Burges, Nathaniel G. ......Lieutenant
                          46th regiment......November 8, 1813

## RECORD OF COMMISSIONS OF OFFICERS

Caldwell, Amos ........... Lieutenant
    46th regiment........... May 19, 1813
Campbell, George ......... Lieutenant
    27th regiment........ October 1, 1813
Cockburn, George ......... Ensign 27th regiment.... October 1, 1813
Coe, Joseph .............. Lieutenant 27th regiment... July 10, 1813
Coffee, Joel .............. Ensign 27th regiment... January 28, 1813
Copeland, Anthony ........ First Major
    27th regiment...... September 10, 1813
Crawford, William ......... Lieutenant 46th regiment... May 19, 1813
Dickey, Benoni ........... First Major
    51st regiment...... November 10, 1813
Dixon, Samuel ............ Captain 27th regiment. February 11, 1813
Dobbins, James ........... Ensign 27th regiment... January 28, 1813
Dobbins, James ........... Captain regiment of cavalry
    5th brigade........ November 8, 1813
Duckworth, John ......... Ensign 46th regiment. November 8, 1813
Fly, William .............. Lieutenant 46th regiment... May 19, 1813
Gurley, Jeremiah ......... Lieutenant Colonel Commandant
    51st regiment...... November 18, 1813
Hanks, George ............ Captain 46th regiment..... May 19, 1813
Herrin, Solomon .......... Ensign 46th regiment. November 8, 1813
Huey, James .............. Cornet regiment of cavalry
    5th brigade........... August 13, 1813
Hughey, John ............. Ensign 46th regiment...... May 19, 1813
Isham, James ............. Second Major
    51st regiment...... November 18, 1813
Isom, George ............. Lieutenant regiment of cavalry
    5th brigade........ November 8, 1813
Jasey, James ............. Lieutenant
    27th regiment....... February 11, 1813
Kendrick, John ............ Lieutenant
    27th regiment....... February 11, 1813
Kenner, Eli ............... Ensign 27th regiment... October 1, 1813
Lewis, Benjamin H. ........ Lieutenant regiment of cavalry
    5th brigade........ November 8, 1813
Looney, John ............. Captain
    27th regiment........ January 28, 1813
McBride, Samuel .......... Lieutenant
    27th regiment........ October 1, 1813
McNeil, Thomas .......... Captain 46th regiment..... May 19, 1813
May, Charles P. ........... Captain 27th regiment.. October 1, 1813
Miller, Daniel B. .......... Lieutenant
    46th regiment...... November 8, 1813
Mitchell, John ............ Captain 46th regiment..... May 19, 1813
Ogelvie, David ............ Lieutenant regiment of cavalry
    5th brigade......... February 18, 1813
Oglevie, David ............ Captain regiment of cavalry

IN THE TENNESSEE MILITIA, 1813 209

|                        |                                              |
|------------------------|----------------------------------------------|
|                        | 5th brigade..........October 9, 1813         |
| Pryor, Peter ..............| Ensign 46th regiment. November 8, 1813   |
| Rees, Joel ...............| Lieutenant                                |
|                        | 27th regiment........January 28, 1813        |
| Rees, Joel ...............| Captain 27th regiment.....July 10, 1813   |
| Secrest, Leroy ............| Ensign 46th regiment. November 8, 1813  |
| Shipley, Benjamin .........| Ensign Light Infantry                    |
|                        | Company attached to                          |
|                        | 46th regiment......November 8, 1813          |
| Stanfield, William ........| Ensign 27th regiment..February 11, 1813  |
| Walker, Thomas ...........| Captain                                   |
|                        | 27th regiment.......February 11, 1813        |

### Montgomery County Commissions

Bailey, Jesse ..............Ensign 50th regiment.....April 27, 1813
Bogard, Joseph ...........Ensign 50th regiment. November 2, 1813
Bridgwater, Richard .......Lieutenant 50th regiment..April 27, 1813
Brown, William L. .........Captain 24th regiment...August 31, 1813
Davidson, Charlton B. .....Cornet regiment of cavalry
                           6th brigade........September 27, 1813
Carney, James W. ........Lieutenant 50th regiment..June 18, 1813
Dean, William ............Ensign Light Infantry Company
                           24th regiment.........August 31, 1813
Hampton, Abner ..........Ensign 50th regiment......June 18, 1813
Hunter, Dempsey .........Ensign 50th regiment. November 2, 1813
Laughridge, Abraham .....Lieutenant 24th regiment.August 31, 1813
Malky, Benjamin .........Lieutenant
                           50th regiment......November 2, 1813
Shammell, Joseph .........Lieutenant
                           50th regiment......November 2, 1813

### Overton County Commissions

Baty, David ..............Lieutenant 35th regiment..April 27, 1813
Boswell, John .............Ensign Volunteer Rifle
                           Company attached to
                           35th regiment.........August 31, 1813
Bradshaw, James .........Lieutenant 35th regiment..April 27, 1813
Burris, John ..............Lieutenant Volunteer Company
                           of men not subject to
                           militia duty............May 3, 1813
Chilton, William ..........Captain Volunteer Company
                           of men not subject to
                           militia duty............May 3, 1813
Copeland, Richard ........Captain (Volunteer) Company
                           of men not subject to
                           militia duty..........August 31, 1813
Fisher, Samuel ..........Ensign 35th regiment......April 27, 1813

Forbes, George ..........Lieutenant (Volunteer) Company
 of men not subject to
 militia duty..........August 31, 1813
Goaro, Henry .............Lieutenant 35th regiment..April 27, 1813
Hearn, Howell ............Ensign (Volunteer) Company
 of men not subject to
 militia duty..........August 31, 1813
Hines, Simeon ............Captain 35th regiment.....April 27, 1813
Hinshaw, Benjamin ........Ensign (Volunteer) Company
 of men not subject to
 militia duty.............May 3, 1813
Hood, Stanwix ............Captain (Volunteer) Company
 not subject to
 militia duty............May 3, 1813
McConnell, Francis .......Captain 35th regiment.....April 27, 1813
Matlock, William .........Ensign (Volunteer) Company
 of men not subject to
 militia duty............May 3, 1813
Miller, John ..............Captain Volunteer Rifle
 Company attached to
 35th regiment.........August 31, 1813
Miller, Samuel ...........Lieutenant Volunteer Rifle
 Company attached to
 35th regiment.........August 31, 1813
Morris, John .............Ensign 35th regiment......April 27, 1813
Ramsey, Alexander ........Ensign 35th regiment.......July 7, 1813
Richardson, Abel .........Ensign 35th regiment.......July 7, 1813
Robb, Arthur .............Ensign 35th regiment......April 27, 1813
Smith, Iri ................Lieutenant 35th regiment...July 7, 1813
Wallis, George ...........Lieutenant (Volunteer) Company
 of men not subject to
 militia duty............May 3, 1813
Weaver, Abraham .........Ensign 35th regiment......July 7, 1813
Weaver, Phillip ..........Lieutenant 35th regiment..April 27, 1813

*Rhea County Commissions*

Berry, Hugh ..............Ensign 30th regiment.September 15, 1813
Brewer, Silvanus ..........Ensign 30th regiment.September 15, 1813
Catchings, Saymore .......Lieutenant
 30th regiment......September 15, 1813
Crumb, David ............Lieutenant
 35th regiment......September 15, 1813
Johnson, John ............Captain
 30th regiment......September 15, 1813
Mitchell, James C. .........First Major
 30th regiment.........March 22, 1813
Patterson, John ..........Ensign 30th regiment.September 15, 1813

IN THE TENNESSEE MILITIA, 1813 211

Shultz, Martin S. .......... Ensign 30th regiment.September 15, 1813

*Roane County Commissions*

Dalton, William .......... Ensign 14th regiment...January 28, 1813
Hall, Garrett ............. Captain 14th regiment...August 31, 1813
Hembery, Benjamin ........ Ensign Volunteer Rifle
  Company attached to
  14th regiment......... August 13, 1813
Ingliss, Mathew ........... Ensign 14th regiment...January 28, 1813
Stockton, Thomas ......... Lieutenant 14th regiment.August 31, 1813
Stout, Abraham ........... Captain Volunteer Rifle
  Company attached to
  14th regiment......... August 31, 1813
Teader, James ............ Lieutenant 14th regiment.August 13, 1813
Williams, Mathew ......... Lieutenant 14th regiment.August 13, 1813

*Robertson County Commissions*

Biddle, Charles ............ Lieutenant
  23rd regiment...... November 23, 1813
Gardner, Dempsey ......... Ensign 23rd regiment..... March 22, 1813
Jones, Thorington ........ Lieutenant 23rd regiment.March 22, 1813
Justice, Alfred ............ Captain 23rd regiment... March 22, 1813
Moore, Joseph ............ Ensign 23rd regiment.November 23, 1813
Payne, Warren ............ Ensign 23rd regiment.November 22, 1813
Wair, George T. ........... Lieutenant 23rd regiment.March 22, 1813
Williams, Samuel ......... Captain 23rd regiment...August 31, 1813
Yeates, James ............ Captain 23rd regiment..... May 3, 1813
Young, William .......... Lieutenant 23rd regiment...June 14, 1813

*Rutherford County Commissions*

Barkley, James ........... Captain 45th regiment..... July 24, 1813
Bass, Benjamin J. ......... Ensign 22nd regiment.February 11, 1813
Bass, Thomas ............. Lieutenant
  22nd regiment...... February 11, 1813
Bethel, John .............. Ensign Light Infantry
  attached to
  22nd regiment......... April 27, 1813
Bole, James .............. Lieutenant 45th regiment...July 24, 1813
Bowman, William ......... First Major
  22nd regiment...... September 3, 1813
Cooke, Hezekiah G. ........ Lieutenant
  22nd regiment....... January 28, 1813
Fleming, David .......... Lieutenant 45th regiment...June 14, 1813
Hollice, M. .............. Lieutenant 45th regiment...July 24, 1813
Kelough, Thomas .......... Captain 45th regiment...August 17, 1813
Knight, John ............. Captain 22nd regiment..October 1, 1813
Lonay, Abner ............ Ensign 45th regiment...... June 14, 1813

# RECORD OF COMMISSIONS OF OFFICERS

McClannahan, Mathew ....Lieutenant Colonel Commandant
    22nd regiment.....September 3, 1813
McEwen, James ..........Ensign 45th regiment.......July 24, 1813
McKinney, John ..........Lieutenant
    22nd regiment........October 1, 1813
McLendon, Bright .........Ensign 22nd regiment...January 28, 1813
Pearce, Stokeley ...........Ensign 45th regiment....August 17, 1813
Porter, Hugh ..............Lieutenant 45th regiment...June 14, 1813
Rhay, John ...............Lieutenant 45th regiment.August 17, 1813
Robeson, Mathew .........Lieutenant 45th regiment...June 14, 1813
Shanks, Archibald .........Captain
    45th regiment.......January 28, 1813
Smith, Luke ...............Lieutenant
    22nd regiment........October 1, 1813
Thompson, John ...........Ensign 45th regiment......July 24, 1813
Tucker, Marady ..........Lieutenant
    45th regiment.......January 28, 1813
Vaughn, William ..........Lieutenant
    45th regiment..........June 14, 1813
White, William ............Captain 22nd regiment..October 1, 1813
Whitsett, Thomas .........Ensign 22nd regiment...October 1, 1813
Yourey, Francis ...........Captain 45th regiment......July 24, 1813
Zacherry, Josiah ..........Captain
    22nd regiment......November 8, 1813

## Sevier County Commissions

Breden, William ..........Ensign 11th regiment......April 27, 1813
Clark, Benjamin ..........Ensign 11th regiment....August 31, 1813
Pierce, John ..............Captain 11th regiment.....April 27, 1813
Porter, John .............Ensign 11th regiment....August 31, 1813
Malcolm, William .........Ensign 11th regiment....August 31, 1813
Sheilds, Robert ...........Ensign 11th regiment....August 31, 1813
Sheilds, Robert ..........Captain 11th regiment.....April 27, 1813
Sively, Absolom ..........Lieutenant 11th regiment.August 31, 1813

## Smith County Commissions

Bartley, Robert ...........Lieutenant
    16th regiment......November 8, 1813
Brown, George ............Ensign 41st regiment......June 14, 1813
Carter, William ..........Captain 41st regiment.....June 14, 1813
Cheek, William ..........Lieutenant 41st regiment...June 14, 1813
Dalton, William ..........Lieutenant 16th regiment...June 21, 1813
Ervetts, Joseph G. ........Ensign 16th regiment.November 8, 1813
Fite, Joseph .............Captain 41st regiment.....June 28, 1813
Ford, Daniel, Junr. ........Ensign 41st regiment......June 28, 1813
Gibson, Samuel ..........Lieutenant 41st regiment...June 14, 1813
Gullick, John ............Captain 41st regiment.....June 14, 1813

Johnston, Thomas .........Captain 41st regiment.....June 14, 1813
Kavinaugh, James P. .......Captain 41st regiment.....June 28, 1813
McClennahan, William .....Captain 16th regiment.....June 21, 1813
McDuffie, Neil ............Ensign 16th regiment.November 8, 1813
Malone, James ............Lieutenant 41st regiment.August 31, 1813
Moore, Lemuel, ..........Lieutenant 41st regiment...June 14, 1813
Nash, Thomas ............Ensign 16th regiment..November 8, 1813
Parker, William ..........Lieutenant 41st regiment...June 14, 1813
Patterson, William .........Captain
          16th regiment......November 8, 1813
Phillips, William ..........Lieutenant 16th regiment...June 21, 1813
Tuggle, Thomas ...........Ensign 41st regiment......June 14, 1813
Ventrass, James ..........Ensign 16th regiment.November 8, 1813
Webster, Peter ............Ensign 41st regiment......June 14, 1813
Woolsey, Thomas .........Ensign 41st regiment......June 14, 1813
Young, Daniel ............Ensign 16th regiment......June 21, 1813

*Stewart County Commissions*

Armour, Robert, Junr. ......Ensign 26th regiment.....April 22, 1813
Armour, William .........Lieutenant 26th regiment..April 22, 1813
Cooper, Robert ...........Lieutenant Colonel Commandant
          26th regiment...........July 24, 1813
Gatlin, Ephraim ..........Captain
          26th regiment......November 8, 1813
Gray, Thomas ............First Major 26th regiment...July 24, 1813
Haglar, John L. ...........Captain
          26th regiment......September 15, 1813
King, William ...........Captain 26th regiment...August 31, 1813
Lightfoot, Henry .........Lieutenant
          26th regiment........August 31, 1813
McAllister, William ........Ensign 26th regiment....August 31, 1813
McClure, William .........Ensign 26th regiment......June 19, 1813
Parker, Nathaniel .........Ensign 26th regiment..November 8, 1813
Randal, James ............Lieutenant 26th regiment..April 22, 1813
Skinner, Nathan ..........Captain
          26th regiment......September 15, 1813
Walker, Robert ...........Second Major
          26th regiment...........July 24, 1813
Ward, Wiley .............Lieutenant
          26th regiment........August 31, 1813
Williams, James ..........Captain 26th regiment...August 31, 1813

*Sullivan County Commissions*

Brownlow, Joseph A. ......Lieutenant Light Infantry
          Company attached to
          2nd regiment..........March 22, 1813
Canale, William ..........Ensign 2nd regiment......May 19, 1813

Cook, Adam ..............Ensign 2nd regiment.....August 31, 1813
Cook, Jacob ..............Lieutenant 2nd regiment.August 31, 1813
Cox, Thomas .............Lieutenant Volunteer Company
of men not subject to
militia duty.............May 4, 1813
Gunning, David ..........Ensign Light Infantry
Company attached to
2nd regiment............June 14, 1813
Hanley, Francis ...........Captain Volunteer Company
men not subject to
militia duty.............May 4, 1813
Jones, Esquire ............Ensign 2nd regiment.....August 17, 1813
Kerr, James ..............Captain 2nd regiment......April 27, 1813
Key, Joel ................Captain Light Infantry
Company attached to
2nd regiment.........August 2, 1813
Lamb, Littlebury .........Captain 2nd regiment....August 17, 1813
Lattern, Christopher ......Lieutenant 2nd regiment...April 27, 1813
Lattern, Samuel ..........Ensign 2nd regiment.......April 27, 1813
Miller, George ............Cornet regiment cavalry
1st brigade.............April 27, 1813
Neideffer, Solomon ........Lieutenant 2nd regiment.August 17, 1813
Ramsey, Samuel ..........Ensign Volunteer Company
men not subject
to militia duty..........May 4, 1813

*Sumner County*

Adams, James .............Ensign 15th regiment......July 7, 1813
Anderson, John B. .........Ensign 15th regiment...October 1, 1813
Nennet, William ..........Ensign 15th regiment...October 1, 1813
Bruce, Robert .............Lieutenant
43rd regiment......September 25, 1813
Gilbert, John .............Captain
15th regiment........October 1, 1813
Harper, Summers .........Lieutenant
43rd regiment......February 11, 1813
Jefferson, Peter F. .........Ensign 43rd regiment.September 25, 1813
Key, Strother .............Captain 15th regiment......July 7, 1813
Montgomery, Daniel .......Captain
43rd regiment......September 25, 1813
Moore, Robert ............Lieutenant
43rd regiment......September 25, 1813
Sanford, George ...........Ensign 15th regiment.......July 7, 1813
Stalcup, James ............Lieutenant
15th regiment........October 1, 1813
Thompson, Joseph .........Captain
43rd regiment......February 11, 1813

## IN THE TENNESSEE MILITIA, 1813

### Warren County Commissions

Banks, Richard ..........Captain 29th regiment...August 20, 1813
Dotson, Elisha ..........Captain
    29th regiment......November 8, 1813
Edge, Henry .............Ensign 29th regiment.....March 8, 1813
Files, Manly ............Captain 29th regiment...March 22, 1813
Gorman, George ..........Captain 29th regiment...August 2, 1813
Graham, Charles .........Lieutenant 29th regiment.March 22, 1813
Hillis, James ...........Captain
    29th regiment......November 8, 1813
Jones, Nathaniel ........Lieutenant 29th regiment.March 22, 1813
McReynolds, William .....Captain 29th regiment...March 22, 1813
Mooney, James ...........Ensign 29th regiment....March 22, 1813
Smith, Amos .............Lieutenant 29th regiment.March 22, 1813
Stringfield, James ......Lieutenant
    29th regiment......November 8, 1813
Vaughn, Daniel ..........Ensign 29th regiment.November 8, 1813

### Washington County Commissions

Bacon, Joseph ...........Captain
    1st regiment.......November 8, 1813
Bean, John ..............Captain 1st regiment......April 27, 1813
Britton, Joseph .........Lieutenant
    1st regiment.......November 8, 1813
Cruckshank, William .....Captain
    1st regiment.......November 8, 1813
Delany, William .........Lieutenant 1st regiment...April 27, 1813
Garner, Griffith ........Lieutenant
    1st regiment.......November 8, 1813
Givin, James ............Ensign 1st regiment.......June 14, 1813
Haire, Joseph ...........Ensign 1st regiment..November 8, 1813
Odel, Bartlet ...........Lieutenant 1st regiment....June 14, 1813
Price, Thomas ...........Ensign 1st regiment.......April 27, 1813
Smith, Richard ..........Lieutenant 1st regiment....June 14, 1813

### White County Commissions

Barton, William .........Ensign 34th regiment......June 21, 1813
Coxsey, Absolam .........Ensign 3rd regiment.......June 21, 1813
Evans, William D. .......Ensign 34th regiment......June 21, 1813
Jones, Zachariah ........Captain 34th regiment.....June 21, 1813
Walker, John ............Lieutenant 34th regiment...June 21, 1813

### Williamson County Commissions

Allen, George H. ........Lieutenant
    44th regiment........January 28, 1813

## RECORD OF COMMISSIONS OF OFFICERS

Armstrong, John .......... Ensign 21st regiment...October 1, 1813
Armstrong, John M. ....... Lieutenant Light Infantry
    attached to
    21st regiment ....... January 28, 1813
Brooks, James ........... Ensign Company Volunteer
    Riflemen attached to
    21st regiment .......... April 27, 1813
Cridle, Andrew ........... Captain Company Volunteer
    Riflemen attached to
    21st regiment .......... April 27, 1813
Dabney, Charles A. ....... Captain 21st regiment ..... June 14, 1813
Dillen, John ............. Ensign 21st regiment ...... July 7, 1813
Dunn, David ............. Second Major
    21st regiment .......... April 27, 1813
Echolas, John ............ Lieutenant 21st regiment.. April 27, 1813
Edmiston, William ........ Captain 21st regiment ..... April 27, 1813
Ellis, James ............. Lieutenant 21st regiment... April 27, 1813
Ellis, John .............. Ensign 21st regiment ...... April 27, 1813
Gunter, Sterling .......... Lieutenant 21st regiment... June 14, 1813
Hargrove, Stephen ......... Ensign 44th regiment...January 28, 1813
Hill, James .............. Ensign 44th regiment...January 28, 1813
Hill, John ............... Captain
    44th regiment ....... January 28, 1813
Hobbs, Joel .............. Ensign 21st regiment ..... April 27, 1813
Holland, Frederick ........ Ensign 21st regiment ...... June 14, 1813
Jackson, Thomas .......... Lieutenant
    44th regiment ....... January 28, 1813
James, Amsey ............ Ensign 21st regiment ....... June 14, 1813
McCutcheon, Robert ....... Ensign 21st regiment ...... April 27, 1813
McCutcheon, Robert ...... Lieutenant
    21st regiment .......... June 14, 1813
McEwen, David .......... Lieutenant 21st regiment... April 27, 1813
McFadden, James ........ Ensign 21st regiment ....... June 14, 1813
McKiney, John ........... Captain 21st regiment ..... April 27, 1813
Maury, Thomas T. ........ Captain Light Infantry
    attached to
    21st regiment ....... January 28, 1813
Nunn, Thomas ........... Ensign 44th regiment....March 22, 1813
Perkins, Nicholas T. ....... Lieutenant Colonel Commandant
    Cavalry regiment
    9th brigade .......... March 17, 1813
Perkins, William O. ........ Captain 21st regiment ..... April 27, 1813
Pope, Thomas A. .......... Ensign 21st regiment ....October 1, 1813
Porter, Thomas .......... Lieutenant
    21st regiment ........ January 28, 1813
Quinllian, William ........ Ensign 21st regiment...January 28, 1813
Reed, Andrew ............ Lieutenant Company Volunteer
    Riflemen attached to

## IN THE TENNESSEE MILITIA, 1813

|  |  |  |
|---|---|---|
| | 21st regiment | April 27, 1813 |
| Reese, Beverly | Ensign 21st regiment | December 1, 1813 |
| Richards, Hiram R. | Lieutenant 21st regiment | July 7, 1813 |
| Richardson, Barnard | Captain 21st regiment | May 19, 1813 |
| Simpson, William | Captain 21st regiment | January 28, 1813 |
| Stewart, John | Ensign 21st regiment | October 1, 1813 |
| Tripp, Samuel | Lieutenant 21st regiment | June 14, 1813 |
| Vaughn, Abner | Ensign 44th regiment | January 28, 1813 |
| Wolf, William | Lieutenant 21st regiment | December 1, 1813 |

### *Wilson County Commissions*

| | | |
|---|---|---|
| Bradberry, Joshua | Ensign 17th regiment | June 14, 1813 |
| Compton, John | Lieutenant 17th regiment | September 24, 1813 |
| Cooper, John | Lieutenant 42nd regiment | May 19, 1813 |
| Cooper, William | Captain 42nd regiment | May 19, 1813 |
| Harris, Fergus | Lieutenant 17th regiment | June 14, 1813 |
| Hill, John | First Major 17th regiment | August 31, 1813 |
| Howell, Levi | Ensign 17th regiment | June 14, 1813 |
| Hunter, Edward | Captain 17th regiment | September 24, 1813 |
| Jackson, Isham | Lieutenant 17th regiment | September 24, 1813 |
| Karr, Walter | Captain 17th regiment | September 24, 1813 |
| McAdow, James | Captain 42nd regiment | September 30, 1813 |
| McVicks, Donald | Ensign 17th regiment | September 24, 1813 |
| Mitchell, Everit | Ensign 17th regiment | September 24, 1813 |
| Perryman, Josiah | Lieutenant 42nd regiment | September 30, 1813 |
| Smith, Bird | Second Major 42nd regiment | January 28, 1813 |
| Taylor, Solomon | Ensign 17th regiment | June 14, 1813 |
| Timmons, Charles | Lieutenant 42nd regiment | September 30, 1813 |
| Wasson, Abner | Captain 42nd regiment | September 30, 1813 |
| Webb, Isham | Ensign 17th regiment | September 24, 1813 |
| Williams, Beverly | Captain 17th regiment | June 14, 1813 |
| Williams, Coleman | Lieutenant 17th regiment | June 14, 1813 |

The following names are included in the Commissions issued in the year 1813 but no reference to the county from which they served is given.

For this reason they are listed here separately:

Johnston, James ..........Lieutenant regiment of cavalry
                          1st brigade.............May 19, 1813
Lyon, William ............Captain regiment of cavalry
                          8th brigade.........February 11, 1813
McAmy, James ............Captain regiment of cavalry
                          8th brigade.............April 23, 1813
McCampbell, John ........First major regiment of cavalry
                          3rd brigade.............April 23, 1813
Payne, William ...........Cornet regiment of cavalry
                          8th brigade.........February 11, 1813
Smith, William ............Lieutenant regiment of cavalry
                          8th brigade.........February 11, 1813
Smith, William ...........Captain regiment of cavalry
                          8th brigade...........August 31, 1813
Thornton, William H. .....Cornet regiment of cavalry
                          5th brigade........November 8, 1813
Warner, John .............Captain regiment of cavalry
                          5th brigade........September 7, 1813

# RECORD OF COMMISSIONS OF OFFICERS IN THE TENNESSEE MILITIA, 1814

### Compiled by Mrs. John Trotwood Moore

*Anderson County Commissions*

| | | |
|---|---|---|
| Barton, Hugh | Captain regiment of cavalry 8th brigade | December 19, 1814 |
| Bowling, Larkin | Lieutenant regiment of cavalry 8th brigade | December 19, 1814 |
| Dunn, Samuel | Captain 13th regiment | October 19, 1814 |
| Oliver, Charles Y. | Second Major 13th regiment | April 5, 1814 |
| Slover, Aaron | Lieutenant 13th regiment | October 19, 1814 |
| Stanley, Rhode | Ensign 13th regiment | October 19, 1814 |

*Bedford County Commissions*

| | | |
|---|---|---|
| Apleby, David | Lieutenant 28th regiment | March 2, 1814 |
| Beasley, Willie | Lieutenant 47th regiment | November 14, 1814 |
| Bylor, John | Second Major 28th regiment | November 22, 1814 |
| Dean, Francis | Ensign 28th regiment | August 21, 1814 |
| Dryden, John | Lieutenant 28th regiment | April 13, 1814 |
| Gillispie, Thomas T. | Lieutenant 28th regiment | March 2, 1814 |
| Hall, Jeremiah | Ensign 28th regiment | March 2, 1814 |
| Hill, Jesse | Lieutenant 28th regiment | March 2, 1814 |
| Hill, Jesse | Captain 28th regiment | August 21, 1814 |
| Hughs, Robert | Ensign 28th regiment | August 21, 1814 |
| Hunter, Ephraim | Ensign 28th regiment | March 2, 1814 |
| Lovens, Hugh H. | Captain 28th regiment | March 2, 1814 |
| McClure, John | Captain 47th regiment | August 3, 1814 |
| McLennan, Hugh | Ensign 28th regiment | March 2, 1814 |
| Martin, Samuel | Lieutenant 28th regiment | August 21, 1814 |
| Montgomery, Thomas | Ensign 47th regiment | November 14, 1814 |
| Morse, Michael | Ensign 28th regiment | April 13, 1814 |
| Murphy, William | Captain 47th regiment | December 16, 1814 |
| Orr, John | Captain 28th regiment | March 2, 1814 |
| Patton, John | Lieutenant 28th regiment | August 21, 1814 |
| Perry, Allen | Ensign 28th regiment | August 21, 1814 |
| Phare, George | Lieutenant in Rifle Company attached to 47th regiment | December 16, 1814 |
| Porter, Samuel | Lieutenant 28th regiment | April 13, 1814 |
| Shockley, T. H. | Ensign 28th regiment | March 2, 1814 |
| Shuffield, Arthur | Ensign 28th regiment | April 13, 1814 |
| Thompson, Thomas F. | Lieutenant 28th regiment | August 21, 1814 |
| Walker, Eneas | Lieutenant 28th regiment | March 2, 1814 |
| Weaver, Joseph | Lieutenant 28th regiment | August 21, 1814 |
| Woods, John | Captain 28th regiment | March 2, 1814 |

## Bledsoe County Commissions

| | | | |
|---|---|---|---|
| Cherry, Benjamin | Lieutenant 31st regiment | September | 5, 1814 |
| Clark, Charles | Ensign 31st regiment | September | 5, 1814 |
| Dever, Alexander | Lieutenant 31st regiment | September | 5, 1814 |
| Igon, James | Lieutenant 31st regiment | September | 5, 1814 |
| Jones, James | Captain 31st regiment | September | 5, 1814 |
| Kee, John | Ensign 31st regiment | September | 5, 1814 |
| Lewis, Jesse | Captain of Rifle Company attached to the 31st regiment | September | 5, 1814 |
| Witten, James | Lieutenant 31st regiment | September | 5, 1814 |

## Blount County Commissions

| | | | |
|---|---|---|---|
| Bonham, Nehemiah | Captain 12th regiment | February | 15, 1814 |
| Boyd, James | Ensign 12th regiment | September | 5, 1814 |
| Boyd, John | Ensign 12th regiment | September | 5, 1814 |
| Carson, John | Ensign 12th regiment | February | 15, 1814 |
| Davis, Andrew | Ensign 12th regiment | November | 2, 1814 |
| Ewing, John | Lieutenant 12th regiment | February | 15, 1814 |
| Gardiner, James | Captain 12th regiment | September | 5, 1814 |
| Little, William | Ensign 12th regiment | November | 2, 1814 |
| Love, James | Captain 12th regiment | February | 15, 1814 |
| Rooker, John | Ensign 12th regiment | September | 5, 1814 |
| Thompson, John | Lieutenant 12th regiment | February | 15, 1814 |
| Thornberry, John | Lieutenant Colonel Commandant 12th regiment | June | 17, 1814 |
| Wallace, Thomas | Captain 12th regiment | November | 2, 1814 |
| Woods, Joseph B. | Lieutenant 12th regiment | September | 5, 1814 |

## Campbell County Commissions

| | | | |
|---|---|---|---|
| Baxter, William | Ensign 33rd regiment | July | 7, 1814 |
| Eisley, John | Lieutenant 33rd regiment | July | 7, 1814 |
| Linville, Richard | Lieutenant Colonel Commandant 33rd regiment | September | 5, 1814 |
| McBraid, James | Captain 33rd regiment | July | 7, 1814 |

## Carter County Commissions

| | | | |
|---|---|---|---|
| Bowers, John | Ensign 5th regiment | September | 19, 1814 |
| Bradley, Daniel | Captain 5th regiment | September | 28, 1814 |
| Bunton, William | Ensign 5th regiment | March | 2, 1814 |
| Carter, George Washington | Captain 5th regiment | December | 10, 1814 |

# IN THE TENNESSEE MILITIA, 1814

Carter, William Blount ..... Lieutenant Colonel Commandant  
    5th regiment .......... August 5, 1814  
Dugger, Abel .............. Captain 5th regiment.. December 10, 1814  
Goodin, Lawson .......... Lieutenant 5th regiment... March 2, 1814  
Harris, Benjamin C. ....... Captain 5th regiment....... May 7, 1814  
McNabb, James .......... Lieutenant  
    5th regiment ....... September 28, 1814  
Proffit, Pleasant .......... Lieutenant  
    5th regiment ....... September 13, 1814  
Sigler, George ............ Lieutenant 5th regiment.. March 21, 1814  
Smith, Ezekiel ............ Captain 5th regiment.... January 8, 1814  
Smith, Ezekiel ............ Second Major  
    5th regiment........ December 10, 1814  
Ward, John ............... Captain 5th regiment.. September 28, 1814  
Wright, John .............. Lieutenant 5th regiment... March 21, 1814  
Wright, John .............. First Major  
    5th regiment ....... September 13, 1814  

### Claiborne County Commissions

Bails, Archibald ........... Ensign 9th regiment...... August 27, 1814  
Bull, George .............. Ensign 9th regiment...... March 30, 1814  
Condray, Dennis .......... First Major 9th regiment. October 4, 1814  
Eaton, James .............. Lieutenant  
    9th regiment ........ February 15, 1814  
Grissum, Robert .......... Lieutenant 9th regiment.. March 30, 1814  
Jackson, Thomas .......... Captain 9th regiment..... March 30, 1814  
McCarty, Thomas ........ Lieutenant  
    9th regiment ....... November 2, 1814  
McGinnis, Robert ......... Captain 9th regiment... February 15, 1814  
Sumpter, William ......... Captain 9th regiment..... August 27, 1814  

### Cocke County Commissions

Campbell, George ......... Ensign 8th regiment...... August 5, 1814  
Holland, James ........... Ensign 8th regiment... December 27, 1814  
Huff, Absolam ............ Captain 8th regiment..... August 5, 1814  
Jester, Isaac .............. Cornet regiment of cavalry  
    2nd brigade........ September 5, 1814  

### Davidson County Commissions

Abernathy, Freeman ....... Ensign 20th regiment...... April 17, 1814  
Anderson, William ........ Lieutenant 20th regiment... April 17, 1814  
Austin, James ............. Ensign company of men not  
    subject to militia duty... April 17, 1814  
Benningfield, James H. ..... Lieutenant 19th regiment... May 7, 1814  
Birdwell, Andrew ......... Ensign 20th regiment.. November 7, 1814  
Camp, John ............... Lieutenant company of men not  
    subject to militia duty... April 17, 1814  
Casselman, Abraham ....... Captain 19th regiment...... June 17, 1814

## RECORD OF COMMISSIONS OF OFFICERS

| | | |
|---|---|---|
| Clemons, James | Lieutenant 20th regiment | July 11, 1814 |
| Colwell, Joseph | Captain 19th regiment | November 14, 1814 |
| Criddle, John | Ensign 20th regiment | November 7, 1814 |
| Criddle, John | Second Major 20th regiment | April 12, 1814 |
| Curry, Isaiah | Lieutenant 19th regiment | March 19, 1814 |
| Demoss, Abraham | Captain 19th regiment | May 7, 1814 |
| Dickenson, Jacob | Captain 20th regiment | January 8, 1814 |
| Dismukes, Daniel | Ensign 20th regiment | July 11, 1814 |
| Dorris, Thomas | Ensign 20th regiment | November 7, 1814 |
| Drewry, John | Captain 19th regiment | November 14, 1814 |
| Drewry, Richard C. | Ensign 19th regiment | November 2, 1814 |
| Earheart, Rodney | Captain 20th regiment | November 7, 1814 |
| Edmiston, Thomas | Second Major regiment of cavalry 9th brigade | July 11, 1814 |
| Felts, George | Ensign 20th regiment | April 17, 1814 |
| Goodrich, Edmund | Captain 20th regiment | July 7, 1814 |
| Hannah, John | Lieutenant 19th regiment | May 7, 1814 |
| Hooper, Nimrod | Lieutenant 20th regiment | January 8, 1814 |
| Hutson, Andrew G. | Lieutenant 20th regiment | August 4, 1814 |
| Hynes, Andrew | Adjutant General | April 5, 1814 |
| Johnson, Charles | Lieutenant 19th regiment | April 17, 1814 |
| Lake, Elijah | Ensign 19th regiment | May 7, 1814 |
| McDaniel, Clement | Captain company of men not subject to militia duty | April 17, 1814 |
| McKann, William | Captain regiment of cavalry 9th brigade | July 25, 1814 |
| Newton, Robert | Lieutenant 19th regiment | June 17, 1814 |
| Patterson, Matthew | First Major 20th regiment | April 12, 1814 |
| Read, Thomas J. | Ensign 19th regiment | November 14, 1814 |
| Ring, Thomas | Ensign 19th regiment | April 17, 1814 |
| Russell, James | Ensign 19th regiment | May 7, 1814 |
| Scruggs, Theophilus | Ensign 20th regiment | January 8, 1814 |
| Taylor, Samuel | Lieutenant Colonel Commandant 20th regiment | April 12, 1814 |
| Vaughn, Paul | Captain 20th regiment | September 13, 1814 |
| Vaulx, William | Lieutenant 19th regiment | June 17, 1814 |
| Waggoner, Cornelius | Lieutenant 20th regiment | April 17, 1814 |
| Willson, Robert | Ensign 20th regiment | September 13, 1814 |
| Wilson, Robert | Lieutenant 20th regiment | November 7, 1814 |
| Woodward, Jesse | Captain 19th regiment | June 17, 1814 |

### Dickson County Commissions

| | | |
|---|---|---|
| Berry, Lewis | Captain 25th regiment | March 2, 1814 |
| McRae, John L. | Captain regiment cavalry 6th brigade | August 29, 1814 |

IN THE TENNESSEE MILITIA, 1814     223

Neisbett, Jeremiah ......... Captain 25th regiment.September  9, 1814
Neisbett, Thomas .......... Lieutenant
                             25th regiment ...... September  9, 1814
Russell, Jesse ............. Lieutenant
                             25th regiment ...... November 15, 1814
Swift, Thomas ............. Lieutenant
                             25th regiment ...... November 14, 1814
Williams, Richard ......... Ensign 25th regiment..September  9, 1814

*Franklin County Commissions*

Anderson, Presley .......... Lieutenant 32nd regiment...July 20, 1814
Anderson, Presley .......... Captain 32nd regiment.November 14, 1814
Brittain, William .......... Captain 32nd regiment.November 21, 1814
Burress, William ........... Lieutenant
                             32nd regiment ........ October 13, 1814
Covey, Joseph ............. Captain 32nd regiment..... May  7, 1814
Davidson, Hugh ........... Lieutenant
                             32nd regiment...... November 21, 1814
Farriss, Joseph ............ Lieutenant
                             32nd regiment ........ October 13, 1814
Finch, Edward ............ Lieutenant
                             32nd regiment...... November 14, 1814
Gotcher, Henry ............ Ensign 32nd regiment...... May  7, 1814
Lewis, Cornelius N. ........ Lieutenant 32nd regiment...May  7, 1814
Lusk, Wilson .............. Ensign 32nd regiment..November 21, 1814
May, John ................ Lieutenant 32nd regiment...May  7, 1814
Moore, Joseph ............ Ensign 32nd regiment....... July 20, 1814
Reggin, John .............. Lieutenant 32nd regiment...May  7, 1814
Smith, Thomas A. ......... Lieutenant 32nd regiment...May  7, 1814
Taylor, James ............. Captain 32nd regiment.November 14, 1814
Wood, Joshua ............. Lieutenant 32nd regiment...July 20, 1814
Woods, Charles ........... Lieutenant 32nd regiment...July 20, 1814
Woods, William ........... Ensign 32nd regiment....... July 20, 1814

*Giles County Commissions*

Abernathy, Charles C. ..... Lieutenant in Volunteer Rifle
                             Company attached to
                             37th regiment....... December 19, 1814
Allen, Richard H. .......... Captain 2nd regiment
                             (52nd) ........... September 28, 1814
Bentley, Richard .......... Captain 37th regiment.... March 21, 1814
Brown, Duncan ........... Ensign 37th regiment..... March 21, 1814
Byler, Abraham ........... Captain
                             2nd regiment (52nd)..... July 20, 1814
Cocke, William B. ......... Captain
                             2nd regiment (52nd)..... July 20, 1814
Cook, David .............. Ensign 37th regiment....... June 17, 1814

Davis, Nathan ............Captain in Volunteer Rifle
                         Company attached to
                         37th regiment.......December 19, 1814
Everet, Larkin ............Lieutenant
                         37th regiment.........October  7, 1814
Fukeway, Nathan .........Lieutenant
                         2nd regiment (52nd).....July 20, 1814
Garrett, William ..........Ensign 2nd regiment (52nd).July 20, 1814
Gordon, Thomas K. ........Lieutenant Colonel Commandant
                         2nd regiment (52nd).....June 21, 1814
Harrelson, Thomas B. ......Captain
                         2nd regiment (52nd).....July 20, 1814
Harvey, Robert ............Ensign 37th regiment....October  7, 1814
Howard, William ..........Lieutenant
                         2nd regiment (52nd).....July 20, 1814
McLemore, Moses .........Ensign 2nd regiment (52nd).July 20, 1814
McMiken, Elisha ..........Lieutenant
                         2nd regiment (52nd).....June 21, 1814
McVay, Claiborne W. ......Captain
                         2nd regiment (52nd).....July 20, 1814
Meadows, Willis G. ........Ensign 2nd regiment (52nd).July 20, 1814
Melton, Elijah ............Lieutenant
                         2nd regiment (52nd).....July 20, 1814
Perry, John ...............Lieutenant 37th regiment..March 21, 1814
Pickens, James H. .........First Major
                         2nd regiment (52nd).....June 21, 1814
Reid, Josiah ...............Lieutenant
                         2nd regiment (52nd).....July 28, 1814
Richardson, May ..........Ensign 2nd regiment (52nd).June 21, 1814
Ruff, John ................Lieutenant
                         2nd regiment (52nd).....July 20, 1814
Scales, Henry .............Ensign in Volunteer Rifle
                         Company attached to
                         37th regiment.......December 19, 1814
Shields, Leander ...........Captain
                         2nd regiment (52nd).....July 28, 1814
Simmons, James M. ........Second Major
                         2nd regiment (52nd).....June 21, 1814
Smith, Hyram M. .........Lieutenant
                         2nd regiment (52nd).....July 20, 1814
Speirs, Nathan ............Ensign 2nd regiment........July 20, 1814
Stephenson, Robert ........Ensign 2nd regiment (52nd).July 28, 1814
Still, James ...............Ensign 2nd regiment (52nd).July 20, 1814
Young, Jaret ..............Captain
                         2nd regiment (52nd).....June 21, 1814

IN THE TENNESSEE MILITIA, 1814     225

*Grainger County Commissions*

Alsup, Henry .............. Cornet regiment of cavalry
                            2nd brigade........ November 21, 1814
Butcher, John ............. Lieutenant
                            7th regiment........ December 14, 1814
Ferguson, John ............ Ensign 7th regiment... December 14, 1814
Hambleton, Alexander ...... Captain 7th regiment.. December 14, 1814
Hightower, Epaphroditus ... Lieutenant
                            7th regiment........ December 14, 1814
Hodge, Phillips ........... Ensign 7th regiment...... March 21, 1814
Hodges, Eli ............... Lieutenant
                            7th regiment........ December 14, 1814
Ivy, Benjamin ............. Lieutenant
                            7th regiment........ December 14, 1814
McGinness, Robert ......... Captain 7th regiment..... March 21, 1814
Moore, Mastin ............. Ensign 7th regiment... December 14, 1814
Read, Thomas .............. Captain 7th regiment.. December 14, 1814
Simmons, Micajah .......... Ensign 7th regiment... December 14, 1814

*Greene County Commissions*

Allison, Ewen ............. Lieutenant Rifle Company
                            attached to
                            3rd regiment .......... August 29, 1814
Brown, Joseph ............. Lieutenant 3rd regiment.. August 29, 1814
Bustard, Michael .......... Captain 3rd regiment..... August 29, 1814
Coatney, George ........... Ensign 3rd regiment... December 20, 1814
Crawford, William ......... Ensign 3rd regiment...... March 2, 1814
Dicky, Christian .......... Captain Rifle Company
                            attached to
                            3rd regiment .......... August 29, 1814
Foles, George W. .......... Lieutenant Rifle Company
                            attached to
                            3rd regiment .......... August 29, 1814
Hunt, Thomas .............. Lieutenant 3rd regiment.... April 27, 1814
Kelly, Samuel ............. Lieutenant
                            3rd regiment........ December 20, 1814
Kelly, William ............ Second Major
                            3rd regiment......... January 8, 1814
Kilgore, James ............ Lieutenant 3rd regiment.. August 29, 1814
McAlpin, Henry ............ Ensign 3rd regiment...... August 29, 1814
McCollom .................. Ensign 3rd regiment...... August 27, 1814
Melekin, Samuel ........... Lieutenant 3rd regiment.... July 7, 1814
Metheny, Elijah ........... Captain 3rd regiment.. December 20, 1814
Mitchel, William .......... Ensign Rifle Company
                            attached to
                            3rd regiment .......... August 29, 1814
Murry, George ............. Ensign 3rd regiment....... April 27, 1814
Murry, Reuben ............. Lieutenant 3rd regiment.... July 7, 1814
Murphy, Edward ............ Captain 3rd regiment....... May 23, 1814

# RECORD OF COMMISSIONS OF OFFICERS

Neal, Strother ............. Lieutenant
    3rd regiment ........ December 20, 1814
Ottinger, Henry ........... Ensign 3rd regiment ...... August 29, 1814
Parker, Caleb J. ........... Captain 3rd regiment ..... August 29, 1814
Robeson, James ........... Lieutenant 3rd regiment .. August 29, 1814
Ross, James ............... Ensign 3rd regiment ...... August 29, 1814
Scruggs, James ............ Cornet regiment of cavalry
    8th brigade ......... December 19, 1814
Scruggs, James ............ Lieutenant
    3rd regiment ........ December 20, 1814
Shavour, John ............. Lieutenant 3rd regiment ... March 2, 1814
Smith, Beverly ............ Ensign 3rd regiment ...... August 29, 1814
Wilson, Gilbert ............ Captain 3rd regiment .. December 20, 1814

## Hawkins County Commissions

Anderson, James ........... Lieutenant
    4th regiment ....... September 5, 1814
Armstrong, Arthur G. ...... Lieutenant Colonel Commandant
    4th regiment .......... August 2, 1814
Bassett, Spencer ........... Captain 4th regiment .. September 5, 1814
Bishop, John .............. Lieutenant
    4th regiment ....... September 5, 1814
Cuming, James ............ Second Major 4th regiment .. June 17, 1814
Davis, James .............. Ensign 4th regiment ... November 2, 1814
Gillenwaters, William T. ... Captain 4th regiment .. September 5, 1814
Groce, James .............. Lieutenant
    4th regiment ....... September 5, 1814
Groves, John .............. Ensign 4th regiment ... November 2, 1814
Harmon, David ............ Lieutenant
    4th regiment ....... September 5, 1814
Laughmiller, Frederick ..... Captain 4th regiment .. September 5, 1814
Laughmiller, Jonas ........ First Major 4th regiment . August 2, 1814
Lawson, Lazarus .......... Lieutenant
    4th regiment ....... November 28, 1814
Lawson, Lewis ............. Captain 4th regiment .. November 28, 1814
Lawson, Stephen ........... Ensign 4th regiment ... November 28, 1814
Molsby, David ............. Ensign 4th regiment ... September 5, 1814

## Hickman County Commissions

Bailey, James ............. Lieutenant
    36th regiment ...... September 5, 1814
Cates, Isaiah .............. Ensign 36th regiment ..... March 2, 1814
Copeland, Joab ............ Ensign 36th regiment ....... June 3, 1814
Gatten, Thomas ........... Captain 36th regiment .... March 2, 1814
Goodwin, George .......... Ensign 36th regiment ..... March 30, 1814
Lieuten, Henry ............ Lieutenant 36th regiment .. March 30, 1814
Lytle, John ............... Captain 36th regiment .... March 2, 1814

## IN THE TENNESSEE MILITIA, 1814

McCaleb, John ............Captain 36th regiment....March 2, 1814
Mason, Warren ............Ensign 36th regiment.....August 8, 1814
Reves, William ............Lieutenant 36th regiment.August 18, 1814
Shelton, Jonathan .........Lieutenant 36th regiment.August 8, 1814
Walker, Elisha ............Lieutenant
                              36th regiment......November 28, 1814
Wilkins, James ............Ensign 36th regiment..November 28, 1814

### Humphreys County Commissions

Anderson, Timothy ........Ensign 38th regiment..November 9, 1814
Black, Stephen ............Cornet regiment of cavalry
                              6th brigade ........September 13, 1814
Brown, Asa ...............Ensign 38th regiment...January 31, 1814
Gaskil, Evan ..............Lieutenant 38th regiment...July 7, 1814
Lain, John ................Lieutenant 38th regiment...July 13, 1814
Lowe, David ..............Captain 38th regiment......May 7, 1814
Mitchell, John G. ..........Lieutenant 38th regiment...July 13, 1814
Murray, Francis ..........Captain
                              regiment cavalry....September 13, 1814
Qualls, William ............Ensign 38th regiment.......June 17, 1814
Qualls, William ............Ensign 38th regiment.......July 7, 1814
Turner, Edward ..........Captain 38th regiment...January 31, 1814
Williams, Joshua .........Captain 38th regiment.September 1, 1814

### Jackson County Commissions

Buford, Seth .............Lieutenant
                              18th regiment ......November 14, 1814
Butler, Bailey ............Captain 48th regiment.September 5, 1814
Cowan, Matthew .........Captain 18th regiment....August 29, 1814
Darwin, George C. ........Captain in Rifle Company
                              attached to
                              18th regiment .........August 29, 1814
Dillard, John .............Ensign 18th regiment.....August 29, 1814
Dillen, Joshua ............Lieutenant in Volunteer Rifle
                              Company attached to
                              18th regiment ......November 14, 1814
Gist, Benjamin ...........Captain 48th regiment...January 31, 1814
Hail, Nicholas ............Ensign 48th regiment...January 31, 1814
Holliday, David ..........Lieutenant
                              18th regiment ......November 14, 1814
Huff, William ............Lieutenant
                              48th regiment ........January 31, 1814
Hutchison, William G. ......Captain 48th regiment...January 31, 1814
Lock, William .............Lieutenant Colonel Commandant
                              48th regiment.......December 10, 1814
Locke, William ...........Captain 48th regiment...January 31, 1814
Mayfield, Luke ...........Captain 48th regiment.September 5, 1814

## RECORD OF COMMISSIONS OF OFFICERS

Montgomery, Fariss ........Ensign 48th regiment..September 5, 1814
Plumby, William ..........Lieutenant
                              48th regiment ......September 5, 1814
Price, Nathan .............Ensign 48th regiment...January 31, 1814
Price, William ............Lieutenant
                              48th regiment ......September 5, 1814
Robinson, Joseph ..........Ensign 48th regiment...January 31, 1814
Sadler, Henry .............Lieutenant 18th regiment.August 29, 1814
Shoemaker, Michael .......Ensign 18th regiment.....August 29, 1814
Short, Caleb .............Lieutenant
                              48th regiment ........January 31, 1814
Skiles, George .............Ensign 18th regiment.....August 29, 1814
Sweezee, John .............Captain 18th regiment.November 14, 1814
Terry, William ............Captain 18th regiment....August 29, 1814
West, Henry ..............Captain 48th regiment...January 31, 1814
Williams, Peter ............Captain 18th regiment....August 29, 1814
Wilson, Ephraim ..........Lieutenant
                              48th regiment ........January 31, 1814

### *Jefferson County Commissions*

Beard, John C. .............Ensign 6th regiment......August 17, 1814
Bradsaws, Richard .........Ensign 6th regiment....... July 20, 1814
Evans, Robert .............Lieutenant
                              6th regiment .......November 21, 1814
Graham, Joseph ...........Ensign 6th regiment........July 20, 1814
Harrison, Peter ............Ensign 6th regiment...November 21, 1814
Hodges, Callaway .........Captain 6th regiment....January 31, 1814
Howard, Samuel ..........Ensign 6th regiment......August 17, 1814
Langdon, Jonathan ........Ensign in Rifle Company
                              attached to 6th regiment..July 20, 1814
Legg, William .............Captain 6th regiment.....August 17, 1814
McCulloch, Joseph .........Ensign 6th regiment...November 21, 1814
Miller, Joseph .............Lieutenant in Rifle Company
                              attached to 6th regiment..July 20, 1814
Moore, Ephraim ...........Lieutenant 6th regiment..August 17, 1814
Mount, Humphrey .........Captain 6th regiment....January 8, 1814
Scott, Andrew .............Lieutenant 6th regiment....July 20, 1814
Sewell, George .............Ensign 6th regiment...September 5, 1814
Taylor, William ...........Captain Light Infantry
                              Company attached to
                              6th regiment .........Januray 8, 1814

### *Knox County Commissions*

Anderson, James ...........Second Major in regiment of
                              cavalry 3rd brigade.September 1, 1814
Bowman, Samuel .........Lieutenant 10th regiment...June 17, 1814
Brasfield, Thomas .........Lieutenant
                              10th regiment.......December 20, 1814

## IN THE TENNESSEE MILITIA, 1814 229

Cavit, Thomas ............Captain 40th regiment.....April 17, 1814
Conner, William ..........Lieutenant 40th regiment...April 17, 1814
Cox, John ................Lieutenant
                          10th regiment......September 7, 1814
Flemming, David ..........Ensign 40th regiment.......May 7, 1814
Frazier, Thomas ..........Captain 10th regiment......June 17, 1814
Galbreath, Thomas ........Lieutenant
                          10th regiment........January 31, 1814
Gammon, Harris ...........Lieutenant 10th regiment...June 17, 1814
Gammon, John ............Lieutenant
                          10th regiment.......December 20, 1814
George, Ruben ............Captain 10th regiment.September 7, 1814
Gillispie, Isaac ..........Ensign 40th regiment.....August 8, 1814
Gillispie, Thomas .........Captain 40th regiment....August 8, 1814
Gillispie, Thomas .........Ensign 10th regiment..December 20, 1814
Godderd, William .........Captain 10th regiment....March 2, 1814
Graves, George ...........Lieutenant 10th regiment..March 2, 1814
Graves, George ...........Captain 10th regiment.September 7, 1814
Harrel, William ..........Lieutenant 10th regiment..March 2, 1814
Haskell, Charles ..........Ensign 10th regiment....January 31, 1814
McCampbell, John ........Lieutenant
                          10th regiment......September 7, 1814
McDanniel, James ........Ensign 40th regiment......April 17, 1814
McMillen, James ..........Captain 10th regiment....March 2, 1814
Pattern, Samuel ..........Ensign 10th regiment.......June 17, 1814
Patton, James C. .........Lieutenant 10th regiment...June 17, 1814
Price, Daniel .............Captain 10th regiment...January 31, 1814
Robertson, Nathaniel .....Lieutenant
                          10th regiment........January 31, 1814
Wallington, George .......Ensign 10th regiment..September 7, 1814

*Lincoln County Commissions*

Adkins, Thomas ...........Captain 49th regiment......July 13, 1814
Bailey, John .............Ensign 49th regiment.......July 13, 1814
Baughman, Daniel ........Ensign 39th regiment.....August 8, 1814
Boaz, Thomas ............Lieutenant in Rifle Company
                          attached to 49th regiment.July 13, 1814
Buchanan, James .........Ensign 39th regiment.....August 8, 1814
Burgess, Richard .........Lieutenant 39th regiment.August 8, 1814
Clark, John ..............Captain 39th regiment...August 8, 1814
Clemment, Benjamin ......Captain 49th regiment......July 13, 1814
Dyer, James .............Ensign 49th regiment.......July 13, 1814
Hinkle, Joseph ...........Captain 49th regiment......July 13, 1814
Hooker, John .............Lieutenant Light Infanty
                          Company attached to
                          39th regiment .........August 8, 1814
Jones, Jesse .............Lieutenant 39th regiment.August 8, 1814
King, John ...............Ensign 49th regiment.......July 13, 1814

Lauderdale, James .........Ensign 39th regiment.....August 8, 1814
Lee, John ................Lieutenant 49th regiment...July 13, 1814
Leehorne, Gabriel ..........Ensign Light Infantry
                           Company attached to
                           39th regiment .........August 8, 1814
McMillen, Joseph ..........Lieutenant Light Infantry
                           Company attached to
                           49th regiment ......November 14, 1814
Miller, Samuel H. ..........Captain Light Infantry
                           Company attached to
                           39th regiment ........August 8, 1814
Odom, Lewis ..............Lieutenant 49th regiment...July 13, 1814
Oyler, Jonathan ...........Ensign 39th regiment.....August 8, 1814
Phelps, Kelan .............Ensign 49th regiment..November 14, 1814
Scoles, Robert ............Lieutenant
                           39th regiment ......November 14, 1814
Slatter, Cornelius ..........Captain Light Infantry
                           Company attached to
                           49th regiment ......November 14, 1814
Smith, James ..............Captain regiment of cavalry
                           5th brigade.........December 10, 1814
Smith, John ..............Lieutenant 49th regiment. .July 13, 1814
Steed, Abner ..............Ensign in Rifle Company
                           attached to
                           49th regiment ......November 14, 1814
Thompson, David ..........Ensign 39th regiment.....August 8, 1814
Thompson, Elisha ..........Ensign 49th regiment.......July 13, 1814
Walker, Carter ............Ensign 49th regiment.......July 13, 1814
Yager, Abner ..............Lieutenant
                           49th regiment ......November 14, 1814
Yarbrough, Robert .........Lieutenant 39th regiment.August 8, 1814

# RECORD OF COMMISSIONS OF OFFICERS IN THE TENNESSEE MILITIA, 1814

COMPILED BY MRS. JOHN TROTWOOD MOORE

*Maury County Commissions*

Burns, Miles ............... Ensign Volunteer Rifle Company attached to 51st regiment ............ May 7, 1814
Carthel, Joseph M. ......... Lieutenant 27th regiment ... July 7, 1814
Cathey, William ........... Captain Volunteer Rifle Company attached to 51st regiment ............ May 7, 1814
Cleaveland, Abner ......... Ensign 46th regiment .. November 16, 1814
Crawford, William ......... Lieutenant 46th regiment ...... November 16, 1814
Dabs, Joel ................ Ensign 51st regiment ....... June 17, 1814
Davidson, James L. ........ Ensign Light Infantry Company attached to 27th regiment. July 7, 1814
Dickey, George ............ Captain Light Infantry Company attached to 51st regiment ....... September 28, 1814
Dobbin, James ............. Lieutenant 27th regiment ... July 7, 1814
Emberson, James H. ....... Lieutenant 27th regiment ....... February 15, 1814
English, Thomas ........... Lieutenant 51st regiment ........ February 3, 1814
Erwen, Ephraim ........... Captain 27th regiment ...... July 7, 1814
Farney, John .............. Captain 27th regiment .. February 15, 1814
Fields, John .............. Lieutenant 46th regiment ...... November 16, 1814
Fleming, John D. .......... Ensign Light Infantry Company attached to 51st regiment ....... September 28, 1814
Foster, Richard ........... Ensign 27th regiment .. February 15, 1814
Garrard, Thomas .......... Ensign 27th regiment .... October 5, 1814
Gholson, John ............ Captain 27th regiment .. February 15, 1814
Gilbreath, John ........... Ensign 46th regiment .. November 16, 1814
Gilchrist, Duncan ......... Lieutenant 51st regiment ......... October 31, 1814
Goforth, William ......... Ensign 46th regiment .. November 16, 1814
Gordon, William .......... Lieutenant 51st regiment ...... September 28, 1814
Graham, Alexander ........ Ensign 51st regiment ....... May 17, 1814
Griffin, Hugh ............. Ensign 27th regiment .. November 14, 1814
Hamblet, James ........... Ensign 46th regiment .. November 16, 1814
Henderson, James ......... Ensign 51st regiment ....... July 20, 1814
Irvin, Ephraim ........... Lieutenant 27th regiment ....... February 15, 1814

| | | |
|---|---|---|
| Johnstone, Samuel | Lieutenant Colonel Commandant 51st regiment | July 27, 1814 |
| Jones, Hezekiah | Lieutenant 27th regiment | November 14, 1814 |
| Kelsey, Robert G. | Ensign 51st regiment | February 3, 1814 |
| Kendrick, Jesse | Ensign 51st regiment | October 31, 1814 |
| Kilcrease, Davis | Ensign in Light Infantry Company attached to 46th regiment | November 16, 1814 |
| Looney, Isaac A. | Captain in Light Infantry Company attached to 27th regiment | July 7, 1814 |
| McAdams, George | Ensign 51st regiment | February 3, 1814 |
| McFall, John | Lieutenant in Light Infantry Company attached to 51st regiment | September 28, 1814 |
| McKean, Eli | Ensign 27th regiment | November 14, 1814 |
| McMacken, Andrew | Lieutenant 51st regiment | February 3, 1814 |
| McNut, Joseph | Captain 27th regiment | October 5, 1814 |
| McNut, Robert | Lieutenant 27th regiment | October 5, 1814 |
| Nelson, Pleasant | Captain in Rifle Company attached to 27th regiment | October 5, 1814 |
| Pace, John | Ensign in Rifle Company attached to 27th regiment | October 5, 1814 |
| Peyton, Moses | Captain 27th regiment | October 5, 1814 |
| Pickens, John | Lieutenant 27th regiment | May 21, 1814 |
| Polk, Eaven | Ensign 46th regiment | November 16, 1814 |
| Porter, William | Captain 51st regiment | May 17, 1814 |
| Ramsey, John P. | Lieutenant 27th regiment | February 15, 1814 |
| Reddin, Abijah | Captain 27th regiment | February 15, 1814 |
| Reed, James | Captain 27th regiment | July 7, 1814 |
| Rice, James | Ensign 27th regiment | February 15, 1814 |
| Richeson, Matthias | Lieutenant 51st regiment | May 17, 1814 |
| Rodgers, William | Captain 51st regiment | May 17, 1814 |
| Rogers, Samuel | Lieutenant Light Infantry Company attached to 27th regiment | July 17, 1814 |
| Secrest, Leroy | Lieutenant 46th regiment | November 16, 1814 |
| Shaw, Samuel | Lieutenant 51st regiment | May 17, 1814 |
| Sibley, Robert | Ensign 27th regiment | October 5, 1814 |
| Stanfield, William | Lieutenant 51st regiment | May 17, 1814 |

IN THE TENNESSEE MILITIA, 1814        233

Thompson, John ...........Lieutenant Rifle Company
                          attached to
                          27th regiment.........October  5, 1814
Walker, Thomas ..........Captain 51st regiment......June 17, 1814
Whiteside, Samuel ........Captain 51st regiment..February  3, 1814
Whitesides, Abraham .......Lieutenant Volunteer Company
                          attached to 51st regiment.May  7, 1814
Whittaker, John ...........Lieutenant
                          27th regiment......November 14, 1814
Wilks, Minor ..............Ensign 27th regiment.......May 21, 1814
Young, Nathaniel ..........Captain 51st regiment..February  3, 1814

### Montgomery County Commissions

Edmondston, Robert .......Captain regiment of cavalry
                          6th brigade..............July 11, 1814
Hagood, Benjamin .........Ensign 24th regiment..September  1, 1814
Hambleton, James .........First Major
                          50th regiment......September  1, 1814
Hendrickson, John .........Ensign 24th regiment..November 13, 1814
King, William .............Lieutenant
                          24th regiment......November 13, 1814
McFall, Henry ............Lieutenant
                          24th regiment......November 13, 1814
McFall, Samuel ...........Second Major
                          24th regiment......September  1, 1814
Morris, Lazarus ...........Lieutenant
                          24th regiment......November 13, 1814
Neblet, Benjamin .........Lieutenant
                          24th regiment......September 14, 1814
Outlaw, Wright ...........Captain 24th regiment.September  1, 1814
Price, Joseph .............Captain 24th regiment.September  1, 1814
Searcy, Robert ...........Lieutenant Colonel Commandant
                          50th regiment..........March 29, 1814
Stallons, Sherrad ..........Ensign 24th regiment..September  1, 1814
Stanford, Lucas ...........Captain 24th regiment.September  1, 1814
Stewart, Nowlan ..........Lieutenant
                          50th regiment......November 17, 1814
Trousdale, James .........Captain 24th regiment.September  1, 1814
Viser, John L. .............Captain Light Infantry
                          Company attached to
                          50th regiment.........August 27, 1814

### Overton County Commissions

Bradshaw, James ..........Lieutenant in company of
                          men not subject to
                          militia duty.........January 31, 1814
Brock, William ...........Ensign 35th regiment....January 31, 1814

RECORD OF COMMISSIONS OF OFFICERS

Calliham, Samuel .......... Lieutenant
    35th regiment ........ January 31, 1814
Campbell, Joseph .......... Lieutenant
    35th regiment......... October 18, 1814
Fisher, Samuel ............ Ensign in company of men not
    subject to militia duty. January 31, 1814
Frogg, Strother ............ Captain 35th regiment... October 18, 1814
Hynes, Simeon ............ Captain in company of men not
    subject to militia duty. January 31, 1814
Keer, John ................ Ensign 35th regiment.... January 8, 1814
Maxwell, John ............. Ensign 35th regiment.... October 18, 1814
Pennycuff, Jacob ........... Captain 35th regiment... October 18, 1814
Totten, Benjamin .......... Captain 35th regiment...... June 3, 1814
Travice, William .......... Lieutenant
    35th regiment ........ January 31, 1814
Ulred, Jonathan ........... Ensign 35th regiment.... January 31, 1814
Williams, John ............ Ensign 35th regiment.... January 31, 1814

### Rhea County Commissions

Blackwell, James .......... Captain 30th regiment...... July 7, 1814
Hubbard, Matthew ........ Lieutenant regiment of cavalry
    8th brigade ........... August 5, 1814
Majors, Absolam .......... Lieutenant 30th regiment... July 7, 1814
Rice, John ................ Second Major
    30th regiment ...... September 5, 1814
Roberson, Mark ........... Ensign 30th regiment....... July 7, 1814

### Roane County Commissions

England, John ............. Ensign 14th regiment.. September 28, 1814
Grigsby, Samuel ........... Captain 14th regiment...... June 17, 1814
Hembery, Joel ............. Lieutenant in Rifle Company
    attached to the
    14th Regiment...... September 13, 1814
McClellan, James W. ....... Lieutenant
    14th regiment ........ January 31, 1814
Pickle, George ............. Lieutenant
    14th regiment ...... September 13, 1814
Pickle, John ............... Ensign 14th regiment... January 31, 1814
Rector, Richard .......... Lieutenant
    14th regiment......... October 13, 1814
Renfroe, John ............. Ensign in Rifle Company
    attached to the
    14th regiment ...... September 13, 1814
Waller, William ........... Captain 14th regiment.. January 31, 1814

IN THE TENNESSEE MILITIA, 1814   235

*Robertson County Commissions*

| | | |
|---|---|---|
| Baldwin, John | Ensign 23rd regiment.. November | 3, 1814 |
| Barbee, George | Lieutenant 23rd regiment... May | 17, 1814 |
| Barbee, George | Captain in Light Infantry Company attached to 23rd regiment...... November | 3, 1814 |
| Cook, James | Captain in regiment of cavalry 6th brigade........... August | 5, 1814 |
| Haley, William | Lieutenant 23rd regiment...... November | 3, 1814 |
| Hunter, Emanuel | Ensign 23rd regiment....... June | 17, 1814 |
| Morgan, William | Lieutenant in Light Infantry Company attached to 23rd regiment...... November | 3, 1814 |
| Payne, Warren L. | Lieutenant 23rd regiment....... December | 8, 1814 |
| Porter, William B. | Lieutenant 23rd regiment... May | 17, 1814 |
| Powell, Matthew | Lieutenant 23rd regiment...... November | 3, 1814 |
| Redfern, Townley | Ensign 23rd regiment.. November | 3, 1814 |
| Sanders, Isaac | Lieutenant 23rd regiment... June | 17, 1814 |
| Steltz, Henry | Lieutenant 23rd regiment... July | 20, 1814 |
| Strickland, Jonathan | Ensign in Light Infantry Company attached to 23rd regiment...... November | 3, 1814 |

*Rutherford County Commissions*

| | | |
|---|---|---|
| Baker, Abraham | Ensign 45th regiment....... July | 20, 1814 |
| Bankhead, John | Lieutenant 45th regiment......... October | 3, 1814 |
| Beaty, William F. | Ensign 45th regiment...... April | 2, 1814 |
| Beaty, William F. | Lieutenant 45th regiment... July | 20, 1814 |
| Berry, James | Lieutenant 45th regiment... April | 2, 1814 |
| Buchannan, George | Ensign 22nd regiment...... May | 7, 1814 |
| Carlee, Calvin | Lieutenant 45th regiment... April | 2, 1814 |
| Davis, William H. | Cornet in regiment of cavalry 9th brigade......... November | 9, 1814 |
| Dement, Cader | Lieutenant Company of Light Infantry attached to 22nd regiment....... March | 2, 1814 |
| Dickson, Ezekiel | Lieutenant in regiment of cavalry 9th brigade......... December | 4, 1814 |
| Dickson, James | Ensign in Company of Light Infantry attached to 22nd regiment....... March | 2, 1814 |
| Dunnaway, Samuel | Lieutenant 22nd regiment....... February | 7, 1814 |

| | | | |
|---|---|---|---|
| Edwards, Presley | Captain 22nd regiment | July | 7, 1814 |
| Fuller, Littleton | Ensign company of men not subject to militia duty | February | 7, 1814 |
| Fortunberry, David | Ensign 45th regiment | April | 2, 1814 |
| Garner, Obediah | Ensign 22nd regiment | July | 7, 1814 |
| Gassaway, Thomas | Ensign 45th regiment | November | 6, 1814 |
| Good, Hugh | Ensign 45th regiment | October | 3, 1814 |
| Griffin, Richard | Ensign 22nd regiment | May | 7, 1814 |
| Haley, Matthew | Ensign 22nd regiment | July | 7, 1814 |
| Hall, John | Ensign in Light Infantry Company attached to 45th regiment | September | 5, 1814 |
| Hoover, John | Lieutenant in company of men not subject to militia duty | February | 7, 1814 |
| Hubbard, David | Ensign 22nd regiment | July | 7, 1814 |
| Jetton, Robert | Second Major 45th regiment | March | 2, 1814 |
| Kavanaugh, Charles | Captain in company of men not subject to militia duty | February | 7, 1814 |
| Kellough, John | Lieutenant in Light Infantry Company attached to 45th regiment | April | 2, 1814 |
| Kirk, Hugh | Captain in Light Infantry Company attached to 45th regiment | April | 2, 1814 |
| McFerrin, Burton L. | Captain 45th regiment | April | 2, 1814 |
| McFerrin, James | First Major 45th regiment | March | 2, 1814 |
| McKee, Ambrose | Ensign 45th regiment | June | 25, 1814 |
| McKee, Ambrose | Captain 45th regiment | November | 6, 1814 |
| McKee, John | Captain 45th regiment | March | 2, 1814 |
| McKnight, David | Lieutenant 45th regiment | May | 7, 1814 |
| Matthews, John | Captain 22nd regiment | May | 7, 1814 |
| Meredith, James B. | Ensign 45th regiment | May | 7, 1814 |
| Murphy, Ezekiel | Ensign 45th regiment | July | 20, 1814 |
| Nash, John | Captain in regiment of cavalry 9th brigade | November | 9, 1814 |
| Noaks, Jesse | Ensign 45th regiment | April | 2, 1814 |
| Patton, David | Captain in Light Infantry Company attached to 22nd regiment | January | 8, 1814 |
| Potts, Oswall | Ensign 45th regiment | May | 7, 1814 |
| Potts, Thomas | Lieutenant 45th regiment | April | 2, 1814 |
| Sharpe, Cyrus | Lieutenant regiment of cavalry 9th brigade | November | 9, 1814 |

IN THE TENNESSEE MILITIA, 1814  237

Smith, Joseph D. ..........Lieutenant
        45th regiment ......November 17, 1814
Thomas, Jidean ............Lieutenant 45th regiment...April 2, 1814
Thompson, George ........Lieutenant 22nd regiment...July 7, 1814
Warnick, William ..........Captain 45th regiment.....May 7, 1814
Warren, James ............Ensign 22nd regiment......May 7, 1814
Webb, Benjamin ...........Lieutenant 45th regiment..March 2, 1814
Webb, Benjamin ...........Captain 45th regiment......June 25, 1814
White, Stephen F. ..........Cornet regiment of cavalry
        9th brigade.........December 4, 1814
Willeford, James ...........Ensign 45th regiment......April 2, 1814
Yardley, Thomas ..........Captain regiment cavalry
        9th brigade.........December 4, 1814

*Sevier County Commissions*

Goforth, Hugh .............Lieutenant
        11th regiment ......September 13, 1814
Huntsman, Lemuel ........Ensign 11th regiment..September 13, 1814
Kincannon, Andrew ........Lieutenant
        11th regiment ......September 13, 1814
Mahon, Archemedes ........Ensign 11th regiment.......June 3, 1814
Pate, Charles ..............Ensign 11th regiment.......June 3, 1814
Perry, Semeon .............Second Major 11th regiment:May 7, 1814
Porter, John ...............Lieutenant 11th regiment...June 3, 1814
Robertson, Elijah ..........Ensign 11th regiment..November 21, 1814
Wear, John ...............Captain 11th regiment......June 3, 1814
Weir, Samuel .............Captain 11th regiment.November 21, 1814
White, William ...........Lieutenant 11th regiment...June 3, 1814

*Smith County Commissions*

Alcorn, John ..............Lieutenant Colonel Commandant
        regiment of cavalry
        4th brigade...........October 7, 1814
Barkley, Robert ..........First Major 16th regiment.March 21, 1814
Bradley, Thomas ..........Second Major regiment of
        cavalry 4th brigade....October 7, 1814
Bruce, Amos ..............Ensign 41st regiment.....March 21, 1814
Burton, Joshua ............Lieutenant
        41st regiment.........October 11, 1814
Byrn, John W. .............Captain cavalry
        4th brigade ........September 5, 1814
Byrn, John W. .............First Major cavalry
        4th brigade...........October 7, 1814
Clibon, John ..............Ensign 16th regiment.....August 8, 1814
Dixon, Tilmon ............Ensign 16th regiment.....August 8, 1814
Ferguson, Patrick ..........Lieutenant 16th regiment.August 8, 1814
Fite, David ...............Ensign 41st regiment....October 11, 1814

Keeling, John ............. Ensign 16th regiment. . September 1, 1814
McFerrin, Thomas ......... Lieutenant
    16th regiment ...... September 1, 1814
Meredith, David ........... Ensign 41st regiment. ... October 11, 1814
Metcalf, Anthony .......... Lieutenant Colonel Commandant
    16th regiment.......... March 21, 1814
Moore, Shadrick ........... Second Major
    16th regiment.......... March 21, 1814
Overall, Abraham .......... Lieutenant Colonel Commandant
    41st regiment............ May 19, 1814
Pate, Jeremiah ............ Ensign 16th regiment.... August 8, 1814
Pursley, Robert ............ Captain 16th regiment. September 1, 1814
Redmond, William ......... Lieutenant
    16th regiment ...... September 1, 1814
Robertson, Edward ........ Captain 41st regiment... October 11, 1814
Sitton, Phillip ............. Captain 16th regiment.... August 8, 1814
Thompson, William ....... Captain 16th regiment. September 1, 1814
Ward, Dicken ............. Lieutenant 41st regiment.. March 21, 1814

*Stewart County Commissions*

Allen, William L. .......... Captain 26th regiment...... June 2, 1814
Andrews, John ............. Ensign 26th regiment..... March 21, 1814
Briges, William ............ Lieutenant
    26th regiment ...... September 1, 1814
Cooley, Cornelius .......... Ensign 26th regiment..... March 21, 1814
Elliott, Ruben ............. Captain 26th regiment. September 1, 1814
James, William ............ Captain 26th regiment. September 1, 1814
Lewis, Benjamin ........... Lieutenant
    26th regiment ...... September 1, 1814
Polk, John ................ Lieutenant
    26th regiment......... October 4, 1814
Randle, Edmund ........... Ensign 26th regiment.... October 4, 1814
Ross, Samuel .............. Lieutenant 26th regiment.. March 21, 1814
Yarbrough, George ......... Ensign 26th regiment.. September 1, 1814

*Sullivan County Commissions*

Booker, William ........... Ensign 2nd regiment........ July 7, 1814
Bowdree, Samuel ........... Captain 2nd regiment....... July 7, 1814
Deyden, Thomas ........... Ensign 2nd regiment.. September 5, 1814
Galloway, James ........... Lieutenant 2nd regiment.... July 7, 1814
Getgood, Alexander ........ Captain regiment cavalry
    1st brigade............ August 29, 1814
Gregg, Nathan ............ Lieutenant
    2nd regiment....... September 5, 1814
Hancher, William .......... Lieutenant 2nd regiment.... July 7, 1814
Hughes, Robert ............ Ensign 2nd regiment... December 10, 1814
Rutledge, William ......... Second Major 2nd regiment. June 3, 1814
Willet, Nathan ............ Ensign 2nd regiment....... April 13, 1814

IN THE TENNESSEE MILITIA, 1814   239

*Sumner County Commissions*

Alderson, James ........... Captain 15th regiment ...... June 8, 1814
Barnes, Turner ............ Lieutenant
                           43rd regiment ........ January 31, 1814
Barret, David ............. Ensign 43rd regiment .... January 31, 1814
Blakemore, John D. ........ Lieutenant 15th regiment ... June 8, 1814
Carr, King ................ Lieutenant 15th regiment. August 8, 1814
Carr, William ............. Captain 15th regiment .... August 8, 1814
Corum, Robert ............. Lieutenant 16th regiment ... April 13, 1814
Cotton, Noah .............. Lieutenant regiment of cavalry
                           4th brigade ........ September 5, 1814
Cranshaw, Kerr ............ Ensign 15th regiment ....... June 8, 1814
Dining, Andrew ............ Ensign 43rd regiment .. December 10, 1814
Everett, Washington ....... Lieutenant 15th regiment ... June 8, 1814
Harris, Matthew H. ........ Captain 43rd regiment. September 21, 1814
Johnston, Jesse ........... Ensign 16th regiment ...... April 13, 1814
Jones, James .............. Ensign 43rd regiment .. September 21, 1814
King, David ............... Ensign 15th regiment ....... June 8, 1814
Lauderdale, Josiah ........ Captain regiment of cavalry
                           4th brigade ....... September 5, 1814
Mallory, Samuel ........... Lieutenant 43rd regiment .. March 23, 1814
Martin, George ............ Lieutenant
                           43rd regiment ........ January 31, 1814
Martin, John .............. Lieutenant 15th regiment. August 8, 1814
Miller, George ............ Ensign 15th regiment ..... August 8, 1814
Sewell, Benjamin .......... Captain 15th regiment ...... June 8, 1814
Stewart, William .......... Ensign Light Infantry
                           Company attached to
                           15th regiment ........... June 8, 1814
Strange, Beverly .......... Captain 16th regiment ..... April 13, 1814
Vinson, Benthle ........... Lieutenant 15th regiment ... June 8, 1814
Willis, Moss .............. Ensign 43rd regiment ..... August 17, 1814

*Warren County Commissions*

Burch, John ............... Lieutenant
                           29th regiment ........ January 31, 1814
Cantrell, Abraham ......... Captain 29th regiment ... January 8, 1814
Conley, John .............. Ensign 29th regiment .... January 31, 1814
Cunningham, John .......... Lieutenant
                           29th regiment ....... February 15, 1814
Graves, John .............. Ensign 29th regiment ....... July 20, 1814
Hillis, James ............. Captain 29th regiment ... January 8, 1814
Thomas, Hamilton .......... Captain 29th regiment ..... April 17, 1814
Watts, Allen .............. Ensign 29th regiment ... February 15, 1814

## Washington County Commissions

| | | |
|---|---|---|
| Barrow, James | Lieutenant 1st regiment | October 31, 1814 |
| Booth, Joseph | Ensign 1st regiment | October 31, 1814 |
| Brown, John | Lieutenant 1st regiment | October 31, 1814 |
| Ensor, Thomas | Lieutenant 1st regiment | December 9, 1814 |
| Fine, Abraham | Captain 1st regiment | October 31, 1814 |
| Garner, Griffin G. | Captain 1st regiment | August 2, 1814 |
| Grimley, William | Captain 1st regiment | October 31, 1814 |
| Gyer, Jacob | Ensign in company of men not subject to militia duty | January 31, 1814 |
| Hanley, Isaac | Lieutenant 1st regiment | October 31, 1814 |
| Hare, Henry | Captain 1st regiment | December 9, 1814 |
| Harris, G. C. | Captain 1st regiment | October 31, 1814 |
| Hartzell, Isaac | Captain 1st regiment | October 31, 1814 |
| **Hartzell**, Jacob | Second Major 1st regiment | August 5, 1814 |
| Hunter, Jacob | Lieutenant in company of men not subject to militia duty | January 31, 1814 |
| Inser, Joseph | Ensign 1st regiment | August 2, 1814 |
| Johnston, James S. | Second Major regiment of cavalry 1st brigade | October 31, 1814 |
| Jones, George B. | Lieutenant 1st regiment | October 4, 1814 |
| McClure, Ewen | Ensign 1st regiment | October 4, 1814 |
| McCracken, John | Captain in company of men not subject to militia duty | January 31, 1814 |
| McCracken, Samuel | Lieutenant 1st regiment | October 4, 1814 |
| Olinger, Samuel | Ensign 1st regiment | October 31, 1814 |

## White County Commissions

| | | |
|---|---|---|
| Car, James | Ensign 34th regiment | August 18, 1814 |
| Denny, William | Captain 34th regiment | June 14, 1814 |
| England, Elijah | Lieutenant 34th regiment | August 18, 1814 |
| Gwinn, William | Ensign 34th regiment | June 14, 1814 |
| Gwinn, William | Captain 34th regiment | November 28, 1814 |
| Hamblet, George | Captain 34th regiment | November 21, 1814 |
| Hawes, William | Captain 34th regiment | August 18, 1814 |
| Hudson, John | Ensign 34th regiment | June 14, 1814 |
| Jones, William | Lieutenant 34th regiment | August 18, 1814 |

IN THE TENNESSEE MILITIA, 1814         241

Kizon, Peter .............Lieutenant 34th regiment.August 18, 1814
Lanie, Henry .............Ensign 34th regiment.....August 18, 1814
Laxton, Jesse ............Lieutenant
                          34th regiment......November 21, 1814
Lewis, Elijah ............Lieutenant 34th regiment.August 18, 1814
McCampbell, James ........Brigade Major
                          7th Brigade........November 24, 1814
Parkeson, Daniel .........Captain 34th regiment....August 18, 1814
Puckett, Robert ..........Lieutenant 34th regiment...June 14, 1814
Smith, John T. ...........Lieutenant 34th regiment.August 18, 1814
Usrey, William ...........Lieutenant 34th regiment.August 18, 1814
Walker, John .............Captain 34th regiment....August 18, 1814
Webb, Martin .............Lieutenant 34th regiment...June 14, 1814

*Williamson County Commissions*

Bell, Joseph .............Captain 44th regiment......July  4, 1814
Brooks, Price W. .........Ensign 21st regiment......April 13, 1814
Bugg, Jesse ..............Ensign 44th regiment.....March 30, 1814
Carson, William ..........Captain 44th regiment....March 30, 1814
Clemm, James S. ..........Ensign Company Light
                          Infantry attached to
                          21st regiment...........July  7, 1814
Dalton, John .............Lieutenant
                          44th regiment......September 24, 1814
Dawson, Hutson ...........Lieutenant
                          21st regiment.......November 19, 1814
Fitzpatrick, Andrew ......Captain 44th regiment...January  8, 1814
Hardeman, Peter ..........Lieutenant
                          44th regiment......September 24, 1814
Johnson, Alexander .......Ensign 44th regiment.....March 30, 1814
Jones, James G. ..........Captain 21st regiment.....April 13, 1814
Lamb, David ..............Ensign 44th regiment.....March 30, 1814
McAlister, James .........Lieutenant 21st regiment....July  7, 1814
McEwen, James ............Lieutenant
                          21st regiment.......December  7, 1814
Madden, Elisha ...........Captain 21st regiment.....April 13, 1814
Manier, Lemuel ...........Ensign 44th regiment.......July  4, 1814
Maury, Thomas T. .........Lieutenant Colonel Commandant
                          21st regiment...........May 16, 1814
Perkins, Hardin ..........First Major 21st regiment.March 21, 1814
Pigg, James ..............Ensign 21st regiment.......April 13, 1814
Ray, John ................Lieutenant 44th regiment...June 30, 1814
Reed, James L. ...........Lieutenant 44th regiment...June 30, 1814
Reess, Beverly ...........Captain 21st regiment......July  7, 1814
Ross, James ..............Lieutenant 21st regiment...April 13, 1814
Rums, Henry ..............Ensign 21st regiment....October 25, 1814
Scott, Arthur ............Ensign 21st regiment....October 25, 1814
Smith, Andrew ............Ensign 21st regiment....October 25, 1814

## RECORD OF COMMISSIONS OF OFFICERS

Smith, William ............Lieutenant Volunteer Company Light Infantry attached to 21st regiment.........May 16, 1814
Stacy, John ...............Lieutenant 21st regiment...April 13, 1814
Stanfield, Goodloe ..........Ensign 21st regiment....October 25, 1814
Stewart, James ............Captain Volunteer Company Light Infantry attached to 21st regiment............May 16, 1814
Taylor, Abraham ..........Ensign 21st regiment.......July 13, 1814
Thompson, James ..........Lieutenant 21st regiment....July 7, 1814
Warren, R. H. .............Lieutenant 21st regiment...April 13, 1814
Williams, Elisha ...........Ensign 21st regiment.....August 18, 1814
Young, William ............Ensign 44th regiment..December 9, 1814

### Wilson County Commissions

Akens, Harrison ...........Lieutenant 17th regiment...May 27, 1814
Alexander, William S. ......Ensign 42nd regiment....August 27, 1814
Alford, Wiley .............Ensign 17th regiment.......May 27, 1814
Braden, John ..............Captain 42nd regiment...August 27, 1814
Braden, Robert ............Captain regiment of cavalry 4th brigade........September 5, 1814
Bradley, Hugh ............Cornet regiment of cavalry 4th brigade........September 5, 1814
Bradley, Thomas ..........Captain regiment of cavalry 4th brigade........September 5, 1814
Campbell, Robert ..........Ensign 17th regiment.......May 27, 1814
Doak, Jonathan ...........Lieutenant regiment of cavalry 4th brigade........September 5, 1814
Dooley, Thomas ..........Lieutenant regiment of cavalry 4th brigade........September 5, 1814
Douglass, Henry L. ........Lieutenant Colonel Commandant 17th regiment...........April 5, 1814
Fake, John ................Lieutenant 42nd regiment.August 27, 1814
Findley, Obediah G. ........Captain 17th regiment......May 27, 1814
Gray, James ..............Captain 17th regiment......May 27, 1814
Hallum, William ...........Lieutenant 17th regiment .....September 13, 1814
Harris, Sloan ..............Captain 17th regiment.September 13, 1814
Hudson, Noah .............Lieutenant 42nd regiment.August 27, 1814
Kirkpatrick, Joseph ........First Major 17th regiment..April 5, 1814
Lucky, John ...............Cornet regiment of cavalry 4th brigade.........December 20, 1814
McKnight, John ...........Ensign 42nd regiment....August 27, 1814
McWhirter, George F. ......Captain 17th regiment...August 18, 1814
Marshall, Robert ..........Ensign 42nd regiment....August 27, 1814
Mitchell, Everet ..........Captain 17th regiment.September 13, 1814
Oakley, William ...........Ensign 42nd regiment....August 27, 1814
Owens, Moses ............Ensign 42nd regiment......April 20, 1814

## IN THE TENNESSEE MILITIA, 1814

Puckett, Charles R. ........Ensign 42nd regiment......April 20, 1814
Shaw, Josiah ..............Captain regiment of cavalry
    4th brigade.........December 20, 1814
Standifer, John ............Ensign 17th regiment.......July 7, 1814
Still, George ...............Second Major
    17th regiment .........August 5, 1814
Stuart, William ............Lieutenant 17th regiment...July 7, 1814
Tarver, Edmund D. ........Lieutenant 17th regiment.August 18, 1814
Turner, James .............Ensign 42nd regiment....August 27, 1814
Walton, Josiah ............Cornet regiment of cavalry
    4th brigade ........September 5, 1814
Warren, Jesse .............Ensign 17th regiment.......July 7, 1814
Williamson, George ........Captain 17th regiment......May 27, 1814
Winstone, William .........Captain 42nd regiment.....April 20, 1814
Woollen, Joshua ...........Ensign 42nd regiment....August 27, 1814

*No County Was Given for the Following Records*

Barnet, Hugh ..............Cornet regiment of cavalry
    5th brigade.........December 10, 1814
Claiborne, Thomas .........Brigade Major
    6th brigade............March 10, 1814
Douglass, Alexander .......Cornet regiment of cavalry
    2nd brigade.........December 18, 1814
Gwinn, William ............Cornet regiment of cavalry
    4th brigade ........September 5, 1814
Tate, Edward .............Lieutenant of cavalry
    2nd brigade ........November 21, 1814
Watkins, Archibald ........Lieutenant regiment of cavalry
    4th brigade.........December 20, 1814
Weaver, Jesse ............Lieutenant regiment of cavalry
    4th brigade ........September 5, 1814
Weims, Briton ............Cornet regiment of cavalry
    6th brigade.........September 13, 1814
West, Samuel .............Captain regiment of cavalry
    2nd brigade ........December 8, 1814
Willie, James .............Cornet regiment of cavalry
    4th brigade ........September 5, 1814

# RECORD OF COMMISSIONS OF OFFICERS IN THE TENNESSEE MILITIA, 1815.

Compiled by Mrs. John Trotwood Moore

## Bedford County

| Name | Rank | Regiment | Date |
|---|---|---|---|
| Anderson, John | Lieutenant | 47th regiment | July 30, 1815 |
| Anderson, Robert | Lieutenant | 47th regiment | July 30, 1815 |
| Beard, John | Ensign | 47th regiment | Nov. 13, 1815 |
| Bolton, Josiah | Lieutenant | 47th regiment | July 30, 1815 |
| Boothe, Benjamin | Captain | 47th regiment | July 30, 1815 |
| Burnet, William | Captain light infantry company attached to 28th regiment | | June 8, 1815 |
| Cooper, Robert | Cornet regiment of cavalry 5th brigade | | June 22, 1815 |
| Crawford, Smith | Lieutenant | 47th regiment | Sept. 23, 1815 |
| Dean, John | Ensign | 47th regiment | July 30, 1815 |
| Elliot, Simon | Ensign | 47th regiment | July 30, 1815 |
| Ferguson, Robert | Lieutenant | 47th regiment | Sept. 23, 1815 |
| Haggard, James | Captain | 47th regiment | July 30, 1815 |
| King, Thomas | Lieutenant regiment—cavalry 5th brigade | | June 22, 1815 |
| Kirkland, Joab W. | Ensign | 47th regiment | Nov. 13, 1815 |
| McCrary, John | Lieutenant | 47th regiment | Nov. 13, 1815 |
| McKisick, James | Captain | 28th regiment | June 8, 1815 |
| Maxwell, John | Lieutenant | 28th regiment | June 8, 1815 |
| Pearson, John D. | Lieutenant light infantry company attached to 28th regiment | | June 8, 1815 |
| Shinault, James | Second Major | 47th regiment | July 30, 1815 |
| Shinault, Walter | Captain | 47th regiment | July 30, 1815 |
| Shuffield, John | Captain | 47th regiment | Sept. 23, 1815 |
| Snelling, Samuel | Ensign | 47th regiment | Nov. 13, 1815 |
| Sutton, John | First Major | 47th regiment | July 30, 1815 |
| Talliaferro, John K. | Ensign | 47th regiment | Sept. 23, 1815 |
| Thompson, Thomas F. | Captain | 28th regiment | June 8, 1815 |
| Watterson, William | Ensign | 47th regiment | Nov. 13, 1815 |
| Webster, Jonathan | Lieutenant Colonel Commander 47th regiment | | July 30, 1815 |
| Yeld, Archibald | Captain | 47th regiment | Nov. 13, 1815 |

## Bledsoe County

| Name | Rank | Regiment | Date |
|---|---|---|---|
| Cherry, Benjamin | Captain | 31st regiment | Nov. 13, 1815 |
| Crabtree, Hiram | Lieutenant | 31st regiment | Nov. 17, 1815 |
| Kelly, John | Lieutenant Colonel Commandant 31st regiment | | Feb. 13, 1815 |
| Myers, Adam | Ensign | 31st regiment | Nov. 17, 1815 |
| Rainey, John | Lieutenant | 31st regiment | Feb. 27, 1815 |

IN THE TENNESSEE MILITIA, 1815  245

| | | | |
|---|---|---|---|
| Seabourn, Richard | Captain | 31st regiment | Nov. 17, 1815 |
| Spring, John | Captain | 31st regiment | Feb. 27, 1815 |
| Tollett, Henry | Captain | 31st regiment | Nov. 13, 1815 |
| Vernon, Thomas | Ensign volunteer rifles company attached to 31st regiment | | Feb. 27, 1815 |
| Vernon, Thomas | Lieutenant | 31st regiment | Nov. 13, 1815 |

### Blount County

| | | | |
|---|---|---|---|
| Allen, Jobe | Lieutenant | 12th regiment | Oct. 31, 1815 |
| Boyd, John | Captain | 12th regiment | Oct. 31, 1815 |
| Campbell, Arthur | First Major | 12th regiment | Sept. 11, 1815 |
| Davis, Andrew | Lieutenant | 12th regiment | Oct. 31, 1815 |
| Dyrus (?) Quentin | Ensign | 12th regiment | Oct. 31, 1815 |
| Easley, Andrew | Lieutenant | 12th regiment | Oct. 31, 1815 |
| Greene, William | Lieutenant | 12th regiment | Oct. 31, 1815 |
| Greenoway, William S. | Captain | 12th regiment | Oct. 31, 1815 |
| Hackney, Samuel | Lieutenant | 12th regiment | Oct. 31, 1815 |
| Hanna, Carolinas | Ensign | 12th regiment | Oct. 31, 1815 |
| James, William | Captain | 12th regiment | Oct. 31, 1815 |
| Jentry, Jacob | Ensign | 12th regiment | Oct. 31, 1815 |
| Kendrick, William | Captain | 12th regiment | Oct. 31, 1815 |
| McCartney, James | Captain | 12th regiment | Oct. 31, 1815 |
| Madden, James | Ensign | 12th regiment | Oct. 31, 1815 |
| Rhea, James | Captain | 12th regiment | Oct. 31, 1815 |
| Taylor, William L. | Second Major | 12th regiment | May 20, 1815 |
| Tedford, James | Lieutenant | 12th regiment | Oct. 31, 1815 |

### Campbell County

| | | | |
|---|---|---|---|
| Campbell, Joseph | Ensign | 33rd regiment | Nov. 17, 1815 |
| Doak, Robert | Captain regiment cavalry 3rd brigade | | April 19, 1815 |
| English, Joshua | Lieutenant | 33rd regiment | Nov. 17, 1815 |
| Glenn, James | Lieutenant regiment cavalry 3rd brigade | | April 19, 1815 |
| Hayter, Abraham | Second Major | 33rd regiment | Dec. 13, 1815 |
| Leviston, Preston | Captain | 33rd regiment | Nov. 17, 1815 |
| Pauley, William | Cornet regiment cavalry 3rd brigade | | April 19, 1815 |
| Porupt, Henry | Ensign | 33rd regiment | Nov. 17, 1815 |
| Rector, Kenner | Lieutenant regiment cavalry 3rd brigade | | April 19, 1815 |
| Sharp, John | Ensign | 33rd regiment | Nov. 17, 1815 |

### Carter County

| | | | |
|---|---|---|---|
| Bailey, Samuel | Lieutenant | 5th regiment | Sept. 11, 1815 |
| Houston, James | Ensign | 5th regiment | Sept. 11, 1815 |
| Johnston, Henry D. | Lieutenant | 5th regiment | Dec. 11, 1815 |
| Sewell, John | Captain | 5th regiment | March 13, 1815 |

| | | | |
|---|---|---|---|
| Smith, William | Lieutenant | 5th regiment | Dec. 11, 1815 |
| Teague, John | Ensign | 5th regiment | Dec. 11, 1815 |
| Tipton, Abraham | Lieutenant | 5th regiment | April 19, 1815 |
| Worley, Hiram | Captain | 5th regiment | Dec. 11, 1815 |

### Claiborne County

| | | | |
|---|---|---|---|
| Brock, George | Captain | 9th regiment | Sept. 23, 1815 |
| Bunch, David | Ensign | 9th regiment | Sept. 23, 1815 |
| Bunch, William | Lieutenant | 9th regiment | Sept. 23, 1815 |
| Cain, Jesse | Lieutenant | 9th regiment | March 17, 1815 |
| Dobkins, Reuben | Ensign | 9th regiment | Sept. 23, 1815 |
| Foster, Mark | Captain | 9th regiment | March 17, 1815 |
| Hoskins, James | Ensign | 9th regiment | Nov. 13, 1815 |
| Hunter, Joseph | Captain | 9th regiment | Sept. 23, 1815 |
| Long, John | Ensign | 9th regiment | Nov. 13, 1815 |
| McReynolds, John | Lieutenant | 9th regiment | Sept. 23, 1815 |
| Roberts, John | Ensign | 9th regiment | Sept. 23, 1815 |
| Vanbibber, Jacob | Lieutenant | 9th regiment | Nov. 13, 1815 |

### Cocke County

| | | | |
|---|---|---|---|
| Blackston, James | Lieutenant | 8th regiment | June 28, 1815 |
| Campbell, Sanders W. | Ensign | 8th regiment | April 7, 1815 |
| Cunningham, David | First Major | 8th regiment | March 13, 1815 |
| Dillen, James | Lieutenant | 8th regiment | Aug. 14, 1815 |
| Grant, William | Captain | 8th regiment | Oct. 30, 1815 |
| Jennings, James | Captain | 8th regiment | Aug. 14, 1815 |
| McClahan, Job | Lieutenant | 8th regiment | June 28, 1815 |
| McMahan, Anderson | Ensign | 8th regiment | Aug. 14, 1815 |
| McPike, Jesse | Ensign | 8th regiment | May 20, 1815 |
| Thompson, James | Lieutenant | 8th regiment | Oct. 30, 1815 |

### Davidson County

| | | | |
|---|---|---|---|
| Cheatham, Samuel G. | Ensign | 19th regiment | Aug. 14, 1815 |
| Cox, Jesse | Lieutenant | 19th regiment | Aug. 14, 1815 |
| Davis, Turner | Ensign | 19th regiment | Aug. 14, 1815 |
| Elam, Samuel | Captain | 19th regiment | Jan. 9, 1815 |
| Fuquay, Joshua | Lieutenant | 19th regiment | Aug. 21, 1815 |
| Goldsberry, Henry | Lieutenant | 20th regiment | April 26, 1815 |
| Goodlet, James E. | Ensign | 19th regiment | Aug. 14, 1815 |
| Hall, Samuel S. | Lieutenant | 19th regiment | Jan. 9, 1815 |
| Hunter, John | Captain regiment of cavalry 1st brigade | | Sept. 23, 1815 |
| Hynes, Andrew | Adjutant General of Tennessee | | Nov. 18, 1815 |
| Matthews, Ebenezer | Cornet regiment of cavalry 1st brigade | | Sept. 23, 1815 |
| Mitchell, Daniel | Ensign | 19th regiment | Sept. 5, 1815 |
| Norvel, Moses | Lieutenant | 19th regiment | Jan. 9, 1815 |
| Prior, Nicholas B. | Ensign | 19th regiment | Jan. 9, 1815 |
| Rarborough, Wm. L. | Captain | 19th regiment | Sept. 5, 1815 |

IN THE TENNESSEE MILITIA, 1815 247

| | | | |
|---|---|---|---|
| Roberts, John | Ensign | 19th regiment | Aug. 21, 1815 |
| Smith, Thomas | Lieutenant | 19th regiment | Aug. 21, 1815 |
| Wright, Thomas | Lieutenant | 19th regiment | Jan. 9, 1815 |
| Yarborough, Wm. L. | Captain | 19th regiment | Sept. 20, 1815 |
| Young, James | Lieutenant | regiment of cavalry 1st brigade | Sept. 23, 1815 |

### Dickson County

| | | | |
|---|---|---|---|
| Anderson, John G. | Lieutenant | 25th regiment | Dec. 16, 1815 |
| Auston, William | Lieutenant | 25th regiment | Dec. 16, 1815 |
| Baker, Charles | Lieutenant | 25th regiment | Dec. 16, 1815 |
| Bernard, John | Lieutenant | 25th regiment | Dec. 16, 1815 |
| Berry, Lewis | Captain | 25th regiment | Dec. 16, 1815 |
| Edwards, Selman | Captain | 25th regiment | Dec. 16, 1815 |
| Fentress, Absolem | Ensign | 25th regiment | Dec. 16, 1815 |
| Higganbotham, Caleb | Captain | 25th regiment | Dec. 16, 1815 |
| Horner, John | Ensign | 25th regiment | Dec. 16, 1815 |
| Hunnals, Robert | Ensign | 25th regiment | Dec. 16, 1815 |
| Lesby, Henry | Lieutenant | 25th regiment | Dec. 16, 1815 |
| Lucas, William | Captain | 25th regiment | Dec. 16, 1815 |
| McMurry, Robert | Ensign | 25th regiment | Dec. 16, 1815 |
| Murrell, Thomas | Captain | 25th regiment | Dec. 16, 1815 |
| Neisbett, Thomas | Lieutenant | 25th regiment | Dec. 16, 1815 |
| Robertson, Christopher | Second Major | 25th regiment | Dec. 16, 1815 |
| Tatum, James | Captain | 25th regiment | Dec. 16, 1815 |
| Teal, George | Ensign | 25th regiment | Dec. 16, 1815 |
| Willy, Willis | Ensign | 25th regiment | Dec. 16, 1815 |

### Franklin County

| | | | |
|---|---|---|---|
| Bean, Robert | Lieutenant | 32nd regiment | July 27, 1815 |
| Burress, Samuel | Ensign | 32nd regiment | July 27, 1815 |
| Caperton, George | Lieutenant Colonel Commandant 32nd regiment | | Aug. 21, 1815 |
| Cowan, Robert | Lieutenant | 32nd regiment | May 21, 1815 |
| Crockett, David | Lieutenant | 32nd regiment | May 21, 1815 |
| Easley, Benjamin | Captain | 32nd regiment | Sept. 23, 1815 |
| Farriss, John | Ensign | 32nd regiment | July 27, 1815 |
| Gates, Phillip | Captain | 32nd regiment | May 21, 1815 |
| Gotcher, Jesse | Captain | 32nd regiment | June 8, 1815 |
| Hunt, David | First Major | 32nd regiment | Aug. 21, 1815 |
| Jones, Brittain | Lieutenant | 32nd regiment | July 27, 1815 |
| Keeton, Reason | Ensign | 32nd regiment | May 21, 1815 |
| Kemp, Nathan | Lieutenant | 32nd regiment | May 21, 1815 |
| Leach, Josiah | Lieutenant | 32nd regiment | July 27, 1815 |
| McCord, James | Ensign | 32nd regiment | July 27, 1815 |
| Montgomery, James | Captain | 32nd regiment | May 21, 1815 |
| Newberry, James | Ensign | 32nd regiment | May 21, 1815 |
| Porter, John H. | Captain | 32nd regiment | July 27, 1815 |

| | | | |
|---|---|---|---|
| Stanley, James | Captain | 32nd regiment | July 27, 1815 |
| Tubb, George, Junr. | Ensign | 32nd regiment | July 27, 1815 |
| Vinzant, Jacob | Captain | 32nd regiment | May 21, 1815 |
| Walker, Andrew | Captain | 32nd regiment | July 27, 1815 |
| Woods, Charles | Captain | 32nd regiment | June 8, 1815 |
| Woods, Peter | Second Major | 32nd regiment | Aug. 21, 1815 |
| Young, Jacob | Ensign | 32nd regiment | May 21, 1815 |

## Giles County

| | | | |
|---|---|---|---|
| Bentley, Richard | Lieutenant | 37th regiment | June 11, 1815 |
| Brooks, William B. | Captain | 37th regiment | April 2, 1815 |
| Brown, Thomas | Lieutenant | 2nd (52nd) regiment | Dec. 20, 1815 |
| Brown, Thomas | Captain | 37th regiment | June 11, 1815 |
| Cook, Lemuel | Lieutenant | 2nd (52nd) regiment | April 29, 1815 |
| Davis, Nathan | Second Major | 37th regiment | Oct. 21, 1815 |
| Dondle, Joseph | Ensign | 2nd (52nd) regiment | April 7, 1815 |
| Evans, John | Ensign | 2nd (52nd) regiment | Dec. 13, 1815 |
| Griffis, Anderson | Ensign | 2nd (52nd) regiment | Sept. 16, 1815 |
| Haile, Butler | Captain | 2nd (52nd) regiment | Dec. 20, 1815 |
| Perkins, James | Lieutenant | 2nd (52nd) regiment | Sept. 16, 1815 |
| Perkins, Robert | Captain | 2nd (52nd) regiment | Dec. 13, 1815 |
| Perkins, William | Captain | 2nd (52nd) regiment | Dec. 20, 1815 |
| Sharpe, Thomas | Lieutenant | 2nd (52nd) regiment | July 4, 1815 |
| Shrader, Henry | Lieutenant | 2nd (52nd) regiment | Dec. 20, 1815 |
| Snader, Henry | Ensign | 2nd (52nd) regiment | Aug. 21, 1815 |
| Swaeringen, William | Ensign | 2nd (52nd) regiment | April 29, 1815 |
| Terrell, James | Lieutenant Colonel Commandant | 37th regiment | Oct. 21, 1815 |
| Welch, Nicholas | Lieutenant | 2nd (52nd) regiment | Dec. 20, 1815 |
| Wharton, Joshua | Ensign | 2nd (52nd) regiment | Dec. 20, 1815 |
| Wilson, Abel | Captain | 37th regiment | June 22, 1815 |

## Grainger County

| | | | |
|---|---|---|---|
| Bradley, Isaac | Lieutenant | 7th regiment | Sept. 23, 1815 |
| Dennis, William | Lieutenant | 7th regiment | Sept. 23, 1815 |
| Feilds, Joel | Captain | 7th regiment | Sept. 23, 1815 |
| Groves, Reuben | Captain | 7th regiment | Sept. 23, 1815 |
| Readen, Alexander | Ensign | 7th regiment | Sept. 23, 1815 |
| Tate, David | Captain | 7th regiment | Sept. 23, 1815 |

## Greene County

| | | | |
|---|---|---|---|
| Adams, David | Captain | 3rd regiment | Nov. 14, 1815 |
| Armontage, John | Lieutenant | 3rd regiment | Nov. 14, 1815 |
| Bible, John | Captain | 3rd regiment | Dec. 13, 1815 |
| Brown, William | Ensign | 3rd regiment | Nov. 14, 1815 |
| Gladden, William | Ensign | 3rd regiment | Dec. 13, 1815 |
| Harmon, Peter | Captain | 3rd regiment | Nov. 14, 1815 |
| Hayes, Lewis W. | Ensign | 3rd regiment | Dec. 13, 1815 |

IN THE TENNESSEE MILITIA, 1815        249

| | | | |
|---|---|---|---|
| Johnston, John R. | Ensign | 3rd regiment | Nov. 15, 1815 |
| McGaffy, John | Lieutenant | 3rd regiment | Nov. 14, 1815 |
| Newman, Jonathan | Captain | regiment of cavalry 1st brigade | Nov. 2, 1815 |
| Pearce, Weston | Ensign | 3rd regiment | Nov. 15, 1815 |
| Robinson, James | Captain | 3rd regiment | Nov. 14, 1815 |
| Ruder, Samuel | Ensign | 3rd regiment | Nov. 15, 1815 |
| Self, Thomas | Captain | 3rd regiment | Dec. 13, 1815 |
| Smith, Beverley | Captain | 3rd regiment | Nov. 14, 1815 |
| Vance, James | Lieutenant | 3rd regiment | Nov. 15, 1815 |
| Wolsey, Mathias | Cornet | regiment of cavalry 1st brigade | Nov. 2, 1815 |

### Hawkins County

| | | | |
|---|---|---|---|
| Cloud, William | Captain | 4th regiment | Sept. 23, 1815 |
| Davis, James | Ensign | 4th regiment | Sept. 23, 1815 |
| Erwen, Edward | Captain | 4th regiment | Sept. 23, 1815 |
| Foster, Winkfield | Captain | 4th regiment | Sept. 23, 1815 |
| Harris, Benony | Ensign | 4th regiment | Sept. 23, 1815 |
| Sphere, Jesse | Lieutenant | 4th regiment | Sept. 23, 1815 |
| Staples, James | Ensign | 4th regiment | Sept. 23, 1815 |
| Tate, Gersham | Ensign | 4th regiment | Sept. 23, 1815 |
| Winager, Jacob | Ensign | 4th regiment | Sept. 23, 1815 |
| Winager, Samuel | Lieutenant | 4th regiment | Sept. 23, 1815 |

### Hickman County

| | | | |
|---|---|---|---|
| Deen, Jacob | Lieutenant | 36th regiment | Dec. 20, 1815 |
| Fisher, William | Ensign | 36th regiment | Dec. 20, 1815 |
| Flinn, Barney H. | Captain | 36th regiment | Sept. 11, 1815 |
| Hail, Job | Lieutenant | 36th regiment | July 17, 1815 |
| Jones, Andrew | Captain | 36th regiment | Dec. 20, 1815 |
| Lytle, John | First Major | 36th regiment | Nov. 29, 1815 |
| Morrison, Miles | Lieutenant | 36th regiment | Nov. 29, 1815 |
| Mullans, James | Ensign | 36th regiment | Dec. 20, 1815 |
| Nunnely, John | Second Major | 36th regiment | Aug. 21, 1815 |
| Rogers, George | Ensign | 36th regiment | July 17, 1815 |
| Shelton, Jonathan | Captain | 36th regiment | Dec. 20, 1815 |
| Wright, William | Ensign | 36th regiment | Dec. 19, 1815 |

### Humphreys County

| | | | |
|---|---|---|---|
| Bakeley, William | Ensign | 38th regiment | Sept. 7, 1815 |

### Jackson County

| | | | |
|---|---|---|---|
| Bennett, Noah | Captain | 48th regiment | Oct. 30, 1815 |
| Hancock, James | Captain | 18th regiment | May 27, 1815 |
| Holloman, James | Lieutenant Colonel Commandant | 18th regiment | Nov. 15, 1815 |
| Jarred, William | Captain | 18th regiment | May 27, 1815 |
| Kerr, James | Lieutenant | 18th regiment | May 27, 1815 |

| | | | |
|---|---|---|---|
| Roberts, Silas M. ...Lieutenant | 18th regiment | Nov. 17, 1815 |
| Williams, James ....Lieutenant | 18th regiment | May 27, 1815 |

## Jefferson County

| | | | |
|---|---|---|---|
| Barton, John ....... Ensign in volunteer rifle company attached to the | | |
| | 6th regiment | Jan. 16, 1815 |
| Brown, William ..... Lieutenant | 6th regiment | Dec. 2, 1815 |
| Clark, Daniel ....... Ensign | 6th regiment | Dec. 2, 1815 |
| Clark, William ..... Lieutenant | 6th regiment | Dec. 2, 1815 |
| Collins, Francis ..... Captain | 6th regiment | Aug. 7, 1815 |
| Copeland, Joseph .... Ensign | 6th regiment | June 22, 1815 |
| Galbreath, William .. Captain | 6th regiment | July 4, 1815 |
| Gibson, William ..... Captain | 48th regiment | Jan. 16, 1815 |
| Kelso, Eliphalet ..... Ensign | 6th regiment | Feb. 3, 1815 |
| Longaver, Richard .. Captain | 6th regiment | Dec. 2, 1815 |
| McDonald, Alexander. Ensign | 6th regiment | Jan. 16, 1815 |
| McFarland, John .... First Major regiment cavalry | | |
| | 2nd brigade | April 11, 1815 |
| McGuire, Thomas ... Lieutenant | 6th regiment | Sept. 23, 1815 |
| Newman, Jonathan .. Lieutenant regiment cavalry | | |
| | 2nd brigade | April 24, 1815 |
| Newman, Robert .... Cornet regiment cavalry | | |
| | 2nd brigade | April 24, 1815 |
| Reece, Joseph M. B. .. Captain regiment cavalry | | |
| | 2nd brigade | April 24, 1815 |
| Sewell, George ...... Captain | 6th regiment | June 22, 1815 |
| Smith, David ....... Lieutenant | 6th regiment | June 22, 1815 |
| Tucker, James ...... Captain | 6th regiment | Dec. 2, 1815 |

## Knox County

| | | | |
|---|---|---|---|
| Armstrong, Aaron ... Captain rifle company attached to | | |
| | 10th regiment | Dec. 13, 1815 |
| Birdwell, George .... Captain rifle company attached to | | |
| | 40th regiment | Dec. 13, 1815 |
| Farquharson, Joel ... Lieutenant | 40th regiment | Dec. 13, 1815 |
| Henderson, Jesse .... Captain | 40th regiment | Dec. 13, 1815 |
| Herrelson, William .. Ensign | 40th regiment | Feb. 13, 1815 |
| Hill, Bowen ........ Ensign rifle company attached to | | |
| | 40th regiment | Dec. 13, 1815 |
| Jackson, Joseph ..... Ensign | 40th regiment | Dec. 13, 1815 |
| Kearns, John ....... Ensign | 10th regiment | June 22, 1815 |
| Lonass, Henry ...... Lieutenant | 40th regiment | Dec. 13, 1815 |
| McCampbell, Wm. A. .Captain regiment cavalry | | |
| | 3rd brigade | April 19, 1815 |
| McMillen, James .... Second Major | 10th regiment | June 5, 1815 |
| McNare, John ...... Lieutenant Colonel Commandant | | |
| | 10th regiment | Dec. 2, 1815 |
| Mahaffy, John ...... Ensign | 10th regiment | April 19, 1815 |
| Price, Daniel ....... First Major | 10th regiment | Dec. 2, 1815 |

IN THE TENNESSEE MILITIA, 1815         251

| | | | |
|---|---|---|---|
| Regney, William .... | Captain | 40th regiment | April 29, 1815 |
| Shell, John ......... | Captain | 10th regiment | June 22, 1815 |
| Stephenson, James .. | Captain | 40th regiment | Dec. 13, 1815 |
| Wolf, George ....... | Lieutenant rifle company attached to 40th regiment | | Dec. 13, 1815 |

*Lincoln County*

| | | | |
|---|---|---|---|
| Bradburry, John .... | Captain | 49th regiment | July 22, 1815 |
| Cunningham, Robert.. | Lieutenant | 49th regiment | Dec. 20, 1815 |
| Dye, William ....... | Ensign | 39th regiment | Aug. 14, 1815 |
| Gamble, Frederick ... | Ensign | 49th regiment | Dec. 20, 1815 |
| Garrott, Westley .... | Lieutenant | 49th regiment | Dec. 20, 1815 |
| Hunt, George ....... | Captain | 49th regiment | July 22, 1815 |
| Leach, Joshua ...... | Ensign | 49th regiment | July 22, 1815 |
| Leonard, William ... | Lieutenant | 49th regiment | Dec. 20, 1815 |
| Lung, James ....... | Lieutenant of volunteer rifle company attached to 39th regiment | | Aug. 14, 1815 |
| McGehe, William .... | Ensign | 49th regiment | July 22, 1815 |
| Milam, Thomas ..... | Captain of volunteer rifle company attached to 39th regiment | | Aug. 14, 1815 |
| Monroe, William .... | Ensign of volunteer rifle company attached to 39th regiment | | Aug. 14, 1815 |
| Philpot, Horatio .... | Captain | 39th regiment | Aug. 14, 1815 |
| Thompson, David .... | Lieutenant | 39th regiment | Aug. 14, 1815 |
| Walker, Carter ..... | Captain | 49th regiment | Dec. 11, 1815 |
| Wilson, John ....... | Captain | 49th regiment | Dec. 20, 1815 |

*Maury County*

| | | | |
|---|---|---|---|
| Abbernathy, Ephraim | Lieutenant | 51st regiment | Feb. 27, 1815 |
| Barnes, James ...... | Lieutenant | 51st regiment | Nov. 30, 1815 |
| Boyd, John ......... | Ensign | 27th regiment | Aug. 8, 1815 |
| Brooks, George ..... | Ensign | 51st regiment | Nov. 30, 1815 |
| Coe, Joseph ........ | Captain | 27th regiment | May 19, 1815 |
| English, Thomas .... | Captain | 51st regiment | March 17, 1815 |
| Flemming, John D. .. | Lieutenant light infantry company 51st regiment | | Nov. 30, 1815 |
| Garner, Lewis ....... | Lieutenant | 51st regiment | July 26, 1815 |
| Gordon, James ...... | Captain light infantry company 51st regiment | | Nov. 30, 1815 |
| Helms, Malaki ...... | Ensign | 51st regiment | Nov. 30, 1815 |
| Herrelson, James .... | Ensign | 51st regiment | March 17, 1815 |
| Lamaster, John W. .. | Ensign | 27th regiment | Aug. 8, 1815 |
| Mallory, Phillip G. .. | Lieutenant | 21st regiment | Aug. 8, 1815 |
| Middleton, Alfred ... | Ensign | 51st regiment | July 26, 1815 |
| Nations, Christopher . | Ensign | 27th regiment | May 19, 1815 |
| Patterson, George ... | Lieutenant | 51st regiment | Nov. 3, 1815 |
| Shaw, Samuel ...... | Captain | 51st regiment | July 26, 1815 |
| Snisher, G. ......... | Captain | 21st regiment | Aug. 8, 1815 |

## Montgomery County

| | | | |
|---|---|---|---|
| Brantley, Hugh | Lieutenant light infantry attached to 50th regiment | | Oct. 30, 1815 |
| Carney, James W. | Captain | 50th regiment | Dec. 20, 1815 |
| Cooley, Wood T. H. | Lieutenant | 50th regiment | May 13, 1815 |
| Crutcher, George | Captain | 50th regiment | Dec. 20, 1815 |
| Foust, Jacob | Captain | 50th regiment | May 13, 1815 |
| Grant, Samuel | Lieutenant | 50th regiment | Dec. 20, 1815 |
| Moore, John | Ensign | 50th regiment | Oct. 30, 1815 |
| Ryburn, Samuel H. D. | Captain regiment cavalry 6th brigade | | July 4, 1815 |

## Overton County

| | | | |
|---|---|---|---|
| Allen, Hiram L. | Ensign | 35th regiment | Nov. 29, 1815 |
| Atkinson, Henry H. | Second Major | 35th regiment | Oct. 10, 1815 |
| Chapin, Paul | Captain | 35th regiment | Nov. 29, 1815 |
| Cherry, Benjamin | Ensign | 35th regiment | March 17, 1815 |
| Davis, Henry | Lieutenant | 35th regiment | Nov. 29, 1815 |
| Evans, Joseph | Lieutenant | 35th regiment | March 17, 1815 |
| Gardenhire, Thompson | Lieutenant | 35th regiment | Nov. 29, 1815 |
| Gilbreath, George | Lieutenant | 35th regiment | Nov. 29, 1815 |
| Greenwood, James | Captain | 35th regiment | Nov. 29, 1815 |
| Harrison, James | First Major | 35th regiment | Oct. 10, 1815 |
| Hord, Thomas | Lieutenant | 35th regiment | March 17, 1815 |
| Maxwell, Simpson | Ensign | 35th regiment | Nov. 29, 1815 |
| Smith, William | Ensign | 35th regiment | March 17, 1815 |
| Travis, William | Captain | 35th regiment | March 17, 1815 |
| Williams, James | Captain | 35th regiment | March 17, 1815 |
| Willis, Abel | Lieutenant Colonel Commandant 35th regiment | | Oct. 10, 1815 |
| Wray, William | Lieutenant | 35th regiment | Nov. 29, 1815 |

## Rhea County

| | | | |
|---|---|---|---|
| Birdsong, William | Captain | 30th regiment | Dec. 13, 1815 |
| Majors, John | Ensign | 30th regiment | Dec. 11, 1815 |
| Neal, James | Lieutenant | 30th regiment | Dec. 11, 1815 |
| Skidmore, John | Captain | 30th regiment | Dec. 11, 1815 |
| Stoner, Michael | Ensign | 30th regiment | Dec. 13, 1815 |
| Wax, Henry E. | Lieutenant | 30th regiment | Dec. 13, 1815 |

## Roane County

| | | | |
|---|---|---|---|
| Crawford, John | Lieutenant | 14th regiment | Nov. 30, 1815 |
| Esery, John | Captain | 14th regiment | April 14, 1815 |
| Esery, John | Captain | 14th regiment | Dec. 13, 1815 |
| Hembre, Joel | Captain | 14th regiment | Sept. 16, 1815 |
| Hembree, Joel | Captain | 14th regiment | Dec. 13, 1815 |
| Lankford, Benjamin | Lieutenant | 14th regiment | Sept. 16, 1815 |

## IN THE TENNESSEE MILITIA, 1815

| | | | |
|---|---|---|---|
| Leftwich, John | First Major | 14th regiment | Jan. 2, 1815 |
| Nail, Joseph | Captain | 14th regiment | Dec. 13, 1815 |
| Nail, Joseph | Captain | 14th regiment | Sept. 16, 1815 |
| Pride, Allen | Ensign | 14th regiment | Sept. 16, 1815 |
| Pride, Allen | Ensign | 14th regiment | Dec. 13, 1815 |
| Rector, Richard | Captain | 14th regiment | Sept. 16, 1815 |
| Rector, Richard | Captain | 14th regiment | Dec. 13, 1815 |
| Renfro, Robert | Captain | 14th regiment | Sept. 16, 1815 |
| Renfroe, Robert | Captain | 14th regiment | Dec. 13, 1815 |
| Scrivner, David | Lieutenant | 14th regiment | Sept. 16, 1815 |
| Scrivenor, David | Lieutenant | 14th regiment | Dec. 13, 1815 |

### Robertson County

| | | | |
|---|---|---|---|
| Anderson, John | Ensign | 23rd regiment | Aug. 21, 1815 |
| Baldwin, John | Lieutenant | 23rd regiment | June 28, 1815 |
| Clarke, Archibald | Ensign | 23rd regiment | June 28, 1815 |
| Cook, James | Second Major | 23rd regiment | Dec. 20, 1815 |
| Cravens, Elisha | Captain | 23rd regiment | Aug. 21, 1815 |
| Elliot, Benjamin | Lieutenant Colonel Commandant 23rd regiment | | Sept. 23, 1815 |
| Jones, Richard | Captain | 23rd regiment | Dec. 20, 1815 |
| Maloy, Daniel | Ensign | 23rd regiment | Aug. 21, 1815 |
| Mason, Phillip | Lieutenant | 23rd regiment | Aug. 21, 1815 |
| Moore, Samuel | Lieutenant | 23rd regiment | Aug. 21, 1815 |
| Payne, Solomon | Captain | 23rd regiment | Aug. 21, 1815 |
| Payne, Warren L. | Captain | 23rd regiment | Aug. 21, 1815 |
| Probitt, Robert C. | Lieutenant | 23rd regiment | Dec. 20, 1815 |
| Rogers, John | Ensign | 23rd regiment | April 3, 1815 |
| Rogers, John | Lieutenant | 23rd regiment | Aug. 21, 1815 |
| Shelton, James | Ensign | 23rd regiment | Sept. 5, 1815 |
| Tucker, John | Ensign | 23rd regiment | Aug. 21, 1815 |
| Williams, Meredith | Lieutenant | 23rd regiment | Aug. 21, 1815 |

### Rutherford County

| | | | |
|---|---|---|---|
| Bellew, Joseph | Captain | 45th regiment | Aug. 30, 1815 |
| Burton, Willie | Ensign | 22nd regiment | April 28, 1815 |
| Byferd, Parker | Lieutenant | 45th regiment | Aug. 30, 1815 |
| Cantrell, Ota | Second Major | 22nd regiment | Dec. 16, 1815 |
| Carnahan, Thomas | Ensign | 45th regiment | Aug. 30, 1815 |
| Caulfield, John | Captain light infantry company attached to 22nd regiment | | Dec. 13, 1815 |
| Colfield, John | Lieutenant light infantry company attached to 22nd regiment | | April 28, 1815 |
| Cooke, Hezekiah G. | Captain | 22nd regiment | Aug. 14, 1815 |
| Cooke, William | Lieutenant | 22nd regiment | Aug. 14, 1815 |
| Covington, David | Ensign | 22nd regiment | June 28, 1815 |
| Crow, John | Captain | 22nd regiment | Dec. 13, 1815 |
| Doyles, Richard D. | Ensign | 45th regiment | Feb. 20, 1815 |

254    RECORD OF COMMISSIONS OF OFFICERS

| | | | |
|---|---|---|---|
| Doyle Richard D. ... Captain | 45th regiment | June 11, 1815 |
| Elam, Solomon ..... Captain | 45th regiment | Aug. 30, 1815 |
| Ganaway, Burwell ... First Major | 45th regiment | May 8, 1815 |
| Ganaway, Walker .... Captain | 22nd regiment | Dec. 13, 1815 |
| Gosset, William ..... Ensign | 45th regiment | June 11, 1815 |
| Graves, Joseph ...... Lieutenant | 45th regiment | June 11, 1815 |
| Haley, Elijah ....... Captain | 22nd regiment | May 19, 1815 |
| Harris, Allsea ...... Lieutenant | 45th regiment | June 11, 1815 |
| Hollis, Micajah ..... Captain | 45th regiment | Jan. 9, 1815 |
| Hutton, Henry ...... Lieutenant light infantry company attached to | | |
| | 22nd regiment | Dec. 13, 1815 |
| Jetton, Robert ...... Lieutenant Colonel Commandant | | |
| | 45th regiment | May 8, 1815 |
| Johnson, Lewis ..... Lieutenant | 45th regiment | Aug. 30, 1815 |
| Johnston, Larkin ... Lieutenant | 45th regiment | June 11, 1815 |
| Kelough, John ...... Captain light infantry company attached to | | |
| | 45th regiment | June 11, 1815 |
| Kindrick, Joseph A. C. Lieutenant | 22nd regiment | June 28, 1815 |
| Kirk, Hugh ........ Second Major | 45th regiment | May 8, 1815 |
| Leathers, William ... Ensign | 45th regiment | June 11, 1815 |
| McGlothlin, Levi .... Lieutenant | 22nd regiment | Dec. 13, 1815 |
| Miller, Isaac ........ Captain | 45th regiment | June 11, 1815 |
| Nance, Allen ....... Lieutenant | 22nd regiment | Dec. 13, 1815 |
| Patten, James ...... Lieutenant | 45th regiment | Aug. 30, 1815 |
| Petty, Alexander .... Captain | 45th regiment | Aug. 30, 1815 |
| Pollard, Joseph ..... Ensign | 45th regiment | Aug. 30, 1815 |
| Potts, Thomas ...... Captain | 45th regiment | June 11, 1815 |
| Powell, G. W. ...... Ensign | 45th regiment | Aug. 30, 1815 |
| Powell, William ..... Lieutenant | 45th regiment | Aug. 30, 1815 |
| Robertson, David J. .. Captain | 22nd regiment | Dec. 13, 1815 |
| Saunders, Elijah .... Ensign | 22nd regiment | Dec. 13, 1815 |
| Scott, Stallard ...... Ensign light infantry company attached to | | |
| | 45th regiment | June 11, 1815 |
| Sharpe, John ....... Captain | 22nd regiment | May 19, 1815 |
| Stanly, James ...... Ensign | 45th regiment | Aug. 30, 1815 |
| Thompson, Abraham . Ensign light infantry company attached to | | |
| | 45th regiment | Feb. 20, 1815 |
| Thompson, Abraham . Lieutenant light infantry company attached to | | |
| | 45th regiment | June 11, 1815 |
| Todd, James ........ Ensign | 45th regiment | Jan. 9, 1815 |
| Tucker, William .... Ensign | 45th regiment | June 11, 1815 |
| Watkins, Thomas G. . Captain | 45th regiment | Aug. 30, 1815 |
| Wimberley, Malachi . Lieutenant | 22nd regiment | Dec. 13, 1815 |

*Sevier County*

| | | |
|---|---|---|
| Benson, Benjamin ... Captain | 11th regiment | Sept. 23, 1815 |
| Clark, John ........ Captain | 11th regiment | Sept. 23, 1815 |
| Ellis, William ...... Lieutenant | 11th regiment | Sept. 23, 1815 |
| Fox, Adam ......... Lieutenant | 11th regiment | Sept. 23, 1815 |

IN THE TENNESSEE MILITIA, 1815   255

| | | | |
|---|---|---|---|
| Friar, William ...... Ensign | 11th regiment | Sept. 23, 1815 |
| Lawson, Andrew .... First Major | 11th regiment | June 28, 1815 |
| Lawson, Robert ..... Captain | 11th regiment | Sept. 23, 1815 |
| Maples, Thomas .... Ensign | 11th regiment | Sept. 23, 1815 |
| Mohan, Archemedes .. Lieutenant | 11th regiment | Sept. 23, 1815 |
| Preston, Alexander .. Lieutenant Colonel Commandant | 11th regiment | June 28, 1815 |
| Sheilds, Robert ..... Lieutenant | 11th regiment | Sept. 23, 1815 |
| Warren, T. W. A. .... Captain | 11th regiment | Sept. 23, 1815 |
| Wear, Samuel, Junr. .. Second Major | 11th regiment | June 28, 1815 |
| Willcockson, John .. Captain | 11th regiment | Sept. 23, 1815 |

### Smith County

| | | |
|---|---|---|
| Bradley, John ...... Lieutenant | 16th regiment | Feb. 13, 1815 |
| Elstane, Jesse ....... Ensign | 41st regiment | Feb. 16, 1815 |
| McClain, William .... Ensign | 41st regiment | Feb. 16, 1815 |
| Nickles, Matthew .... Captain | 41st regiment | Feb. 16, 1815 |
| Tubb, James ........ Second Major | 41st regiment | Dec. 13, 1815 |

### Stewart County

| | | |
|---|---|---|
| Atkins, William R. ... Lieutenant | 26th regiment | July 22, 1815 |
| Blanks, James ...... Lieutenant cavalry | 6th brigade | Sept. 5, 1815 |
| Clarke, Abraham .... Captain | 26th regiment | June 28, 1815 |
| Edwards, John ..... Lieutenant | 26th regiment | June 28, 1815 |
| Folks, Etheldred .... Ensign | 26th regiment | June 28, 1815 |
| Hogan, John ....... Ensign | 26th regiment | July 22, 1815 |
| King, Henry ........ Captain regiment cavalry | 6th brigade | Sept. 5, 1815 |
| McNutt, Benjamin .. Ensign | 26th regiment | June 28, 1815 |
| Palmer, William .... Ensign | 26th regiment | June 28, 1815 |
| Williams, William ... Cornet regiment cavalry | 6th brigade | Nov. 29, 1815 |

### Sullivan County

| | | |
|---|---|---|
| Barb, Abraham ..... Ensign | 2nd regiment | Sept. 23, 1815 |
| Brashear, Sampson .. Captain | 2nd regiment | Nov. 17, 1815 |
| Carson, William ..... Captain | 2nd brigade | Dec. 20, 1815 |
| Cawood, Thomas .... Ensign | 2nd regiment | Nov. 17, 1815 |
| Deck, Jacob ........ Ensign | 2nd regiment | Sept. 23, 1815 |
| Drake, Jacob ....... Lieutenant | 2nd regiment | Sept. 23, 1815 |
| Fink, George ....... Ensign | 2nd regiment | Sept. 23, 1815 |
| Funk, George ...... Lieutenant | 2nd regiment | Nov. 2, 1815 |
| Hale, Lewis ........ Ensign | 2nd regiment | Nov. 2, 1815 |
| Harman, James ..... Ensign | 2nd regiment | Sept. 23, 1815 |
| Keyes, George ...... First Major | 2nd regiment | Sept. 23, 1815 |
| Lacy, Valentine ..... Lieutenant | 2nd regiment | Nov. 17, 1815 |
| Masingale, James .... Captain | 2nd regiment | Sept. 23, 1815 |
| Nicholas, John ...... Lieutenant | 2nd regiment | Sept. 23, 1815 |

# RECORD OF COMMISSIONS OF OFFICERS

| | | | |
|---|---|---|---|
| Owen, Michael | Captain | 2nd regiment | Sept. 23, 1815 |
| Phagan, James | Lieutenant Colonel Commandent | | |
| | | 2nd regiment | Sept. 23, 1815 |
| Phillips, Charles | Lieutenant | 2nd regiment | Dec. 20, 1815 |
| Richards, Richard | Ensign | 2nd regiment | Sept. 23, 1815 |
| Rogers, David | Ensign | 2nd regiment | Dec. 20, 1815 |
| Sevier, John F. | Lieutenant | 2nd regiment | Dec. 20, 1815 |
| Smith, William | Captain | 2nd regiment | Dec. 20, 1815 |
| White, Thomas | Captain | 2nd regiment | Sept. 23, 1815 |
| Willard, Abiah | Lieutenant | 2nd regiment | Sept. 23, 1815 |
| Willet, Nathan | Lieutenant | 2nd regiment | Sept. 23, 1815 |

## Sumner County

| | | | |
|---|---|---|---|
| Anderson, John B. | Captain | 15th regiment | Aug. 28, 1815 |
| Anderson, Lemuel | Ensign | 15th regiment | Aug. 28, 1815 |
| Armfield, Isaac | Captain | 43rd regiment | Nov. 2, 1815 |
| Bowman, Leroy | Lieutenant | 15th regiment | Aug. 28, 1815 |
| Car, King | Captain | 15th regiment | Aug. 28, 1815 |
| Carr, William | Lieutenant | 15th regiment | Aug. 28, 1815 |
| Christian, John | Captain | 43rd regiment | June 11, 1815 |
| Clendening, Ant. B. | Captain | 15th regiment | May 19, 1815 |
| Darr, James | Lieutenant | 43rd regiment | Jan. 30, 1815 |
| Dickinson, Oliver | Lieutenant | 15th regiment | Jan. 2, 1815 |
| Dobbins, Carson | Captain | 15th regiment | July 7, 1815 |
| Dugger, Westly | Lieutenant | 43rd regiment | Oct 31, 1815 |
| Elliott, James | Captain | 43rd regiment | May 1, 1815 |
| Eubanks, William | Ensign | 43rd regiment | July 26, 1815 |
| Fleming, William | Lieutenant | 15th regiment | Aug. 8, 1815 |
| Grimes, Lewis | Ensign | 15th regiment | Aug. 28, 1815 |
| Groves, Thomas | Lieutenant | 43rd regiment | May 1, 1815 |
| Hamilton, Thomas | Lieutenant | 43rd regiment | Nov. 2, 1815 |
| Herondon, William | Ensign | 15th regiment | May 19, 1815 |
| Hodge, Robert | Lieutenant | 15th regiment | July 7, 1815 |
| Johnston, Samuel | Ensign | 15th regiment | May 19, 1815 |
| Kelly, Joseph | Ensign | 15th regiment | Aug. 8, 1815 |
| Lane, William | Ensign | 15th regiment | May 19, 1815 |
| Lauderdale, Samuel D. | Lieutenant Colonel Commandant | | |
| | | 15th regiment | July 30, 1815 |
| McGrady, John | Lieutenant | 15th regiment | Aug. 28, 1815 |
| McKain, Samuel | Lieutenant | 43rd regiment | Nov. 2, 1815 |
| McMurry, James | First Major | 15th regiment | July 30, 1815 |
| Mason, Joseph | Captain | 15th regiment | July 7, 1815 |
| Mires, Miles | Ensign | 43rd regiment | May 1, 1815 |
| Paine, Robert | Ensign | 15th regiment | July 7, 1815 |
| Rice, Elijah | Captain | 43rd regiment | Nov. 2, 1815 |
| Robertson, Hardy | Lieutenant | 43rd regiment | Nov. 2, 1815 |
| Sivey, Jacob | Lieutenant | 15th regiment | Aug. 28, 1815 |
| Smith, John | Captain | 15th regiment | Aug. 28, 1815 |
| Stark, John | Lieutenant | 43rd regiment | Dec. 20, 1815 |

## IN THE TENNESSEE MILITIA, 1815

| | | | |
|---|---|---|---|
| Summers, John | Ensign | 43rd regiment | Dec. 20, 1815 |
| Swaney, John L. | Captain | 15th regiment | May 19, 1815 |
| Townsend, Peter | Lieutenant | 15th regiment | May 19, 1815 |
| Tyre, Richmond | Captain | 15th regiment | Aug. 28, 1815 |
| Vinson, Enos | Captain | 15th regiment | July 7, 1815 |
| Weatheread, Fran. W. | Second Major | 15th regiment | April 19, 1815 |
| Weatherhead, Marcus | Lieutenant | 15th regiment | Jan. 16, 1815 |
| White, Charles | Captain | 15th regiment | May 19, 1815 |
| Williams, James | Ensign | 15th regiment | Jan. 16, 1815 |
| Winham, William | Ensign | 43rd regiment | Dec. 20, 1815 |
| Young, Beverly | Ensign | 43rd regiment | Nov. 2, 1815 |
| Young, James | Ensign | 43rd regiment | June 11, 1815 |

### Warren County

| | | | |
|---|---|---|---|
| Bishop, Stephen | Lieutenant | 29th regiment | Aug. 14, 1815 |
| Brants, Solomon | Captain | 29th regiment | Dec. 19, 1815 |
| Dennis, Thomas | Ensign | 29th regiment | Dec. 19, 1815 |
| Forrest, Richard | Captain | 29th regiment | Dec. 19, 1815 |
| Graham, Charles | Captain | 29th regiment | Aug. 14, 1815 |
| Hammer, Elisha | Lieutenant | 29th regiment | Aug. 14, 1815 |
| Kein, William | Ensign | 29th regiment | Sept. 11, 1815 |
| McGregor, Richard | Ensign | 29th regiment | Dec. 19, 1815 |
| Mitchell, David | Captain | 29th regiment | Dec. 19, 1815 |
| Price, William J. | Captain | 29th regiment | Sept. 11, 1815 |
| Seratt, John | Ensign | 29th regiment | Sept. 11, 1815 |
| Smartt, William C. | Lieutenant Colonel Commandant 29th regiment | | Nov. 9, 1815 |
| Wood, William | Lieutenant | 29th regiment | Dec. 19, 1815 |

### Washington County

| | | | |
|---|---|---|---|
| Bayless, John | Ensign | 1st regiment | Feb. 3, 1815 |
| Church, Robert | Lieutenant | 1st regiment | Oct. 31, 1815 |
| Gibbs, George | Captain | 1st regiment | Oct. 31, 1815 |
| Hunt, Smith | Ensign | 1st regiment | Aug. 28, 1815 |
| Johnston, James S. | Lieutenant Colonel Commandant regiment of cavalry 1st brigade | | Dec. 2, 1815 |
| Martin, Isaac | Lieutenant regiment of cavalry 1st brigade | | Oct. 31, 1815 |
| Millen, Samuel | Ensign | 1st regiment | May 19, 1815 |
| Nelson, John, Sr. | First Major regiment of cavalry 1st brigade | | Dec. 2, 1815 |
| Riley, William | Lieutenant | 1st regiment | Oct. 31, 1815 |
| Smith, Richard | Captain | 1st regiment | Oct. 31, 1815 |
| Tipton, Abraham | Lieutenant regiment of cavalry 1st brigade | | Oct. 31, 1815 |
| Tipton, Samuel | Cornet regiment of cavalry 1st brigade | | Oct. 31, 1815 |
| Walker, John S. | Lieutenant | 1st brigade | May 19, 1815 |

Williams, Leban B. .. Captain regiment of cavalry
1st brigade    Oct. 31, 1815

## White County

| | | | |
|---|---|---|---|
| Harbert, James | Captain | 34th regiment | Aug. 23, 1815 |
| Harris, Thomas K. | Brigadier General | 7th brigade | June 13, 1815 |
| Neville, Joseph | Lieutenant Colonel Commandant 34th regiment | | Sept. 5, 1815 |
| Randals, James | First Major | 34th regiment | Sept. 5, 1815 |
| Smith, John J. | Captain | 34th regiment | Nov. 29, 1815 |
| Taylor, Armstead | Lieutenant | 34th regiment | Nov. 29, 1815 |

## Williamson County

| | | | |
|---|---|---|---|
| Andrews, Jones | Lieutenant in rifle company attached to 21st regiment | | Sept. 16, 1815 |
| Andrews, Sapley B. | Captain | 21st regiment | July 4, 1815 |
| Benton, Samuel | Captain regiment cavalry 9th brigade | | Dec. 2, 1815 |
| Blythe, John | Lieutenant | 21st regiment | July 4, 1815 |
| Bond, Morris L. | Ensign light infantry attached to 21st regiment | | June 5, 1815 |
| Bowder, William | Lieutenant | 21st regiment | Sept. 16, 1815 |
| Bugg, E. M. | Captain in rifle company attached to 21st regiment | | Sept. 16, 1815 |
| Campbell, John K. | Cornet regiment of cavalry 9th brigade | | Dec. 2, 1815 |
| Clemm, James S. | Captain in light infantry company attached to 21st regiment | | April 26, 1815 |
| Dunevant, Leonard | Lieutenant | 21st regiment | July 4, 1815 |
| Dupreast, George C. | Lieutenant | 44th regiment | Oct. 2, 1815 |
| Dupreast, William | Captain | 44th regiment | Oct. 2, 1815 |
| Edmiston, Zebulon | Captain | 44th regiment | Dec. 2, 1815 |
| Foot, Berryman | Ensign | 44th regiment | June 22, 1815 |
| Frost, John | Captain | 44th regiment | Oct. 27, 1815 |
| Goach, David | Ensign | 44th regiment | June 22, 1815 |
| Goodman, Benajah | Lieutenant | 44th regiment | Dec. 2, 1815 |
| Hardeman, Peter | Captain | 44th regiment | Aug. 7, 1815 |
| Helm, Meredith | Captain | 21st regiment | Aug. 7, 1815 |
| Hill, Joshua Cannon | Ensign | 44th regiment | Oct. 27, 1815 |
| Holland Frederick | Captain | 21st regiment | July 4, 1815 |
| Hyde, Richard W. | Lieutenant regiment cavalry 9th brigade | | Jan. 16, 1815 |
| Johnston, Alexander | Lieutenant | 44th regiment | Dec. 2, 1815 |
| Jones, James G. | Second Major | 21st regiment | July 12, 1815 |
| Keggler, Esias | Ensign | 44th regiment | Oct 2, 1815 |
| Little, Joseph H. | Ensign | 21st regiment | Nov. 29, 1815 |
| McClure, Henry | Lieutenant | 44th regiment | June 22, 1815 |
| McEwen, John L. | Captain | 21st regiment | Sept. 12, 1815 |

## IN THE TENNESSEE MILITIA, 1815

| | | | |
|---|---|---|---|
| Orman, Adam | Ensign | 21st regiment | July 4, 1815 |
| Parks, Benjamin | Lieutenant | 44th regiment | Oct. 2, 1815 |
| Pearce, Arthur | Lieutenant | 44th regiment | June 22, 1815 |
| Pinkston, Hugh | Captain | 44th regiment | June 22, 1815 |
| Prewitt, George H. | Ensign | 21st regiment | Dec. 2, 1815 |
| Smith, Samuel | Captain | 44th regiment | June 22, 1815 |
| Smith, William | Captain in light infantry company attached to 21st regiment | | June 19, 1815 |
| Stone, William | Lieutenant | 44th regiment | Oct. 27, 1815 |
| Wilson, Samuel D. | Captain | 44th regiment | June 22, 1815 |
| Young, E. | Ensign in rifle company attached to 21st regiment | | Sept. 16, 1815 |

### Wilson County

| | | | |
|---|---|---|---|
| Alford, Wily | Lieutenant | 17th regiment | Nov. 30, 1815 |
| Bartlet, James | Captain | 17th regiment | July 13, 1815 |
| Check, William | Captain | 42nd regiment | Sept. 16, 1815 |
| Coopwood (Hopwood), William | Lieutenant | 42nd regiment | Sept. 16, 1815 |
| Cotton, Arthur | Lieutenant regiment cavalry 4th brigade | | April 13, 1815 |
| Cotton, Noah | Captain regiment cavalry 4th brigade | | April 13, 1815 |
| Crawford, James | Lieutenant | 17th regiment | July 9, 1815 |
| Crawford, William | Captain | 17th regiment | July 9, 1815 |
| Dooley, Thomas | Captain regiment cavalry 4th brigade | | April 13, 1815 |
| Evans, William | Ensign | 42nd regiment | Sept. 16, 1815 |
| Garrison, Moses | Lieutenant | 42nd regiment | Sept. 16, 1815 |
| Harvey, John | Lieutenant | 42nd regiment | Sept. 16, 1815 |
| Hobby, David | Ensign | 42nd regiment | Sept. 16, 1815 |
| Hodges, William | Captain | 42nd regiment | Sept. 16, 1815 |
| Hopwood (Coopwood), Thomas | Captain | 42nd regiment | Sept. 16, 1815 |
| Keziah, Samuel | Ensign | 42nd regiment | Sept. 16, 1815 |
| McDonald, James | Captain | 17th regiment | July 13, 1815 |
| McSpadden, Thom. C. | Ensign | 17th regiment | July 9, 1815 |
| Parker, William | Captain | 42nd regiment | Sept. 16, 1815 |
| Read, Robert | Captain | 42nd regiment | Sept. 16, 1815 |
| Saunderson, John | Ensign | 17th regiment | July 13, 1815 |
| Saunderson, Thomas | Lieutenant | 17th regiment | July 13, 1815 |
| Scobey, James | Lieutenant | 17th regiment | Jan. 9, 1815 |
| Semlock, Bebly | Ensign | 17th regiment | Nov. 30, 1815 |
| Shannon, James | Lieutenant | 17th regiment | Nov. 30, 1815 |
| Swain, William | Ensign | 17th regiment | Nov. 30, 1815 |
| Swingley, Joseph | Captain | 17th regiment | Nov. 30, 1815 |
| Sypret, Stephen | Ensign | 17th regiment | July 13, 1815 |
| Taylor, Solomon | Captain | 17th regiment | July 13, 1815 |

RECORD OF COMMISSIONS OF OFFICERS

| | | | |
|---|---|---|---|
| Uzzell, Jordan | Cornet regiment cavalry 4th brigade | | April 13, 1815 |
| Webb, Isham | Lieutenant | 17th regiment | July 13, 1815 |
| Whittey, Willie | Lieutenant | 42nd regiment | Sept 16, 1815 |
| Williams, Beverly | Captain | 17th regiment | July 13, 1815 |
| Williams, Charles | Lieutenant | 42nd regiment | Sept. 16, 1815 |
| Williams, James | Captain | 42nd regiment | Sept. 16, 1815 |
| Wright, William C. | Ensign | 42nd regiment | Sept. 16, 1815 |

# INDEX

(Covers pages 169-260 only. For index
to preceding section see page 133 ff.)

-A-

Abbernathy, Ephraim 251
Abernathy, Charles C. 223
  Freeman 221
Adams, David 184,203,248
  James 214
Adkins, Thomas 206,229
Akens, Harrison 242
Alcom, John 237
Alderson, James 239
Alexander, Adam R. 207
  Archibald 175
  Joshia 194
  Robert 194
  William 184
  William S. 242
Alford, Wiley 242
  William 186
  Wily 259
Allen, Goerge H. 215
  Henry D. 207
  Hiram L. 252
  Jobe 245
  Richard H. 223
  Valentine 169
  William 194
  William L. 238
Allison, Ewen 225
  William 196
Alston, James 177
Alsup, Henry 225
Anderson, Audley 171
  James 169,194,226,228
  John 244,253
  John B. 214,256
  John G. 247
  Lemuel 256
  Presley 223
  Richard 183
  Robert 244
  Thomas 184
  Timothy 227
  William 221
Andrews, John 238
  Jones 258
  Sapley B. 258
Anthony, John 179
  William 190
Angean, James 193
Apleby, David, 219

Argentright, George 177
Armbrister, Henry 187
Armfield, Isaac 256
Armontage, John 248
Armour, Robert Jr. 213
  William 213
Arms, Edward 178
Armstrong, Aaron 205,250
  Arthur G. 226
  David 179
  James 194
  John 216
  John M. 193,216
  Josiah 179
  William 179,201
Arnold, Robert 207
  William 186
Arwine, John 202
Asten, James 179
Astin, Samuel G. 179
Atkins, William R. 255
Atkinson, Henry H. 252
  John 196
Atwood, Peter B. 201
Austin, James 221
Auston, William 247
Avery, William 194
Awalt, Michael 206
Aydolott, Thomas W. 207
Ayres, David 179
  Moses 201

-B-

Bacon, Joseph 215
Bailey, James 226
  Jesse 209
  John 229
  Samuel 245
Bails, Archibald 221
Bakeley, William 249
Baker, Abraham 235
  Charles 247
  John 205
  John E. 188
  Martin 176
  Robert 192
  William 173
Balch, Amos P. 181
Balden, Nicholas 203

Baldwin, John 235,253
Bales, Alexander 199
Ballow, William 200
Bankhead, George 207
  John 235
Banks, Richard 215
Barb, Abraham 255
Barbee, George 235
Barecraft, Daniel 196
Barker, Allen 204
Barkley, James 211
  Robert 237
Barkly, William K. 186
Barnade, John 177
Barnard, Jonathan 203
Barnes, James 251
  Turner 239
Barnet, Hugh 243
Barns, Bright 190
Barr, John W. 181
Barret, David 239
Barrett, Isaac 169
Barrow, James 240
Bartlet, James 259
Bartley, Robert 212
Barton, Hugh 219
  John 250
  William 178, 215
Bass, Benjamin J. 211
  Thomas 211
Bassett, Spencer 226
Bateman, William 193
Baty, David 209
Baughman, Daniel 229
Baxter, William 220
Bayless, John 257
Bean, John 215
  Robert 247
Beard, John 244
  John C. 228
·Beasley, Willie 219
Beaty, John 181,184
  William F. 235
Bell, Joseph 241
  Samuel 196
Bellew, Joseph 253
  Bennet, Noah 178
Bennett, Noah 249
Benning, James 173
Benningfield, James H. 221
Benson, Benjamin 254
  Matthias 171
Bentley, Richard 202,223,
  248

Benton, Nathaniel 193
　Samuel 258
　Thomas H. 193
Bernard, John 247
Berry, Hugh 210
　James 235
　Lewis 222,247
Bethel, John 211
Beuford, Thomas 184
Bibb, George 203
　John 203
　Minor 200
Bible, John 248
Biddle, Charles 211
Biles, Stephen 202
Bird, Janathan 179
Birdsong, William 252
Birdwell, Andrew 221
　George 205,250
　Hugh 173
Bishop, John 226
　Stephen 257
Black, George 171
　George G. 175
　Robert 188
　Stephen 227
Blackbourn, John 176
Blackston, James 246
Blackwell, James 234
　Nathan 169
Blair, Samuel Jr. 187
　William 183
Blakemore, John D. 239
Blank, Christian 172
Blanks, James 255
Blanton, James 176
Bledsoe, David 169
Blevins, George 203
Blockner, Elijah 181
Blue, Moses 175
Blythe, John 258
Boatright, William 176
Boaz, Thomas 229
Bobbs, Seth 199
Bogard, Joseph 209
Bogart, Samuel 199
Bohannon, John 177
Bole, James 211
Bolton, Josiah 244
Bond, Morris L. 258
　Stephen 205
Bone, Henry 194
Bonham, Nehemiah 220
Booker, Jacob 190
　William 238
Booth, Joseph 240
Boothe, Benjamin 244
Boring, Greenberry 199
Boswell, John 209
Bowder, William 258
Bowdree, Samuel 238
Bowen, Charles 183
　Robert G. 204
Bowers, John 220
Bowling, Larkin 219
Bowman, Henry 203
　Leroy 256
　Samuel 228
　William 211
Boyd, Bartley 199
　James 181,206,220
　John 220,245,251
　Richard 173
Boyers, David 183
Bradberry, Joshua 217
Bradbury, John 251
Braden, John 242
　Robert 242

Bradford, James 205
　John 169
Bradley, Charles 188
　Daniel 220
　Edward 190
　Hugh 242
　Isaac 248
　John 255
　Thomas 237,242
Bradsaws, Richard 228
Bradshaw, James 209,233
　John 181
Branch, Robert 195
Branson, Thomas 192
Brantley, Hugh 252
Brants, Solomon 257
Brasfield, Thomas 228
Brashear, Sampson 255
Bratton, David 188
Breden, William 212
Breedlove, Charles 206
Brewer, Daniel 188
　Silvanus 210
Bridgwater, Richard 209
Brien, Henry 198
Brigance, William 190
Briges, William 238
Brittain, Joseph 196
　William 223
Britton, Joseph 215
Brock, George 199,246
　William 233
Brooks, George 251
　James 216
　Price W. 241
　William B. 248
Brown, Asa 227
　Duncan 223
　George 202,212
　Hardy 190
　Jesse 171
　John 190,240
　Joseph 190,207,225
　Thomas 175,185,248
　William 248,250
　William L. 209
Brownlow, Joseph A. 213
　William 202
Bruce, Amos 237
　Robert 214
Bruntson, Daniel 176
Bryan, Allen 187
　Henry H. 183
　Thomas 187
Buchanan, James 229
Buchannan, George 235
　John B. 206
Buford, Seth 227
Bugg, E. M. 258
　Jesse 241
Bull, George 221
Bullock, Jonathan 181
Bunch, David 246
　William 246
Bunton, William 220
Burch, John 239
Burdet, Giles 196
Burges, John 169
　Nathaniel G. 207
　William 172
Burgess, Richard 229
　William 179
Burnam, Samuel 196
Burnet, William 244
Burnon, Jesse 169
Burns, Miles 231
Burress, Samuel 247
　William 223

Burris, John 209
Burton, John 179
　Joshua 237
　Robert 203
　Samuel H. 204
　Willie 253
Busby, Thomas 196
Bush, John 171
Butcher, Daniel 196
　John 225
Butler, Bailey 227
　Thomas 204
Byers, William 181
Byferd, Parker 253
Byford, John 186
Byler, Abraham 223
Bylor, John 219
Byrn, John W. 237
Byrne, Rezen 195


-C-

Cage, Edward 169
Cain, James 191
　Jesse 246
Caldwell, Amos 208
　Thomas 181
　William 186
Calhoun, John 196
Calliham, Samuel 234
Cameron, Samuel 176
Camp, John 221
Campbell, Arthur 198,245
　George 202,208,221
　John 172
　John K. 258
　Joseph 234,245
　Phillip 200
　Robert 242
　Sanders W. 246
　William 178,195
Camron, Elisha 198
Canale, William 213
Cantrell, Abraham 239
　Ota 253
Caperton, George 247
Car, James 240
　King 256
Carbet, James 205
Carlee, Calvin 235
Carley, John 177
Carnahan, Thomas 253
Carney, James W. 209,252
Carothers, William 196
Carpenter, James 184
Carr, King 239
　Walter 195
　William 239,256
Carrathers, William 179
Carrell, Clemment 202
Carson, John 220
　William 241,255
Carter, George Washington 220
　William 212
　William Blount 221
Carthel, Joseph M. 231
Caruthers, John 193
Casselman, Abraham 221
Catchings, Saymore 210
Cates, Isaiah 226
Cathey, William 231
Cauley, George 188
Caulfield, John 253
Cavit, Thomas 229

Cavitt, Thomas 179
Cawood, Thomas 255
Chambers, Thomas 172
Chapin, Paul 252
Chapman, John 172
  Robert 206
Cheatham, Samuel G. 246
Check, William 259
Cheek, William 212
Cherry, Benjamin 197,220,
  244,252
Chester, John 190
Childers, Joseph 171
Childress, Nathaniel G.
  200
Chilton, William 209
Chitwood, John 180
Christian, John 256
  William 196
Chumneigh, John 206
Church, Robert 257
Churchman, James 178
Claiborne, Thomas 243
Clanton, Drury 200
Clark, Benjamin 212
  Charles 220
  Daniel 250
  David 195
  John 186,229,254
  Thomas 202
  William 250
Clarke, Abraham 255
  Archibald 253
Clayton, Charles C. 180
Cleaveland, Abner 231
Clemm, James S. 241,258
Clemment, Benjamin 229
Clemons, James 222
Clendening, Ant. B. 256
Clibon, John 237
Clingan, Thomas 202
Cloud, William 249
Coatney, George 225
Coats, John 169,170
Cobler, John 200
Cockburn, George 208
Cocke, James W. 183
  William B. 183,223
Coe, Joseph 208,251
Coffee, Joel 208
Coffer, Reuben 193
Colfield, John 253
Collier, David 184
Collins, Barbe 201
  Francis 250
  William 180
Collom, John 192
Colwell, Joseph 222
Compton, John 217
Condray, Dennis 221
Conley, John 239
Conner, William 229
Cook, Adam 214
  David 223
  Jacob 214
  James 235,253
  Lemuel 248
Cooke, Hezekiah G. 211,
  253
  William 253
Cooley, Cornelius 238
  Wood T. H. 252
Cooper, John 217
  Robert 213,244
  William 217
  Wills 186
Coopwood (Hopwood),
  William 259

Copas, John 192
Copeland, Anthony 208
  Joab 226
  Joseph 250
  Richard 209
  Ripley 204
Coplinger, Samuel 195
Corum, Robert 239
Cosson, John 192
Cotton, Arthur 259
  Noah 239,259
Couch, Thomas 170
Covey, Joseph 201,223
Covington, David 253
Cowan, James 201
  Matthew 227
  Robert 247
  Samuel 171
Cox, Adam 206
  Jesse 246
  John 171,229
  Joshua 185
  Thomas 214
Coxsey, Absolam 215
Crabtree, Hiram 244
  James 191
Crafton, John B. 193
Craig, David 181
Crain, Newel 170
Crane, Jobson 192
Cranshaw, Kerr 239
Cravens, Elisha 253
Crawford, James 259
  John 193,252
  Samuel 181,206
  Smith 244
  William 208,225,231,
  259
Craze, John 180
Creasy, John 181
Criddle, Edward 193
  John 222
Cridle, Andrew 216
Critenton, Henry 171
Crittenton, Thomas W.
  180
Critz, George F. 200
Crockett, David 247
Cross, William 180
Crosswell, Nelson 189
Crow, John 253
Crowson, Jacob 175
Cruckshank, William 215
Cruise, Jacob 203
Crumb, David 210
Crump, George 170
Crutcher, George 252
Cuff, William A. 176
Cuming, James 226
Cumins, James 203
Cummings, John 192
Cuningham, Robert 206
Cunningham, David 246
  John 239
  Robert 251
Currin, Jonathan 193
Curry, Isaiah 222
Curtis, Joshua 193


-D-


Dabney, Charles A. 216
Dabs, Joel 231
Daimwood, Henry 186
Dalton, John 241

Dalton (cont.)
  William 211,212
Dandy, Elancer 196
Daniel, William 181
Darr, Henry 186
  James 256
Darwin, George C. 227
Davidson, Charlton B. 209
  Hugh 223
  James L. 231
  Samuel C. 171
  William Jr. 169
Davis, Aaron 172
  Andrew 220,245
  Henry 252
  James 226,249
  John 180,186
  Nathan 175,224,248
  Turner 246
  William H. 235
Dawson, Hutson 241
Deaderick, David S. 173
Dean, Francis 219
  John 244
  William 209
Dearmond, Thomas 171
Deck, Jacob 255
Deen, Jacob 249
Delany, William 215
Dement, Cader 235
  Thomas M. 175
Demoss, Abraham 222
  John 200
Demsey, John B. 170
Dennis, Thomas 257
  William 248
  Zebedee 183
Denny, William 240
Derrett, John H. 199
Dever, Alexander 220
Deyden, Thomas 238
Dickenson, Abraham 222
Dickey, Benoni 208
  George 231
Dickinson, Oliver 256
Dickson, Ezekiel 235
  James 235
  Robert 174
Dicky, Christian 225
Dill, John 182
Dillard, George 171
  John 227
Dillen, James 246
  John 216
  Joshua 227
Dining, Andrew 239
Dismukes, Daniel 222
Dixon, James 197
  Samuel 208
  Thomas 169
  Tilmon 237
  William 190
Doak, John 186
  Jonathan 242
  Robert 245
Doake, John 195
Dobbin, James 231
Dobbins, Carson 256
  James 208
Dobbs, John 172
  William 199
Dobkins, Reuben 246
Doddy, Alfred 201
Dodson, Elisha 191
Dogget, Thomas 178
Doherty, George 205
  Robert 170
Doke, John 192

Dolton, William 188
Dondle, Joseph 248
Dooley, Thomas 242,259
Dorris, Thomas 222
Dotson, Allen 173
  Elisha 215
Dougan, Sharp 201
Douglas, Alexander 206
Douglass, Alexander 243
  Harry L. 195
  Henry L. 242
Doyle, Richard D. 254
Doyles, Richard D. 253
Drake, Jacob 255
  John Jr. 200
Drewry, John 222
  Richard C. 222
Driver, Thomas 188
Drury, John 173
Dryden, John 219
Duckworth, John 208
Dugger, Abel 221
  Westly 256
Duncan, James 193
  William 191
Dunevant, Leonard 258
Dunkin, John 186
Dunn, David 216
  Samuel 169,219
  William 173
Dunnaway, Samuel 235
Dunwody, Patrick M. 192
Dupreast, George C. 258
  William 258
Durret, J. G. 196
Dyche, Jacob 176
Dye, William 251
Dyer, James 229
Dyrus (?), Quentin 245


-E-


Ealey, Barton 172
  William 173
Earheart, Rodney 222
Easley, Andrew 245
  Benjamin 247
  Drury 177
  Stephen 204
  Washam 177
Easterly, Jacob 173
Eaton, James 221
  William B. 193
Echolas, John 216
Edge, Henry 215
Edmiston, Thomas 173,222
  William 216
  Zebulon 258
Edmondston, Robert 233
Edmonson, John 179
Edmuston, Andrew J. 173
Edwards, John 255
  Presley 236
  Selman 247
  William 190
Eisley, John 220
Elam, Samuel 246
  Solomon 254
Elder, William 186
Eldridge, Benjamin 185
Elles, John 195
Elliot, Benjamin 253
  John 182
  Simon 244
Elliott, Benjamin 186

Elliott (cont.)
  James 256
  Ruben 238
Ellis, James 216
  John 216
  Samuel 190
  William 254
Elstane, Jesse 255
Emberson, James H. 231
England, Elijah 240
  John 234
English, Joshua 245
  Thomas 231,251
Ensor, Thomas 240
Ervetts, Joseph G. 212
Erwen, Edward 249
  Ephraim 231
Esery, John 252
Espey, William 186
Estes, Andrew 201
  John 201
Estis, Samuel 169
Eubanks, William 256
Evans, Cornelius 173
  Evan 185
  John 248
  Joseph 252
  Robert 228
  William 259
  William D. 215
Evens, James 187
Everet, Larkin 224
Everett, Washington 239
Ewing, John 220
Ezell, Timothy 175


-F-


Fake, John 242
Faris, Absolam 201
Farney, John 231
Farquaharson, Robert 179
Farquharson, Joel 250
Farrensworth, David 203
Farrier, Nathaniel 188
Farris, Absolam 201
  Joseph 201
Farriss, John 247
  Joseph 223
Feilds, Joel 248
Felts, George 222
Fentress, Absolem 247
Ferguson, John 225
  Patrick 237
  Robert 244
Fields, John 231
Files, Manly 215
Finch, Edward 223
Findley, Obediah G. 242
Fine, Abraham 240
  L. 199
Fink, George 255
Finly, William 177
Fish, James 201
Fisher, Jacob 170
  Phillip 195
  Samuel 209,234
  William 249
Fite, David 237
  Joseph 212
Fitzpatrick, Andrew 241
Fleming, David 211
  John D. 231
  Samuel 197
  William 256

Flemming, David 229
  John D. 251
Flin, John 204
Flinn, Barney H. 249
Flood, Seth 186
Floyd, Jonathan 206
Fly, William 208
Foles, George W. 225
Folks, Etheldred 255
Foot, Berryman 258
Forbes, George 210
Ford, Andrew G. 188
  Daniel J. 212
  Moses 183
Foreman, Wilson 201
Forrest, Nathan 202
  Richard 191, 257
Fortunberry, David 236
Foster, Enoch 196
  John 188
  Mark 246
  Richard 231
  Winkfield 203,249
Fotherage, David 200
Foust, Jacob 252
Fox, Adam 254
  William 192
Frazier, Thomas 229
French, Joseph 179
Friar, William 255
Frogg, Strother 234
Frost, Ebenezer 183
  John 258
Fukeway, Nathan 224
Fuller, Littleton 236
Fulton, James C. 170
Funk, George 255
Fuquay, Joshua 246
Fusher, Henry 171


-G-


Gains, John S. 179
Galbreath, Thomas 229
  William 250
Gallaway, John 190
Gallion, George 201
Galloway, James 238
Gamble, Frederick 251
  James 198
Gambrell, James H. 170
Gammon, Harris 229
  John 229
Ganaway, Burwell 254
  Walker 254
Gannaway, Walker 187
Gardenhire, Thompson 252
Gardiner, James 198,220
Gardner, Dempsey 211
  John 186
Garner, Griffin G. 240
  Griffith 215
  Lewis 251
  Obediah 236
Garrard, Thomas 231
Garrett, William 224
Garrison, Moses 259
Garrott, Westley 251
Gaskil, Evan 227
Gassaway, Thomas 236
Gates, Phillip 247
Gatlin, Ephraim 213
Gatten, Thomas 226
Gee, Edmond 177
George, John 206

George (cont.)
　Reuben 179
　Ruben 229
Germain, Zacheus 169
Getgood, Alexander 238
Gholson, Benjamin 193
　John 182,231
Gibbons, Samuel 188
Gibbs, George 257
Gibson, Samuel 212
　Thomas 170
　William 250
Giffard, Giddeon 188
Gififes, James 172
Gilbert, John 214
Gilbreath, David 171
　George 252
　John 231
　Thomas 179
　William 178
Gilchrist, Duncan 231
Gilleland, James 187
Gillenwaters, William T. 203,226
Gillespie, Allen 176
Gilliam, Thomas 201
Gilliland, William 173
Gillispie, Isaac 229
　Thomas 229
　Thomas T. 219
Gist, Benjamin 227
Givin, James 215
Gladden, William 248
Glenn, James 245
Goach, David 258
Goad, William 184
Goan, Shadrick 199
Goaro, Henry 210
Godderd, William 229
Goforth, Hugh 237
　William 231
Gold, John 171
Goldsberry, Henry 246
Gomes, Isaiah 173
Good, Hugh 236
Gooden, Jesse 201
Goodin, Lawson 221
Goodlet, James E. 246
Goodman, Benajah 258
Goodrich, Edmund 222
Goodson, Joseph 178
Goodwin, George 226
Gordin, John 202
Gordon, James 251
　Thomas K. 224
　William 182,231
Gorgas, Charles 178
Gorman, George 215
Gosaqe, William 199
Gosset, William 254
Gotcher, Henry 223
　Jesse 247
Gourley, Robert 199
Graham, Alexander 231
　Charles 215,257
　Joseph 228
Grant, James 180
　Samuel 252
　William 246
Graves, George 229
　Henry 206
　John 239
　Joseph 254
Gray, Curtis G. 182
　James 189,242
　Robert 192
　Thomas 213
Greeham, Joseph 203

Green, Elisha 201
　Lewis 190
　Thomas S. 188
Greene, William 245
Greenlee, James 201
Greenoway, William S. 245
Greenwood, James 252
Gregg, Nathan 238
Greggs, Thomas 177
Griffath, Anderson 175
Griffin, Hugh 231
　Richard 236
Griffis, Anderson 248
Griffith, Jacob 196
Griffy, William 189
Grigsby, Samuel 234
Grimes, Jacob 186
　Lewis 256
Grimley, William 240
Grimmer, Henry 189
Grissum, Robert 221
Groce, James 226
Groves, John 226
　Reuben 248
　Thomas 256
Guess, William 180
Guin, John 187
Gullick, John 212
Gunning, David 214
Gunter, Sterling 216
Gurley, Jeremiah 208
Gwin, John 173
Gwinn, William 240,243
Gyer, Jacob 240

-H-

Hackney, Sameul 245
Hagard, James 179
Haggard, James 244
Haglar, John L. 213
Hagood, Benjamin 233
Hail, Job 249
　Nicholas 227
Haile, Butler 248
Hainey, Daniel 203
Haire, Joseph 215
Hale, George 203
　John 203
　Lewis 255
Haley, Elijah 254
　Matthew 236
　William 235
Halfacre, Jacob 178
Hall, Allen 193
　Elisha 197
　Garrett 211
　Jeremiah 219
　John 191,197,236
　Samuel S. 246
　William 191
Hallum, William 242
Hamble, Robert 198
Hamblet, George 192,240
　James 231
Hambleton, Alexander 225
　James 233
Hames, Simon 174
Hamilton, John 170
　Thomas 182,256
Hammer, Elisha 257
Hampton, Abner 209
Hanby, John 180
Hancher, William 238
Hancock, James 249

Hankins, James 178
Hanks, George 208
Hanley, Francis 214
　Isaac 240
Hanna, Carolinas 245
Hannah, John 222
Hansard, John 206
Hanson, William 171
Harbert, James 258
Hardeman, Peter 241,258
Harden, Jeremiah 193
　Jeremiah Jr. 193
Hardgrave, Shelton 200
Hardrige, Zachariah 195
Hare, Henry 240
Hargrove, Stephen 216
Harkins, Joseph 180
Harman, James 255
Harmon, David 226
　Peter 203,248
Harper, Joseph 173
　Summers 214
Harrel, William 229
Harrelson, Thomas 202
　Thomas B. 224
Harris, Allsea 254
　Archibald 187
　Benjamin C. 221
　Benony 249
　Edward 195
　Fergus 217
　G. C. 240
　James 197
　Joseph 172
　Matthew H. 239
　Sloan 242
　Thomas K. 258
　William G. 187
Harrison, Daniel 177
　James 252
　Peter 228
Hartzell, Isaac 240
　Jacob 240
Harvey, John 259
　Robert 224
Haskell, Charles 196,229
Hawes, William 240
Hayes, Lewis W. 248
Hayter, Abraham 245
Hearn, George 184
Howell 210
Helm, Meredith 258
Helms, Malaki 251
Hembery, Benjamin 211
　Joel 234
Hembre, Joel 252
Hembree, Joel 252
Henderson, James 231
　Jesse 250
　Samuel 188
　William 180
Hendrickson, John 233
Henry, Andrew 180
Herbet, Nathaniel 200
Herondon, William 256
Herrelson, James 251
　William 179,250
Herrin, Solomon 208
Hewett, Benjamin 170
Hicks, James G. 200
　John C. 200
Higganbotham, Caleb 247
Higgenbotham, Alexander 204
Higgins, William 187
　William Y. 180
Highbarger, John 176
Hightower, Epaphroditus 225

Hildreth, Reuben 204
Hill, Bowen 250
　Caleb 202
　James 205,216
　Jesse 199,219
　Joab 173
　John 216,217
　Joshua Cannon 258
　Samuel 195
　Thomas 195
Hillis, James 215,239
Hines, Simeon 210
Hinkle, Joseph 229
Hinshaw, Benjamin 210
Hobbs, Collin S. 173
　Edward D. 200
　Joel 216
Hobby, David 259
Hodge, Phillips 225
　Robert 256
Hodges, Callaway 228
　Eli 225
　James C. 195
　William 259
Hogan, John 255
　Richard 171
Hoge, Joseph 197
Holladay, Elliott 172
Holland, Frederick 216, 258
　James 221
　John 186
Hollice, M. 211
Holliday, David 227
Hollis, Micajah 254
Holloman, James 249
Holmes, Josiah L. 201
Holonsworth, Abraham 178
Holt, Irby 171
　Michael 170
Hommell, Daniel 190
Hood, John 206
　Luke 206
　Stanwix 210
Hooker, John 229
Hooper, Absolom 174
　John 200
　Nimrod 222
Hoover, John 236
Hopson, James 173
Hopwood (Coopwood), Thomas 259
Hord, Thomas 252
Horn, Thomas 183
Hornback, Eliot 177
Horner, George 201
　Isaac 205
　John 247
Horton, Archibald 184
Hoskins, James 246
House, James 193
Houston, James 245
　Samuel 198
Howard, Samuel 228
　William 224
Howell, James 200
　Levi 217
　William S. 179
Howerton, Jackson 184
Hubbard, Benneman 188
　David 236
　Matthew 234
Hudeburgh, Lewis 179
Hudson, Edward G. 204
　John 240
　Noah 242
Huey, James 208
Huff, Absolam 221

Huff (cont.)
　William 227
Hughes, Robert 238
Hughey, John 208
Hughs, Buddet 182
　Robert 219
Hulse, William 190
Humphreys, John 206
　Lasley 192
Hunnals, Robert 247
Hunt, David 247
　George 251
　Henry 201
　Nathaniel 175
　Smith 257
　Thomas 225
Hunter, Dempsey 209
　Edward 217
　Emanuel 235
　Ephraim 187,219
　Jacob 240
　John 246
　Joseph 246
　Sherid 180
Huntsman, Lemuel 237
Hurt, Bird J. 182
Huston, William 199
Hutchins, Joseph 183
Hutchison, William G. 227
Hutson, Andrew G. 222
Hutton, Henry 254
Hyde, Richard W. 258
Hynes, Andrew 222,246
　Simeon 234


-I-


Igon, James 220
Ingliss, Mathew 211
Inser, Joseph 240
Irvin, Ephraim 231
　Joseph 173
Irvine, Josephus 170
　Robert 206
Irwin, Joseph Jr. 199
Isaacs, Abraham 180
Isham, James 208
Isom, George 208
Ivy, Benjamin 225
　John 176


-J-


Jack, Samuel 199
Jackson, Hugh 189
　Isham 217
　John 170,173
　Joseph 250
　Robert 173,199
　Thomas 198,216,221
James, Amsey 216
　William 172,238,245
Jameson, Samuel 192
Jarnagan, Preston B. 205
Jarred, William 249
Jasey, James 208
Jefferson, Peter F. 214
Jennings, James 246
Jentry, Jacob 245
Jester, Isaac 221

Jett, Murphrey 187
Jetton, Robert 236,254
Johnson, Alexander 241
　Charles 222
　John 172,210
　Joseph 205
　Lewis 254
　Thomas 182
Johnstone, Alexander 258
　Charles 174
　Christopher 179
　George 191
　Henry D. 245
　James 218
　James S. 240,257
　Jesse 239
　John R. 249
　Larkin 254
　Robert 182
　Samuel 256
　Stephen 203
　Thomas 213
Johnstone, Samuel 232
Jones, Andrew 249
　Brittain 247
　Charles 183
　Esquire 214
　George B. 240
　Harvey 204
　Hezekiah 232
　James 220,239
　James G. 241,258
　Jesse 184,229
　John 171,197
　Nathaniel 191,215
　Richard 253
　Robert 198
　Thorington 211
　William 188,240
　Zachariah 215
Jordan, John 201
Levy 175
Jorden, John 175
Justice, Alfred 211
　Janathan 177


-K-


Kannon, Thomas 185
Karr, Walter 217
Kavanaugh, Charles 193, 236
　Lot 193
Kavinaugh, James P. 213
Kearns, John 250
Keas, James 179
Keathly, Jesse 192
Kee, Benjamin 184
　John 220
Keeling, John 238
Keer, John 234
Keeton, Reason 247
Keggler, Esias 258
Kein, William 257
Kellough, John 236
Kelly, Alfred 170,197
　David 195
　John 244
　Joseph 256
　Nathan 179
　Samuel 225
　William 170,225
Kelough, John 254
　Thomas 211
Kelsey, Robert G. 232

Kelso, Eliphalet 250
Kemp, Nathan 247
Kendrick, Jesse 232
  John 208
  William 245
Kennedy, John 184
  Lemuel 200
Kenner, Eli 208
Kent, William 174
Kerr, James 197,214,249
Key, Joel 214
  Strother 214
Keyes, George 255
Keys, Washington 190
Keziah, Samuel 259
Kilcrease, Davis 232
Kilcrist, John 182
Kilgore, James 225
Kincannon, Andrew 237
Kindrick, Joseph A. C. 254
King, David 239
  Henry 255
  Jacob 197
  James 169
  John 229
  Jonathan 201
  Thomas 244
  William 213,233
Kirk, Hugh 236,254
Kirkland, Joab W. 244
Kirkpatrick, James 169, 196
  Joseph 242
Kizon, Peter 241
Knight, John 211
Kuykindale, James 201


-L-


Lacy, Valentine 255
Lain, John 227
  Samuel 192
Lake, Elijah 222
Lamaster, John W. 251
Lamb, David 241
  Littlebury 214
Landen, James 190
Lane, Garret 204
  Joseph 178
  Roling 175
  William 256
Langdon, Jonathan 228
Langley, Jonathan 188
Lanie, Henry 241
Lanier, Buchannon 174
Lankford, Benjamin 252
Larrimer, James 170
Lassiter, Abner 201
Lattern, Christopher 214
  Samuel 214
Lattimore, James 204
Latty, Eli 187
Lauderdale, James 230
  Josiah 239
  Samuel 191
  Samuel D. 256
  William 191
Laughmiller, Frederick 226
  Jonas 226
Laughridge, Abraham 209
Lawson, Andrew 255
  Lazarus 226

Lawson (cont.)
  Lewis 226
  Robert 255
  Stephen 226
Laxton, Jesse 241
Leach, David 182
  Joshua 251
  Josiah 247
Leatch, James 169
Leath, Isaac 191
Leathers, William 254
Lee, John 180,230
Leehorne, Gabriel 230
Leftwich, John 253
Legg, William 228
Lek, Mathew H. 198
Leonard, William 251
Lesby, Henry 247
Leviston, Preston 245
Lewellen, Charles 196
Lewis, Benjamin 238
  Benjamin H. 208
  Cornelius N. 223
  Elijah 241
  Jesse 198,220
  John 180,190
Lieuten, Henry 226
Lightfoot, Henry 213
Lindsay, Samuel 175
Linville, Richard 220
Little, Joseph H. 258
  William 220
Livingston, Thomas 184
Lock, William 227
Locke, William 227
Lonas, Henry 206
  Jacob 206
Lonass, Henry 250
Lonay, Abner 211
Long, John 246
  John B. 174
Longacre, Richard 178
Longaver, Richard 250
Longimiers, John 172
Looney, Isaac 191
  Isaac A. 232
  John 208
Love, James 172,220
Lovell, Daniel 186
Lovens, Hugh H. 219
Lovins, Hugh G. 170
Lowe, David 227
Loyd, Jordan 170
Lucas, William 247
Lucky, John 242
Luna, Robert 180
Lung, James 251
Lusk, Wilson 223
Luttrell, Mason 185
Lyle, Daniel 178
Lynch, James 182
Lynes, William J. 183
Lyon, Peter Jr. 175
  William 218
Lytle, John 226,249


-Mc-


McAdams, George 232
  William 174
McAdoe, John 196
McAdow, James 217
McAlister, James 241
McAllister, William 175, 213

McAlpin, Henry 225
McAmy, James 218
McBraid, James 220
McBride, John 170
  Patrick 175
  Samuel 208
McCaleb, Ephraim 177
  John 227
McCalister, Garland 188
McCalpin, Robert 203
McCampbell, James 241
  John 218,229
  William A. 169
  Wm. A. 250
McCarley, Andrew 182
McCartney, James 172,198, 245
McCarty, Thomas 221
McCawley, James 201
McCeustian, Thomas 205
McClahan, Job 246
McClain, Charles 187
  William 255
McClanahan, Alexander 205
McClannahan, Mathew 212
McClean, James D. 182
McClellan, James W. 234
McClennahan, William 213
McCliskey, William 175
McClung, James 172
McClure, Ewen 240
  Henry 258
  John 219
  William 213
McCollom, _____ 225
McConnell, Francis 210
McCord, James 247
McCown, Francis 180
McCracken, John 240
  Samuel 240
McCrackin, George 187
McCrary, John 244
  Elisha 192
McCrory, John 197
  Thomas Jr. 193
McCulloch, Joseph 228
McCutcheon, James 174
  Robert 216
  William 200
McDaniel, Clement 222
McDanniel, James 229
McDermott, Jacob 195
McDonald, Alexander 250
  James 259
  William 205
McDowell, Benjamin 206
McDuffie, Neil 213
McEwen, David 216
  James 194,212,241
  John L. 258
McFadden, James 216
McFall, Henry 233
  John 232
  Samuel 233
  Samuel P. 204
McFarland, John 250
  Robert 178
McFerrin, Burton L. 236
  James 236
  Thomas 238
McGaffy, John 249
McGee, Bartley 205
  William 188
McGehe, William 251
McGhan, Eli 194
McGhauy, John 172
McGill, James 197
McGinness, Robert 225

McGinnis, Robert 221
McGlothlin, Levi 254
McGrady, John 256
McGregor, Richard 257
McGuire, Thomas 250
McKain, Samuel 256
McKamey, D. 180
McKamy, John 185
McKann, William 222
McKean, Eli 232
McKee, Alexander 172
  Ambrose 236
  John 236
McKercle, Joel 172
McKiney, John 216
McKinney, John 212
  John V. 180
McKisick, James 244
McKnight, David 236
  John 242
McKnitt, Joseph 182
McKorkel, Henry 185
McLane, Benjamin 192
McLaughlin, Elijah 202
McLemore, Areabel 206
  Moses 224
McLendon, Bright 212
McLennan, Hugh 219
McMacken, Andrew 232
McMahan, Abraham 180
  Anderson 246
McMeans, Isaac S. 185
McMiken, Elisha 224
McMillan, Daniel 199
McMillen, James 229,250
  Joseph 230
McMillin, Thomas 176
McMurry, James 256
  Robert 247
  William 174
McNabb, James 221
McNare, John 250
McNeil, Thomas 208
McNut, Joseph 232
  Robert 232
McNutt, Benjamin 255
  James 179
McPharson, James 172
McPike, Jesse 246
McQuaig, John 187
McRae, John L. 222
McRaken, Samuel 192
McReynolds, James 173
  John 246
  William 191,215
McSpadden, Thom. C. 259
  Thomas 192
McSwiney, Alexander 204
McVay, Claiborne W. 224
  Kinson 175
McVeil, Neil 204
McVerminch, Absolem 175
McVey, Thomas 173
McVicks, Donald 217
McWhirter, George F. 242
McWilliams, John 170

-M-

Maberry, John 187
Madden, Elisha 241
  James 245
Maden, Elisha 194
Mahaffy, John 250
Mahon, Archemedes 237

Majors, Absolam 234
  John 252
Malcolm, William 212
Malky, Benjamin 209
Mallory, Phillip G. 251
  Samuel 239
Malone, James 213
Maloy, Daniel 253
Malton, Elijah 202
Malugin, William 177
Manier, Lemuel 241
Mann, William 204
Maples, Thomas 255
  Wilson 188
Mars, Benjamin 184
Marshal, Gilbert 194
Marshall, Leven 197
  Robert 195,242
Martin, George 239
  George J. 174
  Isaac 257
  James 204
  James L. 191
  John 239
  Samuel 219
  William 188
Masingale, James 255
Mason, David 194
  Joseph 256
  Phillip 253
  Warren 227
Mathews, Abner 182
Matlock, Charles 184
  William 210
Matthews, Ebenezer 246
  John 236
Maughan, James 173
Maury, Thomas T. 216,241
Maxey, Bennet 200
Maxwell, John 234,244
  Simpson 252
May, Benjamin 194
  Charles P. 182,208
  John 223
Mayes, John 176
Mayfield, A. B. 182
  Campbell 202
  Luke 227
Meadows, Willis G. 224
Meales, Lewis 205
Medaris, Washington D. 197
Medlin, Lewis 170
Megill, William 198
Melekin, Samuel 225
Melone, Michael 190
Melony, Robert 192
Melton, Elijah 224
Menefree, Reuben 180
Meredith, David 238
  James B. 236
Meroney, Phillip D. 203
Metcalf, Anthony 238
Metheny, Elijah 225
Middleton, Alfred 251
Milam, Thomas 251
Millekin, Isaac 187
Millen, Samuel 257
Miller, Charles 192
  Daniel B. 208
  George 214,239
  Isaac 254
  James 187
  John 177,178,184,196,210
  Joseph 228
  Loan 177
  Samuel 210

Miller (cont.)
  Samuel H. 230
  William 197
  William S. 200
Milligan, Samuel D. 180
Milliken, Elihu 178
Milton, Michael 170
Mires, Miles 256
Mitchel, William 225
Mitchell, Arthur 184
  Daniel 246
  David 191,257
  Everet 242
  Everit 217
  James C. 210
  John 208
  John G. 227
  Marcus 202
  Michael 183
  Samuel 184
  William 188
Mohan, Archemedes 255
Molsby, David 226
Monroe, William 251
Montgomery, Alexander 204
  Daniel 214
  Fariss 228
  James 247
  John 175
  Thomas 219
Mooney, James 215
Moore, Bennet 182
  Cleon 204
  Ephraim 228
  James 187,204
  John 174,176,200,252
  Joseph 211,223
  Lemuel 213
  Mastin 225
  Reuben 180
  Robert 214
  Samuel 180,253
  Shadrick 238
  Travers 190
  William 174
More, Joel 186
Moreland, John 172
  William 205
Morgan, John 207
  William 179
Morrice, Joseph 179
  William 179
Morris, John 210
  Lazarus 233
Morrison, Miles 249
Morse, Michael 219
Moses, Peter 176
Mosley, Thomas 186
Moss, Reuben 173
Mount, Humphrey 228
Moyers, Henry 176
Mucbery, Archibald 207
Mullans, James 249
Mulvaney, Henry 206
Mumpower, Benjamin 176
Murphy, Edward 225
  Ezekiel 236
  John 207
  Stephen 170
  William 219
Murray, Francis 227
Murrell, Thomas 247
Murry, Bland 189
  George 225
  Reuben 225
Myers, Adam 244

-N-

Nail, Joseph 253
  Samuel 207
Nall, Joseph 253
  William 174
Nance, Allen 254
  Isaac 187
Nash, John 236
  Thomas 213
Nations, Christopher 251
  Nathaniel 175
Nave, Henry 199
Neal, James 252
  Strother 226
Neblet, Benjamin 233
Neelly, Robert 182
Neideffer, Solomon 214
Neighbors, Francis 175
Neighbours, Francis 201
Neil, Grimes 199
  John 197
Neilly, Charles 182
Neilson, William D. 185
Neisbett, Jeremiah 223
  Thomas 223,247
Nelson, John 199
  John Sr. 257
  Pleasant 232
  Nennet, William 214
Nesbitt, Thomas 174
Neuton, Henry 190
Neville, Joseph 258
Newberry, James 247
Newman, James 172
  Jonathan 249,250
  Robert 250
Newton, Kennerry 190
  Robert 222
Nicholas, John 255
Nichols, Solomon 201
Nickles, Matthew 255
Noaks, Jesse 236
Norman, Ezekiel 191
  John 175
  Thomas 197
Norris, Absolem 192
Northcutt, William 180
Norton, John 207
Norvel, John P. 182
  Moses 246
Nunn, Thomas 216
Nunnely, John 249


-O-

Oakley, William 242
O'Callahan, Patrick 207
O'Daniel, John 192
Odean, John 180
Odel, Bartlet 215
Odom, Lewis 230
Offill, James 190
Ogelvie, David 208
Oglevie, David 208
Olinger, Samuel 240
Oliver, Charles Y. 219
  Lunesford 169
Onsley, Stephen 199
Orman, Adam 259
Orr, John 197,219
  Robert 197
Orre, Francis 172

Osborn, George 171
  Thompson 200
Osburn, James 176
  John 207
Osly, Nathan 199
Ostin, Benjamin 173
Ottinger, Henry 226
Outlaw, Wright 233
Overall, Abraham 189,238
Owen, Fain 204
  Michael 256
Owens, Moses 242
  William 171,180,184
Oyler, Jonathan 230


-P-

Pace, James 187
  John 232
Paine, Robert 256
Palmer, Anthony 172
  William 255
Paris, Joel 184
Parish, John G. 175
Parker, Caleb J. 226
  Nathaniel 213
  Noah 197
  Samuel 197
  William 213,259
Parkeson, Daniel 241
Parkison, Daniel 192
Parks, Benjamin 259
Parsons, Enoch 206
Pate, Charles 237
  Jeremiah 238
Paterson, Andrew 197
Patten, James 254
Pattern, Samuel 229
Patterson, Andrew 170,
  197
  George 251
  John 210
  Matthew 222
  Thomas 189
  William 213
Patton, David 187,236
  James C. 229
  John 192,219
  Robert 179
  Samuel B. 197
  Tilman 177
Pauley, William 245
Paxton, James 202
Payne, Greenwood 200
  Joel 207
  Solomon 253
  Warren 211
  Warren L. 235,253
  William 218
Pearce, Arthur 259
  Moses 178
  Stokeley 212
  Weston 249
Pearson, John D. 244
Peck, Moses Looney 178
Pennycuff, Jacob 234
Peoples, William 177
Perkins, Edward 198
  Hardin 241
  James 248
  Nicholas T. 216
  William O. 194,216
Perrin, Matthew 178
Perry, Allen 219

Perry (cont.)
  John 224
  Semeon 237
  William 170,197
Perryman, Josiah 217
Person, George 173
Petty, Alexander 254
Pew, Daniel 206
Peyton, Moses 232
Phagan, James 256
Phare, George 219
Phelps, Kelan 230
Phillips, Charles 256
  Samuel 170
  Thomas 202
  William 213
Philpot, Horatio 180,251
Pickens, James 202
  James H. 224
  John 232
  Joseph 170
  Robert 202
  William 176
Pickle, George 234
  John 234
Pierce, Jeremiah 200
  John 212
Pierfelt, Jeremiah 198
Pigg, James 241
Pinkston, Hugh 259
Pinson, Nathan G. 180
Pipkin, Thomas B. 174,200
Plover, Edward 189
Plumby, William 228
Polk, Andrew 190
  Eaven 232
  John 238
  William 190
Pollard, Joseph 254
Pope, Jacob 188
  Thomas A. 216
Porter, Hugh 212
  John 212,237
  John H. 247
  Joseph 180
  Samuel 219
  Thomas 216
  William 182,232
  William B. 235
Porupt, Henry 245
Potts, Jeremiah 192
  Oswall 236
  Thomas 236,254
Powel, Osborn 174
Powell, G. W. 254
  Matthew 235
  William 254
Powers, Robert 176
Preston, Alexander 188,255
Prewd, John 181
Prewet, Moses H. 170
Prewitt, George H. 259
Price, Daniel 229,250
  Joseph 233
  Nathan 228
  Thomas 215
  William 228
  William J. 257
Pride, Allen 253
Prigmore, Thomas 185
Prior, Nicholas B. 246
Probitt, Robert C. 253
Proffit, Pleasant 221
Pryor, Peter 209
Puckett, Charles R. 243
  Robert 241
Pulloum, William 207

Pursley, James 169
   Robert 238

-Q-R-

Qualls, William 227
Quinllian, William 216
Quinn, James 202
Ragan, Benjamin 174
Ragsdale, David 185
   Edward 194
   John 194
   John Sr. 197
Rainey, John 198,244
Ramsey, Alexander 210
   John P. 232
   Samuel 214
Randal, James 213
Randals, James 258
Randle, Edmund 238
Rankin, David 178
   John 178
Rany, William 198
Rapier, John 207
Rarborough, Wm. L. 246
Ray, George W. 178
   John 241
   Samuel 172
Read, Robert 202,259
   Thomas 225
   Thomas J. 222
Readen, Alexander 248
Reaves, George 177
   Samuel 205
Rector, Kenner 245
   Richard 234,253
Reddin, Abijah 232
Redfern, Townley 235
Redmond, William 238
Reece, Joseph M. B. 250
Reed, Andrew 216
   James 232
   James L. 241
Rees, Joel 209
Reese, Beverly 217
   Isaac 199
Reess, Beverly 241
Reeves, George 203
Regan, John 172
Reggin, John 223
Regney, William 251
Reid, Clement 207
   Josiah 224
Reigle, Jacob 185
Renfro, Robert 253
Renfroe, John 234
   Robert 253
Reves, William 227
Reynolds, William 189
Rhay, John 212
Rhea, James 245
Rice, Elijah 256
   James 232
   John 234
Richards, Hiram R. 217
   Richard 256
Richardson, Abel 210
   Barnard 217
   David 174
   May 224
Riche, James 205
Richeson, Matthias 232
Richmond, Alexander P. 195
Rider, Alexander 172

Riley, William 257
Ring, Thomas 222
Ritcheson, James 176
Roads, Moses 189
Roan, James 195
Robb, Arthur 210
Roberson, James 171
   Mark 234
   William 198
Roberts, John 246,247
   Robert W. 189
   Silas M. 250
Robertson, Christopher 189,247
   David J. 254
   Edward 238
   Elijah 237
   Hardy 256
   Isaac 191
   James 203
   John 201
   Nathaniel 229
Robeson, James 226
   Mathew 212
Robinson, James 249
   Joseph 228
Rodgers, William 232
Rogers, David 256
   Edmund 181
   Elisha 171
   George 249
   John 171,173,174,253
   Joseph 171,190
   Patterson 185
   Samuel 232
   William 179,185
Rook, Adam 176
Rooker, John 220
Ropper, John 205
Ross, Ezekiel 191
   James 226,241
   John 177
   Samuel 190,238
Ruder, Samuel 249
Ruff, John 224
Rums, Henry 241
Rushing, Abraham 190
Russell, Alexander 192
   Andrew 179
   James 222
   Jesse 223
   John 177
   Thomas 169
Rutherford, Thomas 174
Rutledge, William 238
Ryburn, Samuel H. D. 252

-S-

Sadler, Henry 228
Saling, Peter 197
Samuel, John 202
Sanders, Isaac 235
   Robert 186
Sanford, George 214
   Robert 187
Saunders, Elijah 254
Saunderson, John 259
   Thomas 259
Scales, Henry 224
   Robert 207
Scandling, William 201
Scanland, William 205
Scobey, James 259
Scoles, Robert 230

Scott, Andrew 228
   Arthur 241
   George 200
   Hercules 171
   John 177
   Nathaniel 182
   Stallard 254
Scrivenor, David 253
Scrivner, David 253
Scruggs, James 226
   Theophilus 222
Scrugs, James 203
Seabourn, Richard 245
Searcy, Robert 184,233
Sebastian, Isaac 181
Secrest, Leroy 209,232
Self, Jesse 171
   Levy 171
   Thomas 249
Semlock, Bebly 259
Seratt, John 257
Sevier, Archibald 184
   John F. 256
Sewell, Benjamin 239
   George 228,250
   John 245
Shahan, Thomas 188
Shammell, Joseph 209
Shanks, Archibald 187,212
Shannon, James 259
Sharp, Henry 172
   John 245
Sharpe, Alfred 187
   Cyrus 187,236
   John 254
   Richard 175
   Thomas 248
Shavour, John 226
Shaw, Josiah 189,243
   Robert 190
   Samuel 232,251
Sheilds, Robert 212,255
Shelby, William 201
Shell, John 251
Shelton, James 253
   John P. 194
   Jonathan 227,249
Shields, Leander 224
   Robert 188
Shinault, James 244
   Walter 197,244
Shipley, Benjamin 209
Shockley, T. H. 219
Shoemaker, Michael 228
Short, Caleb 228
Shrader, Henry 248
Shropshire, Joel 174
Shuffield, Arthur 219
   John 244
Shultz, Martin S. 211
Sibley, Robert 232
Sigler, George 221
Simmons, James 176
   James M. 224
   Micajah 225
Simms, Bartlett 207
   James 207
Simpson, Nathaniel 177
   William 217
Sims, James 194
   John 182
   Robert 194
Sisk, Elias 199
   James 201
Sitler, James 174
   James W. 200
Sitton, Phillip 238
Sively, Absolom 212

Sivey, Jacob 256
Skidmore, John 252
Skiles, George 228
Skillern, Anderson 171
Skinner, Nathan 213
Slaten, John 204
Slater, Henry 194
Slatter, Cornelius 230
Slover, Aaron 219
  John 178,205
Small, George 207
Smartt, William C. 257
Smith, Aaron 184
  Amos 191,215
  Andrew 241
  Beverley 249
  Beverly 226
  Bird 217
  Daniel Jr. 199
  David 250
  Ezekiel 172,221
  Francis 175
  Hyram M. 224
  Iri 210
  Isaac 179
  James 175,230
  Jasper 181
  Jesse 181
  Joel 207
  John 176,184,230,256
  John J. 258
  John T. 241
  Joseph D. 237
  Luke 212
  Randolph 185
  Richard 184,215,257
  Samuel 259
  Samuel G. 205
  Thomas 176,198,247
  Thomas A. 223
  William 181,190,203,
    218,242,246,252,256,
    259
  William J. 192
Snader, Henry 248
Snelling, Samuel 244
Snisher, G. 251
Snoddy, James 205
Sowder, Jacob 173
Speirs, Nathan 224
Sphere, Jesse 249
Spooner, Jonathan 191
Spring, John 171,245
Spurlock, Josiah 189
Stacy, John 242
Staggs, Felix 194
  Flemmon 194
Stalcup, James 214
Stallons, Sherrad 233
Standifer, James 185
  James Jr. 171
  John 243
Stanfield, Goodloe 242
  William 209,232
Stanford, Lucas 233
Stanley, James 248
  Rhode 219
  Wright 194
Stanly, James 254
Staples, James 249
Stark, James 176
  John 256
Starrot, Joseph 170
Steed, Abner 230
Steltz, Henry 235
Stephens, John 172
Stephenson, Andrew 188
  James 251

Stephenson (cont.)
  Robert 224
Stewart, Bartholemew G.
  184
  James 242
  John 217
  Nowlan 233
  William 239
Still, George 243
  James 224
Stockton, Thomas 211
Stogdon, John 184
Stone, Abraham 185
  John 176
  William 259
Stoner, Michael 252
Story, Henry 174
  Samuel 174
Stout, Abraham 211
Strain, John 172,198
Strange, Beverly 239
Stratton, James 191
Strickland, Jonathan 235
Stricklin, Barnabas 187
Stringfellow, Richard
  174
Stringfield, James 215
Stuart, Andrew 184
  Thomas 192
  William 243
Stull, Samuel 200
Suckler, Jacob 190
Sullivan, Lee 189
Summers, John 257
  Levy 191
  William 191
Sumner, Isaac 207
Sumpter, William 221
Suton, William 178
Sutton, John 178,244
Swaeringen, William 248
Swain, William 259
Swan, John 206
Swaney, John L. 257
Swann, Burch 186
Swanson, Richard 194
Sweezee, John 228
Swift, Thomas 223
Swingley, Joseph 259
Sypret, Stephen 259


-T-


Tallet, Henry 171
Talliaferro, John K. 244
Tarrant, John 201
Tarver, Edmund D. 243
Tate, David 248
  Edward 243
  Gersham 249
  Zedekiah 181
Tatum, James 247
  Nathaniel 181
Taylor, Abraham 242
  Armstead 258
  Daniel Jr. 176
  Harden 175
  James 201,223
  Samuel 169,174,222
  Solomon 217,259
  Thomas 182
  William 208
  William L. 245
Teader, James 211
Teague, John 246

Teal, George 247
Tedford, James 198,245
Temples, John 189
Terrell, James 248
Terry, William 228
Thatch, Thomas 179
Thomas, Hamilton 239
  Isaac Jr. 188
  Jesse W. 174
  Jidean 237
  Tristram B. 177
Thompson, Abraham 254
  Allen 200
  David 230,251
  Elisha 230
  George 237
  James 242,246
  John 202,212,220,233
  Joseph 214
  Reuben 197
  Samuel 172
  Thomas F. 219,244
  William 238
  William W. 183
Thornberry, John 198,220
Thornton, William H. 218
Threat, Howard D. 194
Timmons, Charles 217
Tinman, John 178
Tinnen, John 202
Tipton, Abraham 246,257
  Reuben 179
  Samuel 257
Tittle, James 191
  Samuel 189
Todd, James 254
  William 187
Toff, John 205
Tollett, Henry 245
Tolliver, Charles 170
Tolly, Barnard 204
Toones, John 183
Totten, Benjamin 234
Townsen, William 175
Townsend, Peter 257
Trammel, David 172
Travice, William 234
Travis, William 252
Traylor, James 174
Trimble, John 172
Tripp, Samuel 217
Trousdale, James 233
Trout, Michael 206
Truett, John B. 191
Tubb, George Jr. 248
  James 255
Tucker, James 250
  John 253
  Marady 212
  William 254
Tuggle, Thomas 213
Tunnell, William Jr. 169
Turner, Edward 227
  James 243
  Jesse 206
  Nathan 185
  William 202
Turney, George 189
Tuttle, David 183
Tyre, Richmond 257
Tyree, Richmond C. 191


-U-V-


Ulred, Jonathan 234

Underwood, John 185
Upton, James 185
Uselton, Samuel 187
Usrey, William 241
Uzzell, Jordan 260
Vanbibber, Jacob 246
Vance, James 249
Vanhook, Loyd 189
Vaughn, Abner 217
  Daniel 215
  Paul 222
  William 212
Vaulx, William 174,222
Vaun, Achiles 185
Ventrass, James 213
Vernon, Thomas 245
Vinson, Benthle 239
  Enos 257
  George 204
Vinzant, Jacob 248
Viser, John L. 233

-W-

Wade, Charles 195
  Dabney 183
  William J. 183
Wagg, John 177
Waggoner, Cornelius 222
  Jacob 181
Wair, George T. 186,211
Wait, William 194
Walker, Andrew 202,248
  Carter 230,251
  Elisha 177,194,227
  Eneas 219
  John 215,241
  John S. 257
  Richard 204
  Robert 213
  Thomas 209,233
Wall, Charles 184
Wallace, Benjamin 198
  John 191
  Thomas 220
  William 198
Wallen, Evan 172
Waller, Obediah 181
  William 234
Wallington, George 229
Wallis, George 210
Walt, John A. 181
Walton, Josiah 243
Wamock, Josiah 170
Ward, Anthony 189
  Burrell 187
  Dicken 128
  John 221
  Presley 181
  Wiley 213
Warner, John 218
Warnick, William 237
Warren, Edward 185,194
  James 237
  Jesse 243
  R. H. 242
  T. W. A. 255
Warriner, Thomas 172
Wassom, Jonathan 190
Wasson, Abner 217
Watkins, Archibald 243
  Henry 187
  Isaac 181
  Joel M. 189
  Thomas G. 254

Watson, George 189
Watt, Samuel 181
Watterson, William 244
Watts, Allen 239
Wax, Henry E. 252
Wear, John 188,237
  Samuel Jr. 255
Weatheread, Fran. W. 257
Weatherhead, Marcus 257
Weaver, Abraham 210
  Jesse 243
  Joseph 219
  Phillip 210
Webb, Benjamin 237
  Isham 217,260
  John 186
  Martin 241
Webster, Jonathan 244
  Peter 213
Weeks, Solomon 189
Weims, Briton 243
Weir, Samuel 237
Welch, Nicholas 248
West, Henry 228
  Samuel 243
Wharton, Joshua 248
Whetson, George 174
Whilams, James 199
Whiliss, Herbert 184
White, Alfred 183
  Charles 257
  George 170
  John 199
  Robert 207
  Silas 171
  Stephen F. 237
  Thomas 190,200,256
  William 173,199,212,237
Whiteside, Samuel 233
Whitesides, Abraham 233
Whitsett, Thomas 212
Whitson, John 206
  William 206
Whittaker, John 233
Whittenbarger, Mathew 198
Whittey, Willie 260
Wilkerson, Povy 178
  Thomas 202
Wilkins, James 227
Wilks, Minor 233
Willard, Abiah 256
Willcockson, John 255
Willeford, James 237
Willet, Nathan 238,256
Williams, Beverly 217,260
  Charles 260
  Coleman 217
  Daniel 175
  David 191
  Elisha 242
  Henry 189
  James 171,200,213,250,252,257,260
  James H. 202
  John 185,234
  Joshua 178,227
  Leban B. 258
  Mathew 211
  Meredith 253
  Peter 228
  Richard 223
  Samuel 186,211
  Thomas 176
  William 255
Williamson, George 243

Willie, James 243
Willis, Abel 252
  Elishs 184
  Moss 239
Wills, Archibald 187
  Edward 194
Willson, Robert 222
Willy, Willis 247
Wilson, Abel 248
  Ephraim 228
  Gilbert 226
  Hardin 183
  John 169,181,251
  Robert 222
  Samuel D. 259
  William 207
Wimberley, Malachi 254
Winager, Jacob 249
  Samuel 249
Winant, Vanderpool 172
Winham, William 257
Winkle, Frederick F. 192
Winston, John 171
Winstone, William 243
Winton, George W. 185
Wisdom, William 176
Witt, William 175
Witten, James 220
Wolf, George 251
  George W. 174
  William 217
Wolfenbarger, Phillip 176
Wolsey, Mathias 249
Wood, Joshua 223
  William 257
Woodrow, Joel 171
Woods, Charles 223,248
  John 219
  Joseph B. 198,220
  Peter 202,248
  William 223
Woodward, German 207
  Jesse 222
  William 185
Woollen, Joshua 243
Woolsey, Thomas 213
Woote, Daniel 187
Worley, Hiram 246
Wray, William 252
Wright, John 221
  Peter 174
  Thomas 179,247
  William 249
  William C. 260
Wyrick, Frederick 176


-X-Y-Z-

Yager, Abner 230
Yarborough, Wm. L. 247
Yarbrough, George 238
  Robert 230
Yardley, Thomas 237
Yates, Thomas 197
Yeaqer, James 192
Yeates, James 211
  James Jr. 186
  William 186
Yeld, Archibald 244
York, Jonathan 176
  William 199
Young, Beverly 257
  Daniel 213
  E. 259
  Francis 177

Young (cont.)
  Jacob 248
  James 247,257
  Jaret 224
  Nathaniel 202,233
  Robert 198
  William 211,242
Yourey, Francis 212
Zacherry, Josiah 212

www.ingramcontent.com/pod-product-compliance
Lightning Source LLC
Chambersburg PA
CBHW050341230426
43663CB00010B/1949